# JOEL ZOSS
## and
# JOHN BOWMAN

With an epilogue
by the authors

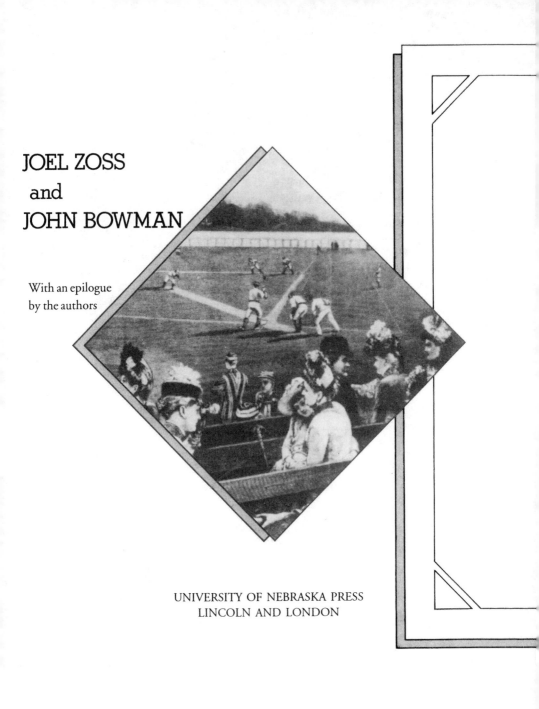

UNIVERSITY OF NEBRASKA PRESS
LINCOLN AND LONDON

# DIAMONDS IN THE ROUGH

*The Untold History of Baseball*

© 1989 by Joel Zoss and John S. Bowman
Epilogue © 2004 by the Board of Regents of the University of Nebraska
Credits for art and photographs appear on pages 423–25.
All rights reserved
Manufactured in the United States of America

⊚

First Nebraska paperback printing: 2004

Library of Congress Cataloging-in-Publication Data
Zoss, Joel, 1944–
Diamonds in the rough: the untold history of baseball / Joel Zoss and John Bowman;
with an epilogue by the authors.
p.   cm.
Includes index.
ISBN 0-8032-9920-6 (pbk.: alk. paper)
1. Baseball—United States—History.   2. Baseball—Social aspects—United States.
I. Bowman, John Stewart, 1931–   II. Title.
GV863.Z67   2004
796.357'09—dc22       2004004965

*Some baseball is the fate of us all.*

Robert Frost

# CONTENTS

*The Professionals • Little League • Throwing Like a Girl •*
*The Oweneresses • The Negro Leagues • Sex and the Game •*
*Female Fans*

# PREFACE

**T**his book is a compendium of baseball, an anecdotal history, not of oddities, but of that side of the game that is not solely concerned with batting averages, statistics, and who won what when. It has often been said that baseball history is 40 percent statistics and 60 percent anecdote, and indeed there are many excellent books covering every conceivable baseball record; more every day, in fact. What we are concerned with is the human side of baseball, with how the game came to be embedded in our society. It has been our experience while working on this book to learn that even when statistics, the obsession of most devout fans, were the point of entry for a lifelong interest in baseball, the realization that baseball is a true reflection of the larger society has dawned with all the force of a major epiphany upon many who would never otherwise consider themselves historians.

There is no doubt that the same historical circumstances that are responsible for the shape of America are responsible for the special place baseball occupies in the hearts of Americans. The United States is a country of recent origin populated with diverse immigrant groups, and in a nation without a common religion or ethnic heritage, the game of baseball, one of America's oldest cultural artifacts, has almost by default taken on a metaphysical function and become a source of legend that exemplifies those virtues supposedly unique to the American character. Its history, like that of the American Dream, is one of pristine vision menaced by corruption and greed. As baseball's visionary deviant, Jim Bouton, has pointed out, "There's pettiness in baseball, and meanness and stupidity beyond belief, and everything else bad that you'll find outside of baseball . . . yet there's been a tremendous amount of good in it."

At a more personal level, playing baseball is an experience shared by almost every American child before grown-up responsibilities and cares have taken hold. And since baseball, unlike other common shared activities, such as school and church, was fun for most who played it, for adults it represents a mythical, golden age of childhood and has become an approved cultural retreat from weighty realities that few other American institutions afford. Indeed, the idea that a man can make a living (or a fortune) playing a boy's game is an enticing accommodation to the unforgiving business of being alive and working for a living. Baseball provides a soothing, undemanding, predictable identity for Americans. To disturb it—whether by adding franchises or by questioning its heroes—is to encounter the reaction one might expect from challenging one of society's most entrenched conservative institutions.

It is this phenomenon that we address in *Diamonds in the Rough.* We feel it is important to point out that any responsible researcher who gets his feet wet in baseball soon realizes that in a very real sense myth is *truer* than history, and that what people *think* is true about baseball is at least as important as what *is* true about baseball. *Diamonds in the Rough* is not intended to be a comprehensive history, but if we have been successful, it will reveal to the reader enough about what is not usually told about baseball to indicate the main driving forces behind our perception of the national pastime. The anecdotal structure of our book was suggested by the pattern of baseball history, which, apart from statistics, does indeed consist of little modules of legend, as yet unhomogenized.

We hope our efforts in this game of the imagination meet with your approval. One fact working much to your advantage is that the authors do not consider themselves baseball experts. We play no favorites, have no hidden agenda, leave nothing out and gloss nothing over to preserve cherished illusions or to spare embarrassment to favorite teams and eras. Insofar as possible, we have confined our own views to this preface and to the chapter introductions and have tried to let the facts speak for themselves. As professional writers with a love of baseball, we hope only to have brought to this history certain commonsense powers of observation that are easily lost in the heat of the factional moment, and we will feel justified if we have somewhat succeeded in supplying a fresh overview to the great metaphor of American life that is baseball.

John Bowman
Joel Zoss

# ACKNOWLEDGMENTS

**T**he authors were profoundly impressed during their work on this book by the willingness of baseball scholars to share information. In a society that leans toward secrecy, we found the community of baseball writers to be a caring family that routinely placed concern for accuracy, accessibility, and integrity ahead of personal career and publishing priorities. It is impossible to acknowledge everyone who helped with a kind or informative word.

Top of the batting order for anyone doing serious research in baseball these days is the Society for American Baseball Research (SABR), which, during the period we were working on this book, was administered by its constantly helpful and knowledgeable executive director, W. Lloyd Johnson. SABR's members and publications, meetings and communiqués, committees and projects, have revolutionized the study of baseball in the last two decades; any book such as this owes many debts and details to SABR members, some of whom are given special thanks below.

Among the institutions to which the authors owe special thanks are the University of Massachusetts Library, especially to research librarian Marjorie Karlson, and to Eric Esau, Richard Morrill, Virginia Craig, and others who helped with the computer search; the Springfield College Library; Forbes Library in Northampton, especially research librarians Elise Feeley and Elise Dennis, and Charlotte Leighton at the desk; the New York Public Library, particularly its Rare Books and Reprographic Services; the National Baseball

Library, especially librarian Thomas R. Heitz, Bill Deane, and Patricia Kelly; the Boston Public Library, McGreevy Collection; Smith College Library; the Harvard University Library System, especially Millard Irion; *The Sporting News* archives; and the librarians and archivists at Vassar College, Mount Holyoke College, Wesleyan University, Oberlin College, and Syracuse University.

We especially wish to acknowledge the following individuals for their advice, readings, generous conversations, and detailed expertise in illustrations, music, board games, and history: John Thorn, Amos Blinder, Jim Kaplan, John Holway, Happy Chandler, Michael Stein, Thomas Lesser, Esq., William Weiss, Joseph Overfield, Mark Rucker, Peter Reich, Denny Goldstein, Kelly Candaele, J. Richard Seitz, Dick Clark, Professor Richard H. Miller of Brooklyn College, Mike Mumby, Bette Wright, Leonard Koppett, Mohan Baum, Harrington E. "Kit" Crissey, Jr., Mel Gussow, Thomas Aylesworth, Aaron Mintz, Victor Pearlin, Bill Kozack, George Moonoogian, Ellen Miller-Mac, Sherwin Dunner, Robert Peterson, Peter Bjarkman ("The Baseball Professor"), Matthew Zakrzewski, and Dr. Robert E. Smith, president of the International Baseball Association. Others who have contributed are acknowledged at specific places in the text. We would also like to thank our literary agent, Elizabeth Frost Knappman, and David Wolff.

Last but not least, we offer our very special appreciation to our loving support systems, our wives and families, who put up with us during the past two years, and especially to Alex Bowman, who constantly reminded us that the real game is still the one played out there in the ballpark.

# DIAMONDS IN THE ROUGH

# POP CULTURE

**P**ractically everyone who writes five sentences about baseball these days turns one of them over to Jacques Barzun's famous, "Whoever wants to know the heart and mind of America had better learn baseball." Barzun was right and his quoters are right. No one needs any further convincing that baseball is part of the warp and woof of America's culture: "The national pastime" has become one of the trinity of our popular mythology—along with Mom and apple pie. But whenever Barzun is quoted, there is at least the potential for misunderstanding the true role of baseball in our society. There is something a bit ethereal, abstract, remote about intellectuals verbalizing their appreciation of baseball: To paraphrase Hermann Goering, whenever baseball fans hear talk of heart and mind, they should reach for a bat.

To put it another way, can a man who didn't collect baseball cards in his youth *really* know what he is talking about? The Taiwanese and Koreans may win every Little League Championship from now to the Final Out, but can they have a true feel for baseball until Bob Feller shows up regularly at local fairs to sign autographs? For there is the game of baseball as it is played on the field, and there is baseball as it pervades American popular culture. Indeed, baseball has become such a part of our way of life that, as with the air we breathe, few are aware of it.

## A Good Decision

BASING its decision on performance and proven superiority, that great umpire, the American Public, has declared for Firestone Tires.

The figures of Firestone Sales indicate the preference of a great majority of seasoned motorists. And this decision was fairly won on all the essentials of tire service: safe, easy riding and the economy of Most Miles per Dollar.

It is to your interest to follow the "motoring fans" and order Firestones.

Firestone Tire and Rubber Company, Akron, Ohio—Branches and Dealers Everywhere
America's Largest Exclusive Tire and Rim Makers

# Firestone Tires

The terms and expressions of baseball were taken into popular speech from the very outset of the game, for they have a resonance that Americans find both familiar and suggestive. Advertisers have always been adept at exploiting this type of speech, as demonstrated by this tire company advertisement from the 1920s.

To be sure, many fans don't pay all that much attention to anything beyond the current season and the players. Which is how it should be. But outside the ballparks there exists an incredibly elaborate superstructure involving vast numbers of products and publications, stores and sales, manufacturers and dollars, a world of shows and conventions, swaps and auctions, newsletters and catalogues, collectibles and limited editions, exhibitions and parks, cruises and camps. By and large, it is self-generated; that is, the fans themselves have called this world into being and support it with their own energies, ingenuities, and hard-earned bucks. Its sheer dimensions and pervasiveness stagger the imagination.

*Baseball Talk*   One of the truest measures of just how popular something has become is its impact on everyday speech. Baseball more than passes this test, for it long ago entered our language on several levels, generating its own terminology and jargon. One of the earliest glossaries of baseball terms came out in 1888—*The Krank: His Language and What It Means* (and most Americans today would need a glossary to understand that *krank* meant "baseball fan"). Dozens of similar books and articles have been published in the last century, including a special book for Little League lingo. There are also numerous books and articles that reproduce baseball's colorful quotations—"the wit, wisdom, and wisecracks" as one such compilation titled itself: "It ain't over till it's over," "You can look it up," "Say it ain't so, Joe."

But the real impact of baseball on our language is seen in the many words and phrases that have by now become part of our everyday speech: "He threw me a curve." "Her presentation covered all the bases." "That's a judgment call." "He's really out in left field." "The kind of inside baseball talk that loses most of us." "He tried to score with her but struck out instead." Again, many people have commented on this phenomenon (among them, William Safire, who writes the "On Language" column for *The New York Times Magazine*), but it is singled out here just to touch base before we begin a circuit through some of the ways Americans have made baseball part of their language and lives.

One of the wonderful things about the language of baseball is its adaptability. It seems to lend itself easily to metaphorical use in many areas, perhaps because baseball terms themselves are such familiar words—"home plate," "infield fly," "curveball"—they all seem to explain themselves. From the earliest days of baseball songs, lyricists exploited the familiar imagery of baseball for romantic themes. In the 1877 song "Tally One for Me," the

# Get in the Game—"Roll Your Own"

When the umpire shouts, "Play Ball!" light up a fresh-rolled "Bull" Durham cigarette and settle down to root for the home team—the one best way to enjoy a ball game, as millions of "fans" will testify.

### GENUINE

# "BULL" DURHAM

## SMOKING TOBACCO

has been identified with the great national pastime for so many years that it has practically become a part of the game itself—the spectators' part. No other game can ever supplant baseball—no other tobacco can ever supplant "Bull" Durham—in the enthusiastic favor of sport-loving, enjoyment-loving America.

*Ask for FREE package of "papers" with each 5c such*

The *unique fragrance* of this pure, mild, mellow tobacco—the *smoothness* and *freshness* of "Bull" Durham hand-made cigarettes—afford *distinctive*, wholesome enjoyment and thorough, *lasting satisfaction.*

**FREE** An Illustrated Booklet, showing correct way to "Roll Your Own" Cigarettes, and a package of cigarette papers, will both be mailed, *free*, to any address in U. S. on request. Address "Bull" Durham, Durham, N. C., Room 1269.

THE AMERICAN TOBACCO COMPANY

*A classic example of how the language of baseball interacts with Americans is exemplified by "Bull" Durham tobacco. The tobacco brand was simply* Durham *with the bull as a trademark or logo. To solidify its ties with then mostly male smokers, the company advertised widely in minor league ballparks and in turn used the language of baseball in its ads (as in this one from 1915). Most recently a popular movie about minor league ballplayers took this name to evoke all these images.*

player says his heart was "stolen by a nice young girl/By her exquisite play." By 1935, people were singing "I Can't Get to First Base with You" (dedicated to Lou Gehrig, its words allegedly by his wife). It all sounds very natural and innocent.

But baseball lingo also slips easily into more raunchy talk. In 1950, for instance, there was a recording of Bill Williams's "Baseball Boogie," sung by Mabel Scott; like many black rhythm and blues tunes (certainly not to be heard on mainstream radio stations), the song used baseball imagery with thinly veiled sexual innuendo:

> I mean, baby, do you know the game?
> I'm a big league player. . . .
> Get that bat ready, baby,
> Let's see what you can do. . . .
> I need a pitcher
> 'Cause my last man wore out. . . .
> When I wind up,
> I'm pitchin' my all to you. . . .
> Play ball!

What's amazing is that baseball lingo also lends itself so naturally to religious sentiments. Billy Sunday may have been the first to realize this when he gave up baseball and became a revival preacher, but in 1907 there appeared a song, "Brother Noah Gave Out Checks for Rain," in which Deacon Jones tells us that "Eve stole first and Adam second/St. Peter umpired the game." This song probably drew on black American religious musical traditions; in any case, American blacks soon took the imagery of baseball into their own preaching and gospel songs, a tradition they have kept alive to this day, as attending or listening to black gospel meetings will confirm. "Life Is a Ballgame," one of the more striking black gospel songs, was written and recorded by Sister Wyonna Carr in 1953:

> For Jesus is standing at the home plate
> Waiting for you to come in.
> Yes, you know, life is a ballgame.
> But you've got to play it fair.

The imagery here sounds just as natural as it does in the barrelhouse, in the boardroom, or in the mouths of millions of ordinary Americans, not to mention those who make their living on the diamond.

*Souvenirs*  In the beginning there was the game, and the game produced souvenirs. Every kid who takes home the program from his first big-league ballgame and stashes it in a drawer is on the way to becoming a collector. (There is a brisk market for programs to World Series, All-Star Games, and other special games.) Ticket stubs don't fetch much (unless they turn out to be from some significant game), but a foul ball is a great souvenir, a home-run ball is a prized possession, and an autographed ball is a true valuable.

Most fans never have much chance to get even a thread from a player's uniform (Jim Rice was willing to put himself at risk by running right up into the stands at Yankee Stadium to take back his hat when a fan got hold of it). A glove or a bat is beyond their wildest dreams, although twelve-year-old Michael Smith of New York, who retrieved Don Mattingly's record-setting sixth grand-slam homer of the '87 season, was rewarded with a bat—in return for handing over the ball. Mets fans ripped up chunks of turf from Shea Stadium in 1986: Do they adorn walls in bars and trophy rooms?

Team pennants aren't truly necessary to the game, but they are so traditional that they count, at least if bought at a game. A truly specialized artifact is the World Series press pin, which can be collected and traded. Since clubs must have the pins made up well in advance, this has led to "phantom" World Series press pins—pins made for teams that thought they might make it to the Series but didn't: the 1986 Houston Astros phantom press pin already brings $75, while the 1950 Brooklyn Dodgers phantom press pin goes for $1,600. Among true rarities is a Hall of Famer's ring: Casey Stengel's somehow showed up at a New York auction in 1988, where it fetched $18,000.


*Collectibles*  Of more dubious significance are the various items that have been made and distributed specifically to take advantage of the fan's desire to own something associated with the game. Posters are now a part of every kid's bedroom. Sticker pictures of players can be pasted into special albums, team logo stickers can be pasted just about anyplace a kid finds inviting, and bumper stickers proclaim one's loyalty (or that of the car's previous owners). The sale of baseball caps, T-shirts, sweatshirts, jackets, and various other items of clothing that bear a team's name is a multi-million-dollar business: Look at the crowd at a typical ballgame and notice how many people are wearing such copyrighted items. (Baseball-style caps, by the way, are now part of most American males'—and some American females'—wardrobe, whether or not they have any interest in baseball.)

Baseball players began endorsing products and lending their names to items from almost the earliest days of the game. Here is "Hack" Wilson, a star in the early 1930s—still the holder of the National League's single-season home-run record—looking somewhat amused to find his name on a line of wagons. Even he, though, would have drawn the line at appearing in underwear ads.

## The Pete Rose Platinum Edition

Own the first collection of Pete Rose personally autographed collectibles. The 10¼ '' collector plate features Rose and Ty Cobb, the man whose record stood until Rose wielded his prolific bat. Rounding out this magnificent collection is a 9'' by 11'' ceramic plaque with hardwood frame; a 6¾ '' porcelain figurine; and a 3¼ '' by 5'' ceramic baseball card. All are limited to worldwide distributions of 4,192 and are personally signed by Pete. All are sequentially hand numbered.

PRP4 10¼'' collector's plate, signed . . . . . . . . . . . . . . . . . . . . . . . . $525.00*
PRP3 Ceramic plaque, frame included, signed . . . . . . . . . . . . . . . . $175.00*
PRF5 Porcelain figurine, signed . . . . . . . . . . . . . . . . . . . . . . . . . . . . $600.00*
PRC2 Collector ceramic baseball card, signed . . . . . . . . . . . . . . . . $ 50.00*
PRC1 Miniature ceramic baseball card . . . . . . . . . . . . . . . . . . . . . . $ 9.95
PRFF Miniature collector plate . . . . . . . . . . . . . . . . . . . . . . . . . . . . $ 14.50
*Secondary Market Price

*In the relatively new field of manufacturing so-called fine-art collectibles, Gartlan U.S.A. is probably the leader. This is their advertisement for the Pete Rose series. Like most of these Gartlan sets, many of the items are issued in limited editions and personally signed by the stars.*

Moving over (if not up) to the world of collectibles, there are statuettes of star players, issued years ago by the Hartland firm but more recently by the Kondritz company. For superstars and special occasions, there may be ceramic plates and porcelain figures. (A new six-inch porcelain figurine of Pete Rose costs $125; the original Hartland statuettes now bring several times that.) Several firms now issue reproductions or prints of original paintings of baseball subjects and ask hundreds of dollars. And then there are the "Slurpee Discs," colored discs (one and three quarters inches in diameter) each picturing a player and offered since 1983 by 7-Eleven Stores with the purchase of a large Slurpee drink.

As original souvenirs and memorabilia vanish into museums and collectors' displays, entrepreneurs have moved in and begun to issue replicas of old posters, programs (of, for instance, World Series games), manuals, and classic texts. This trend does no harm so long as the artifacts are clearly labeled as replicas or reprints, but in the case of some more valuable rarities it can be tricky for the inexperienced.

Back in 1888 the J. & E. Stevens Company (of Cromwell, Connecticut) put out a metal mechanical bank that collectors of mechanical banks know as the Dark Town Battery. As its name suggests, it was issued at a time when many Americans thought that anything involving Negroes was inherently funny. The metal bank has a ten-inch base and its figures rise to seven and a quarter inches. The pitcher stands to the left, and when a penny is placed in his right hand and a lever is pressed, his arm springs forward and releases the coin; the batter swings and misses, and the coin is "caught" by the crouching catcher. The movements and the timing make for a surprisingly lifelike action. Originally sold to stores for $8.50 a dozen, today a single "first edition" in top condition brings up to $1,500. This bank has been reproduced many times over the years, however, and replicas may cost the inexperienced collector much more than they're worth.

*Cartoons and Comics*   One of the surest tests of acceptance by Americans is to be taken into the world of cartoons and comic strips, the vernacular mediums through which Americans anoint their popular heroes from Uncle Sam to Superman. Many of the earliest drawings of baseball games and players, those of the 1860s and early 1870s, mildly mocked the game or used the game to mock other topics, but no one seems to have made topical drawings of actual baseball games before Christopher Smith of Buffalo, New York. Born Christoff Schmidt in Germany, he changed his name in his adopted land and became a sign painter. In 1877, Buffalo got its first professional baseball team, and Smith began to draw a series of cartoons that provided a humorous commentary on the season as it was played out. Done in ink on poster paper and signed "Christo," they were not published in a newspaper but were displayed in the window of a downtown clothing store. Thirty-four of these cartoons survive from that season of 1877, and Smith

*This is the design submitted by J. H. Bowen when he took out a patent in 1888 on a mechanical bank he called "Dark Town Battery": The coin is placed in the pitcher's hand, and when it is pitched, the batter swings and misses, and the coin goes into the catcher's midsection and down into a box. Original copies of this ingenious bank are quite valuable, but there have also been many subsequent "editions."*

never seems to have done any others, but "Christo" probably deserves to be known as the first baseball cartoonist.

Early in the twentieth century, sports cartoonists began to appear in various American newspapers. One of the best-known of the first generation was Theodore A. Dorgan, who signed his work "Tad"; his cartoons first appeared about 1905 in the New York *Evening Journal* and then appeared nationally until his death in 1929. Dorgan was long credited with introducing numerous popular usages such as the "hot dog," now a part of baseball culture; although he may have popularized it, authorities have shown that he did not invent the term for this popular food. By the 1930s and 1940s, there were numerous sports cartoonists working for newspapers and magazines around the country, but the three who had the greatest following—and whose

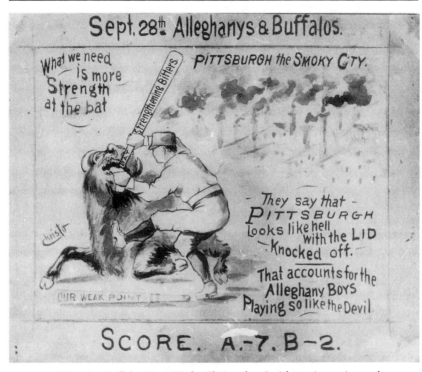

*In 1877, in Buffalo, New York, Christopher Smith, a sign painter, drew a series of cartoons about the local baseball team's games. Smith signed his work "Christo," and these cartoons, of which this is a typical example, probably qualify as the first American baseball cartoons. As clever as Christo's work was for its day, it still used more words than modern cartoonists find necessary.*

best baseball cartoons still "work"—were Lou Darvas, Willard Mullin, and Leo O'Mealia. Their cartoons, which appeared in different newspapers as well as in *The Sporting News,* seemed to "fix" the game and its players in an era before the TV image took over. Mullin was especially known for the cast of characters he used to represent each team—the Brooklyn Bum for the Dodgers, St. Louis Swifty (a riverboat gambler) for the Cardinals, a Quaker for the Phils, a hillbilly for the St. Louis Browns. Darvas and Mullin continued to work into the 1970s, and others gained reputations—Alan Mayer, Murray

Olderman, Gene Mack, just to single out three—but by then the Golden Age of Sports Cartoons was over.

Individual comic books and series have been issued to honor major stars—essentially biographies—but strangely, the only comic strip (at least with a national following) built around a baseball player was "Ozark Ike." But there remains one special case: the longest-running (since 1952), most beloved, and probably best-known game of baseball in any medium is the one being played by Charlie Brown and his pals in "Peanuts."

*Autographs*    A special aura attaches to souvenirs and memorabilia that have been personally signed by baseball players. The most authentic autographed items—balls, programs, pictures, and so forth—are those on which an individual fan obtained the signature in person, ideally at a game, but this gets harder and harder as the players become less and less accessible. For most fans, then, the easiest way to obtain a signature is to send the item to the player and ask him to return it autographed. (There is a published directory of ballplayers' addresses.) For best results, a stamped, self-addressed envelope or package for returning the item should be included.

Inevitably the question arises how many of these signatures are truly the autographs of the players and how many are done by "assistants." Gene Karst, who served as the public relations man for several major league teams, claims that many of the signatures are forgeries. He tells how back in the 1930s, the Cardinals' trainer, Doc Weaver, wanted to save his players' arms and signed baseballs for them with eight or more fountain pens filled with different colored inks to give the impression that each player had an individual style. Jim Bouton tells of a superstar who refused to sign baseballs in the clubhouse before games, "So there are thousands of baseballs around the country that have been signed not by Mickey Mantle, but by [the clubhouse crew]." Joe Morgan, an obscure coach and ex-player until he managed the Red Sox in 1988, says that for years he received baseball cards with the picture of Joe Morgan, the great infielder, with the request for an autograph: "I learned his signature," says Joe, "so I sign [the cards] and I send them back."

Up to a point, providing autographs is regarded as good public relations for the team and the individual player. Beyond that, things get more difficult. Players naturally resent being asked to come up with envelopes or stamps, even if a picture or card has been provided. (They especially resent being asked to sign baseball cards issued illegally.) Players tell tales of receiving large bundles of photographs and other memorabilia with a request that they all be autographed. This almost certainly means that a dealer or at least a professional collector is on the other end, and a player is not about to oblige when he knows that someone is simply seeking to make money on his signature. In an effort to thwart such dealings, Fred Lynn is reputed to give only personalized autographs (that is, "To Bill Jones, from Fred Lynn").

But players aren't exactly Innocents in the Ballpark when it comes to profiting from autographs these days. Good money is to be made from personal appearances at the endless round of shows and conventions and fairs where players are paid to autograph pictures, balls, and other artifacts. Sponsors of these occasions usually put up large appearance fees for the athletes and in turn charge the individuals who want to get the autographs. Some autograph hounds are genuine fans and collectors who want the autograph of an admired player, but increasing numbers are simply out to collect in order to trade or sell. Once Johnny Mize was sitting at a show signing autographs for a line of fans when seconds after he had signed two original pictures for one man, the man began to sell one to another collector. And recently Frank Robinson complained that he was getting a bit annoyed at seeing some of the same faces at these autograph sessions year after year—many of them having passed from youth to adulthood while soliciting his autograph.

Personal appearances at these major shows and conventions have become such a good source of income for both retired and active players that no one seems too aloof to show up. Even—"Say it ain't so, Joe!"—the Yankee Clipper himself put in an appearance at the 1987 national convention of National Sports Collectors, where for $10 he signed photographs. Joe DiMaggio's signature on a ball cost $29—for fans who had already paid $3 or $4 to gain entry to the convention. At this same event, Hank Aaron's or Willie Mays's signature on a picture cost $7; on a ball, $19. Duke Snider's, Willie McCovey's, Ernie Banks's, and Al Kaline's on a picture were each $5; on a ball, $15. Eddie Mathews, Warren Spahn, and Bob Feller got only $4 apiece for signing a picture and $12 for a ball. (An official ball with all ten of the Hall of Famers' signatures was $129. All autographs, by the way, included an official certificate verifying how the signature was obtained.)

This sliding scale of fees is in itself intriguing: Joe DiMaggio at the top is not surprising, but who has determined that Duke Snider gets $5 and Warren Spahn only $4? Mickey Mantle gave autographs at a New York City show that same June of 1987 and also got $10, while Sandy Koufax got only $8. (Mantle was advertised as giving out *only* twelve hundred autographs on each of the two days of the show, so the sums involved can be calculated.)

Numerous players make regular appearances at these shows, although none has carried it on for so long or with such dedication as Bob Feller; for decades now, Feller has been driving the highways and byways of the land to keep his name alive. Hank Aaron also appeared at the Northwest Indiana Baseball Card Show in June 1987, and autographed pictures for $6; at that same show, Hall of Famer Eddie Mathews autographed pictures for $4.

Even if you can't get to a show or convention in person, they are equipped to sell autographed items by mail. These cost considerably more because the object signed is included in the price. A mail order sent to the national convention, for instance, got Hank Aaron's or Willie Mays's autograph on an official baseball for $69, and as with in-person autographs, there was a sliding scale for the other players. (Joe DiMaggio, Warren Spahn, and Bob Feller did not sell autographed baseballs through the mail, perhaps to maintain their value, more likely because of prior contractual arrangements.) Mickey Mantle's signature on an official baseball ordered by mail from the New York City show cost $24, Koufax's cost $20. A bat autographed by Mantle cost $80.

There are hundreds of such shows and conventions going on all over the country and throughout the year, so anyone who wants an autograph should be able to buy one. And if there's no show nearby, there are always dealers: a ball autographed by Aaron bought through a dealer lists at $20, one from Mantle at $23, and one from Mattingly for $29. Clearly the new generation of players know their value.

*Cards: The First Hundred Years*  Everything claimed for souvenirs, collectibles, memorabilia, and autographs pales in comparison with collecting baseball cards. By now, this phenomenon has been so well publicized that every schoolboy knows the latest price for the 1952 Topps Mickey Mantle card (although only a true connoisseur knows the price of the 1951 *Bowman* Mantle rookie card). However, the Mantle card is far from the most expensive baseball player's card these days: A 1909 T-206 card picturing Honus Wagner fetched up to $150,000 in 1988, while the 1952 Topps Mantle was going for only $9,000. And even the Wagner card may not be the most expensive: In 1988 a dealer was asking $1 million for U.S. Caramel's 1932 card of Fred "Lindy" Lindstrom on the grounds that this was the only known copy in existence.

Purists may decry this development—that young fans know more about the price of a Mantle card than about Mantle's stats. But a still more sobering development is the report that in 1987 a record-breaking 52 million fans spent $350 million on major league tickets, while spending more than twice that—$750 million—on new baseball cards and $350 million on resales of pre-1987 issues.

Copyright. 1887.
Goodwin & Co.

~Johnston. C.F. Boston.

CLD JUDGE CIGARETTES Goodwin & Co.,
New York.

The "Old Judge" brand of cigarettes issued what is now a famous and valuable set of "cabinet" cards in the late 1880s—photographs of players to be displayed at a tobacconist's cabinet. They were not sold with each pack of cigarettes but could be obtained by saving coupons that came with each pack.

Baseball cards, it is true, moved in on the game very early in its history, although the first ones, in the 1880s, were given away to adults with packs of cigarettes. The first cards were smaller—one and three quarters by two and three quarters—than cards of recent decades and had nothing but a picture of the player (that is, no statistics or other data on the back). But even before these small cards were being issued, tobacco sellers often displayed larger "cabinet cards"—black-and-white (actually, sepia) photographs of prominent players. Most were plain studio portraits, but some used props to suggest pictures taken outdoors or in a ballpark. Another curiosity of those early years was the folding cards issued by the Mecca Cigarette Company in 1911; these showed one player—usually in a fielding pose—but the top half of the card folded back to reveal a teammate (sharing the same legs) hitting, pitching, or fielding.

Cards continued to be issued by tobacco companies for several decades, a fact that explains the astronomical price of the Honus Wagner card. He was an adamant nonsmoker. When the American Tobacco Company issued his picture and a brand of cigarettes named after him without his permission, Wagner forced them to withdraw both the card and the cigarettes, and relatively few (perhaps fifty) of the Wagner cards have survived. Even the Cooperstown Hall of Fame Museum doesn't own one—the card on display there is on loan from a private collector.

Tobacco companies gave up issuing baseball cards about 1918, but the Red Man Tobacco Company revived them briefly, from 1952 to 1955. Red Man cards claim another distinction—an attached coupon that could be redeemed for a cap or some such item. Meanwhile, other companies had long since begun issuing baseball cards with their products, one of the less publicized being the Zeenut Candy Company of San Francisco, which from 1911 to 1939 issued the longest continuous series of baseball cards before Topps (begun in 1951 and still going strong).

Zeenut cards also rate a distinction beyond sheer longevity. In 1916 the San Francisco Oaks of the Pacific League signed Jimmy Claxton, a black pitcher who passed as an Indian, during the week that the Zeenut photographer took the pictures for that year's set of cards. Although Claxton was dropped from the team, his card was issued, and Claxton, not Jackie Robinson, rates as the first black player to have appeared on a baseball card.

There were many variations on the basic cards with tobacco or candy products—pictures of players, for instance, on a regular fifty-two-card set of playing cards. Contrary to the usual story, the Goudey Gum Company in 1933 was not the first to combine baseball cards with chewing gum. A company named John H. Dockman and Sons sold the first gum packaged with a card

*One of the more unusual set of baseball cards was issued by the Mecca Cigarette Company in 1911. One player was shown (usually bent down to field), and when the top was folded up and over, a teammate was pictured (sharing the same legs from the knees down). These cards were also among the first to provide statistics on the back.*

about 1910. But these never caught on and it was the Goudey Gum Company in 1933 that first realized that the great market for baseball cards lay in exploiting several irresistible forces: a sweet product associated primarily with kids, compact enough to be placed on view at every candy counter, gimmicky enough to intrigue like a lottery (the sealed product did not reveal whose pictures would be inside), and all for a penny. Other gum companies soon took this up, and bubblegum-and-baseball-cards became instant Americana. Bowman Gum cards appeared in 1948 and Topps in 1951; in 1959, Fleer began to issue occasional sets, moving into annual production in 1981, the same year that Donruss got into the game; Sportflics and Score Cards are more recent entrants. There are other firms, but Topps, Donruss, and Fleer now account for most of the sales, with Topps far and away the dominant player.

The cards are still sold in waxed and sealed packets—but now with as many as ten in a packet with gum or a puzzle or a sticker (or nothing)—and the purchaser has no way of knowing whose pictures will show up.

In any case, 99 percent of all baseball cards used to be bought by boys who accumulated and traded cards until they outgrew the hobby; then their mothers, in a room-cleaning mood, threw out the old cards. Here and there some people managed to hold on to their cards, and here and there more serious collectors and dealers appeared, but buying and selling was done with restricted resources. This was the story of baseball cards and card collecting during the first century of their existence.

*Wild Cards*   Since the late 1970s and early 1980s, baseball card collecting has changed. For one thing, there are far more cards on the market than ever before. Not only have more firms entered the market, but they issue more sets: In 1987 there were 4 billion cards printed, but in 1988 this figure jumped to 5 billion. Moreover, the major firms often reissue whole sets from current or previous years to satisfy demand. In addition to cards sold in stores, scores of others are given away by manufacturers of various food products popular with kids, such as Mother's Cookies, M&M Candies, Kahn's Wieners, Drake's Bakeries, Gatorade, Kraft Macaroni, Coca-Cola, Burger King, and Jiffy Pop Corn. Some of these are one-time issues of only one team, with limited distribution, while others have begun to be issued as fairly complete sets; some are given out on one-time promotional occasions, others are released for extended periods with the product.

There are also special sets issued by the major card makers—such as those of the USA Olympics baseball teams of 1984 and 1988, and the glossy-coated Topps "Tiffany Edition"—as well as all kinds of special commemorative sets. Two firms now issue sets of minor league players—TCMA Ltd. and ProCard; local entrepreneurs occasionally issue sets of college teams. And in 1988 a California businessman issued a set of umpire cards showing all the active major league umpires; it seemed like a first, but in fact the Bowman Gum Company had issued umpire cards back in the mid-1950s. As to the latest baseball cards that feature two and a half minutes of talk by the player pictured (essentially they are small vinyl records that play in a special unit), they are so gimmicky and expensive that true collectors will probably give them a pass.

Not only is the country awash in baseball cards, the hobby is now completely commercialized—and, more to the point, self-conscious. Among the several publications devoted just to collecting is the *Beckett Baseball Card Monthly,* which costs $18.95 for a year's subscription and has a paid circulation

# COMMENTARY

## BY DAN ALBAUGH

In the last issue of *Baseball Card Price Guide Monthly* we listed the 1988 Traded/Update sets. The Score and Topps Traded sets have proven to be very popular with collectors.

The 110-card Score Traded set is a premiere edition and, as a result, is seeing a lot of action much the same way the initial Topps Traded (1981), Fleer Update (1984) and Donruss Rookies (1986) sets did. Score is one of the two card companies who included Ricky Jordan in their post-baseball card season sets. Jordan cards in the Score Traded and Fleer Update sets are selling for $2 or more and are proving to be hotter than Sabo cards.

The 132-card Topps Traded set includes 19 players from the U.S.A Olympic baseball team. The U.S.A team won the gold medal in the Olympic games held this summer in Seoul, South Korea. Besides the United States, seven other teams competed in the round-robin tournament.

Five Olympians in the Traded set are extremely popular with collectors and are selling for $1 or more. Jim Abbott, the 1987 Golden Spikes Award winner as the top amateur player in the U.S., was the winning pitcher in the finals against Japan. Abbott has signed with the California Angels.

Andy Benes, the #1 draft pick in the nation in 1988, pitched the U.S. to a victory over Australia in Game 2 of the Olympic competition. Benes has signed with the San Diego Padres. Robin Ventura batted .407 in the Olympics and was recently named the Golden Spikes Award winner for 1988. Ventura has signed with the Chicago White Sox.

Ty Griffin, second baseman on the Olympic team, will be playing in the Chicago Cubs organization next summer. Tino Martinez, who hit two home runs in the gold medal game, has signed with the Seattle Mariners.

Martinez and Ventura could reach the majors soon and others will follow. The hobby will be watching their progress.

# HOT CARD CORNER

#371 — 1985 Fleer
MT Value — $5.00

After posting a league-leading 23 victories in 1988, the righthander captured the National League Cy Young award. Hershiser notched two wins in the 1988 World Series and was named the Series' Most Valuable Player.

---

### 1948 Bowman

This 48-card set includes 12 card. (#'s 7, 8, 13, 16, 20, 22, 24, 26, 28, 29, 30 and 34) which were short-printed. Cards measure 2-1/16" by 2-1/2" with black and white photos.

| | | NR MT | EX |
|---|---|---|---|
| | Complete Set | 1500.00 | 525.00 |
| | Common Player 1-36 | 10.00 | 5.00 |
| | Common Player 37-48 | 15.00 | 7.50 |
| 1 | Bob Elliott | 60.00 | 7.00 |
| 2 | Ewell (The Whip) Blackwell | 18.00 | 9.00 |
| 3 | Ralph Kiner | 60.00 | 30.00 |
| 4 | Johnny Mize | 50.00 | 25.00 |
| 5 | Bob Feller | 90.00 | 45.00 |
| 6 | Larry (Yogi) Berra | 275.00 | 110.00 |
| 7 | Pete (Pistol Pete) Reiser | 32.00 | 16.00 |
| 8 | Phil (Scooter) Rizzuto | 125.00 | 44.00 |
| 12 | Johnny Sain | 20.00 | 10.00 |
| 13 | Willard Marshall | 30.00 | 15.00 |
| 14 | Allie Reynolds | 30.00 | 15.00 |
| 16 | Jack Lohrke | 22.00 | 11.00 |
| 17 | Enos (Country) Slaughter | 50.00 | 25.00 |
| 18 | Warren Spahn | 90.00 | 45.00 |

| | | NR MT | EX |
|---|---|---|---|
| 19 | Tommy (The Clutch) Henrich | 25.00 | 12.50 |
| 20 | Buddy Kerr | 22.00 | 11.00 |
| 22 | Floyd (Bill) Bevins (Bevens) | 30.00 | 15.00 |
| 24 | Emil (Dutch) Leonard | 22.00 | 11.00 |
| 26 | Frank Shea | 30.00 | 15.00 |
| 28 | Emil (The Antelope) Verban | 22.00 | 11.00 |
| 29 | Joe Page | 35.00 | 17.50 |
| 30 | "Whitey" Lockman | 22.00 | 11.00 |
| 34 | Sheldon (Available) Jones | 22.00 | 11.00 |
| 36 | Stan Musial | 375.00 | 150.00 |
| 38 | Al "Red" Schoendienst | 35.00 | 17.50 |
| 40 | Marty Marion | 25.00 | 12.50 |
| 47 | Bobby Thomson | 35.00 | 17.50 |
| 48 | George "Dave" Koslo | 40.00 | 9.00 |

### 1949 Bowman

This set consists of 240 cards (2-1/16" by 2-1/2") which feature black and white photos overprinted with various pastel colors. Twelve major variations can be found in the set. The

| | | NR MT | EX |
|---|---|---|---|
| | Complete Set | 9600. | 3500. |
| | Common Player 1-36 | 10.00 | 5.00 |
| | Common Player 37-73 | 12.00 | 6.00 |
| | Common Player 74-144 | 10.00 | 5.00 |
| | Common Player 145-240 | 45.00 | 20.00 |

| | | NR MT | EX |
|---|---|---|---|
| 1 | Vernon Bickford | 70.00 | 7.50 |
| 4 | Jerry Priddy (name on front) | 30.00 | 15.00 |
| 11 | Lou Boudreau | 35.00 | 17.50 |
| 18 | Bobby Thomson | 18.00 | 9.00 |
| 19 | Bobby Brown | 20.00 | 10.00 |
| 23 | Bobby Doerr | 35.00 | 17.50 |
| 24 | Stan Musial | 275.00 | 110.00 |
| 26 | George Kell | 35.00 | 17.50 |
| 27 | Bob Feller | 80.00 | 40.00 |
| 29 | Ralph Kiner | 40.00 | 20.00 |
| 33 | Warren Spahn | 80.00 | 40.00 |
| 35 | Vic Raschi | 20.00 | 10.00 |
| 36 | Harold "Peewee" Reese | 90.00 | 45.00 |
| 46 | Robin Roberts | 100.00 | 45.00 |
| 50 | Jackie Robinson | 450.00 | 180.00 |
| 60 | Larry "Yogi" Berra | 200.00 | 80.00 |
| 65 | Enos "Country" Slaughter | 40.00 | 20.00 |
| 69 | Tommy "The Clutch" Henrich | 25.00 | 12.50 |
| 70 | Carl Furillo | 30.00 | 15.00 |
| 78 | Sam Zoldak (name on front) | 30.00 | 15.00 |
| 82 | Joe Page | 16.00 | 8.00 |
| 83 | Bob Scheffing (name on front) | 30.00 | 15.00 |
| 85 | Roy Campanella | 350.00 | 140.00 |
| 85 | Johnny "Big John" Mize (no name on front) | 40.00 | 20.00 |
| 85 | Johnny "Big John" Mize (name on front) | 100.00 | 45.00 |
| 88 | Bill Salkeld (name on front) | 30.00 | 15.00 |
| 98 | Phil Rizzuto (no name on front) | 65.00 | 33.00 |
| 98 | Phil Rizzuto (name on front) | 125.00 | 50.00 |
| 100 | Gil Hodges | 100.00 | 45.00 |
| 109 | Ed Fitzgerald (Fitz Gerald) (printed name on back) | 30.00 | 15.00 |
| 110 | Early Wynn | 65.00 | 33.00 |
| 111 | Al "Red" Schoendienst | 20.00 | 10.00 |
| 114 | Allie Reynolds | 25.00 | 12.50 |
| 124 | Danny Murtaugh (printed name on back) | 30.00 | 15.00 |
| 126 | Al Brazle (printed name on back) | 30.00 | 15.00 |
| 127 | Henry "Heeney" Majeski (printed name on back) | 30.00 | 15.00 |

| | | NR MT | EX |
|---|---|---|---|
| 128 | Johnny Vander Meer | 16.00 | 8.00 |
| 129 | Bill "The Bull" Johnson | 16.00 | 8.00 |
| 132 | Al Evans (printed name on back) | 30.00 | 15.00 |
| 143 | Bob Dillinger (printed name on back) | 30.00 | 15.00 |
| 162 | Elwin "Preacher" Roe | 75.00 | 38.00 |
| 175 | Luke Appling | 80.00 | 40.00 |
| 194 | Ralph Branca | 70.00 | 35.00 |
| 209 | Charlie "King Kong" Keller | 70.00 | 35.00 |
| 214 | Richie Ashburn | 350.00+ | 140.00 |
| 224 | Leroy "Satchel" Paige | 950.00 | 380.00 |
| 225 | Gerry Coleman | 70.00 | 35.00 |
| 226 | Edwin "Duke" Snider | 700.00 | 280.00 |
| 229 | Ed Lopat | 75.00 | 35.00 |
| 233 | Larry Doby | 100.00 | 45.00 |
| 238 | Bob Lemon | 175.00 | 75.00 |
| 240 | Norman "Babe" Young (photo actually Bobby Young) | 80.00 | 25.00 |

### 1950 Bowman

Cards (2-1/16" by 2-1/2") in this 252-card set are beautiful color art reproductions of actual photographs.

---

*This is a typical page from a 1988 issue of* Baseball Card Price Guide Monthly, *one of the major publications for baseball card collectors. Along with all the other factors that can affect price, the physical condition of a card is crucial: MT refers to "mint" condition, NR MT means "near mint," and EX is "excellent."*

of 157,000. Another one, the *Baseball Card Price Guide Monthly,* treats collecting more like investing in the stock market than in nostalgia; each month it devotes page after page to the prices of cards (over 45,000), charting the ups and downs (usually emphasizing only the ups) of various cards. "A proven track record" goes the title of an article that opens, "Look at the phenomenal price surges these cards have enjoyed in a few short years," and the accompanying charts seem straight out of a stock investor's newsletter. The magazine boasts of employing "the hobby's only full-time pricing analyst . . . monitoring card prices nationwide *on a daily basis.*" Cards are graded—"Mint," "Near Mint," "Excellent"—and incredible amounts of trivia and details are tracked: "I'm having trouble understanding which variation cards might be included in a 1988 Topps set I would buy," writes a troubled reader to *Baseball Card Price Guide.* "Will I get the blue or white letter variation of the Keith Comstock card? Or do I have to buy wax packs to get both varieties?"

Prices of older cards and of retired players tend to have stabilized, depending mostly on the demand of collectors, but values can take an upward leap when a player is elected to the Hall of Fame. Current players cards' prices rise and fall depending on what they do or don't do during the season (batting average, home runs, and so forth), while special risks and profits attach to the cards of rookies. All serious collectors want to own the first, or "rookie," card of a player who eventually becomes a popular star—but who can predict this with certainty? For every Wade Boggs '83 and Don Mattingly '84 card, collectors can be stuck with a Mark Fidrych or a Joe Charboneau or a Ron Kittle. A Gregg Jefferies, the "hot" rookie in 1988, rose from its wax-pack cost of three cents to five dollars during a few months in 1988, but who can be sure where he'll be a year or two from now?

It must be admitted that the prices of cards are influenced by the players' off-field behavior—drug problems, for instance—and their attitudes, at least as perceived and reported in the media. (Dwight Gooden's rookie card shot up to $120 in 1984, plunged to $30 in 1987, then moved back to $65.) Some players clearly are more popular than others, for reasons that cannot always be traced to stats. This at least suggests that there are some personal enthusiasms, some true fans, behind this business.

But a business it has certainly become. Where once there were only a few dealers and shops in major cities in the United States, there are now an estimated thirty-five hundred retail card stores throughout the land, many of them run by collectors who think they can turn their hobby into a profit-making operation. In addition, there are another estimated ten thousand dealers who buy and sell through the mail. Most of these are small part-time operations, but a number of major dealers traffic in complete sets, even whole cases of cards. (Like stamp collecting, baseball card and memorabilia collecting requires a certain amount of supporting material—albums, holders, and the like—that are also sold by dealers.) The most publicized dealer, Alan Rosen of Montvale, New Jersey, is known as "Mr. Mint," a pun on his interest in cards in the best condition and the vast sums of money he has invested in cards (over $2 million in 1987 alone).

Then there are the endless shows, fairs and conventions where many of the one million collectors in North America get together to buy, sell, and trade, primarily cards but also other sports memorabilia. (These are where the players, active or retired, show up to sign pictures, balls, bats, or whatever.) Incredibly, *The New York Times* reported there are about one hundred such get-togethers in North America—each week!

Realizing that it could capitalize on this great surge of interest in baseball cards, Topps Chewing Gum Company went public in 1987 (inevitably raising the question of whether their stock would perform better than their cards). That same year, Score Board, Inc., raised $2.7 million on the stock market to issue yet another line of baseball cards. Meantime, at least two card-investment clubs have been formed: in one, the Baseball Card Society, for a minimum of $30 a month, members acquire cards specially selected by "Advisors" who are supposed to be adept at picking promising rookies and potential Hall of Famers. (The top class of members are asked to invest $125 each month.) In the Rookie Card Club, sponsored by *The Sporting News,* members sign on for as little as $19.95 or as much as $99.95 a *month,* and get monthly sets of only rookie cards.

The surest sign of success is the attempt by the unscrupulous to exploit it. While legitimate card companies negotiate contracts with the players, who get a flat fee plus royalties, illegal companies just print cards of current players and reprint those of older players. Because a man can be a rookie only once, there is particularly good money to be made by reissuing the rookie cards of players who have made it. Unscrupulous dealers sometimes carefully open packs and replace valuable cards with commons, then reseal the packs. Speculators hoard cards with the goal of driving up prices. Cards are also sold with forged autographs of the players. An extraordinary variant on this scam arises when star players appear at autograph sessions at fairs or conventions; the sponsors of these events must sell tickets in order to make back the appearance fees they pay the players, but unscrupulous people have been known to counterfeit the admission tickets! Meanwhile, a Massachusetts man has been charged with embezzling $88,000 to build his baseball card collection, and an Oregon man, according to some reports, was murdered for his valuable collection of cards and other baseball memorabilia.

More than one observer of this current baseball card craze has compared it to the "tulipomania" that seized Europe in the 1630s, when thousands of people invested increasingly larger sums of money in new varieties of Dutch tulips—until the whole bubble burst. There is indeed some question about how much longer this baseball card investing spree can go on. The original basis for the rising prices of these cards was that *(a)* there were limited numbers printed in the first place and *(b)* even most of these were thrown out. Now there are billions being printed every year and countless people save them with the idea of cashing in.

Compare this situation to another collecting hobby such as rare books: the number of first editions can never be increased and gradually volumes vanish into libraries—thus the increase in the price of those that remain on the market. People who buy later editions have no expectations that their copies will ever have much value. But since each contemporary player may have as many as 5 million cards issued, it is hard to believe that these will accrue in value like the cards of earlier decades. In 1987, Fleer issued a special commemorative set in a tin box; it sold for $40 to $50, and because it was promoted as a "limited edition" its price quickly shot up to $125; then it turned out that the edition was not all that limited, and the price collapsed to $40 again.

People promoting the trade in cards talk ceaselessly about the increase in prices of the same few cards, implying that all cards will follow an endlessly upward curve. "One Hundred Dollars Invested in Rookie Baseball Cards in 1980 Is Worth $2,449 Today," claims *The Sporting News Rookie Card Club*. "No Black Monday in Baseball Cards" boasts the Baseball Card Society in soliciting members for its investment plan. But the stock market has to average out hundreds of stocks before it can claim to be going up. The promoters of card collecting constantly trumpet such great deals as the 1984 Donruss Mattingly card, trading at $75 by 1988, or the 1973 Mike Schmidt, selling for $170, but neglect to point out how many cards you would have had to buy in 1984 and 1973 (and all the years between) to be sure of obtaining such standouts. (The complete Topps set in each recent year comes to 792 cards.) The famous 1952 Mantle card owes its high value to the fact that it was issued late in the year and that, when Topps found itself stuck with too many unsold cards, it dumped them into the ocean. Now collectors and dealers buy up whole cases of cards, thereby precluding the very scarcity they hope to capitalize on.

Stamp collecting, it can be argued, has remained in fashion for over a hundred years and shows no sign of collapsing; but only a few collectors can be sure of seeing their investment appreciate in value—most are content with enjoying their collection. That is what must happen sooner or later to card collectors. Dealers and publications that promise otherwise are almost certainly guilty of misrepresenting their product.

*Table Games*  In a land where Monopoly is a major pursuit, baseball table games might at first seem strictly bush league. Read on. To begin with, there are table games and there are table games. In 1988, Parker Brothers came out with Starting Lineup Talking Baseball, a fancy game involving baseball cards, a large plastic model of a baseball stadium, some electronic wizardry that allows over 250,000 possible plays, and a taped announcer who calls them all. Only a year before, the Hegman Toy & Game Company of Ohio came out with The Big-League Baseball Game, with baseball cards, a fold-up paper stadium, and old-fashioned dice to control the flow of the game. Such games are clever fun but look suspiciously like the type that get played on Christmas Day and are then sent to the closet.

But these games are simply updated versions of baseball table games that have been around for well over a century, specifically the type that tries to replicate the physical action of the game, usually by moving tiny figures, pegs, cards, or whatever around the field. In the late 1950s and early 1960s there was one made by the Tudor Company that moved magnetized players around the ballpark by mechanical (and later, electric) devices, but no one except specialized collectors now knows of it. And there have been hundreds of other mechanical games that involve some kind of miniature bat striking a ball or a disc, plus hundreds of others that involve dice, spinners, cards, or some other activator to guide the movements of the players on the board. The patents and copyrights for such games tally in the thousands.

Many of these games use cards as part of the game. Lawton's Patent Game of 1884 used a deck of thirty-two cards, each one directing the players what to do next. Tom Barker produced a game in 1913, using a traditional fifty-two-card deck but with pictures of baseball players. Other baseball card games followed and continue to this day (and provide a double-whammy for baseball card collectors). Inevitably, many of the great stars of baseball had their names attached to these games, often with the suggestion that they had somehow invented them; in most cases they were simply selling the celebrity. Two of the most original baseball games, however, were invented by baseball players.

Ethan Allen of Cincinnati was a major league outfielder from 1926 to 1938 and although he may never make the Hall of Fame, he deserves recognition for inventing the All-Star Baseball Game about 1948. Allen realized that the drawback of all the table baseball games was that because they relied on dice, a spinner, the turn of a card, or some mechanical device, all players had the same chances; there was no way of accounting for variability among the players' real-life abilities. Allen's innovation was to provide a separate disc for each player with different segments on the rim to reflect the player's tendency to hit singles or home runs, to strike out or walk. The spinner placed over each disc has a greater or lesser chance of stopping within the proportioned segment, thus reflecting the player's real actions.

*This illustration appeared in an 1868 issue of* Frank Leslie's Illustrated Newspaper *with an article on Frances Sebring's newly invented "Parlor Base-Ball Field," which the genteel Victorians are shown playing. Note that women are already assumed to be interested in the game and that the children are playing their own game. Since no known copies of the game exist, it may never have gone into production.*

Ethan Allen was ingenious but by no means the first baseball player to invent a table game. That honor belongs to Frances C. Sebring, of Hoboken, New Jersey, home of the Elysian Fields where the Knickerbockers and other New York City teams played beginning in 1845. Sebring pitched for one of those teams, the Empire Club (founded in 1854), and by 1866 he had come up with the "Parlor Base-Ball Field," the first baseball table game of any kind. He claimed to have invented the game to help an invalid player-friend, and it is remarkable how much Sebring was able to contain in this first table game. The board covers the space of some two square feet and is shaped, by coincidence, almost exactly like a modern home plate. A coin about the size of our quarter is laid on the board in front of a small spring at the pitcher's position; a small bat that lies flat on the board at home plate is attached to another spring; the person serving as pitcher releases the spring that sends the coin sliding and the person controlling the bat-spring releases it; the coin (unless it is missed, in which case a strike is called) slides forward and either drops into holes at the positions of the infielders and outfielders or comes to rest on circular spots or marked spaces. If the coin slides into a hole, it is an automatic fly out, while printed instructions on the spots and spaces give other calls: "double," "home run," and the like. When a batter gets on base, he is represented by a small wooden circle (which, if knocked off by a batted ball, is regarded as an out).

The rules contain numerous other analogies to a real game; for instance, if the pitched coin doesn't reach the bat, it is a balk; if it goes out of reach of the bat's swing, it is a ball. But its complexity and price—five dollars, at a time when many people still made only ten dollars a week—may have limited its success, because the game never did catch on. Although announced in 1866 in *Frank Leslie's Illustrated Newspaper* as though it were available (and patented in 1868), it may never have gone into production, for no copies are known to exist today. Variations on Sebring's game did appear later in the nineteenth century, one of which added a device that traps a ball or object hit directly at a player. This version eventually showed up as the sturdy spring-action game long popular in penny arcades. Apparently Sebring was ahead of his time.

*Rotisserie Ball*  In 1980 a group of young-middle-aged men in New York City launched the first season of a new baseball league. Taking the name of their league from the small restaurant on New York's East Side where they often gathered to eat while talking baseball, they concocted the notion of forming their own "dream teams" of active players and pitting them against

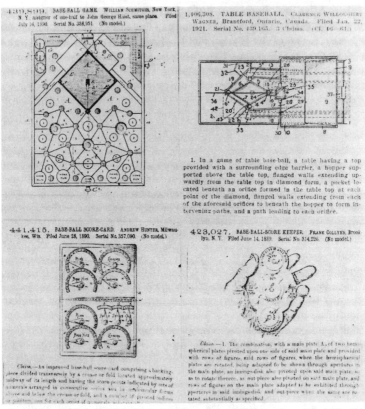

*In the years following Sebring's 1866 patent application for a baseball table game, literally hundreds of applications have been filed for similar games; many, like these (top row), involve incredibly complicated ways to make the game more closely replicate the real game's mental strategies and physical tactics. Meanwhile, there have been countless patents taken out on other baseball paraphernalia, these mechanical scorekeepers being only two of many.*

each other during the upcoming season. The performance and ultimate standings of each team would depend on a point system that in turn was based on eight crucial statistics (four for batting, four for pitching) based on the actual performance of their team's players during the current season. Thus was Rotisserie Baseball born.

The phenomenon has swept the country. There are now an estimated 125,000 individuals in North America who manage their own teams, and the original Rotisserie League concept has become so popular that a number of competing leagues have set up shop, offering similar action with minor variations. Since widely scattered individuals now participate in a season's play, there is a certain amount of administration involved—for announcements, mailings, and so forth—and this also means fees are charged by those who run the leagues. The original Rotisserie League still tends to garner most of the publicity—several of its members are New York media types and write books and articles promoting the game—but throughout the continent, on the first weekend after the season begins in April, thousands of participating managers gather (American Leaguers on Saturday, National Leaguers on Sunday) in small groups—ten teams if you're within the National League, twelve for the American—to make up that season's teams in Rotisserie-style baseball. The names they give their leagues and individual teams now reflect the origins and identities of the members; in New York City, for instance, the original league now calls itself Tony's Italian Kitchen League. At the annual meeting, each manager puts together a team of fourteen batters and nine pitchers for the coming season, drawing only on players from that one of the two major leagues with which they have chosen to be affiliated and limited to players not already owned by other managers.

When starting a new league, all players in the "parent" major league are up for auction. Most leagues place a maximum on how much each manager may have invested in the team—$260, for instance, is the sum set by Tony's Italian Kitchen League—with the players going to the highest bidder. Thus, the Blood Brothers of Tony's Italian Kitchen League paid a dollar for players such as Jerry Browne or Chris Bosio, but forty-five dollars for Dave Righetti and forty-seven dollars for Joe Carter. Once a league gets going, trades are made, players are claimed on waivers, and farm-team players may be activated if they are actually called up by their real-world teams. (Each manager also maintains a minor-league team composed of players not on the active rosters of any other team.) During the actual season, each manager must follow the status of the real players on his team, and if a player is placed on the disabled list or sent down, the manager is allowed to activate other players. There are many other ways in which a team's composition reflects the actual goings-on in the majors: For example, a player is lost if he actually moves to the other league, and rosters may be expanded to twenty-four in September. The two limiting factors at all times, if it isn't clear, are that each team is limited to active players in one of the two major leagues, and each owner-manager is limited to an agreed-upon sum of money to invest in all players. Thus, if you have forty-five dollars invested in an ace pitcher and he leaves the league, you have that same forty-five dollars to spend on other players through some combination of purchases and trades.

As the actual season proceeds, managers are expected to follow the daily stats of their team members in the relevant statistical categories: home runs, RBIs, stolen bases, and batting average for position players; wins, saves, ERA, and "ratio" (walks plus hits divided by innings pitched) for pitchers. Points are awarded on the basis of where your players stand in these categories, with 10 (12 in the American) points awarded for being first, 9 (11 in the American) for being second, and so on down the line; final standings in a Rotisserie league are not determined until the last out is recorded in the season's actual major league play. Most leagues reward managers for their standings, with the top five teams getting at least their investment back. The tradition set by the original Rotisserie League is for the managers to get together and pour a bottle of Yoo-Hoo, the chocolate-flavored drink once promoted by Yogi Berra, over the head of the winning manager. Then the managers spend the winter trading, drafting, and planning how to improve their teams for next season.

There is more to the Rotisserie League, but not much. Clearly there are elements of Cutesy and Yuppie and Egghead to all this, but it is harmless fun and games. The originators dislike the label "fantasy baseball," preferring to call it "ultra-real," and for the active participants, it is evidently just that. They report spending many of their waking hours thinking about their team's performance, trying to make trades that will be to their advantage, haunting the sports pages to make sure they have not missed some obscure injury or release that would allow them, for instance, to get a nondrafted player still in the pool. But the fact is, once they have selected their team, they are pretty much at the mercy of statistics. For that is the point about this Rotisserie League baseball: its appeal is to would-be owners or general managers, not to field managers. Everything depends on how well you have done in assembling your team, although smart trading throughout the season can greatly improve your standing; but there is little you can do to affect your team's standing. It all lies in the real players' performances and the occasional vagaries of a season (such as an injury). Tip-sheet publications help to fill those months with information on preseason reports, drafts, player comparisons, and strategies.

Since it would be incredibly time-consuming to compute your players' performance and your team's standings (it takes hours to go through the newspapers to pin down your players' statistics and to rank them with others), there are now numerous aids. Computer software exists to provide statistics and other information to help a manager plan a team. Computer spread-sheet programs aid managers in working out the statistics and standings as the season proceeds. And for those who find even that too time-consuming, there are now a number of firms that provide support services: For fees, they will compile all the stats for your team's players, record transactions, and provide weekly standings. A random issue of *The Sporting News* carries ads from at least twelve such firms. Many grown people these days are paying good money to find out how their imaginary team stands each week in relation to other phantom teams, and Rotisserie League ball seems firmly established as another American pastime.

*Doppelgamers*  As big a phenomenon as Rotisserie baseball has become, it is not really in the same league with a still older form of statistical baseball gaming. This "other game" has gone on quietly for almost four decades in a world parallel to the baseball that is known and played and loved by millions of Americans. Real baseball is played in the light before masses of people; Rotisserie-type baseball is played by articulate, upscale individuals; and simpler table games involve some simulation of the physical action of the game. But this "other" baseball exists in a shadowy underworld of serious, dedicated players who seek neither light nor crowds nor publicity nor physical simulations: They know that the true game lies in one's head and in the numbers.

The story of this form of baseball is usually traced only as far back as 1931 but it really began in the early 1920s when Clifford A. Van Beek of Green Bay, Wisconsin, invented a truly new type of baseball game. He filed for a patent in 1923 and received it in 1925, but it was 1931 before he was able to produce the first commercial version of the game. It was called National Pastime and was advertised in several magazines, but whether because of its expense, its complexity, or just the mood of the Depression, it did not catch on. When the printer went bankrupt, the artwork was locked up by the foreclosure process so there was no second edition. Clifford Van Beek seems to have totally vanished—and he has never received the credit due for inventing the game that has spawned the modern phenomenon, and industry, of statistically based games.

Meanwhile, a teenager in Lancaster, Pennsylvania, J. Richard Seitz, had seen an ad for National Pastime in *Baseball Magazine.* Seitz had been a baseball fan since he was taken to his first game in 1926; he had been playing one of the many mechanical games but was already thinking about a more imaginative game that would reflect the actual players and plays. Seitz sent for National Pastime and found that it involved a pair of dice, a set of play sheets, and cards picturing players active in 1930; on each card was a list of numbers that bore some relation to that player's career performance, while the play

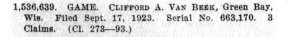

1,536,639. GAME. CLIFFORD A. VAN BEEK, Green Bay, Wis. Filed Sept. 17, 1923. Serial No. 663,170. 3 Claims. (Cl. 273—93.)

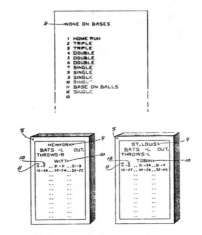

1. A game comprising a set of dice each of which indicates a digit of a number, a set of cards each representing players having two columns of numbers, one column having numbers which may be indicated by the dice and the other column having selected numbers, and a set of play sheets having a column of numbers corresponding to the last mentioned numbers and having plays marked opposite such numbers.

*These are the original patent drawings submitted by Clifford A. Van Beek in 1923 in support of his baseball simulation game. The elements that were so novel at that time—the dice to obtain numbers by chance, the cards for players, and the play sheets—have since been incorporated into the various statistical baseball games, of which the APBA is the oldest and best known.*

sheets governed what occurred in standard game situations (such as bases full, or runners on first and third). When the dice were thrown, their numbers led to a number on the card of the batter and this in turn led to a number on the play sheet that directed what the player did. Despite its primitive elements, this game was close to what Seitz had been imagining: Unlike any baseball table game until then, it was not limited to the random results of a spinner or dice; it depended to some extent on the player's knowledge of actual major leaguers, and its progress reflected their actual statistical performance. In other words, the player of the game could exercise something of the control of a real manager.

Van Beek's game soon faded from public view, but Seitz and some of his friends continued to play this game, and eventually they organized a small "league" they called the American Professional Baseball Association (APBA). Since only the 1930 cards existed, Seitz began to make his own cards; more important, he began to incorporate new elements on the charts and cards to reflect the realities of the game, such as factoring in differences between hits with two out or less than two out, and particularly the differences among pitchers.

When he went off to the army in 1942, Seitz introduced the game to his buddies and found they liked to play it. After the war, Seitz returned to Lancaster and had to go to work, but he didn't abandon his dream of marketing his game. Finally, with a set of player cards based on 1950 statistics, Seitz issued the APBA Major League Baseball Game. It would still be several years before Seitz could sell enough copies of the game to enable him to quit his job and devote himself fulltime to his game, but the modern age of statistical baseball games began in 1951 with the appearance of the first APBA game.

What has happened since makes the Rotisserie League addicts seem like little old ladies holding tea parties. The APBA game itself has become increasingly refined over the years, so that, for instance, the cards can account for statistical probabilities that occur only once in every 1,296 plate appearances by a player; pitchers' control and strikeout stats have likewise been factored in. APBA now has a Master Baseball Game version, which incorporates far more complex strategies and statistics for the more serious game players, and it also issues cards for the pre-1950 seasons. Meanwhile, others began to get into the act with games that vary enough to avoid copyright suits. The best known of these is the Strat-O-Matic Baseball Game, introduced in 1963; it boasts that its player cards have factored in a still wider range of elements of the game—clutch hitting, for instance, hit-and-run and bunting ability, and throwing range and error frequency; for pitchers, such factors as stamina, hold ratings, and record against lefties and righties; and even the effects of particular ballparks on individual batters. The newest entry in this market, Pursue the Pennant, boasts of being still more sophisticated; drawing on the newly available work of statistical experts such as Bill James and the Elias Bureau, it factors in such elements as artificial turf or grass, wind direction, whether the batter is a straightaway or a pull hitter, and how frequently the pitcher throws home-run balls to right-handed or left-handed hitters. It even has a special HOT symbol on cards of temperamental players so that a certain combination of dice may result in a fight, a confrontation with the umpire, and a suspension. Clearly these new games are for serious players.

And the players are out there, all over North America. The APBA game began with individuals who liked to play solitaire or with neighborhood friends. Many statistical baseball game players continue this way; some carry on through the mail with old friends or pen pals. All of these thousands of players take sets of cards for each team and play out entire previous seasons, competing against their opponents but, more essentially, matching their managerial savvy against the actual manager's.

APBA, meanwhile, has grown far beyond this replaying of games of previous seasons to play-by-mail draft leagues; instead of just using the cards of real teams, it operates much like the Rotisserie League, pooling all players in the National or American League and allowing a manager to select a team that plays against other selected teams in their new league—either in face-to-face groups or through the mail. (When a manager sends his team "on the road," he sends instructions, some of which can be incredibly intricate.) Because the draft-league games cannot be played out against past seasons but require new teams and managers, they have given birth to still more supporting apparatus such as the *APBA Journal,* a monthly newsletter that keeps new and old managers in touch with one another. Strat-O-Matic and Pursue the Pennant players naturally have their own newsletters. Many baseball magazines now devote columns and articles to this form of baseball and occasionally the results of league play will even surface in newspaper sports pages, meaningless to all except the initiated. Managers within leagues also find ways to keep in touch, often putting out their own little newsletters in which they discuss, debate, and sometimes argue over their teams' strengths and weaknesses, rules changes, and anything else that managers worry about.

Much of the appeal of these statistical baseball games is that they allow Everyman to sit in his kitchen and go beyond replaying countless baseball games to fantasizing being the owner, general manager, and field manager of a baseball team. This is one reason why the diehard statistical-game players look with contempt at the newer computer versions of these games. However, it was inevitable that this type of game would also be computerized. These computerized games (and they include other team sports such as football and basketball) are now a major subdivision of software, and basically they incorporate Van Beek's original insights. Some of these computer games go far beyond statistical replays; they provide elaborate graphics for arcadelike animated effects that show the actual play in action, depict different stadiums, or shift perspective depending on which side of the plate the batter stands. Some even have sound effects—playing "Stars and Stripes Forever" at the outset, sounding the "charge" theme, and announcing each batter with a digitalized voice. Clever, but not for the purist.

All over North America, then, thousands of people, mostly young men but not limited to them (George Bush is reputed to have been an avid player), spend thousands of hours playing and replaying these games of baseball. (Unlike the Rotisserie League habit, though, which can cost $800 or more per season to sustain, APBA-type games do not require much money to play.) Understand this: Some managers replay every single game of a major league's previous season, throwing the dice and recording the moves called for by the player cards until all twenty-seven outs for both teams have been attained. (A typical game takes only about a half hour to play, but a 162-game season needs eighty-one hours.) The top-ranked table baseball player in North America in 1987 was Jim Battista, a twenty-seven-year-old financial executive from Yeadon, Pennsylvania; he plays more than six hundred games a year in face-to-face leagues as well as many solitaire matches. Young men have been known to drop out of college, not to mention life, in their addiction to these games: Robert Coover expressed some of the obsessive quality of the game in his 1968 novel, *The Universal Baseball Association, J. Henry Waugh, Prop.*

On the back pages of *The Sporting News,* along with all the ads for the baseball games and supporting services, one ad stands out: "Men's Divorce Rights," it announces, "Protecting Men's Rights. Custody, Support, Property." Presumably this lawyer knows something about the role of table baseball games in contemporary life.

*Fan-Antics*   There are many other ways by which people express their attachment to the game of baseball. Barry Halper, in New Jersey, has gathered in his basement a veritable museum of baseball memorabilia, generally conceded to be the largest and most meaningful such collection outside the Cooperstown Hall of Fame. Halper has been collecting baseball memorabilia since he was fourteen years old and got Cy Young's autograph on a baseball. Since then, he has collected not only the autographs of every man, living or dead, in the Hall of Fame, but numerous unusual autographs, including on one piece of paper the signatures of all players who have hit over five hundred home runs. But autographs are only one part of Halper's collection; he has over a million baseball cards (including complete sets of every series of cards issued since 1890); nine hundred players' uniforms; programs of all the

All-Star Games and World Series back to 1914; hundreds of press pins, commemorative buttons, tie clasps, and cufflinks; scores of posters, books, paintings, photographs, letters, and trophies; plus countless individual objects such as the batting helmet Hank Aaron wore when he hit his 715th home run. (Halper once had the actual pine tar bat used by George Brett to hit the controversial pine-tar home run; he gave it back to Kansas City, but he owns the ball itself—autographed by the man who threw it, Goose Gossage.)

Halper, admittedly, is a fairly wealthy man—he even owns a share in the

*The grandfather of all fanatic fans was the Boston saloonkeeper Michael T. "Nuf Ced" McGreevy, who from the 1890s to about 1918 led the "Royal Rooters," a group of Boston fans, first in support of the Boston National League team and then in support of the new American League team, the Red Sox. McGreevy's saloon, called "Third Base," was covered with Red Sox memorabilia (note the lights—made to look like bats and balls); the photographs now form the famous collection in the Boston Public Library.*

Yankees—but wealth is not a prerequisite for being a dedicated fan. People of modest means all over the country maintain small one-room "museums" or shrines filed with baseball memorabilia, often focused on a particular team or player. One man tapes every game of baseball he can get access to, on radio and TV; he maintains a library of thousands of games and has members of his family, now scattered throughout the country, also taping games; he is especially proud that he can sometimes produce three or four broadcasts of the same game, taped from different stations and with different sportscasters.

Other fans now sign on for special cruises, usually to the Caribbean, with the lure of hearing and meeting several baseball stars on the ship. Specialized tours visit spring training camps or include tickets to games in all the major league cities. There have long been summer baseball camps

*Surely the greatest coup for any baseball fan—better than any baseball card, any autograph—would be to have "bagged" Babe Ruth. The men in this rare family photograph could boast of just this: They stand with Babe Ruth after he had joined them for deer hunting in 1941 in a small community in western Massachusetts. Babe Ruth stands alone to this day among baseball's pop icons, in part because of the natural way he could go off on such expeditions.*

for young boys, sponsored by some star who may put in a brief appearance and pass on a few pointers, but the latest variation on this is baseball camps for grown men, where for a few thousand dollars aging frustrated jocks can get into the uniform of their favorite team, mix with some of the former players, and play ball. The Chicago Cubs introduced the first such "Fantasy Camp" in 1983; it has drawn an average of sixty "campers" each year since (four of them have been women), and even at $2,995 a week shows no sign of running out of campers. Several other teams now run similar camps. Or if you really want to go first class, you can hire an ex–major leaguer (such as Jack Aker) to "tutor" your child in baseball.

Cooperstown, of course, has attracted fans for some fifty years, but with the exception of a batting cage and a pitching speed recorder, it is designed to foster passive nostalgia, not activate fantasies. But there now exists a theme park, Boardwalk and Baseball, located in Florida to take advantage of fans who are attracted to the region by the spring training camps. In addition to a display of some memorabilia and showings of baseball films, it has a batting cage, a pitching speed recorder, and a fielding cage; it will even print up a baseball card with your own picture. Two men associated with the Oakland A's have come up with yet another novelty, Fantasy Play-by-Play. The fan gets to sit in a special booth at a regular major league game and is taped (twenty dollars for audio, thirty dollars for video) as he "calls" a half inning of an actual game. So far only the A's and the Pirates offer this copyrighted attraction, but an imitator has already appeared in San Diego.

Perhaps the ultimate is something called Bingham Baseball: for twenty-two dollars, the fan gets to pick a position he'd like to play, and then is reported in a monthly magazine as though he were an active player in the major leagues. His season's career is covered in considerable detail as he moves from spring training through the pennant race and possibly into the World Series, and all his batting or pitching feats are recorded as he contends for the MVP or the Cy Young Award. Surely this must be the fanatic fan's most fantastic fantasy, the grand slam of pop culture.

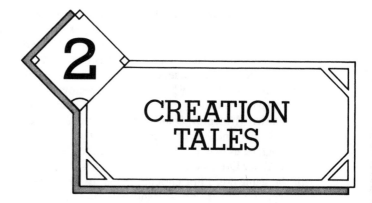

# CREATION
# TALES

One of the most endearing qualities of baseball is its role in human imagination. Very few of a club's most devoted fans ever get to attend even one tenth of its games, which means that for most people, baseball is experienced primarily in the newspapers, through writers' interpretations; on the radio, which leaves everything to the imagination; or on television, which creates its own reality. As such a product of the imagination, baseball very easily takes on the attributes of a mythological system, and as Civil War historian Bruce Catton has pointed out, baseball's "legends are, in some ways, the most enduring part of the game. Baseball has even more of them than the Civil War, and its fans prize them highly." In the United States, which as a nation is largely defined by its lack of any sense of history or tradition, the citizens turn to myths for continuity, and to sports for myths. Baseball is not only America's oldest popular team sport, but one of the oldest institutions in American society.

In the postcard-lovely village of Cooperstown, New York, a statue of a barefoot boy in overalls and a straw hat holding a baseball bat stands proudly on the spot where Abner Doubleday never invented baseball. Like so many other elements of America's manufactured past, this shrine is not entirely without problems, for not only did Abner Doubleday never invent baseball in Cooperstown (the town, appropriately, was founded by the father of one of our greatest creators of fictional folklore, James Fenimore Cooper) or anywhere else, but the corollary myth that baseball was a product of rural American life does not stand up under the unequivocal documentation that baseball came into existence among young New York City businessmen in the 1840s and was purely a product of an urban environment. Until after the Civil War, when baseball spread to small villages and towns, the game continued to grow almost exclusively in manufacturing centers.

Legends that have been consciously created might properly be considered fraudulent, or worse, but in baseball, which has always been a source of enjoyment for so many, and in which reality and illusion have always been so far apart, somehow it doesn't seem to matter much. Baseball has indeed committed the unforgivable sin of locating its creation myths in historical time, so that their inaccuracies are verifiable, but its scribes have been able to convince us that if children can have their Santa Claus, grown-ups can have their Abner Doubleday. Baseball needs its mythology, almost as if the playing of the game were not enough; hence its dependence upon statistics, which constantly compare present and past, and its corresponding dependence on rules. In 1860, when Porter's *The Spirit of the Times* reprinted the latest update of the rules, it admonished, "Every Base Ball player shall have a copy by him at all times."

At first glance rules and mythology might seem antithetical, but as a practical matter they have served each other well. When statistics indicated that there were not so many .300 hitters as there used to be, the rules were changed to lower the pitcher's mound, so that new heroes and legends might be created. On other occasions the ball has been made more lively—or less so—to produce the same effect. Baseball officialdom never admits when it has altered the ball, just as pitchers never admit to doctoring the ball, because the great unwritten code of baseball is that anything goes if it helps you win, just as the great unwritten rule of American society is that nothing is illegal if you don't get caught. Even the aura of disrepute that has always clung to baseball and to those who play it professionally has become a traditional part of its charm.

Be that as it may, thanks largely to the machinations of Albert G. Spalding, by 1939 baseball achieved the status of a cult with all the paraphernalia of a religion. Its predominant creation myth, firmly adhered to by legions of the devout despite incontrovertible proof to the contrary, required that it build a shrine at Cooperstown, a monument to devotion and shrewd public relations, to which millions of pilgrims have since come to gaze reverently on its relics. One might almost say that if no Abner Doubleday had existed, baseball would have had to invent one.

Most artifacts and institutions are the result of a long process of evolution. Basketball may indeed have had its inventor, the hula hoop had an inventor, and our Constitution and the atom bomb had committees of inventors, although they did not work in a vacuum. But baseball *insists* on *one* inventor because it is a mythological system, and because mythological systems abhor natural processes. Absurd and embarrassing as the Abner Doubleday story is, baseball's peculiar affinity for mythology still animates its fans. The question now seems to be, "Well, if Abner Doubleday didn't invent baseball, then who did?" As we have tried to demonstrate, this is really not a very good question, but from those with a little knowledge, the answer is invariably, "Alexander Cartwright." Too bad he didn't invent baseball either.

*"No Rounders!"*   Abner Doubleday was a man of parts. He was a West Point graduate, a Civil War general, and after his retirement from active service, a contributor to newspapers and magazines. He never mentioned baseball in his articles. He never claimed that he invented baseball. No contemporary records have ever been discovered that connect him to baseball, and no one ever saw him play baseball or attend a baseball game (only one person claims to have seen him play, as a child). None of his sixty-seven diaries mentions baseball. His obituary in *The New York Times* makes no mention of baseball, nor does a memorial volume published by the New York State Monument Commission in 1918. He never mentioned baseball to A. G. Mills, fourth president of the National League and a comrade in arms. It may be that he was an extraordinarily modest man who did not choose to take credit for his great invention, but as far as anyone has yet been able to discover, his name was never in any way associated with baseball during his lifetime, and it seems reasonable to conclude that Abner Doubleday went to his grave in 1893 without any idea that his name would forever be linked with the invention of baseball.

Doubleday's curious beatification began in 1889 at the banquet held at Delmonico's in New York City to celebrate the somewhat less than triumphant return of A. G. Spalding and his all-stars from a global baseball tour; Mark Twain and future president Theodore Roosevelt were among the three hundred worthies in attendance. National League president A. G. Mills spoke on the occasion and excited the diners when he told them that "patriotism and research" had established that baseball was uniquely American and not, as generally believed, descended from the English rounders or any other foreign game. It is significant that Mills, a lifelong baseball enthusiast, failed to mention Doubleday, whom he knew; he also failed to mention what "research" he had in mind. But the "patriotism" in the room was palpable; the audience was so pleased that they cheered Mills wildly, and grown men took up the chant of "No Rounders!"

Quite likely the matter would have ended there, but in 1905 Henry Chadwick, baseball's oldest and most respected journalist and for decades the editor of Spalding's *Base Ball Guide,* wrote an article in the *Guide* that described his own youthful play at rounders (he was born in England) and mentioned that rounders was the game from which baseball had evolved. This was by no means a revolutionary statement; before the 1880s it was generally accepted that baseball had evolved from the English children's game of rounders, and had received its essential American character when its rules were codified by the Knickerbocker Base Ball Club in 1845. In 1878, Spalding himself had written in his *Guide* that Englishmen watching Americans play baseball who "accused them of playing rounders" were not far wrong because "the game unquestionably thus originated." But in 1905, Spalding, by now convinced by his own rhetoric that a game so fundamentally representative of American values had to be exclusively of American origin, took exception to Chadwick's assertion and published a rebuttal; more than that, he created a special commission to discover that baseball was entirely of American origin. He made Mills its chairman.

Spalding reveals in the final report of this commission, dated December 30, 1907, that among his motives for instigating the inquiry was a growing irritation at the "sneering comments" he and the boys had been subject to in 1889 from English audiences in "New Zealand, Australia, Ceylon, Egypt [and] England. . . . 'Why, this American game of Base Ball is nothing more than our old English game of "Rounders" that we used to play with the girls when we were boys, you know!' " For Spalding, this was apparently too much to bear; at any rate, his quarrel with Chadwick concerning baseball's origins was chimerical, at least in terms of Spalding's patriotic goals, because Chadwick, while maintaining that baseball had descended from the English rounders, also steadfastly maintained that this did not detract "one iota from the merit of its now being unquestionably a thoroughly American field sport, and a game too, which is fully adapted to the American character." But Spalding's belief in baseball's special responsibility for shaping American character compelled him to go to great lengths to demonstrate its impeccably American pedigree. Doubtless his insistence on this point was also mixed with commercial considerations—he was a multimillionaire in the baseball equipment business—and with a simple desire for attention. After taking almost three years to gather its evidence, the so-called Mills Commission concluded *"that Base Ball is of American origin, and has no traceable connection whatever with 'Rounders,' or any other foreign game."* (The emphasis is from the original; the operative words here are "any other foreign game.")

The final report of the Special Base Ball Commission consists of four letters with an introduction by Secretary James E. Sullivan that delineates "who fought on the American side of this 'Origin' controversy," and who didn't. In his letter, Chadwick briefly reiterates the accepted rounders theory but doesn't offer any documentation (he thought the whole thing a waste of time); John Montgomery Ward begins by pointing out that "the circumstances surrounding [baseball's] inception were undoubtedly such that no written records or memoranda of any kind were ever made," and does not mention Abner Doubleday, but ends by asserting that baseball is "a purely American game"; and Spalding and Mills distinguish themselves with such a fluidity of invention and mendacity that one wonders why anyone ever said that businessmen were dull. Mills claims that he subscribed to the belief that the Knickerbockers were responsible for baseball until he read about Abner Doubleday.

Those fighting on the American side of the controversy, as it were, rested their case on a letter about Abner Doubleday from "a reputable gentleman" named Abner Graves who shot his wife to death and ended his days in an institution for the criminally insane. This letter no longer exists—all the evidence gathered by the commission was lost in a fire in 1911—but to judge by excerpts that were printed in press releases, Graves never made half of the claims for Doubleday that Spalding and Mills did, including Spalding's famous assertion that Graves "was present when Doubleday first outlined with a stick in the dirt the present diamond-shaped Base Ball field" in 1839.

Forgetting for a moment that at least four diamond-shaped baseball plans had been published by 1839; that Graves was five years old in 1839 and Doubleday was twenty; that Doubleday would have had to be AWOL from West Point to be in Cooperstown in 1839; and that Doubleday's family had moved away two years earlier anyway, what we do know from Graves's statement is that "Doubleday's game" had eleven men on a side and that "anyone getting the ball was entitled to throw it at a runner between the bases and put him out by hitting him with it." Since both of these rules are classic rounders, even if Doubleday had invented them, he did not invent baseball; baseball is almost defined by dropping the centuries-old rule that a man between bases may be put out by being hit with a thrown ball. These factual inaccuracies and more are documented in a number of fine books, especially by Robert W. Henderson, who first published a researched refutation of the Doubleday hoax in 1937. To anyone who takes the time to examine the "evidence," it is clear that "the first" game of baseball and its inventor never existed anywhere but in Spalding's fertile imagination, and that if Spalding had never existed, Abner Doubleday would never have existed as the inventor of baseball.

The rest, as they say, is history. Spalding's scheme to establish Abner Doubleday as the inventor of baseball did not succeed so well as his promotion of baseball as the national game, but it received little resistance, and it picked up steam in the early twenties when the citizens of Cooperstown purchased the pasture where baseball wasn't invented. A few years later, as luck would have it, someone discovered a battered old ball in a trunk associated with Abner Graves. Local historians determined that this was in fact the Original Ball; Stephen C. Clark, heir to a large part of the Singer Sewing Machine empire and a Cooperstown booster, purchased the ball for five dollars and put it on display, where it amazed those who wished to believe. (Voltaire once remarked that if all the pieces of the true cross in Europe were gathered in one place, they would build a sizeable cathedral.)

The modest success of the "Abner Doubleday Baseball" gave Clark the idea of putting Cooperstown on the map with a full-scale baseball museum. It was an idea whose time had come. Clark enlisted the enthusiastic collusion of the baseball establishment, which was eager for any publicity that might help baseball out of its Depression attendance doldrums, and elaborate plans were made for a centennial celebration of the birth of baseball. National League president Ford Frick suggested that a Hall of Fame be instituted as well. An Alexander Cartwright Day was added to the 1939 celebration as a concession to those who were already debunking Doubleday and promoting Cartwright as baseball's inventor, and the American public's general acceptance of the Doubleday myth was secured at the investiture. Today it is still a good bet that many, if not most, Americans who have any opinion *still* believe that Abner Doubleday invented baseball. In 1988, the *Hall of Fame Program* felt it necessary to include an article by Lowell Reidenbaugh, corporate editor of *The Sporting News,* entitled, "Doubleday's Legend: Did He or Didn't He?" A special celebration at Cooperstown in commemoration of the "alleged" 150th birthday of baseball took place in 1989.

Shortly after Spalding's special committee published its findings in the 1908 *Guide,* Henry Chadwick sent a revealing note to A. G. Mills: "Your decision in the case of Chadwick vs. Spalding . . . is a masterly piece of special pleading which lets my dear old friend Albert escape a bad defeat. . . . The whole matter was a joke between Albert and myself." It may well have been a joke, but Chadwick could hardly have foreseen that baseball's need for a creation myth was so great that the joke would endure; and that when the Doubleday myth began to wobble and Doubleday became increasingly unacceptable as baseball's inventor, Alexander Cartwright would be summoned from the Elysian Fields to fill the breach.

### Rounders

An elaborate form of this game has become the national game of the United States.
 —Alice Bertha Gomme, *Traditional Games of England, Scotland, and Ireland,* Volume II, 1898

\*     \*     \*

. . . the verdict of the spectators is almost universally against it as a competitor with our national game; and in our own individual judgment, it has so many inherent defects that it has not the slightest pretensions to be considered superior to, even if it is equal with, our own juvenile amusement "rounders," on the basis of which it has been modelled.
 —*The Field,* England's leading sporting journal, August 8, 1874

\*     \*     \*

Three hot dogs, two bags of peanuts, three glasses of beer and nine innings later, I was amazed to find out how much I already knew about baseball. In fact I'd played a simpler form of it as a schoolgirl in England, where it was called rounders and was played exclusively by rather upper class young ladies in the best public schools, which in England of course means the best private schools. Yet though we played on asphalt and used hard cricket balls, and played with all the savagery that enforced good breeding can create, we never dreamed of such refinements as I saw that afternoon. The exhilaration of sliding into base! That giant paw of the glove! The whole principle of hustle! A world awaits the well-bred young Englishwoman in the ballpark. But for me the most splendid of these splendors was to watch the American language being acted out.
 —Lesley Hazleton, reflecting on her first visit to a baseball game, Yankee Stadium on Catfish Hunter Day, 1979

\*     \*     \*

**The Cartwright Myth**   As David Voigt has pointed out, baseball's myth-makers apparently have a penchant for immaculate conceptions. Baseball was prepared to reject the indefensible Cooperstown-Doubleday myth, but only

*This illustration of boys playing rounders on the Boston Common first appeared in Robin Carver's* The Book of Sports, *published in Boston in 1834. Note the small bat used in rounders and the State House in the distance; two catchers are prepared to stop the ball from going too far if the batter misses. Carver's book marks an epoch in the history of baseball in America because although the game depicted and described in the text is rounders, reprinted essentially unchanged from the English edition of* The Boy's Own Book *(London, 1829), for the first time the rules are headed, "Base, or Goal Ball."*

on the condition that it could replace it with the rational, democratic, politically sound, and almost equally false Knickerbockers-Cartwright myth. Remarkable thematic similarities exist between the two, but only because they are two of a kind. Cartwright, for instance, like Doubleday, never claimed that he invented baseball, but unlike Doubleday, Cartwright really was a baseball enthusiast who played a significant role in the development of the game. This historical circumstance has opened the door to endless opportunities for obfuscation on the part of the scribes, who are apparently always on the alert for the entrance of another baseball Moses with his inscribed tablets of rules. They did their job well, as is attested by this typical formulation of the "enlightened" version of baseball's creation myth that appeared in the *Minneapolis Review of Baseball* in 1987: "Cartwright invented baseball. Spalding invented Abner Doubleday."

No less an authority than Macmillan's *Baseball Encyclopedia* (1985 edition), known affectionately throughout the baseball industry as "the Big Mac," perpetuates the modern myth this way:

> . . . on June 19, 1846 . . . two amateur teams met and played a form of baseball no one had ever seen before. Under the rules established by Alexander J. Cartwright, a surveyor and amateur athlete, who umpired the game, the Knickerbockers were beaten by the New York Nine, 23–1. Cartwright's game, which included guidelines to the field as well as the playing rules, served to mark the only acceptable date of baseball's beginning.

Anyone who cares to scratch the surface will soon find that Cartwright was not a surveyor, that there is no evidence that he umpired this game, that he is nowhere listed as a member of the Knickerbockers' Committee on Rules and Regulations, and that baseball games were played under the Knickerbockers' rules at least eight months previous to this game. But the salient feature of the Big Mac version is its quasi-official assertion that this game marks "the only acceptable date of baseball's beginning." As a mythological system, baseball may insist on a discrete moment of birth, but when historians insist on mingling their "histories" with theology, they are treading on shaky ground.

How Cartwright became credited with the invention of baseball is something of a mystery, even if it is not quite so groundless a theory as the Doubleday saga. His beatification apparently began with an innocent statement by Charles A. Peverelly, one of the earliest historians of the game, that Cartwright "one day upon the field proposed a regular organization, promising to obtain several recruits." The mythmakers evidently took this matter-of-fact statement and ran with it. As it happens, the young New York City businessmen who eventually formed the Knickerbocker Base Ball Club—including Colonel James Lee, Dr. Ransom, James Fisher, Abraham Tucker, W. Vail, Charles H. Birney, Fraley C. Nichols, Charles S. DeBost, Henry T. Anthony, W. R. Wheaton, Alexander J. Cartwright, D. F. Curry, W. H.

Tucker, and E. R. Dupignac—had been playing a baseball-like game for three years before Cartwright allegedly made the proposal to form a regular organization in 1845. There is no reason to believe that Cartwright, who had the reputation for being something of a sparkplug, did not make the initial suggestion to form a social/sporting club along the lines of those already in existence and gaining in popularity. Wheaton, Cartwright, Curry, W. H. Tucker, and Dupignac were appointed by their mates to organize the club.

They rounded up a certain number of members, and after some casting about the players settled on a permanent playing field across the Hudson in Hoboken, New Jersey, where they hoped they would be free from the encroachments of the New York developers who had already forced them to move their site in Manhattan at least once. The origin of their rules is no mystery; since 1744 several books had been published with rules for games called baseball, primarily directed at children, some with diamond-shaped fields. As Peverelly pointed out as early as 1866 in *The Book of American Pastimes,* baseball was a descendant of the English children's game of rounders, forms of which were played by many boys in eighteenth- and nineteenth-century America. Baserunning bat-and-ball games played on a diamond with rules such as three-strikes-you're-out were therefore well-known to many American youths, and while the Knickerbockers' Committee on Rules and Regulations listed no bibliography, the general idea of their game and some of its specific rules undoubtedly came from childhood memories and popular books such as *The Boy's Own Book* (1829) and the *Boy's and Girl's Book of Sports* (1835). When the Knickerbocker Club rules, which were probably the first created by and for adults, were finally agreed upon, they were signed, "William R. Wheaton, William H. Tucker, Committee on By-Laws"; the other three founding members, Cartwright included, did not sign. As a founder, Cartwright may well have had a hand in formulating the rules, but there is no evidence that he played a particularly important or exclusive role. Since he left town to move west three and a half years later, on March 1, 1849, and never returned, no claim can be made that he influenced the development of baseball through his continuing presence. Dr. D. I. Adams, who joined the Knickerbockers a month after they were organized and chaired the Committee on Rules and Regulations for the next decade and a half—in 1895 *The Sporting News* called him "The Father of Base Ball"—makes no mention of Cartwright in his reminiscences as recorded in the *News.*

The majority of today's serious baseball histories repeat that Cartwright "laid out the first diamond" and that the distinguishing feature of "Cartwright's game," aside from its prohibition against baserunners' being put out by being hit with a thrown ball, was that it prescribed nine men to a side, nine innings to a game, and ninety feet between bases. Unfortunately, none of these multiple-of-nine features are true either for any nonexistent code of "Cartwright's Rules" or for the Knickerbockers' code, which made no mention of how many men could play on a side or how many innings would be played; their game was won when one side got twenty-one runs, although each side had to have the same number of players at bat before the game was ended.

As for the distance between bases, the Knickerbockers' rule number four gives this formula: "The bases shall be from 'home' to second base, forty-two paces; from first to third base, forty-two paces, equidistant." In 1845, at least two standard-length paces were in use in the Eastern United States, two and a half feet and three feet. Neither would, by the Knickerbockers' formula, yield ninety feet between bases. By the time the club fixed the distance at thirty yards between bases, Cartwright was living and playing baseball in Hawaii. The commonly repeated inaccuracy that he was a draftsman, surveyor, or engineer—he was a teller at the Union Bank when the Knickerbockers were organized—was apparently made to bestow upon him the special powers necessary to conceive, formulate, and lay out the baseball diamond, and to create the rules with their mystical rhythms of threes and nines.

Another indispensable element in the Cartwright myth is that he umpired "The First Game." Even if the game of June 19, 1846, was "The First Game," a matter that modern scholarship has cast into serious doubt, neither Cartwright nor anyone else signed the umpire's blank in the game book that day. This does not mean that he *didn't* serve as umpire—several matches in the Knickerbocker game book are without an umpire's signature—but it doesn't mean that he did, and no primary evidence exists that indicates that he did. These and other circumstantial matters (the Cartwright myth also features an Original Ball) not only cast a pall over "the only acceptable date of baseball's beginning" and its unwitting inventor, but Henry Chadwick, writing in 1877, didn't think much of the Knickerbockers' primitive rules anyway, which he claimed made the game "tediously dull and uninteresting."

As far as Chadwick is concerned, baseball, which "dates its origin from the old English game of rounders, to which, however, it now bears as much resemblance as chess to draughts or 'chequers' . . . can only date its rise from the establishment of the National Association of Base-Ball Players, organized in 1857, from which time only has [baseball] been played under a specially authorized set of rules. . . . The changes in the rules introduced . . . in 1857, were such as to materially improve the game; but these revised rules were nothing in comparison with the complete code of laws by which base-ball is now governed, and which now characterizes it."

It is interesting to note that when the only acceptable date of baseball's beginnings shifted to Abner Doubleday and Cooperstown in 1839, A. G. Mills and A. G. Spalding, the principal perpetrators of the Doubleday hoax, made no attempt in their special committee to repudiate the evolutionary role of the Knickerbockers. The caption for an early diagram of a baseball diamond in the Spalding Collection at the New York Public Library thus reads,

> Eighteen players (nine on a side) with a ball and bat, playing the American Game of Base Ball, as it was originally designed and named "Base Ball," by Abner Doubleday, of Cooperstown, N.Y., in 1839, and subsequently formulated in a printed code of Playing Rules by the Knickerbocker Base Ball Club of New York City in 1845.

Spalding credits Cartwright and other founding members of the Knickerbockers for their role in the game's evolution, both in his special commission report and in his 1911 history, *America's National Game,* but makes no claim for any special role played by Cartwright. Mills, in his portion of the commission report, tries to preempt the Knickerbockers' contribution to baseball's evolution by asserting that a Mr. Wadsworth delivered the diagram of Doubleday's diamond-shaped playing field to the Knickerbockers when they were organizing their club; this claim is allegedly based on the recollection of D. F. Curry, one of the Knickerbockers' founding members. How else to explain the manner by which the same game of baseball, invented in rural upstate New York, became the game of a group of Manhattan businessmen six years later? A Wadsworth in fact did appear in some of the Knickerbocker lineups, but no one in 1908 had much of a stomach for this story and Mills never followed it up; since the only acceptable date of baseball's beginning has switched back to the Knickerbockers, it has become even more unpalatable.

So it was that baseball's probable genesis, which throughout the nineteenth century was believed to have occurred when the Knickerbocker rules acted on the ancient game of rounders, was replaced by the Cooperstown-Doubleday creation myth, which was replaced by the Knickerbockers-Cartwright myth. The modern version of the Cartwright myth has serious flaws, not the least of which is Cartwright's nonrole and the greatly exaggerated role of the Knickerbockers, who were in no hurry to play by their rules and ignored most of them for years. But baseball scholarship, which some people date from the publication of Harold Seymour's landmark dissertation in 1956, is still in its infancy; and it appears that we are finally approaching a golden age of research that will regard the origin and history of baseball and its place in American society on a factual, if not altogether dramatic, basis.

### The First Club

The Knickerbocker Club, organized in 1845, was the pioneer organization, and for several years the only one in the field. Its first competitor was the Washington Club, which, however, only existed for a short period, many of its members taking part in the formation of the Gotham Club, in 1852. The Eagle Club was organized in 1854, but for several seasons the three clubs above mentioned were the only ones playing in the vicinity of New-York. They adopted a series of rules and regulations to govern the game, and these rules were adopted by all the clubs organized prior to 1857.
   —Preface to the *National Association of Base-Ball Players Constitution and By-Laws,* 1858–64

There is no reason to believe that the broad outline of the history of the formation of baseball clubs in New York as summarized above is not essentially correct. Still, there is considerable room for quibbling, particularly since both the National Association of Base-Ball Players (NABBP) and its individual clubs indulged in the sort of self-aggrandizing promotion that leads to fudged dates. It is clear that by the mid-1850s amateur clubs were springing up like mushrooms; before that, things are less certain. There are reports that a baseball club was formed in Rochester, New York, as early as 1825, but it is important to remember that many games that didn't have much to do with the "New York Game of Base" were called baseball (or "base") from 1744 on; and for some time after the Knickerbockers were organized, baseball played a poor third to cricket and town ball in popularity, so that contemporary information about it is sparse.

An association of town ball players existed in Camden, New Jersey, in 1831, where "so great was the prejudice of the general public against the game . . . that the players were frequently censured by their friends for indulging in such a childish amusement." This Camden group merged with the Olympic Ball Club and formed the Olympic Town Ball Club of Philadelphia in 1833. After twenty-seven years of town ball, in May 1860, the Olympic Club "adopted the National Association [NABBP] game of base ball, resulting in the honorable retirement of most of their old members," who quit, among other reasons, because the adoption of NABBP ball enlarged "their sphere of action with a vengeance" by increasing the distance between bases from forty to ninety feet. Another variant, the Massachusetts game, with sixty feet between bases, held sway to the north (and in many Eastern states), where thirty-two Boston area clubs were organized into an amateur association in 1860. Baseball under the New York rules was first played by a Boston club, the Tri-Mountains, in 1857.

It is generally agreed that the Knickerbocker Base Ball Club of New York City was the first properly organized baseball club. But while it deserves "the honor of being the pioneer of the present game of Base Ball," as Henry Chadwick wrote in 1861, the Knickerbocker Club was known to have been preceded by at least one other baseball club, the New York Nine. Chadwick acknowledges the prior existence of the New Yorkers, as does Alexander Cartwright himself, who mentions in a letter from Honolulu in 1865 that the Knickerbockers were truly the first baseball club in New York because "the old New York Club never had a regular organization." Dr. D. I. Adams, who joined the Knickerbockers one month after they were organized, claimed in 1895 in *The Sporting News* that it was in fact younger members of the New York Base Ball Club who "got together and formed the Knickerbocker Base Ball Club" in September 1845. They were "merchants, lawyers, Union Bank clerks, insurance clerks, and others who were at liberty after two o'clock in the afternoon"; Dr. Adams also claims that "there was then no rivalry, as no other club was formed until 1850." But according to the New York *Herald* for November 11, 1845, the New York Club on that day gathered on their grounds at the Elysian Fields, later the home field of the Knickerbockers, to celebrate their second anniversary with an intrasquad game and postgame dinner. This implies that they had been meeting regularly since 1843; if so, the Knickerbockers' claim to primacy rests only on the brevity of the New York Club's lifespan and its apparent lack of a formal constitution or extant records.

Whether the New York Club ever reached its third anniversary is indeed a problematic but significant consideration. We know that several members of the New York Club who played in a game on October 24, 1845, later turned up on the Washington Club, organized in 1851, then on the Gothams; and it seems reasonable to believe that other loosely organized or short-lived clubs, such as the Brooklyn Club that played the New Yorkers on October 24, may also have predated the Knickerbockers. The Eagle Club, which the NABBP lists as the third club chartered, published a booklet entitled *By-Laws and Rules of the Eagle Ball Club* in 1852; on its title page is clearly printed, "Organized, 1840." But no further evidence to support the Eagles' prior claim has ever been produced, and unless new evidence does turn up, it still

*The making of a match during the amateur era of baseball was attended with punctilious etiquette. This imposing document is an invitation to the Lowell Base Ball Club of Boston from the Wamsotta Base Ball Club of New Bedford, October 9, 1868. The club proposing the match usually provided a collation; if a "forfeiture" was agreed upon in advance, the losing club might be required to pay for a supper, or for drinks.*

*This two-page spread from* Harper's Weekly, *October 15, 1859, contains one of the earliest drawings of adults playing baseball. In this era baseball was still treated as an adjunct to cricket. Note the tepeelike pavilion to the left of the diamond, where ladies could take shelter from the sun and all could take refuge in the event of inclement weather; spectators in the foreground watch from their carriages. Both matches depicted were played at the delightful Elysian Fields, Hoboken, home grounds of the Knickerbockers and of the New York Club before them.*

seems, as Chadwick put it, that "we shall not be far wrong" in granting the Knickerbockers primacy.

*The First Game*   The date that the first game of baseball was played is also a hotly disputed item in the archeological hot-stove league. Much of the controversy stems from different opinions on just what was and was not baseball and when it began, but in the balance, the designation of June 19,

1846, as the date for "the first game" seems a questionable choice. Not only has the repeated claim that it was the first game promulgated yet another apparent baseball inaccuracy, but it has resulted in the theft of the pages recording this game from the original Knickerbocker game book, which is at present a valued part of the priceless Spalding Collection at the New York Public Library. The relevant pages—and no others—were evidently cut from the book sometime about 1983, when the entire game book was committed to microfilm at the urging of John Thorn; such is the price of fame.

One central problem with the game of June 19, 1846, is that statements from Dr. Adams and the preface to the NABBP constitution, among other

*Panoramic view of New York City in a lithograph first published in 1866 after an earlier drawing by John Bachmann. In the lower left-hand corner on the near side of the river a baseball game is in progress at the Elysian Fields. The popular cricket and baseball grounds belonged to the Stevens estate, part of which is now the Stevens Institute of Technology; the Stevens palace with its flag flying is to right center. Lower Manhattan was already so built up that baseball clubs had to look uptown, to Brooklyn, or across the Hudson for places to play.*

sources, cast serious doubt on whether there were any other baseball clubs in New York from about the time the Knickerbockers were organized in 1845 until 1850. Harold Seymour states that the Knickerbockers played in the June 19, 1846, game against a team that, "for the sake of having a name, called themselves the New York Base Ball Club"; and that this New York Club may have predated the Knickerbockers, but lasted only a season. A comparison of the lineups seems to indicate that the game of June 19 was most likely an intrasquad game that included some players who were not Knickerbocker members. Such a contingency was provided for in rule six of the Knickerbocker code, which concerns when and how "gentlemen not members may be chosen in to make up the match." Others who have studied this game and its problems, including Tom Heitz, librarian at the National Baseball Library, have come to the conclusion that someone, probably a club member, went back at a much later date, perhaps in the 1860s, and wrote "1st Match of the Club" on the appropriate game book page, for reasons that are not entirely clear.

According to the game book, a game that may cast some light on this problem was played on June 17, 1846, two days before the famous game. On the game book pages for this date someone has crossed out the pre-printed *Knickerbocker* at the top of the left page and written in *New York,* which is the same way the New York Nine was designated two days later. The team on the left-hand page is also designated *White* while the team on the right is designated *Black,* a usage that otherwise does not appear until May 17, 1849. Except for a player named Thompson, who played with the New York Club on June 19, most of the names of the players for both the New York and Knickerbocker squads on June 17, 1846, are familiar Knickerbocker names. In the first complete game after June 19, 1846, played on June 20, 1846, members of the New York team of the nineteenth are interspersed among Knickerbocker players on both teams, and no designations—neither Black nor White nor any club names—are used to indicate that this game was other than the usual Knickerbocker intrasquad game. (Some researchers claim that there was a second game played on June 19; indeed, *20* was apparently written over *19* in the June date, or vice versa.) The lineups in the games immediately preceding and following the game of June 19, 1846, are perhaps the most convincing evidence of all that the putative first game of June 19, 1846, was a regular intrasquad game. Since there is as yet no determination of when "1st Match" was written in the game book record for the game of June 19, 1846, how it became known as "the first game" may even have something to do with the New Jersey boosters who erected a plaque in its commemoration in Hoboken in 1946. As we have seen at Cooperstown, sometimes plaques speak louder than words.

If *first game* is to be understood as the first game played under the Knickerbocker rules, rather than the first intersquad match under the rules, the simplest approach is to look up the first game recorded in the official Knickerbocker game book, which was played on October 6, 1845, thirteen days after the official founding of the Knickerbockers on September 23, 1845. This game had seven players on each side; that the game of June 19, 1846, had nine men on each side gives it no greater claim to being "the first game," since an undated game in late October 1845 also had nine men per side, and in 1846 the Knickerbocker Club rules did not stipulate *any* particular number of players. For years the number of players was coincidental; well into the 1849 season, scores sometimes go over seventy runs per team, and games last two to ten innings with anywhere from four to thirteen men per side. Of the dozen games recorded in the game book in the fall of 1845 after the Knicker-bockers were organized and the half dozen recorded in the spring of 1846 before June 19, none were apparently played with any overwhelming faithful-ness to the Knickerbockers' rules, and it has been pointed out that there are serious problems with the way the game of June 19, 1846, is scored as well.

*Facing pages from the Knickerbocker Base Ball Club game book. The match of October 6, 1845, in which two teams of seven men played for three innings, is the first complete, dated game in the book. The squad listed under Curry beat the squad listed under Cartwright, 11–8. The club rules, which were formally adopted on September 23, 1845, did not specify the number of innings or players. The first team to score twenty-one runs, or "aces," won.*

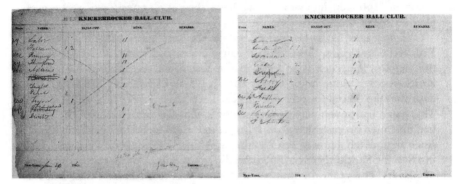

*Facing pages from the game book for the first game after the game of June 19, 1846. The Knickerbockers at times seemed almost obsessed with fines, which rated their own column in the game book along with* Hands Out *(outs) and* Runs. *Someone has written* KBC *for Knickerbockers and* NY *for New York Club, apparently to indicate the club affiliations of some of the players. Ten men played on each squad.*

According to the game book, the first game besides an undated contest in October 1845 to end when one team scored twenty-one runs—a game was over when one team reached twenty-one runs *and* when all members of both teams had had an equal number of at-bats—was played on September 16, 1847. This is also the first contest in the game book, excepting the game of June 19, 1846, that is designated "Match Game." Was the game of September 16, 1847, the first game? It seems that even from the intrasquad point of view, the first Knickerbockers game may not have taken place until the club started playing consistently by its own rules, several years after it was organized.

Compounding the difficulties in determining the date of the first Knickerbockers' game is the recent discovery that a series of games were played in October 1845 between two outfits called the New York Ball Club and the Brooklyn Club. The members of the Brooklyn Club belonged to the Union Star Cricket Club of Brooklyn; the New York Club is evidently the same or some permutation of the same organization that, if it still existed, allegedly faced the Knickerbockers on June 19, 1846, or otherwise supplied the name for the Knickerbockers' opposition on that date. According to the lineups given, at least four New York Club players played in both the 1845 and 1846 games; indeed, at least two of the October 1845 New Yorkers later reappear on the Knickerbocker nine. Since the October 1845 games were played on the same Elysian Fields used by the Knickerbockers after the Knickerbockers were fully organized and the players of all three clubs obviously knew one another, it is quite possible that they were played under the Knickerbockers' rules—as much as any games were at the time—and therefore that the first game of this series was the elusive "first game." According to the New York *Herald,* both the Knickerbockers and the Stars were present at the New York Club's second anniversary dinner on November 11, 1845. If the New York Club indeed ceased to exist between this date and next June 19, the Knickerbockers may not have played in the first intersquad match under their rules. There is a growing school of modern researchers that maintains that the first true interclub match involving the Knickerbockers could not have taken place before 1851. Perhaps it would be simpler, as Chadwick maintains, if we didn't call what was being played before 1857 *baseball.*

*The First Report*   The report of the 1845 New York–Brooklyn games in the New York *Herald* brings us to yet another disputed category of firsts. Before Melvin Adelman's publication of a paper in the 1980 winter edition of the *Journal of Sport History,* baseball historians had agreed that the first newspaper references to a game called baseball appeared in 1853. While in this case there was at least consensus on the year, different dates were given for the first newspaper account, including May 1, 1853, and July 10, 1853, both in the New York *Mercury;* the confusion here may have been that the *Mercury* mentions baseball in general on May 1 but gives the first account of a match on July 10. But the *Herald's* October 21, 1845, announcement that a baseball game was to be played between the New York Club and the Brooklyn Club predates the previously first-known newspaper reference to baseball by eight years, just as, if one of these games *was* the first intersquad game, it pushes the date of the putative June 19, 1846, "first game" back by eight months. To date only one challenger to the October 21, 1845, newspaper reference has emerged, this being a mention of a baseball game in an October 1844 edition of the Bangor, Maine, *Whig.* However, since the game referred to, regardless of what it was called, was a form of town ball of the "round ball" variety (there is no record that either Abner Doubleday or Alexander Cartwright ever traveled to Maine to teach baseball to the natives), this reference is not, as of this writing, a serious contender.

Scholarship, even in baseball, is a progressive affair, and what is in good

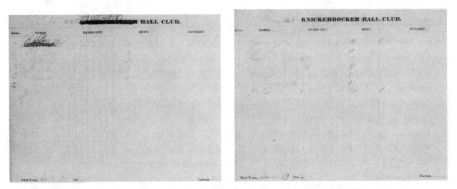

*Facing pages from the game book for the game preceding the game of June 19, 1846. New York has been substituted for Knickerbocker (then crossed out?) on the left-hand page. The squads have been designated "White" and "Black." Six men played on each side; "Jack" seems to have played for both sides.*

KNICKERBOCKER BALL CLUB.

KNICKERBOCKER BALL CLUB.

*Photocopy of facing pages from the game book for the game of June 19, 1846. These pages were cut out and stolen from the game book sometime in the early 1980s and are probably now in the hands of a wealthy private collector who believes they record "the first game." Note that the space for the umpire is blank. New York and KBC designate the squads; "1st Match of the Club" is written at the top of the KBC page.*

BASE BALL PLAY —The subjoined is the result of the return match between the New York Base Ball Club and the Brooklyn players, which came off on the ground of the Brooklyn Star Cricket Club yesterday. Messrs Johnson, Wheaton and Van Nostrand were the umpires.

| NEW YORK BALL CLUB. | | | BROOKLYN CLUB. | | |
|---|---|---|---|---|---|
| | *Hands out.* | *Runs.* | | *Hands out.* | *Runs* |
| Davis,...... | 2 | 4 | Hunt...... | 1 | 3 |
| Murphy ... | 0 | 6 | Hines....... | 2 | 2 |
| Vail....... | 2 | 4 | Gilmore... | 3 | 2 |
| Kline...... | 1 | 4 | Hardy...... | 2 | 2 |
| Miller...... | 2 | 5 | Sharp....... | 2 | 2 |
| Case....... | 2 | 4 | Meyers..... | 0 | 3 |
| Tucker.... | 2 | 4 | Whaley.... | 2 | 2 |
| Winslow... | 1 | 6 | Forman..... | 1 | 3 |
| | — | — | | — | — |
| | 12 | 37 | | 12 | 19 |

*The first baseball account and box score, as it appeared in the New York Herald on October 25, 1845, the day after the "return" or rematch. For years baseball and cricket scores appeared together. New York Club players Davis, Murphy, Case, and Winslow played on the New York squad that beat the Knickerbockers on June 19, 1846.*

faith determined to be the first club, game, or newspaper reference today may not be tomorrow. No responsible historian would ever be so reckless as to say with confidence that his research has been thorough and comprehensive enough to settle any matter for all time; such absolutes are the province of supernatural systems. Unsatisfying as this state of affairs may be, historians often must content themselves with merely outlining the problems involved in exploring their topic. This may seem no great accomplishment, but in terms of baseball history—which is strewn with legends, misconceptions, inaccuracies, wishful thinking, and deliberate falsehoods—it is a step in the right direction of the first magnitude.

*Cricket Versus Baseball*   These days cricket is played in the United States on such rare and rarefied occasions that Americans would be justified in thinking the game never had a chance against baseball. Cricket is the Englishman's game par excellence and, by extension, a game played where the British Empire once held sway. Americans long ago got rid of everything associated with the British style of life—crumpets with tea, bowlers on bankers' heads, endless cricket matches on the lawn, all that sort of thing was discarded when Americans declared their independence and set off on the road to "life, liberty, and the pursuit of baseball." Who would dare to suggest that cricket was played by redblooded Americans, let alone that the game challenged baseball as our national pastime!

It is all a bit more complicated and interesting than that. Specialized historians of sport know the story but it is one of the best-kept secrets of America's social history. To begin with, cricket *was* long played by many Americans; although the first reference to a game (in New York City) comes in 1751 (about the same time, by the way, that cricket was becoming popular in England), there must have been informal games before that; by 1809, the first cricket club had been organized in Boston; by the late 1840s—when baseball was just beginning to appear in any organized way—cricket and cricket clubs were to be found in many cities in the Northeast. It is true that most of the players in the recorded games up to this time were of English origin, but this did not mean that cricket was confined to the upper classes. Quite the contrary; by the 1850s, when baseball was just beginning to break out of the "gentlemen's" club mold, cricket was very much a sport of the blue-collar class in most of the industrial and commercial cities across the Northeast to the Midwest, from Portsmouth, New Hampshire, to Cincinnati, Ohio. Cricket, in fact, was explicitly praised by the American sporting press for its democratizing influence. As Steven Gelber has written (in one of the finest articles on the social history of early baseball):

> Far from seeing [cricket] as a symbol of old world social stratification, both Englishmen and Americans praised the game because it rewarded skill, not status. . . . [A] *Clipper* [the prominent American sporting journal] correspondent called on all Americans "whose occupation is sedentary" to patronize this "invigorating" game because it is a "great means of bringing into friendly intercourse all classes of society."

So by 1860, when baseball was just beginning to explode on the American scene, cricket was actually well established. George Kirsch, a professor of American history at Manhattan College, says that cricket was being played by three hundred to four hundred clubs in more than 125 cities in at least twenty-two states, including Savannah, New Orleans, Chicago, Milwaukee, and San Francisco, and flatly states: "Cricket was America's first modern team sport." Professor Melvin Adelman of the University of Illinois, another authority on this subject, puts it this way: "By 1855 cricket was still more frequently played and attracted more public attention than baseball."

Cricket's role in a history of baseball goes beyond even its precedence. Many of the leading figures in those early years of baseball bridged the worlds of cricket and baseball. In baseball's earliest phase—the time of the Knickerbockers and other early New York City clubs—many of the players participated in both games and many of the teams used the already-established cricket club grounds; the most notable instance, referred to earlier, was the game of October 24, 1845, at the Union Star Cricket Club, the first game reported in a newspaper. The first reports of baseball games in *The New York Times* and the *Spirit of the Times,* a leading sporting journal, treated them as sort of an afterthought or appendage to the game of cricket (and at first baseball was even indexed under cricket articles). In their fascinating account of the evolution of baseball statistics in *The Hidden Game of Baseball,* John Thorn and Pete Palmer point out how the first box scores for baseball simply carried over the categories from cricket—"hands out" and "runs"; Thorn and Palmer also recount how Henry Chadwick, English born and committed to playing and reporting cricket, witnessed a game of baseball in 1856 and experienced a sort of "conversion" and then long continued to record baseball games under the influence of cricket.

A curious but long-forgotten reflection of this phase shows up in the account of the famous first "convention" of the New York baseball clubs in January 1857. Some of the delegates seemed annoyed that the commissioners of the newly planned Central Park had made "provision . . . for the English national pastime of cricket, but none for base ball," and they appointed a committee to "put itself in communication with the authorities on the subject." The editor of the *Spirit of the Times,* however, assured the delegates and public in a footnote that the commissioners had simply referred to setting aside "a Cricket Ground, for the encouragement of, and indulgence in, athletic and manly sports, . . . This, we should suppose, would include Base Ball, Quoits, etc." The two sports were clearly getting ready for a grudge match.

In baseball's next phase, after the Civil War, as teams became more organized and then professional, some of the leaders were also linked to cricket—particularly Harry and George Wright, brothers whose father was a leading English cricketer and who themselves had begun by playing cricket in America. Cricket had even shown the way to professional baseball: It is estimated that there were at least eleven paid cricketers working for teams in the Northeast by 1859. And in many of the public discussions of the new game of baseball—from issues such as its impact on workers' time and energy to techniques of pitching—cricket served as the yardstick, the touchstone: Baseball games took less time than cricket matches, baseball was or wasn't more "scientific" than cricket. It appeared that cricket was to hold the lead in the competition for Americans' sporting favors.

Then, by 1870, cricket had all but collapsed as a serious contender for America's national pastime. There were several reasons for this, and Professor Adelman has identified four of what he calls the "interacting elements":

> Since cricket required more skill at this time, Americans did not engage in this sport because with their limited ballplaying tradition they lacked the talent to participate enjoyably in this complex sport. Control of cricket by Englishmen further inhibited the growth of the sport in this country. Since cricket clubs functioned as a means of preserving English identity, little effort was made to popularize the sport among Americans. Two structural differences—the batting system and the length of an inning—made baseball a more action packed sport and a better spectator and participatory sport. Finally, that cricket had emerged as a modern and mature sport with well established institutional structure made it virtually impossible for the sport to be modified to meet American needs and conditions.

That seems to say it all. Cricket had lost out to baseball.

*It Isn't Cricket*   Histories of sport in America tend to sign off on cricket about 1870, thus failing to convey the long denouement that followed the demise of cricket as a contender with baseball for our nation's popular devotion. English cricket teams, for instance, continued to visit the United States and often played both cricket and baseball against American teams—the implication being that any decent cricket player could immediately master such a simple boys' game. Throughout the rest of the nineteenth century and even into the first years of the twentieth, countless articles and editorials in newspapers and magazines and sections of books felt compelled to hold forth on baseball versus cricket, always reassuring Americans that the right sport had won. Some of the explanations offered by the authors now seem quite unexpected.

An A. Sedgwick, writing in *The Nation* in 1869, jokes around with the notion that "Providence, it appears, at length answers us (with the usual Providential derision of lofty aspirations) with a truly American game of ball"; Sedgwick then proceeds to examine the differences in the English and American character that might explain the diversity in their two chosen national games, and concludes:

> Now, in two points at least, it may be said with certainty that the American character differs from the English—in being less brutal, and in being more fond of novelty, of change, of the excitement which novelty and change produce.

A love of novelty most Americans would subscribe to, but "less brutal" than the English? Sedgwick, however, proceeds to show how physically punishing the game of cricket can be, with its hard ball and hard drives.

Richard Proctor, an Englishman writing in several publications in 1886–87, devotes endless paragraphs to analyzing the difference between the curve of a pitched baseball and the "break" of a bowled cricket ball, all in order "to decide whether baseball or cricket is the more scientific so far as relations of the batsman and the bowler or pitcher are concerned," only to arrive at a quite unexpected conclusion:

> I cannot say that I quite appreciate the qualities of baseball regarded as a game. It seems to me it would have no chance with cricket in America, but for the circumstances that cricket can never be properly practised there, the time being so short during which there is any grass. Baseball requires no grass, as the ball does not touch the ground between the pitcher and the batsman, and so can be played nine months out of the twelve.

Here it is, 1887, and someone is still suggesting that cricket might replace baseball if only the grass were greener!

Proctor was an Englishman, to be sure, and the mass of Americans had by then made up their minds that they wanted no more to do with cricket. But this rivalry between the two people's national pastimes continued throughout the nineteenth century, and the arch-exponent of this rivalry was Albert G. Spalding. When he led two teams to England in 1874, they were forced to play some cricket matches and although they won, it was by playing in an unorthodox manner; the English didn't appreciate this and let it be known that they regarded baseball as a crude game, but Spalding didn't concede a point.

When he returned to Britain at the end of the round-the-world tour in 1889, Spalding was still feeling the need to compete with cricket—by this time, though, he was on the offensive, thinking he might win the British over to baseball. Even in 1911, when he came to publish his book, *America's National Game,* Spalding still seemed obsessed by this rivalry:

> It seems impossible to write on this branch of the subject—to treat Base Ball as our National Game—without referring to Cricket, the national field sport of Great Britain and most of her colonies.

Spalding couldn't resist calling attention to those "colonies," and then he proceeds to show how ill-suited cricket is to the American spirit:

> Cricket is a splendid game, for Britons. It is a genteel game, a conventional game—and our cousins across the Atlantic are nothing if not conventional. They play cricket because it accords with the traditions of their country so to do; because it is easy and does not overtax their energy or their thought.

Spalding goes on and on in this vein, not so subtly bashing the British, all the while setting up baseball as the opposite of cricket:

> I claim that Base Ball owes its prestige as our National Game to the fact that as no other form of sport it is the exponent of American Courage, Confidence, Combativeness; American Dash, Discipline, Determination; American Energy, Eagerness, Enthusiasm; American Pluck, Persistence, Performance; American Spirit, Sagacity, Success; American Vim, Vigor, Virility.

But Spalding, however embarrassingly chauvinistic he may now sound, was not really the originator of this line. Starting as far back as the 1850s, numerous editorials and articles began to celebrate the intrinsic Americanness of baseball, and this often led to its contrast with cricket. Just to cite one, more or less at random, an 1888 article from *Outing,* a sports magazine of the late nineteenth century, recounts this anecdote:

"Why is it," asked a distinguished subject of Queen Victoria upon a recent visit to this country, "that your people support with such astonishing liberality the game of baseball?"

"Because," rejoined the equally distinguished Yankee (Governor Hill of New York), "baseball, like the average American, has more dash, more enterprise, more vim and more 'git-up-en-git' to it in a minute than anything else of its kind that any other nation on earth ever attained to in a lifetime. That's the secret of the national game's success in the United States, and in every other enterprising country in which it has been introduced."

This, of course, was implicit in Mark Twain's address to the returning round-the-world ballplayers in 1889, when he characterized baseball as "the very symbol, the outward and visible expression of the drive and push and rush and struggle of the raging, tearing, booming nineteenth century." And to this day, whenever a sports columnist has a slow schedule, although he may be unaware of belonging to this great tradition, he's apt to write yet another article pointing out why cricket may be all right for the slow-tempered English but would never do for us "git-up-en-git" Americans.

*Baseball and Chess*   As mentioned earlier in this chapter, in its very early years baseball was treated as a sort of appendage to cricket, even to the extent that newspapers and weeklies carried and indexed baseball stories under cricket games. But there is another curious footnote to this. Perhaps the most popular American sporting journal of the middle decades of the nineteenth century was the *Spirit of the Times* (sometimes with the publisher's name in front, as *Porter's* or *Wilkes' Spirit of the Times*). This weekly catered not to today's "sports fans" but to the tastes and image of a sportsman rooted in the English tradition—a country gentleman and man-about-town interested in horse racing (this was its strongest suit), hunting, fishing, boating, and billiards; the only team sport that was allowed into its clubby columns, until baseball forced itself in, was cricket. But it was accepted that the readers did have some other interests, so there were regular reports on such urban pursuits as music, theater—and chess. Chess matches were regularly reported in *Spirit of the Times,* and it was for the readers of such reports that baseball had to compete for space and attention.

Long after this association between chess and baseball vanished (chess columns are as apt to be with the entertainment or gardening sections as with sports in most of today's newspapers), baseball is still on occasion compared to chess: "a thinking man's game," balancing long-range strategy and short-range tactics, a contest between two opponents who try to put each other's men out of combat, one by one, until the final out/checkmate. Baseball managers, at least, must occasionally feel like grand masters, and baseball fans probably like to think that if chess players are attracted to any team sport, it is baseball as opposed, say, to football. But by and large, baseball fans and chess players go their own ways these days.

All the more surprising, then, to discover that on at least one other occasion baseball and chess teamed up. By now historians of the game are well aware that the first intercollegiate game of baseball was the one played at Pittsfield, Massachusetts (a neutral "intermediate" city being regarded as desirable), between Amherst and Williams on July 1, 1859. But a closer focus on the headline of the *Amherst Express* that reported the event shows this:

EXTRA
WILLIAMS AND AMHERST
BASEBALL AND CHESS!
MUSCLE AND MIND!!

The full story comes out in the article. Amherst had challenged Williams simply to a baseball game, but "in turn Williams challenged to a game at Chess, that there might be a 'trial of mind as well as muscle.'" Amherst accepted, and it was agreed that the baseball game would be played on July 1 and the chess game on July 2, also in Pittsfield. Amherst soundly defeated Williams at baseball, 73–32, and when news reached Amherst at about eleven that evening, the victory was celebrated with a "general jubilee" that included the chapel bell, a bonfire, and "a copious display of enthusiasm and rockets." When the Amherst baseball team arrived back in town on July 2, they were met with a "coach and four" and escorted by cheering students to a reception that included "congratulations, speeches, and familiar accounts of interesting incidents."

Meanwhile, the Amherst chess team was defeating the Williams team that very day—in an eleven-hour match!—but probably because the next day was Sunday the news of the outcome did not reach Amherst until Monday, July 4. Once more, "There was a universal ringing of bells, and firing of cannons; and throats already hoarse shouted again amid the general rejoicing." When some of the chess team arrived later that day (interestingly, not a word is said in the account of the Fourth of July as a patriotic holiday), "they were saluted by a storm of cheers, conducted to a barouche, in which they were drawn by their fellow students, with the sound of music, to the residence of President

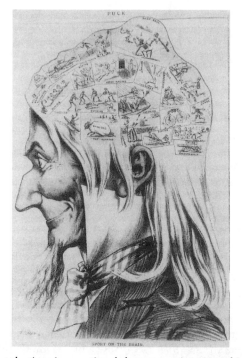

*A wry look at the American national character as it appeared in the popular late-nineteenth-century American magazine* Puck. *According to the apostles of phrenology, a pseudo-science of the day, proclivities and abilities could be determined by examining the bumps on the skull. Uncle Sam clearly has sports on the brain, as well as eating and gambling. Baseball, enormously popular during the 1880s, occupies the largest, most prominent and baroque spot.*

Stearns." Speeches and more receptions ensued, and when the rest of the chess team arrived back the next day, they too were greeted by their fellow students. The newspaper's long article concluded:

> The students of Amherst rejoice not merely in the fact that in this contest their Alma Mater has borne away the laurels; but also in the belief that by such encounters as these, a deeper interest will be excited in those amusements, which, while they serve as a relaxation from study, strengthen and develop body and mind.

In fact, the Amherst catcher, James Claflin, was also captain of the chess team, so at least he lived up to this final ideal. This seems to have been the first and last publicized pairing of chess and baseball; it is hard to imagine any college today giving such a reception to its baseball team, let alone its chess team.

*The Curveball*   Richard A. Proctor, the Englishman who in 1887 was claiming so confidently that cricket would probably prevail in America if only the grass-growing season were longer, also wrote a number of articles in 1886–87 trying to explain to both his British and American readers some of the differences in their two nations' pastimes. In particular, he focused on "the scientific qualities" behind the pitching of balls in the two games and concluded that "in baseball pitching, a more difficult scientific problem is involved." The problem was one that was exercising many minds at that time: how to explain, if it even existed, what Proctor called "the curving of the ball."

Explaining the curveball, and the many related pitches such as the slider and the spitball, has long been a small industry in America. In addition to countless articles analyzing the nature of the curveball and its cousins, not to mention all the "how to pitch" books by pitchers and coaches, there is one entire book devoted to a history of these phenomena, *The Crooked Pitch: The Curveball in American Baseball History* (1984), by Martin Quigley (also known for a couple of fine novels about baseball). In his humorous, anecdotal way, Quigley sets forth pretty much everything that need be said about "the Great Equalizer," at least as far as tracing its role in the game. Although he considers some of the many candidates put forth as the first to pitch a curve, Quigley settles on the one who is generally regarded as the first, William Arthur "Candy" Cummings; he claimed to have pitched his first curve in 1864 and then introduced it into organized baseball in 1866 when he pitched for the Fulton Hercules team of Brooklyn. Although Cummings later boasted that he amazed some students and professors of physics at Harvard by his 1867 demonstration of his curve, Quigley says that the first authenticated report of a pitched curve came in 1870, when the great Henry Chadwick set up a test for Fred Goldsmith to demonstrate that he could pitch a baseball that sped past opposite sides of two stakes on the exact straight line between the pitcher's mound and home plate. Such public demonstrations were quite popular for many years; one of the more notable ones occurred in 1879 when Will White of the Cincinnati Reds allegedly threw a curve that "bent" around alternating sides of *three* posts on its way to home plate.

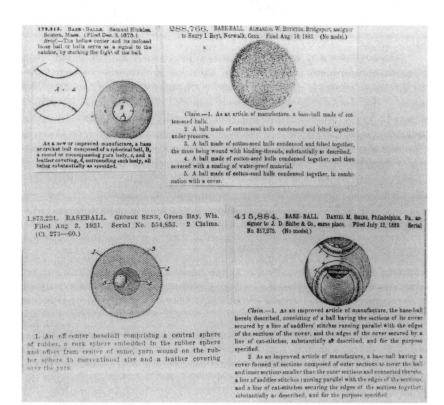

As baseball's possibilities began to capture the American imagination, inventors inevitably jumped in to see if they couldn't improve the game with technology. These are only a few of the many patents applied for to improve the ball itself: top left, *a bell in its center so that batters could hear the ball coming;* top right, *a ball made of cottonseed, presumably to give it some sort of velocity;* bottom left, *a small rubber sphere off center to aid in pitching a curve!;* bottom right, *a prototype of what would be the modern ball as proposed by Daniel Shibe in a patent filed in 1889.*

Such evidence and incidents, however, have never stopped people from nominating themselves or others as the first to pitch curves: Many years after the first intercollegiate contest between Amherst and Williams in 1859, for instance, the Amherst second baseman claimed that Amherst's "thrower," Henry D. Hyde, "had a wonderful knack of making the ball curve in to the catcher." Presumably such recollections can be found from all over America from that era. More likely, no one man "invented" the curve: It was probably one of those things that was "in the air" and a lot of men began to try to pitch curves about this time. Remember, too, that all baseball pitching in those days was underhand—and that balls were nothing like the baseball of today—so that whatever technique produced these curves would be quite different from today's curveball pitching.

Quigley discusses these matters and provides lots of good evidence and stories about the controversies that have surrounded pitching. The most revealing section for many people will be his second chapter, which reviews some of the modern "scientific" experiments and demonstrations designed to explain whether and how a pitched ball does curve; Quigley has special fun with three articles that appeared in *Life* (in 1941), *Look* (in 1953), and *Science 82* (1982), all drawing on sophisticated technology, photography, and scientists to conclude that a ball cannot curve the way ballplayers and baseball fans claim to have been seeing it for over a century now. But Quigley did not choose to get into the original controversy that surrounded the notion of a curve, the controversy that Proctor was participating in back in 1887.

"Candy" Cummings seems to have been one of the few pitchers who was able to throw a curve with any consistency in the years following its introduction—say, by 1870. It must have been especially hard to master, considering that there was a rule against releasing the ball with a "jerking" motion or a twist of the wrist (a rule abolished in 1872), not to mention that only gradually over the years did the pure underhand delivery give way (in 1882) to a rule that allowed the hand to rise up to the hip and then (in 1883) up to the shoulder. Not until 1884 (at least for teams playing in the major leagues) were all such restraints removed and true overhand pitching allowed. Pitchers were now free to exploit power, speed, and trick pitches, and when in 1887 the rule was abolished that required the pitcher to place the ball high or low at the request of the batter, the pitcher emerged as the pivotal figure he has been ever since.

So it was no coincidence that about this time a debate arose over whether it was physically possible for a pitched ball to curve. Many quite knowledgeable people, often appealing to the laws of science, had been denying that a pitched baseball could be made to curve; Chadwick dismissed them as "old fogy individuals." One such in 1886 was the editor of the Grand Rapids *World,* and he concluded his claim that "the curves are in the imagination of [the pitcher's] admirers" by inviting the most prestigious scientific magazine of the day, *Scientific American,* to decide the matter. The magazine thus commissioned an article (in the issue of July 31, 1886) by none other than Henry Chadwick, who with technical drawings and careful prose tried to explain just how a pitched baseball is made to curve. The editor of *Scientific American* evidently was not entirely convinced, because in an editorial in the same issue he referred to it as Chadwick's "theory of the curved ball, which so many have watched with interest and so few have attempted to explain," and concluded: "If any one can advance any better theory as to the way the ball is held or thrust from the hand, the editor will be glad to hear from him."

The Chadwick article did elicit "a large number of communications," the editor reported some weeks later; he also admitted that most of these letter-writers had found a basic flaw in Chadwick's explanation: The ball *does* curve, they agreed, but in the direction opposite to that shown by Chadwick. Although these letter-writers may not all have used precisely the language of modern physics, many of them basically got it right: As a ball spins, one side spins against the air so that greater pressure builds up there than on the side spinning with the air's force, and the ball curves in the direction where the pressure is lower. At least one letter-writer to the *Scientific American* (October 9, 1886), a K. E. E. Munson of Millerton, New York, came up with a surprisingly modern explanation, referring to "molecules being forced aside" and the "rapid rotation" that "produces a thinning out, or what resembles a partial vacuum."

What is amusing now, though, is to read some of the long and involved explanations of how the curve worked. Also, most of them failed to note the role of the raised stitches and other nonsymmetrical elements of the ball itself, and also the role of the pitcher's positioning of his fingers on the ball seams. So although these "scientific" types explained the ideal curveball, they failed to anticipate all the possible variations, including the illegal pitches resulting from "doctoring" a ball in some way. But just as pitchers had discovered the curve without knowing anything about the physical laws behind it, they would gradually discover these variations on the theme of the curve.

*The Damnable Curve*   It did not take long, of course, for pitchers to realize that they could make the ball perform in various unpredictable

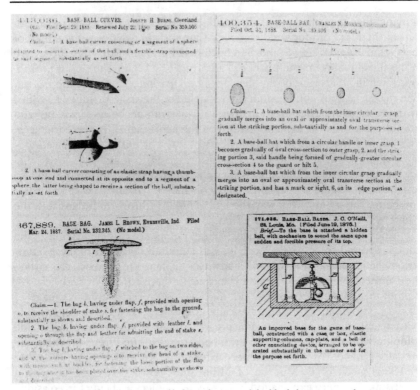

*Hundreds of patents were filed in the second half of the nineteenth century by Americans determined to help the game of baseball become more efficient. Among them were these:* top left, *an elastic strap that a pitcher would use in some way to put a curve on the ball!* top right, *a different shaped bat that was supposed to increase the hitting power;* lower left and right, *two ideas for bases (which base stealers would regard as lethal weapons).*

ways if they could increase the asymmetry of its surface. It would be 1919 before things got so bad that the spitball and other "freak" deliveries were abolished (with that strange exception, the "grandfather clause," which allowed spitball pitchers already established in the major leagues to continue using it). But long before that many people were objecting to the advantages given to the pitcher by allowing so many variants on old-fashioned pitching. In fact, the history of baseball from the very first rules of the Knickerbockers to this day is the story of attempts to find some balance between the power of the pitcher and the power of the hitter.

Not surprisingly, if you accept that poets are seers, one of the few who saw this coming was Walt Whitman. The full story of his lifelong attachment to baseball is told as a part of American literature's involvement with the game. But on this one particular issue, the role of the pitcher, Whitman showed especial foresight. Ed Folsom deserves credit for resurrecting this footnote (in his article, "The Manly and Healthy Game") to American baseball history: how a friend, Thomas Harned, visited Whitman after a game in May 1889 and Whitman questioned him closely about the new development:

> In baseball, is it the rule that the fellow pitching the ball aims to pitch it in such a way the batter cannot hit it? Gives it a what-not—so it slides off, or won't be struck fairly?

When Harned confirmed this, Whitman expressed his dismay in vivid language:

> The wolf, the snake, the cur, the sneak all seem entered into the modern sports, though I ought not to say that, for a snake is snake because he is born so, and man is snake for other reasons, it may be said. And again he went over the catalogue: "I should call it everything that is damnable."

For as Folsom explains, Whitman had been working himself up over this matter for some time, the increasing dominance of the pitcher in a contest Whitman felt should be between equals, "a fair and open and democratic game."

Some would say that Whitman's fears have been borne out, that long before such episodes as Jay Howell and his pine tar in the 1988 NL championship game, pitchers did come to assume far too great a role in the game through their tricky pitching. A 1978 poll asked the field managers and general managers or chief executives of all twenty-six major league clubs as well as twenty-six sportswriters and baseball broadcasters what percentage of winning baseball they assigned to pitching. They came up with an average of about 60 percent (leaving, that is, only 40 percent to everything else—batting, fielding, managing, attitude, and ballpark). Almost all the rules added and changed in the years since 1845, as well as much of the equipment and many of the adjustments in the layout of the diamond and the ballparks, involve attempts to fine tune this relationship, to strike some better balance. To straighten out the curve.

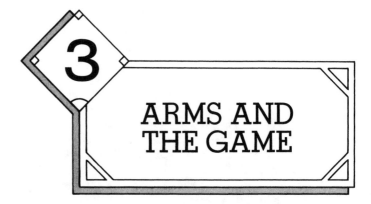

# 3

## ARMS AND
## THE GAME

**T**he idea that the military and baseball have been connected from remotest antiquity is quite close to the truth—this is what the Doubleday myth was supposed to establish—even if not for the reasons usually given. All sporting matches are at bottom forms of ritualized combat that also prepare the participants for the mayhem of the real thing, but in baseball, at a crucial moment in its establishment as the national game, a particularly conscious effort was made to invest it with a martial character, partly to make it appear more grown-up and less like rounders, the game's boyish antecedent. This effort culminated in the almost entirely groundless assertion by baseball equipment tycoon Albert Spalding that a career soldier named Doubleday, who sighted the first gun fired against the Confederacy in the Civil War, invented baseball in 1839.

Albert Spalding liked to refer to baseball as "a bloodless battle." His push to connect baseball with the military was spearheaded in the 1880s by sportswriter Henry Chadwick, the "Father of Baseball," who edited the *Spalding Guide*s and set the tone for most of the writers and commentators during the formative stages of baseball's development. During this time, baseball grew up with rule changes that brought it close to the modern game, but most of all through an intelligent application of strategy—often called "mental combat" at the time—which resulted in the "scientific game."

In Chadwick's *How to Play Base Ball* (1889), the most influential work promulgating the scientific approach, military metaphors abound. Chadwick stressed the importance of a well-paced attack, with tactics coordinated by the captain, or "commander of the field," who was responsible for the overall strategy. The *battery,* a term still commonly used today for the pitcher and catcher, was to the team "what the battery of a regiment is to the the line of infantry." The pitcher, as the squad's artillerist, lays siege to the batting team's "home base," and "is the main reliance of the attacking force of the field corps," also known as infielders, who "are the immediate supporting force of the 'battery'" and "the defenders of the citadel of the field."

To violence-jaded citizens of the late twentieth century it is easier to see football as a metaphor for warfare, but in the nineteenth century baseball was construed after eighteenth-century warfare, which, like baseball, was genteel and based on rigid rules. Chadwick's martial language exploited an identification of baseball with warfare that was quite understandable at a time when, according to historian Harold Seymour, professional baseball games "resembled miniature wars more than athletic contests." During the 1880s, contemporary observers likened the feverish enthusiasm for baseball to the feverish fascination of the Civil War, pointing out, for instance, that fans gathered at town newspaper offices to await news from their team just as they did when awaiting news from the front; others complained that there was already enough regimentation in life "without making one's very sport a kind of West Point drill."

Baseball had long since established itself as a relatively bloodless outlet for village-to-village warfare; even today we refer to Boston when we mean the Red Sox, New York when we mean the Mets or Yankees, as if they were warring city-states; and the workaday world of entire cities can grind to a halt during a tight Series or pennant campaign. The clubs and rocks that as civilized human beings we have transmuted into bats and balls and that we use only according to the strictest rules apparently still have the power to evoke some vestigial memory of a time when violent disputes were settled with their primitive prototypes.

In fact, it was only with the advent of football and modern warfare that baseball came to represent a simpler, more mannered pastoral past and that baseball lost its commonplace resemblance to war. But curiously enough, in the great conflicts of the twentieth century, baseball was time and again invoked to represent the moral and physical superiority of the United States and the purity of its mission. Its martial essence was resurrected in all its glory to restock the ideological arsenal with the virtues of courage, teamwork, loyalty, and leadership; and to quicken and restore the national spirit.

*This illustration of a major match and some of New York's leading players from* Frank Leslie's Illustrated Newspaper *for November 4, 1865, demonstrates how popular baseball had become by the end of the Civil War. All players at the time were supposedly amateur, but the cult of the baseball hero, as illustrated by the crepe-draped central figure of deceased superstar James Creighton, was clearly on the rise. Creighton received payment for his services as early as 1860; some of these other "amateur" players were professional as well.*

**The War Between the States**   Whatever else may be said about the U.S. Civil War, its influence on the development of baseball was profound. In the words of Albert Spalding, the leading proponent of baseball as the national game as well as its first millionaire:

No human mind may measure the blessings conferred by the game of Base Ball on the soldiers of the Civil War. A National Game? Why, no country on the face of the earth ever had a form of sport with so dear a title to that distinction. Base Ball had been born in the brain of an American soldier [Abner Doubleday?]. It received its baptism in the bloody days of our Nation's direst danger. It had its early evolution when soldiers, North and South, were striving to forget their foes by cultivating, through this grand game, fraternal friendship with comrades in arms. It had its best development at the time when Southern soldiers, disheartened by distressing defeat, were seeking the solace of something safe and sane; at a time when Northern soldiers, flushed with victory, were yet willing to turn from fighting with bombs and bullets to playing with ball and bat. It was a panacea for the pangs and humiliation to the vanquished on one side, and a sedative against the natural exuberance of the victory on the other. It healed the wounds of war, and was balm to stinging memories of sword thrust and saber stroke. It served to fill the enforced leisure hours of countless thousands of men suddenly thrown out of employment. It calmed the restless spirits of men who, after four years of bitter strife, found themselves all at once in the midst of a monotonous era, with nothing at all to do.

Spalding goes on to express his vision of baseball as a transcendent "beacon" guiding mankind to "a future of perpetual peace," but for once, so far as the evolution of baseball goes, he wasn't too far from the truth. Without the Civil War, baseball—the New York Game—might never have become the national pastime, or might at least have taken a much different route to get there.

Folklorist Tristram Potter Coffin tells us, in an exemplary expression of the standard history, how the New York game swept "like dysentery through the Army camps, down the South Atlantic coast, and out into the Midwest," to become, "by the time the nation's wounds were bandaged . . . the most popular game in the land." But the game was far from unknown in the South before the war. In fact, the Mexican War, in which future officers of North and South fought side by side, had already established the pattern by which baseball would be spread by the American military, and the game was popular in New Orleans and several other Southern cities, which also had baseball clubs, well before Union troops arrived with their bats and balls.

But perhaps even more important than the geographic expansion of baseball was the social leveling that occurred during the war, a process by which control of the game passed from the young professionals with gentlemanly pretensions who played it in the Northeast—now officers—to men of all backgrounds who earned their places on the diamond according to skill. This eminently democratic development gave momentum to the growing movement, underway since the 1850s, which placed emphasis on competition and winning—rather than "exercise"—and made postwar professionalism inevitable. By 1866, the New York *Herald* was calling baseball "The National Game," and the first professional league was organized in 1871, only six years after the cessation of hostilities.

Many Union troops "took their Base Ball implements with their war accoutrements and camp equipage to the front," and since many a town's commons or parade grounds was also its ballfield, ballplayers as well as Union soldiers mustered at the Armory Parade Grounds in Syracuse. A. G. Mills of Cincinnati, fourth president of the National League, packed his bat and ball with his field equipment before going off to war; he recalls that these implements of sport received as much use as his side arms. Another future National League president, Nick Young, whose regiment sported a cricket team of which he was a member, was introduced to baseball by the Twenty-seventh New York Regiment in 1863. After the war he helped found the Olympic Base Ball Club in Washington. Young's battlefield conversion illustrates the process—now long forgotten—by which baseball vanquished cricket in the struggle for the title of national game.

Northern prisoners sometimes organized teams and taught the game to their guards, as depicted in a lithograph of two Union teams playing at a Confederate prison camp in Salisbury, North Carolina; and Southern prisoners returning from Northern camps brought the game into areas of the South it had not yet penetrated. Altogether over one million soldiers had the opportunity to return home with new knowledge or appreciation of the game.

For Union troops, baseball supplied a poignant reminder of home, especially on major holidays, when it took the place of family gatherings; and in this way baseball became for many soldiers permanently entwined with feelings for family and country. On Christmas 1862, over forty thousand Union soldiers, possibly the largest crowd of spectators at any sporting event in the nineteenth century, gathered to watch a game in Hilton Head, South Carolina, between the 165th New York Volunteer Infantry and an all-star Union team that included A. G. Mills. Diaries and letters contain myriad accounts of matches at the front and there are even reports, highly touted by Spalding, that a series of games were played between Union and Confederate troops during McClellan's Peninsular Campaign.

*The baseball game taking place behind this portrait of a New York State regiment on parade at Fort Pulaski, Georgia, during the Civil War qualifies as one of the oldest photographs of men playing baseball in existence. Fort Pulaski fell to Federal forces in November 1861. The pitcher, in a white shirt, is close to the middle of the frame behind the men at attention.*

On the home front, the game was comparatively stagnant during the war years, but popular enough to stay afloat. As might be imagined, baseball clubs in the border states had particular problems; the Pastime Club of Baltimore prevented friction between Northern and Southern sympathizers by banning all talk about the war. The National Association of Base-Ball Players, baseball's first league, could count forty-nine clubs among its members in 1859 and sixty-two in 1860, but for the next four years it averaged only thirty-one clubs, bottoming out with a low of twenty-eight in 1863.

Several developments that would prove significant to the evolution of baseball occurred up North while the New York game caught on with the Union troops and spread to the Southerners. On October 21, 1861, three months after the first battle of Bull Run, over ten thousand fans gathered in Hoboken to watch a game between New York and Brooklyn all-stars (Brooklyn won), which was promoted by Henry Chadwick, who arranged for the prize of a silver ball. The next summer, on July 10, 1862, the Brooklyn Excelsiors became the first New York club to play in Boston when they bested the Bowdoin team, 41–15. By this time the Excelsiors were paying pitcher Jim Creighton—and probably others—under the table, a trend that grew rapidly among baseball's "amateur" clubs as a means to insure excellence. Box scores continued to be a regular feature of Northern newspapers; *The New York Times* reported on crowds of over "four thousand spectators, including a large number of ladies," at matches in the summer of 1864.

But perhaps the most significant home-front development occurred in 1862 when William Cammeyer, who owned the field used by the Union Club of Brooklyn, decided to fence in the field and charge each spectator ten cents admission; until 1958 there was no regulation in major league ball governing the distance to the outfield fences, because fences have always been, and still primarily are, a business, not a sporting, consideration. Cammeyer let the Unions play for free, but a year later the club discovered its business potential and successfully sued Cammeyer for a cut of the gate by threatening to strike. Commercialism was on the horizon.

*Ice Baseball* One of the real oddities of Civil War baseball began in the winter of 1861 when the Atlantics and the Charter Oaks of Brooklyn played four innings on skates before eight to ten thousand spectators. In 1863 the Atlantics again figured in an ice match, this time against a team composed of Charter Oaks and Star club members, and from then on into the 1870s ice baseball continued to be popular. The Atlantics and the Gothams (of New York) played a championship series in January 1865. The ice game, which employed a soft ball and special rules dispensations that permitted a runner to skate through a base for the distance of five feet, otherwise adhered strictly to the rules of the National Association, to which all the clubs that played in the New York area belonged.

*Abe Lincoln and Baseball* The newly reunited United States' need to define itself resulted in the invention of a common American folklore with recognizable myths and heroes. Abraham Lincoln, safely dead, as all the best heroes are, suddenly became Abe Lincoln of Illinois, who would walk miles through sleet and snow to return a few pennies. If they did not already exist, fables connecting Abe Lincoln of Illinois to the national game were necessary, including compulsory vignettes of his playing catch with his and other people's sons. It may be that not all of these tales were outright lies, but perhaps some embodied wishful thinking more than others.

In 1860 Lincoln became the Republican nominee for president. The committee that was sent to Springfield, Illinois, to notify him of his selection reportedly found the "great leader . . . engaged in a game of Base Ball." According to Albert Spalding, Lincoln remarked to the messenger who had been sent ahead to inform him of the committee's imminent arrival, "Tell the gentlemen that I am glad to know of their coming; but they'll have to wait a few minutes until I make another base hit." Clearly, to a man of Lincoln's stature, baseball was just as important as affairs of state. Unfortunately, Spalding, who set this tale to paper in an age when an impassioned appeal to patriotism was enough to end any argument, spoils his case for its accuracy by citing as his authority a letter he received in 1908 ("which letter is in my possession"); Spalding's "proof" that Abner Doubleday invented baseball also rested on a letter that was written seventy years after the fact, and its author was a well-known liar who murdered his wife with his revolver shortly after informing Spalding of the true origin of baseball and spent the rest of his days in an institution for the criminally insane.

Winfield Scott Larner of Washington remembered attending a game in Washington in 1862, which was already underway when Lincoln arrived with his son Tad in a modest two-horse carriage. Lincoln took Tad by the hand, "modestly and unobtrusively" made his way to a spot along the first-base line, sat down in a pile of sawdust left over from a recent circus, and with Tad between his knees watched the rest of the game, sometimes cheering boisterously like any other enthusiastic fan. Before he left, he and Tad accepted three loud cheers from the crowd. Clearly, Lincoln was a man of the people; even in the midst of his crushing responsibilities as commander-in-chief of a great nation at war, he took time out, as would any common man, to refresh himself by attending the great national pastime. Mr. Larner's eyewitness report, recorded fifty years after the fact, would be more convincing if it were supported by contemporary evidence—its combination of classic mythic elements is almost too pat—but one has to admit, with no reluctance whatsoever, that it is quite possible that it happened just this way.

Perhaps the most reliable account of Lincoln's participation in a ballgame—also long after the fact—comes from one Frank B. Blair, who in a book suspiciously titled *"Abe" Lincoln's Yarns and Stories* (Chicago: John C. Winston Company, 1904) tells how he and eight or ten other lucky boys used to gather during the Civil War at the estate of their grandfather Frank P. Blair, in Silver Springs, Maryland, where the president was a frequent visitor. Lincoln's rides out to the estate were memorable to the boys because he liked to join in with them when they played town ball on the vast lawn. "I remember vividly how he ran with the children; how long were his strides, and how far his coat-tails stuck out behind, and how we tried to hit him with the ball, as he ran the bases. He entered into the spirit of the play as completely as any of us, and we invariably hailed his coming with delight."

Clearly, the great man's genius lay in his simplicity and enthusiasm, which never deserted him even when he was beset with the cares of a nation on the brink of destruction. Because this yarn is not set among those who would necessarily have related to him as a powerful adult, it seems to carry a louder ring of truth, but at any rate, Lincoln and the boys were playing town ball, in which a player could be put out by being hit with a thrown ball, and not the national pastime. So even if Mr. Blair's account is factually correct, it does little to document the general belief that Lincoln was mildly interested in baseball.


*The Postwar Decade*  To say that baseball grew to impressive proportions during the Civil War era is to say that its commercialization resulted in large part from the increased emphasis that was placed on winning by both Union troops and players at home during the war years. After all, the idea of war was to win; the gentlemanly, English model of play, which could never be wholeheartedly embraced by a democratic nation anyway, did not survive the conflict that reunited the United States. When the fighting stopped, baseball was in the right place at the right time to combine with the newly fused nation's patriotic quest for national identity and its dire need for a new kind of hero—the self-reliant, self-made man—who would inspire this brave new world that promised both industrialism's cornucopia of material goods and its total dislocation of community and sense of place. Professional athletes, in filling the spiritual vacuum that the new age created, became keepers of the national morality, a role as incredible then as it is now. And it is from this concatenation of forces that baseball heroes attained a status equal to political and military leaders.

In 1864, while the war still raged, the National Association, baseball's first league, counted only 30 member clubs, less than half of its 1860 enrollment, but in 1865 this number shot up to 91, and in 1866, when Johnny really came marching home, the number of clubs reached 202, almost four times its prewar high. The phenomenal baseball mania that gripped the Northeastern cities in the late 1860s was echoed even in the shattered South, where by the end of 1866 baseball clubs had popped up in Charlottesville, Richmond, Staunton, and Washington, and at the University of Virginia. Amateurism, the *raison d'être* of the National Association, which had steadily been going by the boards since the early 1860s when association clubs began charging admission, continued to evaporate after the war as ballooning gate receipts demonstrated to baseball clubs that they could do without the support of their amateur members, who increasingly found themselves relegated to the sidelines by paid professionals who drew ever larger crowds and accelerated the cycle of commercialization. Three years after Appomattox the first openly all-professional club, the Cincinnati Red Stockings, was organized, and two years later, in 1871, major league baseball was born with the formation of the first professional league.

Not everyone was happy with the commercialization of baseball, but it was too late to turn back the clock. When the Athletic Base Ball Club of Philadelphia owned up to hiring four professional baseball players to increase their prospects for victory in the summer of 1866, an irate amateur player sent a letter to the Philadelphia *City Item* that read in part, "What must be the contempt for those who would degrade our great 'National Game,' and make it a *business*. When such becomes the case, farewell to base ball; the excitement, which is, at present, attendant on these contests, will cease, then the game itself will gradually, but surely, die out." But the winning of games, rather than the taking of exercise, became the motivation for baseball; and winning became a matter of civic pride and prestige. When the Union Base Ball Club of Morrisania defeated the Atlantics of Brooklyn in 1867, they announced themselves Champions of the United States.

So it was that the idea of the "baseball epidemic" took on different connotations to different factions. By those who believed that baseball had won the war and continued to attribute to it the most remarkable psychic and physical powers, baseball was even promoted as a preventative for the cholera epidemic that threatened the nation in the spring of 1866: ". . . no sanitary measure that can be adopted . . . is so calculated to induce that healthy condition of the system which acts as a barrier to the progress of this disease as base ball exercise every afternoon."

Baseball was similarly promoted as a balm to heal sectional wounds—for years it appeared to be the only thing North and South did have in common—and as an analogue for an older, presumably more civilized form of war. For many men who were brutally thrust into the mayhem and irrationality of the Civil War, the practice of a game supposedly based on the genteel strategy of eighteenth-century warfare provided a cathartic opportunity both to deny their wartime experience and to assert it as something kinder and more rational than it had been.

The healing of the United States lasted for decades, indeed is still going on; but once baseball became identified in the popular imagination as the national game, almost before the war was over, it also became inextricably entwined with nationalism and the "mission" of America to expand and spread its marvelous form of government, by sword if necessary, all over the world. As a manifestation and an exemplar of American values, baseball began to mirror major national political and ideological shifts, both good and bad.

When the Republican party accepted a disputed presidency in 1876 in return for agreeing to permit states to handle blacks in their own way, thereby closing the door on equality and ushering in the horrid reign of Jim Crow, the national pastime responded by squeezing blacks out of the major leagues and all but out of organized baseball in little more than a decade; some sixty years later, when the pendulum swung the other way, it begrudgingly admitted Jackie Robinson back into its fold. But in 1876, one decade after the Civil War, the possibilities for America seemed endless. One major league had already come and gone, but a new one was patched together and launched, and this one, the National League of Base Ball Clubs, came to stay, laying the basis for the current two-league system and supplying a continuity almost unique among American institutions.

The peculiar sway baseball continues to exercise in American life derives at least partly from its timely establishment on the ground floor of a nation finally united under one Constitution, which it was in a position to do because it combined so many elements of whatever it is to be American. To a giddy post–Civil War America teetering on the brink of full industrialization, baseball represented something that is hard to imagine, but in the words of an 1866 *City Item* article, "What a blessing is conveyed by those two words, base ball."


*The Spanish-American War*   The "splendid little war" of 1898 lasted about the length of the baseball season and had minimal impact at home, but when American military missions replaced Spanish governors in former Spanish colonies in the Caribbean and the Philippines, American soldiers brought baseball as well as democracy. In the Caribbean, baseball flourished in Puerto Rico, Cuba, and the Dominican Republic; Mexico and Venezuela also regularly saw some of the finest major league and black players from the States when they came down to play in the winter Latin leagues. Puerto Rico eventually produced the incomparable Roberto Clemente, and even the far-flung American military presence in the former Spanish colony of the Philippines nurtured an American baseball legend, for it served as a staging area for Hall of Famer Oscar Charleston, who began to realize his potential as a player while serving in the Army there from 1911 to 1915.

*The Great War* For most Americans, the war that started in Europe in 1914 had no real meaning for another three years and seemed so foreign and far away that it was almost like a game they could follow in the newspapers. But in Canada the war was a reality. When the Providence Grays, a tributary that fed the Red Sox, arrived at Montreal in the summer of 1914 with a nineteen-year-old southpaw named Babe Ruth, they discovered that the evening editions of the newspapers were so filled with war bulletins that they had to wait until the next morning for the box scores (in those days the newspapers were the only way to learn the results of the day's games). War was hell.

One of Ruth's teammates, a pitcher named Wallace Shultz from Pennsylvania, became a rooter for the German side. He was promptly nicknamed "the Kaiser," and suffered a great deal of teasing and practical joking. On one occasion, when the Montreal papers carried a headline announcing that 75,000 Germans had been killed in France, Shultz's teammates sent numerous copies of this news to his room, left them for him at the front desk, stuffed them into his shoes and socks, hid them under his dinner plate, and even wrapped one around his bat. Shultz saved every copy, wrapped them around a brick, and sent the bulky package express collect to one of his chief tormentors, infielder Matty McIntyre, whom he knew was expecting a package from home. McIntyre willingly shelled out forty-eight cents for the parcel—in those days the price of a good meal—and flew into a rage when he realized he had been tricked. Shultz declared a satisfying victory for the Germans.

An Illinois district judge named Kenesaw Mountain Landis developed a particular dislike for the Germans, and found a convenient outlet for his patriotism and a way to make headlines by declaring that after the war he would try Kaiser Wilhelm for the murder of a Chicago resident killed on the *Lusitania*. Unfortunately, Secretary of State Robert Lansing informed Judge Landis that under existing treaties, the extradition of the kaiser would be impossible.

Another enterprising American who was unafraid to take the law into his own hands and who would also make a name for himself, Captain Larry MacPhail, had other plans for the kaiser. After the armistice the young captain and seven members of his artillery battery staged an unauthorized attempt to kidnap Wilhelm from the Dutch castle in which he had taken refuge. The attempt failed, but MacPhail did manage to snatch the kaiser's ashtray, which for many years occupied a prominent position in his office.

World War I, it has often been observed, was the last of the great fun wars, but in February 1942, as president of the Dodgers, MacPhail came up with the fun idea that baseball should put up the money—about three hundred thousand dollars—to buy an Army Flying Fortress "to carry our compliments overseas." The huge, state-of-the-art bomber, he proposed, could be named the *Kenesaw Mountain Landis* and be crewed by former major leaguers. The owners decided against it, but the awesome breadth of MacPhail's creative genius as here demonstrated may help explain why some owners were reluctant to endorse some of his less startling suggestions, including night games and radio broadcasts.

*Work or Fight*   Major league baseball attendance climbed steadily during the first decade of the twentieth century and hovered around 6.5 million during the second, except for the slump caused by the competing Federal League, but in 1917, apparently as an effect of America's involvement in the foreign war, attendance fell to 5 million and some baseball men began to panic. Uncertain even that the game would continue in the face of conscription, the Phillies sold Grover Cleveland Alexander to the Cubs in November of 1917 for sixty thousand dollars and two players—he was indeed drafted and grievously wounded—and Harry Hempstead sold the Giants to Charles Stoneham the following year. In the shortened 1918 wartime season attendance fell to 3 million, the lowest since 1902. The owners had no precedent by which to predict the effects on the game of a national emergency—the Spanish-American War could hardly qualify in that respect—and the outlook was uncertain and rather gloomy at best. Baseball was about to learn that its status as America's national game sometimes required it to be compliant while clever politicians manipulated it for personal image enhancement or the advancement of their military policies.

In the spring of 1917 talk of war, or more properly, war hysteria, was everywhere. *Preparedness* was the watchword. In baseball it was generally believed or at least widely promoted that if the United States entered the war, players might be left alone if they appeared to be receiving military instruction at their place of work. Accordingly, American League President Ban Johnson announced that teams would do close-order drills, using bats as rifles, during spring training; as an incentive, he put up a five-hundred-dollar prize for the club that won a drill competition to be held during the season. But by mid-March the players had had enough, and on March 20 the Dodgers voted to end drill practice, followed by the Tigers and Indians, on the grounds that they didn't have enough time.

The drill teams were quickly reinstated when the United States declared war on Germany five days before the opening of the 1917 season; in New York, the Red Sox and the Yankees marched before their opening game of the season. Registration for the draft began in June. Although only eligible

*A baseball game at Camp Gordon, Georgia, during World War I. Army outfits like this depended on major league baseball's Ball and Bat Fund to supply them with equipment.*

single men who drew a low number were likely to be called up before fall, and the status of ballplayers was as yet unknown, there was much speculation about whether enough players would be left to take the game into the World Series. Meanwhile, throughout this season of jingoistic excitement, ballparks staged patriotic extravaganzas almost daily. Sometimes games were interrupted in midinning to sell war bonds; Heinie Zimmerman of the Giants and Heinie Groh of Cincinnati both became "Henry"; teams sent a percentage of profits from one week out of every month to the Red Cross for European War Relief. In St. Louis, the Browns won Ban Johnson's five-hundred-dollar prize in a well-publicized drill-off with the Red Sox.

Baseball's moment of truth came in the spring of 1918 with the promulgation of Provost Marshal General Crowder's "work or fight" order, a puritanical decree that served notice on draft-age men previously deferred that they were liable to be drafted if they were engaged in "nonproductive" work. No labor shortage in essential industry existed, and the order, ostensibly designed to keep the factories and mills turning, was specifically designed to prevent otherwise draftable men from enjoying themselves while their comrades might be fighting and dying.

Yankees pitcher Joe Finneran, previously deferred as a husband and a father, was drafted and appealed his induction under the work-or-fight order to his New Jersey draft board on the grounds that after ten years as a professional there was no other occupation at which he could earn a comparable income. His plea echoed baseball's stance (perhaps its undoing) that it wasn't seeking special exemptions, but that if an individual player was deferred on the merits of his own case, he should be permitted to keep playing—uh, *working*—at baseball. Finneran was deferred and permitted to continue playing, but other draft boards did order players out of baseball and into serious jobs.

Resolution of the entire dilemma would have to await the disposition of the case of Eddie Ainsmith, a catcher with the Senators, who was deferred, then called up under the work-or-fight order, and had finally appealed all the way up to Secretary of War Baker. Organized baseball, invoking its status as the national game, had indeed appealed first to the president and then to Secretary Baker and General Crowder not to be classified with nonessential "amusements" when the order was first issued; and had its balancing act between patriotism and self-interest been more skillful, baseball players might well have been classified with actors, opera singers, and movie folk, who were deferred for providing essential public entertainment.

Meanwhile, more and more baseball players, convinced that the mood of the country would not tolerate men playing a children's game while their countrymen died overseas, enlisted in various reserve units or found work playing baseball in industrial leagues. Others enlisted hoping to play for service teams or to serve as physical education instructors. Although Chief Bender, then pitching for the Phillies, worked himself into nervous exhaustion in the shipyards, very few major leaguers entered war-related work; and of those who did, most spent most of their time playing ball. Red Sox southpaw ace Dutch Leonard jumped to the Fore River Shipyards in Quincy where his job at the shipyard remained a mystery, but everyone knew that he pitched for the Fore River baseball team.

In early July, Babe Ruth, already deferred as a married man and a reservist, reached an impasse with Red Sox manager Ed Barrow. He left the club in Washington, traveled to his father's place in Baltimore, and began negotiating with the Chester Shipyards in Pennsylvania to see what they would pay him if he jumped to the shipyard team. Apparently it wasn't enough; at any rate Boston wooed him back and swallowed a five-hundred-dollar fine their manager had levied against him. But the newspapers, exploiting rumors that Ruth was jumping to Chester to avoid being drafted, had such a field day with the incident that Ruth's alleged draft-dodging remains a staple of Ruthian folklore to this day. Baseball players were indeed assumed by their contemporaries to be "slackers," a most undesirable thing. In September 1918, workers at Philadelphia's Cramp Shipyard went out on strike over ballplayer employees who received foreman's wages, drove to work in cars, and spent most of their time playing baseball.

When Secretary of War Baker finally decided on July 19, 1918, that baseball was not an essential occupation under the work-or-fight order, baseball faced the imminent loss of almost all of its players. League president Ban Johnson, without bothering to consult the team owners, announced that the American League season would end two days later, a decision most American League club owners would have nothing to do with; the same was true for his subsequent plea to have the season end on August 20. The National League chose to continue, and baseball's attempt to delay the order until after the October Series, or at least long enough to enable the industry to disband in an orderly fashion, finally resulted in an agreement that the 1918 season would end on Labor Day, September 2. On August 22, after another appeal, the War Department agreed to permit an early World Series, provided 10 percent off the top was donated to war charities.

Wartime travel restrictions and the flip of a coin determined that the earliest World Series ever played (and the last one without a home run; the ball was really dead that year) would begin in Chicago on September 5; after the first three games the Cubs would travel to the Red Sox's Fenway Park for as many more games as were necessary. To display patriotism and encourage attendance, ticket prices were cut in half, but attendance was worse than terrible. Since this was the first Series in which a share of receipts would be allocated to other first-division players and a cap had been set on winner's and loser's shares, which would be calculated after the War Department's cut, by the time the clubs traveled to Boston, where attendance continued to be miserable, it was questionable whether the guaranteed shares would be met. Players of both teams, already smarting over pay lost during the shortened "regular" season, agreed on the train to approach the National Commission, which agreed to meet with them after the fourth game when the players threatened to strike.

The fifth game was delayed—Ban Johnson was late to the pregame meeting—while players and officials conferred. The commission refused to defer the plan to include other first-division clubs or even to guarantee the players shares of $1,500 and $1,000 (they had been expecting $2,000 and $1,500), and the players decided to strike. However, the strike crumbled when Johnson astutely pointed out that with wounded servicemen in the stands and men dying overseas, ballplayers who whined for more money could not expect to receive much sympathy from the public. Indeed, boos as well as cheers greeted the players when they took the field. Boston's winning share, $1,102, was the smallest in history; the 1919 losing share was worth $3,254.

No one at the time knew there would be a 1919 season—many later wished that there never had been—and some baseball writers went so far as to assert that the only way baseball could cleanse itself would be to voluntarily shut down operations for 1919 and turn its parks over to the military for storage depots. The end of the war put a stop to all that, and when Hank Gowdy, the first major leaguer to enlist, returned to the States, he was offered $1,500 a week for thirty-six weeks to tell the vaudeville world how he stopped the Hun; Johnny Evers, who had represented the Knights of Columbus as a baseball instructor in France, went on a lecture tour to relate his experiences. Attendance would double in 1919 and hit a new high of 9 million in 1920, reflecting a pattern of increased interest and attendance following a war that has held true in baseball since the Civil War.

*Servicemen's Baseball* So many servicemen played baseball in the Great War that Ban Johnson could attribute the postwar surge in major league attendance in part to the thousands of soldiers who first came into contact with baseball in the service, or who had found a deeper appreciation for the national game on the playing fields of France. Before the United States entered the fray, Canadian units in the British Army were already playing baseball and teaching the game to their English and Australian allies, and by the time the first American troops began to ship out in the fall of 1917, 101 teams were locked in battle in England for the Canadian overseas military championship. After the Americans arrived, the Anglo-American League was organized in London with help from veteran major leaguer Arlie Latham. Each American or Canadian club in the league included four or five professionals and participated in a regular weekend schedule throughout England and Scotland; Sunday league ball remained so popular that it was continued for another three weeks after the regular season ended on September 7, 1918. On the Fourth of July, 1918, American Army and Navy teams, perpetuating an ancient rivalry, played a benefit game at Chelsea, this one attended by the king of England and over forty thousand spectators.

Once the Americans arrived in Paris, Sunday baseball became a regular feature in the Bois du Boulogne. The YMCA organized a French Association League made up of thirty clubs that played a fifteen-game Sunday schedule; they had the official rule book translated into French. According to the YMCA overseas representative, former major leaguer Bill Lange, the Americans had taught the Europeans how to fight, and now would teach them how to play. To this end the Knights of Columbus sent former superstar Johnny Evers to France on a special instructional mission, and by the end of the war, whether out of the French command's respect for the American fighting spirit or a

*In this wonderful period piece, Franklin Delano Roosevelt, then assistant secretary of the Navy, marches into Griffith Stadium in Washington, D.C., with the Senators' team in 1918. During World War I, major league players hoped that displays of patriotism and "preparedness," especially evidence that they were receiving military training on the job, would exempt them from the draft.*

bemused willingness to humor their somewhat baseball-crazed allies, French soldiers were ordered to learn baseball. In addition to these larger movements, ad hoc leagues sprouted up among smaller units, such as the eight-club circuit that the 471st Aero Construction Squadron organized in its part of England.

Much of the equipment for these and other programs was supplied by the Clark C. Griffith Ball and Bat Fund, brainchild of the Washington Senators' manager, which began in 1917 to supply servicemen with baseball equipment. Baseball executives also hoped that their generosity and patriotism would convince the American government to protect baseball as a maintainer of morale. The first fund consignment went down with the *Kansan* when she was torpedoed by a German submarine, but the Ball and Bat Fund rallied to supply $95,104.41 worth of baseball essentials to American servicemen. Each outfit sent by the fund consisted of a catcher's mask, a catcher's mitt, a catcher's chest protector, a first baseman's mitt, three bats, twelve balls, three bases, three base pins, a book of rules, and twelve score cards (total cost: about thirty dollars). In its *Final Report* (1919), the Ball and Bat Fund congratulated itself for helping to give the American soldier the kind of "punch" he needed to knock out the Hun.

Much equipment purchased by the Ball and Bat Fund was also distributed in the States, where it was put to good use by such outstanding service teams as the one fielded by the Second Naval District, Newport, Rhode Island, which featured several major leaguers; the 85th Division, Battle Creek, Michigan, which featured pitcher Urban Shocker; the Great Lakes Naval Station club, which would become even more famous in World War II, featuring Hall of Famer Red Faber; the Camp Dodge, Iowa, nine; San Antonio's Kelly Field club; and the San Diego Naval Training Camp team. The top service club of World War I was probably the 342d Field Artillery of the American Expeditionary Force, which featured Grover Cleveland Alexander among its undefeated players.

Two hundred forty-seven major leaguers had donned military uniforms by the end of the war, and the American presence in England and France once again raised expectations that baseball might become a major sport in these countries. This prospect, long dear to the hearts of Al Spalding and the horsehide missionaries whose visions of worldwide democracy and Christianity included baseball as the international game, was corroborated by Colonel Tillinghast L'Hommedieu Huston, co-owner of the Yankees, who commented after his return from France that if the war had gone on for another year or so, baseball might have taken root. His analysis may well have been correct; wherever American military presence has been lasting, as in the

*French soldiers playing baseball at La Valbonne during World War I. By the end of the war French soldiers were under orders to learn baseball, but the American Expeditionary Force that succeeded in making the world safe for democracy had less success when it came to creating European baseball franchises.*

decades-long U.S. Marine presence in Nicaragua, baseball has tended to establish itself even better than democracy; and it is axiomatic that wherever American servicemen have gone, baseball has gone, too, following the flag. By the end of the war the flag of baseball had been planted not only in England, France, Belgium, Italy, and Germany, but in such far-flung ports of call as Guam.

*The Star-Spangled Banner* Due primarily to sectional bickering, the United States entered World War I without a national anthem. Congress did not agree to formally adopt "The Star-Spangled Banner" until 1931, but with a war on its hands, President Wilson decreed that "The Star-Spangled Banner" would have to do. Bands undoubtedly played the tune on occasion at the patriotic extravaganzas that tended to precede or interrupt major league games in 1917–18, but the first time the song took root in baseball was at the first game of the disastrous 1918 World Series, when the band unexpectedly started playing "The Star-Spangled Banner" during the seventh-inning stretch. Most of the Cubs and the Red Sox, accustomed to drilling in the hope that it might keep them out of the draft, snapped to attention and faced the flag flying above center field; one player, on leave from the Great Lakes Naval Training Center, spontaneously raised his hand in salute. Most of the fans were already on their feet anyway, and the crowd began to sing along. When the song ended, everyone burst into applause. To the spectators in the half-filled park the truly incredible sight of six insectlike biplanes, the weapons of the future, flying in formation perilously close to Wrigley Field during the eighth inning made a more lasting impression, but the warm, spontaneous singing of "The Star-Spangled Banner" did not go unnoticed, and the tune was played again at the next two games in Chicago. When the teams moved to Boston to complete the Series, Red Sox owner Harry Frazee, a showman at heart, ordered his band to play "The Star-Spangled Banner" to open the contests.

"The Star-Spangled Banner" continued to be played on Opening Day and at World Series games, on national holidays, and for other patriotic occasions that warranted the presence of a band after President Hoover signed it into law as the national anthem in March 1931. By the beginning of World War II, when baseball parks again became arenas for patriotic spectacles, sophisticated public address systems made it possible to play the anthem with or without a band, and to invite vocalists of greater or lesser reknown to lead the crowd or to solo on this song that is not particularly singable; and by the end of World War II, it was an expected ritual that the national anthem would be sung before the playing of the national game, at least at the major league level. The lyrics, which describe warfare, with "bombs bursting in air," have nothing in particular to do with base-ball, but baseball has something to do with war. So it seems appropriate that this warlike melody, which gained currency as the national anthem in ballparks where athletes marched, bands played, and fireworks burst in the air, and which is as difficult to perform well as the game it precedes, should be played in ballparks as a reminder of the national pastime's long connection to the military; or at least it seems more appropriate that it be played before a game that is in some ways a legacy of the Civil War, that for decades promoted itself as a model of nineteenth-century warfare, and that was carried to other lands by American soldiers, than that song about "amber waves of grain," which seems to have more to do with farming than winning.

*Green Light*   "Uncle Sam, we are at your command!" *The Sporting News* announced after Pearl Harbor, promising that baseball would close down if necessary. "You're Gonna Win that Ball Game, Uncle Sam," proclaimed a popular song by former Detroit third baseman, manager, and umpire George Moriarity. As in World War I, the fate of the patriotic national game was in Washington's hands, but this time the pastime had some idea of what it might expect, and the loyalty it expressed to its government was returned with a greater feeling for the role the game played in American life and in America's self-proclaimed mission.

Owners and players must have spent some anxious moments wondering how they were going to spend the war, but they cannot have been too surprised when President Franklin Delano Roosevelt's letter of January 15, 1942, to Commissioner Landis acknowledged that baseball played an important part in sustaining national morale and should continue. Players would still be drafted, or expected to enlist, and baseball would not be sheltered from wartime restrictions on travel and materials, but Roosevelt was on the whole correct when he wrote that "Even if the actual quality of the teams is lowered by the greater use of older players, this will not dampen the popularity of the sport." And he was sensitive enough to suggest that "I hope night games can be extended because it gives an opportunity to the day shift to see a game occasionally." Baseball was not listed among the essential occupations, but unlike General Crowder of the work-or-fight order, Manpower Commissioner Paul V. McNutt permitted players to leave winter factory jobs to report for spring training—it would cost them their draft-proofing—and he threw out the first ball in lieu of the president on Opening Day 1943.

The Japanese sneak attack on Pearl Harbor had forced the American baseball establishment to reconsider its contention that Japan's enthusiasm for baseball was an index of its affinity for Christian democracy. In 1932 National League President John Heydler said he hoped to see a Japanese World Series winner in the near future, but in his New Year's message for 1942, J. G. Taylor Spink, publisher of *The Sporting News,* called the attention of all "civilized, democratic peoples of the world" to the unworthiness of the Japanese to possess baseball. He withdrew the gift from them, cautioned that it should be bestowed more carefully in the future, and suggested that the major leagues apologize for permitting the Japanese to "share the benefits and the God-given qualities of the great game with us" (apparently not satisfied that baseball was invented by Abner Doubleday, Spink attributed its invention to the Deity Himself).

Mr. Spink was most likely unaware that baseball had initially caught on in Japan because its warrior class considered it a martial art, like judo, and wished to learn it to understand the American fighting spirit; and he felt it necessary to denigrate the Japanese character in order to counter what was

*American soldiers playing baseball in Luxembourg during World War II. Note explosions taking place just beyond the right-field fence. Most of the military baseball in World War II took place far from the fighting.*

perceived in some quarters as a failure of baseball to fulfill its mission. But such claims for baseball would run out of steam in a more skeptical age; those who observed that black and white baseball players in the United States had to play on separate teams would begin to wonder what claim baseball had to democracy anyway. For baseball, too, the war signaled the end of a more naive, more idealistic age. In the new era, rhetoric about the alleged moral authority of baseball would take a back seat to clinical exposés of players and behind-the-scenes practices.

After the long night of Depression-era woes, things had just begun to look good again for baseball in 1941: Ted Williams hit .406 and Joe Di-Maggio had his fifty-six-game streak. But by the end of 1942 Williams and DiMaggio were both in the service, and by the end of 1944, 60 percent of all major leaguers—over 1,000 players—had joined them. According to *The New York Times,* as of January 1945, 5,400 of the 5,800 men playing professional baseball at the time of Pearl Harbor had exchanged baseball for military uniforms. The implications of this exodus for the game were clear, and much has been made of the quality of play during the war, but it is a matter of record that when attendance slumped the worst, in the 1942–43 seasons, plenty of regular players were still on hand, while in 1944–45, when attendance topped all records since 1930, few contemporary professionals, not to mention stars, were in baseball uniforms.

The Browns won their first pennant in 1944 with eighteen 4F players, but the Yankees and the Cardinals, who topped their leagues in 1942 and 1943, and had considerable depth in their farm systems, played real ball; the Cardinals club that upset the Yankees in the 1942 World Series took four pennants in five years and remains one of the National League's more memorable teams. Pete Gray, the one-armed outfielder who played for the Browns in 1945 and whose name, along with that of fifteen-year-old Cincinnati pitcher Joe Nuxhall, has become synonymous with the era, was a qualified player who, although normally excluded from the majors because of his handicap, was voted MVP by the Southern Association in 1944. Nuxhall, who pitched *two-thirds* of an inning in the years 1942–45, returned to the majors for a fifteen-year career after he grew up. No one claims that Eddie Gaedel, the midget who had one major league at-bat in 1951 and was much more purely a gate-attraction player than Pete Gray or Joe Nuxhall, was representative of the quality of players in the early fifties.

While no attempt need be made to minimize the decline in the quality of wartime ball, it does not seem fair to maximize it either, for this was by no means an age only of grotesqueries. The roster of players who came up during the war and stayed on after it is impressive, and as the surges in attendance in 1944 and 1945 attest, the games were interesting. Relief pitching became more important, base-stealing experienced a revival, and there was less dependence on the home run.

Most important for the future, wartime conditions led to innovations and changes in attitude that profoundly marked the course of baseball. Clark Griffith initiated the influx of Latin Americans by hiring them because they were draftproof (he refused to consider qualified black Americans). The federal salary freeze of 1942 permanently affected relations between owners and players, who expected their salaries to reflect their abilities, and tensions increased when after the war some returning players had to threaten or bring legal action to get their jobs back at former pay as guaranteed by the GI Bill of Rights. It is no accident that the first effective major league ballplayers' union was organized after the war by players who had learned to be less timid about demands for pensions, tenure, and collective bargaining. Umpires, who suffered similarly, followed suit. Night games, a relative rarity before the war, became a baseball institution; radio broadcasts of games also took a quantum leap, creating legions of new fans; General Eisenhower himself had arranged for the 1943 Yankees-Cardinals World Series to be broadcast to the troops. But perhaps most significant of all, the conflict had the effect of enhancing awareness of racial inequity in baseball. The old era was over, but one of the signs that a new era had begun was Branch Rickey's signing of three blacks to the Dodger organization, one of whom, Jackie Robinson, would become the first black American to play in the major leagues since the Walker brothers in 1884.

*Jim Crow Uncle Sam* During World War II, black ballplayers in the military were segregated from white ballplayers in the continental United States just as they were in civilian life, but according to the peculiar logic of racism, or perhaps to fulfill propaganda goals, blacks played on white teams overseas. Pete Reiser, who played for the Fort Riley, Kansas, baseball team, recalls that one day a Lieutenant Jackie Robinson came out for the baseball team, but a white officer told him he'd have to play with the colored team. There wasn't one.

Nowhere was the grim irony of racism in the military lost on black players. Nate Moreland, a black pitcher who tried out with Robinson at the Chicago White Sox Pasadena training camp in 1942, remarked, "I can play in Mexico, but I have to fight for America where I can't play." Larry Doby, the first black to play in the American League, was denied a shot at the famous Great Lakes Naval Training Station ball club, managed by Mickey Cochrane, and forced to play for the black team; he was permitted to play softball with white professionals on Ulithi Atoll in the Pacific.

Leon Day, one of the greatest black pitchers in America, was too old to play in the majors when integration finally arrived, but during the war he drove trucks and played for George Patton's Third Army team; Willard "Home Run" Brown of the Kansas City Monarchs also played with white professionals on Patton's club, which was managed by John Quinn, the Phillies' peacetime general manager. In 1945, Day pitched for the Third Army against Ewell Blackwell before one hundred thousand GIs at Hitler's Nuremburg Stadium. Day took that game, 2–1, and when he faced Blackwell again before fifty thousand GIs in Marseilles, he shut him out, 8–0, with able assistance from Brown, who hit Blackwell for a couple of home runs.

Monte Irvin recalls, "When I was in the Army I took basic training in the South. I'd been asked to give up everything, including my life, to defend democracy. Yet when I went to town I had to ride in the back of a bus, or not at all on some buses." Irvin was an established Negro leagues star when he went to France in 1943 with an all-black engineering unit, and he was the acknowledged choice among both black players and executives to be the first black to break the major league color line. But he never got a chance to play in the service, and by his own estimation was not the same coming out as when he went in: "I lost my timing and I was three years older."

When Branch Rickey approached Irvin in 1945, ostensibly to ask him to join his new Negro leagues club, Irvin excused himself to get back in shape playing winter ball in Puerto Rico. Had he known that the Dodger president was preparing to integrate the majors—he did sign with Rickey—the history of integration might have been written differently. Ironically, Rickey's eventual choice of Robinson took into consideration that his record as an officer made his claim to equality that much stronger; Rickey may not have known that it was only the intervention of heavyweight champion Joe Louis that made it possible for Robinson to attend Officers' Candidate School, and that Robinson was released from the service in 1944 after he protested segregated seating on military buses at Fort Hood, Texas. Once, when Robinson telephoned a superior officer to complain about segregated seating at Fort Riley's PX, the officer, who didn't know Robinson was black, asked him how he'd like to have *his* wife sitting next to a nigger.

Perhaps the crowning irony of the period was that World War II provided the only real era of prosperity for the segregated Negro leagues. According to Buck Leonard, "During the war when people couldn't get much gas, that's when our best crowds were." Satchel Paige recalls, "Everybody had money and everybody was looking around for entertainment. Even the white folks was coming out big." Attendance at the annual East-West all-star game, established in 1932, reached fifty-one thousand in 1943. But postwar integration siphoned off the black leagues' best players and destroyed them completely within a decade.

Integration had been in the air just before the war, but it became inevitable principally because the blatant hypocrisy of an American policy that fought racist ideologies in Europe and the Pacific but maintained racist policies in its national game—and even in the armies that fought to make the world safe for democracy—lent moral authority to the growing movement to end discriminatory practices in American life. World War II served as a catalyst to open the game to minorities by enhancing expectations among all Americans that their country should live up to its claims of equal opportunity and justice for all; and black soldiers, like their white counterparts, returned home less hesitant to demand their fair share from a country they had been asked to die for. The death in 1944 of Commissioner Landis, an implacable foe of integration who never hesitated to use the weight of his office to crush any tendency toward racial tolerance, accelerated this process. His successor, Happy Chandler, undoubtedly expressed the sentiments of a majority of Americans when he said in March 1945, "If a black boy can make it on Okinawa and Guadalcanal, hell, he can make it in baseball."

*Service World Series*    The baseball tradition in the military that began with the Civil War reached a flowering in World War II that will probably never be seen again, not only because military policies and attitudes about

*Boston Braves manager Casey Stengel apes the professor on the opening day of spring training. Wartime travel restrictions and tight budgets landed the Braves at Choate Preparatory School in Wallingford, Connecticut, in 1943, hence the idea for this publicity photo. Pitcher Lefty Gomez stands second from right.*

baseball have changed, but because warfare has changed, and extended global conflict with conventional weapons involving millions of soldiers seems a fairly remote possibility. But in World War II the various branches of the service actively competed with one another for professional players, built outstanding teams, and even created all-star teams for important interservice and benefit games.

While by no means all of the professional baseball players in the service played baseball, a great many did. Clubs such as that assembled by the Norfolk Naval Training Station, which for the first two years of the war had its pick of the professional athletes passing through Gene Tunney's athletic specialist training course, often fielded major leaguers at every position; in 1943, Norfolk had its pick of Pee Wee Reese and Phil Rizzuto for shortstop. The famous Great Lakes Naval Training Station team, often referred to as "the seventeenth major league team," sometimes fielded more career major leaguers than contemporary civilian major league teams; their headliners included future Hall of Famers Bob Feller, Billy Herman, and Johnny Mize. The Navy's Norfolk Naval Air Station nine and the Bainbridge and Sampson Naval Training centers' clubs were in the same league, as were the Army's Fort Riley and Texas Army Flying School squads, the Marines' Quantico and Parris Island nines, and the Coast Guard's New London and Curtis Bay clubs. There were many other outstanding teams, and since the military didn't desegregate until 1948, some military centers, such as Great Lakes, had excellent all-black clubs as well.

In 1944 the Army and the Navy played a World Series in Hawaii that was, with some justification, billed locally as that year's "real" World Series. Both starting lineups were composed entirely of past or future major leaguers, and the Navy in particular spared no expense to beef up its club. Dom DiMaggio and Phil Rizzuto were flown in from Australia; Virgil Trucks and Schoolboy Rowe were shipped in from Great Lakes; and Johnny Vander Meer was requisitioned from Sampson, in New York State. All were placed under the management of Bill Dickey. The Army featured Joe Gordon at shortstop, first-class fielder and heavy hitter Ferris Fain at first base, and Cardinals pitcher Johnny Beazley, who in 1942 won twenty-one games and took two games from the Yankees in that year's upset Series win (Beazley's arm became a war casualty as the result of a superior's command to pitch when he was not ready).

The Navy's superior lineup paid off and the bluejackets took the first four contests before crowds of thousands. The games were staged at different bases to give as many servicemen as possible a chance to attend; and a full seven-game schedule was played for the same reason. Admiral Nimitz threw out the first ball at the opening game. Since the motive for the Series was entertainment and morale boosting, not profit—the Navy's scramble for star players made it clear that there was honor at stake, too—after the seventh game, which was attended by sixteen thousand, four more games were played on three more of the Hawaiian islands in the first half of October. Final score: Navy eight games, Army two, one tie. Rizzuto and DiMaggio flew back to Australia, but other World Series performers stayed on, and some eventually joined a contingent of Army and Navy stars from the best mainland teams that traveled to forward areas of the Pacific and played exhibitions for the troops during 1945.

In the fall of 1945, the Navy staged its own World Series in the Hawaiian Islands with the best players from the ten-team 14th Naval District League grouped into American League and National League clubs according to their civilian affiliations. The American League club, which included such giants as Ted Williams, was so heavily favored to win that Bill Dickey reportedly initiated arrangements to have it play the winner of the major league World Series, but the Navy Senior Circuit club took the military classic in six games. Following the lead of the previous season's Service World Series, the seventh game was played anyway for the benefit of the servicemen, and the American League won to make it a 4–3 series.

*Benefits and Bedfellows*  During World War II support for the war effort in baseball ranged from multimillion-dollar benefits to free admission for kids who donated scrap iron. On September 26, 1942, youthful scavengers admitted at the Polo Grounds in return for scrap metal cost the Giants a win when they swarmed the field in the eighth inning and umpire Ziggy Sears awarded the game to the Braves, who were trailing, 5–2 (the home team must maintain order or is liable to forfeit). Other modest wartime efforts included the return of balls hit into the stands for shipment to soldiers, an extremely inefficient practice with the chief aim of public relations. (When exhortations to throw the balls back resulted in injuries to other patrons, most clubs asked their patrons to give any balls they caught to an usher.)

Even before the United States entered the war, a major league benefit had been staged in Florida for the Finnish Relief Fund during spring training in 1940. On July 7, 1942, a much-anticipated American League All-Star–Service All-Star benefit was staged at Cleveland's Municipal Stadium. The highly touted match pitted such luminaries as Ted Williams and Joe DiMaggio, most of whom would soon be playing for the other side, against a service team managed by Lieutenant Mickey Cochrane, USN, and assembled from the best players at Great Lakes and Norfolk Naval Training Sta-

*Catcher Vince Lombardi watches helplessly as Stan Musial races home. Lombardi is with the 1945 New York Giants, Musial with the Navy's Bainbridge Training Station team, one of the Navy's finest. During World War II top service teams such as the Bainbridge, Maryland, squad often featured major leaguers at every position. Benefits between service and major league teams were common.*

tions and select Army squads. Navy Chief Bob Feller topped the service pitching staff.

As would become customary at such gatherings, before the game the crowd of 62,904 was entertained for almost two hours by a seemingly endless array of military bands, marching Marines, tanks, and anti-aircraft equipment; several hundred servicemen were still in the outfield when the game began, and as a further reminder that there was a war on, the crowd experienced a two-minute trial blackout between halves of the sixth inning. Feller and the servicemen, fine professionals, were apparently not able to keep their baseball skills honed in the service, and the major leaguers shut them out, 5–0. Of the $143,571 gross, $100,000 went to the major leagues' servicemen's Baseball Equipment Fund, known as the Ball and Bat Fund by those who remembered World War I, and the rest to Army and Navy relief funds.

Such competition at the all-star level was not repeated, but numerous other benefits took place between service and major league teams and between champions of the innumerable intraservice leagues. In June 1942 the Norfolk Naval Training Station team played an Army team at the Polo Grounds. On May 24, 1943, the Norfolk Naval Training Station team beat the Washington Senators at Griffith Stadium, 4–3, in a benefit that generated $2 million in war bond purchases; on July 12, 1943, the Service All-Stars, featuring Ted Williams and managed by Babe Ruth, beat the Braves at Fenway Park, 9–8; on July 28, 1943, the Navy's North Carolina Pre-Flight team beat an aggregation of Yankees and Indians called the "Yank-lands" and managed by Babe Ruth at Yankee Stadium; and at the Baseball War Bond Show of August 26, 1943, where fans who purchased eight hundred thousand dollars in war bonds got to see Frankie Frisch, George Sisler, Eddie Collins, Connie Mack, Honus Wagner, Roger Bresnahan, and Walter Johnson, a team assembled from Dodgers, Yankees, and Giants players, beat an Army all-star club, 5–2.

On April 20, 1944, a team of former major leaguers serving in the Navy beat a Hawaiian all-star team, 4–2, in a benefit that raised over $1 million in war bonds (to put these figures in perspective, one state-of-the-art Flying-Fortress bomber cost about three hundred thousand dollars). That same year the Sampson Naval Training Center club beat the Red Sox by the wide margin of 20–7, and the Indians by 15–2; Great Lakes lambasted the Indians, 17–4. By 1944 the professional teams were hardly at their best—most of their regular players were in the service—and since they traveled with pared-down rosters and were cautious about using their better players in purely benefit situations, and many players performed at positions other than their usual ones, it would be unfair to say that they entirely lay down for the service clubs. The attitude they held toward such games might more fittingly be characterized as generous—Satchel Paige and Josh Gibson admitted that in Negro league games against the Marines, the professionals kept their winning margins small, and tried to insure that the soldiers scored at least one run to save face.

One of wartime baseball's truly unique occurrences was the three-sided game that was conceived by New York's sportswriters and played at the Polo Grounds before fifty thousand spectators on June 26, 1944. In this enor-

*Bob Feller in his Great Lakes Naval Training Center uniform. Most professional athletes got to play or coach during World War II. The Navy was famous for sparing no expense to ship top players anywhere in the world for important games, a practice no longer permitted.*

mously successful fundraiser, New York's three major league teams, the Yankees, Giants, and Dodgers, faced each other in one nine-inning round-robin game; each club sat out one inning, then played two consecutive innings, for a total of six innings per club. The Dodgers and the Yankees shared the visitors' dressing room, and during the first, fourth, and seventh innings shared the same dugout while they played against each other. The final score was Dodgers 5, Yankees 1, Giants none. Forty-one-year-old Paul Waner played in the Dodgers outfield, and the Giants' defense featured veterans Joe Medwick, Mel Ott, and third baseman Billy Jurges, all of whom had been persuaded to put off long-overdue retirements for the duration of the war. Milton Berle was master of ceremonies at the pregame show, which featured field events and an assemblage of baseball immortals, clowns, and local dignitaries. At the end of the night it was announced that the crowd had purchased $6.5 million in war bonds.

In 1945 the All-Star Game, canceled due to travel restrictions and an overwhelming lack of stars, was transmuted into a two-day series of exhibition benefits. In addition, many baseball stars who for one reason or another remained in the States traveled the globe under USO auspices, entertaining the troops; in 1944 and 1945, five units of baseball stars stumped military bases in the Far East, the Pacific, the Middle East, the Mediterranean, and Europe. When the war ended, professional players in Europe had German and Italian prisoners build baseball fields; an Army all-star team toured Austria, Italy, France, and Germany. In certain occupied territories excellent facilities already existed and were put to good use, notably at the Nazi Stadium at Nuremberg, Olympic Stadium in Berlin, Victory Stadium near Frankfort, Rizal Stadium in Manila, Meiji Shrine Park in Tokyo, and Lou Gehrig Stadium in Tokyo.

A great deal of the money raised at home went to supply equipment to ordinary soldiers, who continued to play baseball everywhere they went. In the Army, almost no funds existed for sports programs before the war, but vast amounts of sporting equipment were on hand by the war's end. Among the mountains of Ping-Pong balls and volleyball nets "stored in advance against the needs of a post-hostilities letdown," enlisted men were happy to count 100,000 baseballs, 360,000 baseball bats, 100,000 baseball gloves, and 288,000 baseball shoes. According to the Hillerich & Bradsby Company, manufacturers of Louisville Sluggers, before the cessation of hostilities a shipment of sporting equipment reached a German prison camp in Upper Silesia, and American prisoners dumbfounded their captors by crying at the sight of bats.

*Pete Gray, the one-armed outfielder who played with the St. Louis Browns in 1945, has become symbolic of the unusual wartime players of the "care-taking era." Gray was primarily a gate attraction, but he was a real professional, voted MVP by the Southern Association in 1944.*

*Besuboru* Baseball arrived in Japan with American missionaries in the 1870s some twenty years after Commodore Perry's gunships opened up the island nation to the West. The game was originally perceived by the Japanese as an American martial art. When it became a high school and college sport, Japanese adepts sharpened their skills by playing—and usually beating—Navy teams from battleships that put in at Yokohama. By the 1930s, Japanese baseball fans were familiar with American teams and stars such as Babe Ruth and Lou Gehrig, who toured their country, but as relations between the two countries deteriorated and Japan's nationalism became increasingly virulent,

American names and terminology were rigorously expunged from Japanese baseball, and the name of their national game was itself transformed from *besuboru* to *yakyu,* by which it is still called today (all Japanese also know baseball as "baseball").

Japan was at war with China in 1937 and professional Japanese baseball players were subject to the draft at least by 1938; the great pitcher Sawamura, for whom a Cy Young–like award now exists, was killed in action in 1944. After Pearl Harbor, radio broadcasting of professional baseball in Japan was terminated, and in 1942 an attempt to abolish the game achieved partial success in the military, which catalyzed the more xenophobic elements of the population in its wish to eradicate any outside influences. During the war the Japanese leagues struggled and muddled through much as professional baseball did in America; in 1944 only six clubs competed for the professional championship in a thirty-five-game season, and in 1945 *yakyu* stopped altogether as the economy collapsed.

American soldiers who faced Japanese troops in the Pacific learned that the enemy was no stranger to baseball when they heard battle cries of "Fuck Babe Ruth!" Numerous stories are told of victorious Japanese soldiers fighting over copies of *The Sporting News,* and of Japanese prisoners asking for the results of the World Series. American airmen sometimes dropped baseballs with obscene messages over Japanese cities. After the war, the occupying Yanks judged that baseball was consistent with the fostering of democratic principles and actively assisted in the restoration of Japan's professional organizations, which were reorganized in principle barely three months after the empire surrendered. General Douglas MacArthur personally issued the order to refurbish the Tokyo Giants' Stadium, which had served during the war as an ammunition dump (as some Americans had proposed for American ballparks in World War I).

Limited professional play resumed in the 1946 season, grew to eight clubs by 1948, and in 1950 resulted in the institution of Japan's current two-league system. So it was that with curious symmetry, the American military, which had opened Japan up to baseball in the nineteenth century and destroyed it with a violent eruption into the nuclear age in the twentieth century, helped restore and reimplant baseball in Japan, where it flourished with a greater vigor than it had previously known.

*Baseball in the Cold War*    After World War II the United States chose for the first time in its history not to disarm but to define itself as being against something called communism, and in failing to release the military's vast wealth and energy into the private sector, watched its expectations for peace and prosperity evaporate into the tensions of a Cold War and the insatiable demands of the military-industrial complex. As a bastion of traditional American values, baseball sought and found its place in the emerging postwar ideology and even, if the stories are to be believed, provided cover for one of the Cold War's greatest spies.

The strange tale of Moe Berg, baseball's master spy, is far from typical baseball fare, but his career in espionage and intrigue, real or imagined, eloquently captures the spirit of the new era. Berg was a rather lackluster catcher in the majors from 1923 to 1939—it was in reference to Berg that the famous "good field, no hit" was coined—but was a summa cum laude graduate of Princeton, master of a dozen languages, and probably the best-educated man ever to play in the major leagues.

Berg first visited Japan, on a baseball instructional tour, in 1932; his observations of Japanese society were supposedly of interest to his secret sponsor, the American intelligence community, which was growing increasingly alarmed by Japan's militarism. In 1934 Berg was incongruously included on the all-star tour to Japan that featured Babe Ruth. His covert mission was to photograph Tokyo; the movies he took of the capital were allegedly used by General Jimmie Doolittle in the air raids that began on April 18, 1942. In the book *Moe Berg: Athlete, Scholar, Spy,* the authors credit Berg with taking the photographs that the U.S. military used in planning the 1945 firebombing of Tokyo, which caused more deaths than the atomic blast at Hiroshima. Berg is also alleged to have made propaganda broadcasts in Japanese.

Another source credits him with surreptitiously gaining intelligence from Nazi scientist Werner Heisenberg during a 1944 visit to Switzerland that materially influenced the progress of the Manhattan Project. Some claim Berg was an OSS officer and that he also served in Latin America, where his baseball credentials again worked magic, and that after the war he continued his work in espionage as a CIA Cold War agent. While there is apparently good reason to suspect that his travels in Japan and elsewhere encompassed more than baseball, baseball lectures, and linguistic studies, the final word on his alleged career as a spy must await a thorough examination of intelligence agency records.

America's entry into the Korean War, a direct outgrowth of its postwar anticommunist ideology, was initially viewed with dread by the baseball establishment, but neither Korea nor the American involvement in Vietnam were to have anywhere near the effect on baseball of the two previous wars. Korea, in fact, gave baseball executives a chance to demonstrate their belief that baseball represented the values for which America's young men were fighting, and so to align the national game with the postwar anticommunist consensus. A year before the conflict Jackie Robinson had compliantly denounced Paul Robeson before the House Un-American Activities Committee for making the un-American, un-baseball suggestion that blacks would not fight against Russia for a country that still oppressed them. General Eisenhower contributed a letter to the committee testifying to "the irrefutable proof of the loyalty of our Negro troops" during World War II. And when the owners started looking for someone to replace Commissioner Chandler, General Douglas MacArthur was their first choice. In Venezuela, Ambassador Walter Donnelly made news when he used baseball bats to attack alleged communist demonstrators in front of the American embassy.

In the end only a handful of players were inducted during the Korean era, and then only for two years. The Giants suffered when Willie Mays was inducted after the beginning of the 1952 season, but he came back in 1954 stronger than ever and captured the National League MVP title. Of all the service branches only the Marines had a general recall of World War II veterans, which meant that Ted Williams, a Marine flyer, got the call in 1952. After an emotional farewell at Fenway Park from fans who never expected to see the thirty-three-year-old slugger play again, the Splendid Splinter left for Korea to fly thirty-nine combat missions, where one of his mates was John Glenn, first American to orbit the earth. Williams elected to crash-land rather than risk breaking his kneecaps by ejecting through the canopy when his Panther jet was hit by small-arms fire in 1952. When he returned to the Red Sox after being discharged on July 28, 1953, he hit .407 in thirty-seven games with thirteen home runs.

Almost all of the players drafted before the cessation of hostilities in 1953—Whitey Ford, Billy Martin, Johnny Antonelli, Dick Groat, Faye Throneberry—ended up in the Army, which consequently fielded the best service teams at home and abroad. Service competition was not what it used to be, but since Japan was a staging area for American activities in Korea, some American players became part of the United States' continuing baseball mission to Japan, where they saw action with and against Japanese professionals. Air Force Major Robert Neighbors, who played briefly with the Browns in 1939, was the only former major leaguer to die in combat in Korea, and as far as is known was the sixth and last major leaguer to die in a foreign war.

The impact of the Vietnam War on baseball was even less than that of the Korean conflict, particularly because the availability of reserve programs requiring only six months of continuous active duty enabled most players and executives to avoid any disruption of their careers. Many reserve units under-

stood the public relations potential of professional players and made exceptions. In 1967, Red Sox pitcher Jim Lonborg drew his two-week reserve duty
in Atlanta in the middle of that year's tight American League pennant race,
but was permitted to practice with the Atlanta Braves and received passes that
prevented him from missing any of his turns in the rotation. The draft, which
loomed large in the lives of many young American men throughout the
1950s, came to an end in the '70s, and is no longer an issue in professional
baseball.

Service baseball also came to an end in the Cold War. By the time the
Korean War was winding down the Army and the Department of Defense
had initiated major policy changes in service athletics that prohibited special
treatment for "athletes, entertainers and other nationally known personalities," forbade the "appearance of 'professional' type athletic teams," and
stressed that the primary purpose of service sports programs was to provide
"the maximum opportunity for all military personnel to participate in a balanced program of planned leisure-time activities," regardless of ability or
previous experience. In 1953 the Army explicitly forbade the strengthening
of teams participating in the All-Army Baseball Championship "through personnel transfers" and reiterated that "known 'name' athletes [would] not
receive preferential treatment solely because of their athletic ability." Baseball competition was reduced to low-level intramurals. Navy baseball had
effectively been out of contention since the end of the draft after World War
II. When the Army discontinued the All-Army Baseball Championship in
1957, high-level baseball in the military was officially over.

Softball is now the serviceman's game, and since it seems unlikely that
military considerations will ever again foster serious service baseball or affect
the civilian game, the future of military baseball is not bright. The next war,
it is often proclaimed, will last only a few days. But those who hold this view
would do well to remember that every war has been considered the last by
many of its participants, and that no less a military genius than General
William Tecumseh Sherman believed that the Civil War would be the last war
because modern weaponry rendered warfare too horrible to contemplate.
History of course has its own laws, and no doubt the end of the venerable
connection between baseball and the military is a small price to pay for peace,
but it seems a Cold War indeed that banishes top-flight baseball from its
barracks.

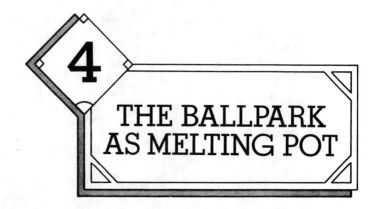

# THE BALLPARK AS MELTING POT

**I**n recent years, the image of the United States of America as the great "melting pot" society has come under attack, by both those who deny it ever worked and those who say it worked all too well. According to the traditional theory, people from all over the world have arrived on these shores, either individually or in large waves of immigrants, and then proceeded to be acculturated and assimilated—sort of "melted down" to an amalgam, your all-purpose American. Obviously numerous factors contribute to and reflect this homogenization process, and one of them could be the game of baseball: The assumption is that if people are going to be "regular Americans," they should give up their cricket or soccer or bullfighting or whatever and "relate" in some fashion to the National Pastime.

But the linking of baseball and the melting pot has gone beyond this to incorporate a more focused claim: Namely, that professional baseball itself has historically been quick to welcome and absorb the various national and ethnic groups as they have appeared on our shores. In this version, baseball began as a game played essentially by WASPs and then took onto its teams and into the game each wave of immigrants—the Irish, for example, being the first to be so absorbed, with the other major groups "signed up" as they got off the boats, a sort of reversal of Noah's accepting each species onto his ark.

Serious historians and sociologists write articles and books about this,

*This is widely reproduced as a photograph of some of the members of the early Knickerbocker Base Ball Club; there is no question that the man in the center of the top row is Alexander Joy Cartwright. If it is the club, since he left it in March 1849, it must have been taken sometime between 1846 (when the Knickerbockers apparently adopted straw hats) and 1849.*

although most usually subsume the question of the ethnic and national origins of baseball players under the broader categories of socioeconomic classes and forces. (A notable exception is Steven A. Riess, who discusses the ethnic backgrounds of early players in *Touching Base.*) Even the more popular accounts of baseball venture into this subject when they debate whether baseball owes more to urban sources than to agrarian roots. It is understood that if baseball was largely an urban sport then immigrants may have played as great a role in its development as old-stock Americans. Ultimately, too, the question of the assimilation of immigrants crosses paths with the whole notion of baseball as part of America's national myth, and certain inconsistencies hover behind both: Americans want to believe in a simpler rural society that produced baseball, but Americans also want to believe that they have always been receptive to different types.

There are many testimonials and tributes to this role of baseball as a "mainstreamer" of awkward aliens. On the face of it, there is nothing outrageous about such a version of the history of the game. Look at the rosters of professional teams these days and for at least a few decades past, and the sheer diversity does seem to echo those Hollywood wartime roll calls that celebrated America as a melting pot. But just how baseball got from those few WASP gentlemen to the present rainbow coalition bears examination.

*All-WASP Baseball* The question of whether the first baseball teams were essentially composed entirely of WASPs is inextricably involved with some of the other questions about the early years of the game. Even setting aside the Doubleday-Cooperstown–rural America theory as no longer credible, there are still historians of baseball who speak as though the game was invented by a group of WASP gentlemen in New York City. Some accounts go even farther, referring to them as upper-class and a "social aristocracy." What these writers have in mind, of course, is the famous Knickerbocker Base Ball Club of which Alexander Cartwright was a founding member. The first thing that must be stated is that, as shown in Chapter 2, this club shouldn't really be credited with "inventing" baseball any more than any single club or individual should. Many baseball teams and players contributed to the development of the game, and some of the individuals are known and some are forgotten, but there is no reason to assume they were either all "gentlemen" or all WASPs.

Even when we know a fair amount about the men who made up the Knickerbocker Club in those early years, there is some doubt as to just how many of them were WASP gentlemen in the strict sense of that term. (Indeed, if that term is taken literally, it is not even known how many were Protestants.) Some of the Knickerbockers in the first years were, to be sure, lawyers, physicians, stockbrokers, and merchants, but many more were mere clerks—Alexander Cartwright being one of them. (Someone counted the members who listed their occupations in the club's book between 1845 and 1866 and found that of the eighty-three, eight were professionals—lawyers, doctors, and a dentist—seventy-three worked in the business world at some level, and only two listed themselves as "gentlemen.")

To be fair, a clerk in a bank or commercial office in those days was often on the ladder to higher positions—there were no business schools or MBAs to prepare one for the business world. It can also be admitted that these early clubs were relatively small and had a semisocial basis; clearly each had its own sense of self that would limit membership to congenial types. But it seems unnecessary, and undemocratic, to overemphasize the careers or social status of these early Knickerbockers and the other New York clubs that quickly sprang up. Some of those other clubs were, in fact, deliberately made up of what we today would call blue-collar workers: the Eckfords and Atlantics, two of the earliest New York clubs (founded in 1856) were specifically composed of manual laborers. And if one considers that by 1860, say, there were several hundred baseball teams in the Northeast alone, it would be silly to pretend that the game belonged to some WASP gentlemen. Quite the contrary: By this time, most of the teams were organized by men in different occupations and workplaces—telegraphers, government clerks, commercial clerks, factory workers.

Above all, the notion that at least the Knickerbockers were some exclusive club of old New York aristocracy should be thoroughly rejected. This is a confusion of the ball club's name with the old Dutch aristocracy of the Hudson River. There may be some "aristocratic" New Yorkers today who trace their ancestry back through the baseball club, especially due to intermarriages over the years, but the Knickerbocker Base Ball Club should not be confused with the Social Register.

As to the national or ethnic roots of the Knickerbockers and the other early clubs and teams, this question also dissolves in the sheer number of individuals involved. True, given the makeup of America up to 1850, most of the names that survive in the records seem to have British (that is, Welsh and Scottish as well as English) origins. And if "WASP" is understood as also including some related Northern European groups such as Dutch and Germans, there are a fair number of these, too—DeWitt, Niebuhr, Falmayer (or Fallman), Brinker, Vredenburgh, and Van Nortwick, for instance, show up in the first year of the Knickerbockers. But so does Dupignac—and two O'Briens. And there is George Cassio, Cartwright's brother-in-law, a distinctly Italianate name.

And these are among the earliest Knickerbockers, allegedly the "aristocracy" of the New York baseball world. As soon as one looks into other records of that era, numerous national and ethnic names crop up. There is an E. G. Saltzman, for instance, who played with the New York Gothams and is then credited by some as being the first to introduce the New York game to a Boston team in 1857. And in the very first baseball game for which there is a newspaper account, that in the New York *Herald* of October 25, 1845, one player's name is Kline and another's is Meyers.

In fact, it soon becomes both impossible and misguided to try to attribute the first years of baseball to some elite group of WASPs. Yes, most of the names of the men on the earliest teams seem to have a British and Northern European ring. And no, these early clubs probably didn't post notices all over large cities and invite just anyone to join in the game. But rather than boasting about some WASP elite, baseball and its supporters should be proud that the game so early found room for men from a number of origins. Both before and after Albert G. Spalding, many have been asserting that baseball is "the American game." True enough, and therefore all the more reason to recognize the contributions of many different national and social groups.

*Up the Irish!* By 1870, many baseball teams were openly professional and many large and medium-sized cities were supporting teams. Young North Americans (because Canadians were also among the early players) from many a national-ethnic origin and socioeconomic status could now begin to envision themselves making careers in baseball—farmboys, shopboys, office clerks, factory hands, dockworkers, just about anyone. A look at some of the names of prominent players in 1870 suggests some divergence from the predominant WASP origins, but nothing really that conclusive. Zettlein was the Atlantics' star pitcher, Sweasy was the Cincinnati Red Stockings' star second baseman, Sensenderfer was the Philadelphia Athletics' star left fielder; the New York Mutuals had Wolters, Flanley, and Eggler. And so on through team after team.

Conventional accounts of baseball tend to emphasize that the Irish were the first large non-WASP group to be accepted into American baseball. Ethnically speaking, of course, the Irish were not that much different from the Welsh and Scotch—all being Celts, if they must be distinguished from the English—but it is a fact that their Roman Catholic religion and their national history led to the Irish being perceived as different. (Just to eliminate any misunderstanding, no claim is being made here that this religious or national background had any known effect on the ability to play baseball.) And unlike the Protestant British, the Catholic Irish hadn't begun to show up in North America in large numbers until the great famine of the mid-1840s. But if by "Irish" baseball players it is meant that a lot of them were recent immigrants, this does not seem to be the case. Two Irish-born players joined professional teams in 1876—Fergy Malone with the Phillies, and Tommy Bond with the Hartfords. (Bond went to Boston in 1877 and became famous as one of the first to pitch overhand and to throw a curveball.) Tony Mullane joined Detroit in 1881 and Mike Hines joined Boston in 1883, but there do not seem to have been any more Irish-born major leaguers until Jimmy Archer, the famous catcher, appeared with Pittsburgh in 1904.

No, the Irish ballplayers of the first decades were almost all American-born—the O'Briens who played for the Knickerbockers, the famous Peter

O'Brien and Dickey Pearce of the Atlantics, and countless others with names that might not jump out as Irish but who were undoubtedly Roman Catholic Irish-Americans. The trouble with this version of baseball as an assimilator of a sequence of ethnic groups is that we simply do not know enough about most of these men—just who both parents were, how they were raised as boys, which group they identified with. A man could have an Irish name and parentage yet not be a Roman Catholic. Or be born in England, like Marty Hogan, and probably regard himself as Irish. Still, Irish-Americans were an increasing presence in the large cities of the Northeast where baseball was also definitely on the rise, the same cities where signs that read "Irish Need Not Apply" were appearing. Some of the many editorials criticizing baseball for harboring rowdies and worse were probably thinly veiled attacks on Irish-Americans; there was an old Puritan tradition of condemning public entertainments and this melded nicely with many Americans' distaste for the new urban immigrants. A *New York Times* editorial on September 3, 1897, went so far as to refer to baseball players as "degenerates."

Curiously, in 1896 Cardinal Gibbons of Baltimore, one of the most prominent Roman Catholics of his day, went out of his way to put his imprimatur on baseball: "I am not what you might call a crank [a fan], but . . . without hesitation [I] say that these young men, who have obtained such prominence in their chosen profession, are worthy of the praise bestowed upon them." This about the Baltimore team that many people then and now regard as one of the dirtiest ever! Gibbons then went on to say, "It is necessary that there should be popular amusements, and in consequence it is wise that the most generally patronized of these amusements should be innocent, since, were the opposite the case, the opportunity of committing sins of greater or less degree would be too openly set before the public. Base ball is a clean sport. It is an innocent amusement. Never have I heard that the games were being used as vehicles for gambling." At the time, however, some felt that gambling was undermining the whole edifice of professional baseball! No wonder that more straitlaced Americans might think that the Roman Catholic element was a threat to society at large.

Be that as it may, by the 1890s, it has been reliably estimated, at least one third of the major leaguers were Irish-Americans; by 1915, eleven of the sixteen managers were also Irish-Americans. So in that sense professional baseball does deserve credit for accepting and absorbing Irish-Americans from the earliest days of the game. Still another way of putting it is that Irish-Americans contributed to the development of baseball from the earliest days of the game. Once that accolade is accepted, of course, certain responsibilities go with it, as will later be seen.

One other word on the Irish-American baseball contingent: If they had felt discriminated against in the earliest years of baseball—and there is no evidence they had been—they certainly got their revenge. In the early years as baseball was making its way into America, it had to compete with cricket, an outright import from England and eventually regarded as a more upper-class sport. Soon, though, the game of baseball virtually wiped out cricket except in a few isolated cities or situations, and although there is no known record of the Irish-American baseball players taking any explicit glee in this, they might well have been aware that they were eliminating this vestige of the imperial English. Albert Spalding, however, would years later gloat most explicitly over the defeat of the British game of cricket by the all-*American* baseball.

But the Irish triumph over the English went beyond this. Among the early promoters of baseball were several Englishmen, including some former cricketers. The Wright brothers, Harry and George, were sons of a well-known English cricketer and themselves had begun playing cricket. Richard Higham and Al Reach were from English families. And the man who did the most to systematize and promote the game, Henry Chadwick, was also English-born. Chadwick, who was also the first historian of the game, was quite sure that baseball was directly descended from the ballgames familiar for centuries to English youths. This version of baseball's history was accepted through the second half of the nineteenth century by most who knew or cared about such questions (although most baseball players, Irish-American or otherwise, could not have cared less).

Then along came Spalding and the Special Baseball Commission to investigate the origins of the game. As with many such commissions composed of important people to give it prestige and authority, the actual work was done by subordinate staff, and Spalding pretty much left the work to James E. Sullivan, his secretary and a known booster of things Irish. It has since been suggested by more than one knowledgeable student of this episode that Sullivan took the occasion to disown any English influence on the game and give all the credit to indigenous American sources, Cooperstown and Doubleday. Thus did the Irish get back at the British and save baseball for Americans.

*The Next Waves*   By the end of the nineteenth century, Irish-Americans had made their way into the majors in great numbers and many of them had emerged as the stars of the game—Mike "King" Kelly, Edward "The Only" Nolan, Ned Hanlon, and scores of others. Not for nothing did the old Yankee Ernest Thayer name his archetypal ballplayer "Casey." But with a few exceptions, the major leagues, at least, had not yet become the great assimilator of all the national and ethnic groups that were making their way to America. (In the minors and semipro teams, there were many players from diverse backgrounds, but most were never going to get a chance in the majors.) It has been calculated that over 90 percent of the professional baseball players into the early 1900s were from only three groups—old-stock Americans, Irish-Americans, and German-Americans.

Partly, perhaps mainly, this lack of diversity was due simply to the fact that other groups had not yet come to North America in sufficient number and for long enough to participate in the culture that included baseball. Even when they came in large numbers, immigrants at that time tended to settle among their own. They weren't apt to join or start baseball teams—let alone learn the game from their fathers, who were too busy just trying to survive; it takes a lot of boys playing a lot of baseball over many years to produce a major leaguer. But part of it must have been due to built-in discriminatory attitudes and practices. This was definitely true when it came to pushing black Americans out of the majors and organized baseball—a story that rates its own chapter. Even if the best light is put on things—that it was a simple economic motive, the desire to reserve the limited number of jobs in professional baseball for one's own circle—a career in major league baseball must have seemed a somewhat unattainable goal for certain young Americans until well into the twentieth century.

Along with the Irish-Americans and German-Americans so prevalent in the majors by the turn of the century, there were some Scandinavian-Americans and French-Americans, and even a few Czech-Americans. (The Chicago teams were especially open to Czechs because of the large Slavic population in the area.) As for Italian-Americans, they were present in large numbers in major cities by the end of the nineteenth century, but not on the rosters of the majors (again, assuming that family names reveal the true heritage). There had been George Cassio, to be sure, an early Knickerbocker, but he was Alexander Cartwright's brother-in-law. And there was that curious game of June 25, 1849, when the Knickerbocker scorebook records a "Mr. Donato" as scoring nine runs and being put out only once. Donato never appears again in the club records: Perhaps he played too seriously for the Knickerbockers, too much like a . . . foreigner? The WASP code of gamesmanship throughout the nineteenth century called for a somewhat cavalier attitude toward winning. This would eventually be pushed aside by the image of the "hungry" immigrant, anxious to claw his way up the ladder of financial independence if not social acceptance. "Mr. Donato" may have been a bit pushy for his time.

In any case, obviously Italian names are missing from the rosters of the professional teams of the early decades. The first to appear in the majors seems to have been Ed Abbaticchio, who joined the Phillies in 1897, but he was born in Latrobe, Pennsylvania. There are explanations that bypass prejudice—Italian boys were too small to play against the big boys, Italians stuck together in a few city neighborhoods and weren't exposed to the game. This might work into the first decade of the twentieth century, but it wouldn't explain the paucity of Italian-Americans in the majors from 1910 on. Everyone can quickly name some outstanding Italian-American players of decades past, aside from Joe DiMaggio—Tony Lazzeri, Ernie Lombardi, Frank Crosetti, Dolph Camilli, Phil Rizzuto—but note that most of the names don't go back much before the 1930s. There were a few Italian-Americans before then, to be sure—Mike Balenti and Joe Giannini came on in 1911—but again, it is pushing things to claim that professional baseball turned the flame up under the melting pot in assimilating Italian-Americans.

This is even more marked when it comes to various other ethnic and national groups. Again, it can be explained away—they were not physically suited to the game, they chose to live among their own countrymen, they simply didn't care that much about the game. All of these are undoubtedly factors when it comes to explaining why there have been so few Russian-Americans aside from Lou "the Mad Russian" Novikoff and no Chinese-Americans, but they are certainly not the only reasons. (In 1915, two Pacific Coast League managers wanted to use Asian-Americans on their teams, but both were forced to abandon their plans because of the objections of other players and the fans.) As for the scarcity of Greek-Americans—Harry "The Golden Greek" Agganis is one of the few who comes to mind—we should resist turning the theories of one of their true countrymen, Al Campanis (born on a Greek island), against them and accept that Greek-Americans simply have had other things to do with their energies and time.

Lest some think that this is an "invented" problem, ask all the oldtime ballplayers who felt compelled to change their names to avoid discrimination or abuse. (Someone once counted at least seven Cohens who disguised themselves.) Or read the sports pages and newspaper accounts of baseball from the 1870s through till quite recently. Again, black Americans were spoken of so viciously ("coons," "niggers," and worse) that they rate a chapter to themselves, but it was not uncommon, even in the 1930s, to read something like this reference to Joe Glenn, a Polish-American catcher born Joseph Gurzensky: "It is not the impression of the writer that Glenn will ever develop into a real great catcher. He hasn't sufficient speed afoot and it may be that around the slag piles on the wrong side of the tracks Joe's schooling was neglected." Simply some crude provincial talking? How about an article on Joe DiMaggio that opens, "On a rainy afternoon of May 3, 1936, a tall thin Italian youth equipped with slick black hair"; which goes on to explain why Joe is so good at baseball: "Italians, bad at war, are well-suited to milder competitions"; which says that like "heavyweight champion Joe Louis, Di-Maggio is lazy, shy and inarticulate"; and which ends up describing him as follows:

> Although he learned Italian first Joe, now 24, speaks English without an accent and is otherwise well adapted to most U.S. mores. Instead of olive oil or smelly bear grease he keeps his hair slick with water. He never reeks of garlic and prefers chicken chow mein to spaghetti.

That was in a *Life* magazine story on DiMaggio (May 1, 1939), and by a literate writer (note the "mores") who believed he was being complimentary!

And such stereotyping was mild compared to what went on in some quarters. Fans, ballplayers, and managers were appallingly vicious in certain situations: Even before blacks came along to be pilloried, Latin Americans, Jews, and others were sometimes subjected to vicious epithets that simply cannot be dismissed as the good old tradition of "bench jockeying." (Calling a Jewish umpire "Christ-killer," for instance, is in a different class of insult from "kraut" or "mick.") Such crude stereotyping has generally disappeared, but not entirely: Italian-American players are still often regarded as Romeos or Casanovas by well-meaning fans.

This whole matter of deciding which ethnic and national groups have been a part of major league baseball can be tricky. What about the many individuals who must have had mixed parentage—like a certain A. Bartlett Giamatti today? And there have always been those players who have hidden, for a variety of reasons, their origins behind more familiar names. Everyone today presumably knows that Billy Martin is actually Alfred Manuel Pesano, but who remembers that Babe Martin was born Boris Martinovich or that Joe Mack was born Joe Maciarz, that Cass Michaels started out in the majors as Casimir Kwietniewski, that Leonidas Lee was born Leonidas Pyrrhus Funk-houser, and Lee Magee was originally Leopold Christopher Hoern-schemeyer?

Just going by the apparent origins of a player's name can lead to prob-lems, but it is a game that many who love baseball are fond of playing in one form or another. The trivia buffs, for instance—and this is a major subdivision among baseball fans—are fond of making up lists of all-star teams of only Polish-Americans or only Italian-Americans and such. All very well, but these teams have to be weighted toward the more recent decades or they don't have too many choices for certain positions.

Meantime, more official spokesmen for organized baseball like to boast of how the game has been one of the front burners under the melting pot. What emerges from a close reading of the roster of all who have made the majors since 1876, however, is how exclusive baseball long was. To that extent, the Irish-Americans who were so much a part of the earliest years of baseball have to take some of the responsibility for the slow assimilation of Americans of other ethnic and national persuasions; they were part of the Baseball Establishment and they did not let others in. It is pretty much what we are witnessing in our own day, with the reluctance of that establishment to let blacks into management and administrative positions. Perhaps the motives are more economic than anything else, more a case of positive fraternity than negative prejudice, more unconscious decisions than deliberate, but the end result for those left out is much the same. Organized baseball has much to be proud of when it comes to assimilating young men of many backgrounds into today's teams, but it should not imagine that it has always been in a class by itself. There has been more than enough prejudice and discrimination to go around in America, and baseball has been very much a part of that scene.

*Native Americans at Bat*    American Indians occupy a special niche in the history of baseball, one that reflects the special niche they occupy in American history and society. Again, on the face of it, Americans can point with pride to the fact that Indians were accepted in professional baseball from early on—accepted, in fact, at the very time that the last Indian wars were being fought (Wounded Knee was in 1890) and that blacks were being pushed out of organized baseball. Beneath that cozy surface, however, all is not necessarily so congenial.

To begin with, there are Indian baseball players and there are Indians who play baseball. The former include those more or less full-blooded Indians who, due to upbringing and self-identification, presented themselves as Indians or were publicized and perceived as such. This group tends to include most of the best-known Indian baseball players: Louis Sockalexis (the first known Indian in the majors), Charles Albert "Chief" Bender, John "Chief" Meyers, Jim Thorpe, Moses "Chief" Yellowhorse, Pepper "The Wild Horse of the Osage" Martin, Allie "Big Chief" Reynolds. But there is a still larger group of men, now largely forgotten except by students of baseball history, who were of at least partial Indian descent: Louis Bruce, Elon Hogsett, Bob and Ray Johnson (brothers), Frank Jude, Louis LeRoy, Cal McLish, Ben

Tincup, John Whitehead, Rudy York, and others, some of whom never made it up to the majors from the minors, not to mention many other players who had some Indian in their ancestry but never made anything out of it (Jack Aker, for example). In terms of numbers, though, it does seem that baseball has been good to Indians (although ironically it was Jim Thorpe's summers with minor-league baseball that cost him his Olympic gold medals).

But look more closely at some of these men's stories, starting with the very first, Louis Sockalexis. Born in 1871, a Penobscot Indian from Maine, Sockalexis was playing in summer-league baseball in Maine when he was discovered and invited to attend Holy Cross College; from there he went to Notre Dame, but in 1897 he joined the Cleveland team, then known as the Forest Citys or the Spiders. Sockalexis was hailed at once as a superman and an Indian, and it was even suggested that the team be named the Indians. In his first weeks with the Cleveland team, Sockalexis lived up to his reputation as a heavy hitter, but by August he was already being fined and suspended by the club's owner; he ended the season with a .338 batting average and appeared in only twenty-one games in 1898 and seven games in 1899, when he was released; he spent a couple of years in the minors, returned to Maine, and died in 1913, only forty-two years old.

Yet in 1915, when a Cleveland newspaper held a contest for a new name for the team, the winning suggestion was the Indians, at least partially in honor of Louis Sockalexis. And in the years that followed, various stories accrued to Sockalexis to turn him into an almost mythical Indian-athlete. In 1956 Holy Cross made him the first member of their Athletic Hall of Fame, and the State of Maine set up a monument at his grave in the Penobscot tribal cemetery. Some sources even claim that he was the model for Gilbert Patten's Frank Merriwell, the all-American sports hero. Could any ballplayer be more honored, any Indian more respected?

In fact, as recounted in Chapter 12, Sockalexis had a serious drinking problem, and this, coupled with a foot injury in his first season in the majors, led to his rapid decline. He was probably exploited from the time he was taken into Holy Cross as a "special student," much like so many minority athletes at colleges today, and for all the headlines and popularity that attended his first weeks in Cleveland, he was discarded when he was unable to produce runs. No different from all players then as now, it may be said, and certainly no one in those days had much time to play social worker or therapist to any baseball player. But the myths that grew up around Sockalexis were at least as self-serving to white society as they were flattering to him.

This is true generally of the history of Native Americans in baseball, as of so many other players of varied ethnic and national origins. Traditional versions of baseball have always liked to publicize the backgrounds of special groups like the Indians who have been part of the game, as this shows how "American" it is. But there is the version of the perceivers, and there is the version of the experiencers. Most of these American Indian players have never been sounded out as to how they felt they were treated, but some at least have gone on record. John Meyers, interviewed by Larry Richter for *The Glory of Their Times,* indicated he had been treated as a "foreigner," and odds are that most of the Native American baseball players would confirm at least that description. Even the term *Chief,* applied so goodnaturedly to many of these men, is not regarded in quite the same way by Indians themselves. As for the honor to Sockalexis of having the Indians named after him, there is a movement among some Native Americans to force Cleveland to drop that name, along with the Braves of Atlanta, for these contemporary Native Americans now find such words degrading.

Yet these are the same people who, when blacks were being totally locked out of baseball during the early decades of this century, could play baseball in the majors. Indeed, several owners and managers tried to slip blacks onto teams by passing them off as Indians. Isn't that a sort of tribute to Indians? Where's the disrespect? How to explain the paradox?

Probably it lies in the fact that Indians could be admitted precisely because, as "Chief" Meyers put it, they were regarded as "foreigners"—or more to the point, as exotics. The teams could count on Indians to sign on, play as long as they could produce, and then move on and vanish back to the reservation, so to speak. There were no concentrations of Indians in cities where major league teams played, and the presence of the odd Indian or two on a baseball team would not excite expectations in any large group of citizens or spectators—unlike blacks, for instance, who, if one or two players had been allowed, might have turned into uncontrollable lines of both players and spectators expecting admission. Thus the nickname "Chief" for so many of the stars; this reminded everyone that these men were "sports." Thus, too, the honors heaped on Louis Sockalexis after his death: a variation on "the only good Indian is a dead Indian."

*The Jewish Connection*    If Native Americans occupy their own niche in American history and baseball, American Jews also occupy quite a special one. For one thing, where the story of the Indians in baseball is still largely being told by Caucasians, the story of Jews in organized baseball has very much been told by Jews themselves. Indeed, there is now a major league of writings by and about Jews and baseball, with both fiction and nonfiction divisions, plus several farm-league "feeder" teams. All these writings look back to a Jewish world in which physical achievements were denigrated while the cerebral were elevated, an attitude best expressed by Eddie Cantor in his autobiography when he tells of his grandmother shouting at him: " 'Stop! You—you—you baseball player you!' . . . That was the worst name she could call me. To the pious people of the ghetto a baseball player was the king of loafers." Yet all now seem to agree with the conclusion reached by Walter Harrison in his article, "Six-Pointed Diamond: Baseball and American Jews," in *Journal of Popular Culture,* Winter 1981:

> Baseball certainly did not supplant Judaism as the religion of American Jews. Rather baseball was one of the aspects of American life that many Jews quickly and earnestly assimilated and mixed with Judaism to form a new, secular faith. Within this new faith—by the middle of the 20th century at least—baseball was providing the mythic link that Morris Raphael Cohen had earlier defined: "unity with a larger life of which we are a part." This was not the larger life of the Jewish people, which it had traditionally been, but the life of America.

Baseball fiction by Jewish writers is discussed in Chapter 9, but as for nonfiction, there are at least two major books about Jewish ballplayers, not to mention a number of minor works. The history of Jews in America can be traced through some of the magazine articles: "Why Not More Jewish Ballplayers?" one asked back in 1926; by 1954, another was describing "Anti-Semitism in Baseball"; yet by 1973 another could proclaim, "Jewish Players Have Excelled in the Majors." In 1984, noted literary critic Eric Solomon could eloquently convey both his personal and literary insights in "Jews, Baseball, and the American Novel." By 1987, a Jewish teenager, Louis Jacobson, could write for his Bar Mitzvah project, "A Vanishing Breed: The Jewish Experience in Major League Baseball, 1876–1986." Meanwhile, that same year Shapolsky Books could publish *The Jewish Baseball Hall-of-Fame*—"the perfect gift for anyone who thinks they know everything about Jewish baseball stars. . . . Do you know: Which Phillies Jewish pitcher surrendered Honus Wagner's 3,000th career hit? . . . for every baseball buff who wants the ultimate in entertaining, sophisticated, brain-teasing erudition."

No, there is no danger that Jews will leave *their* role in the game of baseball to be written by others. Indeed, turning the ploy of racists to their own advantage, Jewish writers have managed to record every single player who can claim a drop of Jewish blood, starting with such early New York amateurs as Lipman and Boaz Pike; the first Jewish professionals (Nick Bertonstock and Lipman Pike, in 1871); the first major leaguers (Lipman Pike and his brother Jacob); and down through the greats (Hank Greenberg, Sandy Koufax), the not-so-greats (Ken Holtzman, Ron Blomberg) and the all-but-forgotten (Moses Solomon, Sid Schacht). Many of the early players encountered open hostility and anti-Semitism, of which John McGraw's "no Jewish Babe Ruth" was the politest form. Yet the New York Giants of the 1910s and 1920s actively sought out Jewish ballplayers to sign up because Jews were moving into the neighborhood near the Polo Grounds; by 1940 there had been at least fifty-five Jewish major leaguers, and since then about eighty-five more. Eric Solomon says that, after turning through the *Encyclopedia of Jews in Sports,* the impulse is to exclaim, "I didn't know *he* was Jewish!" Another exclamation might be that of the many Jewish ballplayers as they came to the plate: "How do I bat Jewish!"

For throughout all these writings about Jewish baseball players, few claims are made that their "Jewishness" had any particular effect on their ball-playing. One exception to this is the fact that Hank Greenberg would not play on Yom Kippur and Sandy Koufax would not pitch on any of the high holy days. The most notable instance of this came in the 1965 World Series, where the Dodgers faced the Twins and Koufax would have been expected to pitch the opening game; instead, Don Drysdale opened—and the Dodgers lost. When Koufax lost the second game, things looked bad for Jewish pitchers, but in the end, Koufax won the fifth and seventh games and the Dodgers were World Champions: probably nothing would have happened to Jewish-Americans had the Dodgers lost that Series, but one can't help wondering what anti-Semitics would have made of it.

Hank Greenberg's Jewish roots had another impact on the game, when in 1940 he was one of the first major leaguers to go into the military—there was a decided sense that he had to set an example, both as a Jew and as a professional athlete. But aside from such impacts on the peripherals of the game, no one has claimed that there is a "Jewish" way to play baseball, any more than there is a Roman Catholic Irish way or a French-American way or a Polish-American way. (There is thought to be an African-American way of playing the game, but that is a story told in Chapter 5.) Much is made of the fact that Morris "Moe" Berg, a catcher through most of his fifteen-year career (1923–39), was an intellectual among the untutored: "most erudite of all pro players," he is described in one reference work, "student of foreign languages who was an important O.S.S. figure in Europe during World War II and a noted attorney afterward." There is an element of nervous condescension whenever Jews are paid such tributes. They seem caught somewhere between Dr. Johnson's epigram about women preaching ("not done well, but you are surprised to find it done at all") and Richard Nixon's praise for Jews' abilities with figures and money.

But American Jews themselves no longer hide their pride in Jewish ballplayers. There is now a Jewish Sports Information Service that sits at the center of a network of people interested in one aspect or another of Jewish sports figures. Some, for instance, specialize in collecting baseball cards of Jewish players or related memorabilia, others just receive the newsletters to keep informed about the latest discoveries. The service's list of Jewish baseball players is coded to distinguish among the following categories: Jewish mother, Jewish father, converted in, converted out, possible convert, unconfirmed, and disputed. So long as such Talmudic hairs are being split, the sense will linger that Jewish baseball players bring something distinctive to the game, even if no one knows what it is.

*The Hispanics*    Perhaps the most surprising and remarkable chapter in the history of hyphenated Americans in baseball is that written by Hispanic-Americans. Whether they come from South America or Central America, from Caribbean islands or Mexico, from United States affiliates or from the fifty states, they seem omnipresent and indispensable on team after team these days. Yet once again, on the face of things, this might not have been predicted.

Physically, it might be assumed, Hispanics as a group would not be as large or powerful as so many of today's players (although don't tell that to José Canseco); meanwhile, the physical appearance of many might make them easy targets as "foreigners" to be discriminated against. Aside from that, some of them don't speak much English, and many, especially those from outside the fifty states, don't share much of the United States' mainstream culture and society. It could even be argued that if simple economics governs to some extent the exclusion of "outsiders" from the baseball establishment—the "Take Care of One's Own" theory—the foreign-born Hispanics should be the first to be kept out: They have no voice in the baseball establishment, and besides, they have their own teams back where they come from.

Yet here they are, in considerable numbers, and here they have been for much longer than might be realized. When the first professional league, the National Association of Professional Base Ball Players, was formed in 1871, among its members was the Cuban-born Esteban Bellan, then playing with the Troy (New York) Haymakers. He turned out to be way ahead of his times, for although there may well have been players with some Hispanic ancestry, the first to be identified as such in the majors were two Cubans taken on by the Cincinnati Reds in 1911, Rafael Almeida and Armando Marsans. In 1912, the Cuban Mike Gonzalez began his seventeen-year career as a catcher and would eventually manage several games for the Cardinals in 1938 and 1940. In 1913, another Cuban, Merito Acosta, joined the Washington Senators, but he played in only 175 games over five years; Acosta's brother José pitched in some twenty games over three years, 1920–22. Also in 1913, Al Cabrera, born in Spain's Canary Islands, played in one game for St. Louis, but he went hitless for two at-bats and was never seen again in the majors. The first big Latin American baseball star was the pitcher Dolf Luque, "The Pride of Havana," who joined the Boston Braves in 1914 and ended up with a 193–179 record for his twenty years in the majors.

Between Luque and Jackie Robinson's arrival, another forty or so Latin Americans played in the majors, but as is recounted in Chapter 5, the whole issue of who was a Latin American and who was a black and who was both or neither is extremely complicated. Meanwhile, there were scores of Hispanic-Americans playing in the minors and on semipro teams throughout the United States, and no one can ever know or prove how many of them might well have deserved to be brought up to the majors. So it is not that Hispanics, foreign-born or native-born, were treated entirely differently from other hyphenated Americans. Far from it. Even when they made the majors, many of these Hispanic players were subjected to ridicule (and far worse), some of it of the merely insensitive variety but a lot of it crudely deliberate—wisecracks about their stereotypical eating habits, appearance, and such. Allowing for this, though, it seems fair to say that, for a mixture of motives, both foreign-born and native-born Hispanics have been treated better than might have been expected, given the discriminatory practices of professional baseball throughout most of its history.

And now United States major league baseball is participating in the extraordinary phenomenon of the boys of San Pedro. San Pedro de Macoris, a city of some eighty thousand on the southeast coast of the Dominican Republic, is the country's third-largest city and has been known until fairly recently for its sugar factories. But today it has gained for itself the distinction of being the one city in the whole world's history to have produced the most major league baseball players per capita. (At any given moment, many more are in the minors.) There are apt to be three or four dozen Dominicans on the rosters of the major leagues these days, including coaches, and in recent years as many as seventeen of them have been from this one city, San Pedro de Macoris. Outstanding players, too—Pedro Guerrero, George

Bell, Alfredo Griffin, Rafael Santana, and many more. It has been suggested that an all-star Dominican team might be able to win the World Series; a San Pedro team could certainly give most major league teams a run for the pennant.

The explanations for this are several. One is that the sugar factories that support the town also sponsor baseball teams, semipro teams that take their baseball very seriously and compete strenuously among themselves and against similar teams from all over the Dominican Republic to win the country's championship. As for San Pedro's special eminence, one theory is that the boys are so poor there that they have had to make their own equipment—improvising bats, balls, and gloves from any available material—so that once a youth becomes good with such crude gear (on rough fields), he is an absolute whiz when he gets to play on a good field with real equipment. In the end, the explanation for Dominican baseball prowess is probably the most obvious one: the classic "hungry athlete" syndrome. The poverty and lack of opportunity of San Pedro and the Dominican Republic mean that baseball provides young boys with one of the few ways out to a better life. What bullfighting has been in Spain, for instance, what boxing is for many youths around the world, and what baseball used to be for certain youngsters in the United States.

One other facet to the role of Hispanics in North American baseball: There are already six major league clubs that provide Spanish-language play-by-play (radio) broadcasts of their teams' games, and the Boston Red Sox may by now have joined them as the seventh. In addition to these local broadcasts, CBS provides Spanish-language coverage of the League Championships and the World Series for some thirty-five stations in the United States and some two hundred in Latin America. Los Angeles claims the largest Hispanic "market area"—over a million—but the Hispanic population is one of the fastest-growing and most upwardly mobile ethnic groups in the United States and, given the prominence of Hispanic-American and Latin American players, it seems that baseball will increasingly take on a Spanish accent.

*Warming Up the Melting Pot*   Is the last word on hyphenated Americans in baseball that, given the "discriminatory practices of professional baseball throughout most of its history," they've done pretty well? It would be easy to compile a section on the demeaning, unjust, and downright vicious cases, and some contemporary baseball researchers are turning them up. Nor should these instances be explained away entirely on the grounds of being no worse, if no better, than the spirit of American society at large.

But there might be a few points that the other side could make. Yes, the majors were slow to let these hyphenated Americans into the locker room, but by 1941 teams were made up of some 9.3 percent Slavic-Americans and 8 percent Italian-Americans, percentages over twice those in the white population of the United States at large. It might be hard to think of any occupational group with a "positive charge" that to this day can point to such figures. Today the major league player rosters are about as totally integrated as one could expect, with men from every possible socioeconomic, national, ethnic, and racial slice of society playing alongside one another.

Where else do college graduates and graduate students labor shoulder to shoulder with high school dropouts, where else do white boys from Middletown U.S.A. work out and shower with blacks from L.A. and Hispanics from Cuba? Yes, they tend to go their own way after work, and there is no need to romanticize relations or gloss over the problems among various groups on the diamond or in the dugout. There is an undercurrent of racial animosity in baseball today that is to be deplored. But give organized baseball some credit. To this day the U.S. military likes to boast of taking the lead in integration, but it didn't really start desegregating until 1948. Professional football has had occasional blacks on teams since 1902, but none between 1933 and 1945, suggesting it had capitulated to segregation; it was 1946 before the modern NFL became truly integrated, by which time Jackie Robinson had already been playing for the Dodgers' farm team for a year. The NBA didn't have its first contracted black player on the floor until 1950.

Allowing for its slow start, baseball has been one of the few occupations where young men of any background—Native Americans, slave descendants, Puerto Ricans—could work alongside and compete with white Americans. In a world of so many newscasts and headlines that feature the Willy Hortons and Colombian drug lords, where else outside professional baseball do most Americans see and read about so many blacks and Hispanics in possession of such admirable skills and in positions of approved prominence? There's only one Native American in baseball's Hall of Fame, but that's one more than is living in most Americans' neighborhoods.

Steven Riess, one of the toughest critics of the myths and ideologies that the conventional histories of baseball have perpetuated, concludes:

Baseball by the 1920s was probably more successful in helping socialize and integrate Americans than ever before. Sunday baseball and an improved standard of living made it possible for more fans to participate in the rituals of spectatorship. The game finally became the democratic spectator sport its ideology had long proclaimed it to be. The realities of baseball were beginning to catch up to its myths.

There are still a number of myths floating about and still some realities to catch up to, but that's the national pastime. Organized baseball has a way to go before it is truly integrated, especially at the executive and managerial levels, but probably no farther than the whole of American society.

# DON'T LOOK BACK . . .

**O** f all the immigrants who came to these shores and learned to play baseball, blacks are unique because, with few exceptions, they came here not to seek greater prosperity, freedom from religious persecution, or surcease from famine, but to work as slaves. They came here against their will, and it is as much for this reason as for the darkness of their skin that the history of Afro-Americans in the land of the free has been so peculiar, and rates a special chapter in this book. It will be seen that the experience of blacks in organized baseball is a particularly accurate and subtle reflection of the experience of black folk in American society at large, a society that, according to sociologist David Fabianic, "implies a degree of bigotry, discrimination, and fear, as well as business decisions made at the expense of social progress." The incredible wealth of material on the topic is one indication of how central the issue is to the American social landscape.

It is only recently that black participation in the national pastime has begun to be documented and to receive its historical due and that great black players whose careers took place during baseball apartheid have been recognized for their skill. It may be that one day all records achieved when organized baseball was white will have asterisks next to them, as Roger Maris's does now, to remind us that Babe Ruth never had to compete against Josh Gibson or Satchel Paige. Many of the stories in this chapter will strike the enlightened reader as extremely strange, or pathetic, with the poignance and nostalgia of long-gone practices that no civilized man or woman would countenance nowadays. Unfortunately, many other stories will document that racism, here in America, is not only a thing of the past.

*Cap Anson and Jim Crow*   In 1867 history's first baseball league, the National Association of Base-Ball Players, passed a resolution barring blacks and the teams they played for from membership. The resolution reflected the racism and segregation that were rapidly becoming facts of life in the North after the Civil War. While none of the *major* leagues that came after the National Association ever adopted a *written* resolution barring blacks, the precedent set by the National Association served as the basis for what became known as the "gentleman's agreement," an ironclad rule excluding blacks from organized ball. Many whites simply came to believe that there was a law barring blacks from playing major league ball.

Such a one, apparently, was Cap Anson, one of the all-time greats of baseball and baseball's most prominent figure in the nineteenth century. The first player to reach three thousand career hits—he still holds a National League record for hitting .300 or better in twenty seasons—Anson was also a bigot of fierce conviction who pressed to insure that blacks would find no permanent place in the major leagues.

At least fifty-five blacks are known by name to have played in organized baseball before 1900. It will come as a surprise to many to learn that two black men, Moses Fleetwood Walker and his brother Welday Wilberforce Walker, played major league ball last century in the American Association, which shared major league status with the National League during the 1880s.

Fleet Walker, who in 1884 became the first black to play in the majors, was a catcher for the Toledo club of the Northwestern League in 1883. According to an agreement that the Northwestern League signed with the National League and the American Association in the spring of 1883, Toledo played lucrative exhibition matches that season against the New York Nationals, the New York Metropolitans, Columbus, and St. Louis. But when Anson brought his Chicago White Stockings to play the strong Toledo club on August 11 and Walker appeared on the diamond, he bellowed, "Get that nigger off the field!" and refused to play unless Walker was removed from the game. On this occasion Anson was forced to back down when threatened with forfeiture of his team's share of the gate. In fact, Toledo had not intended to play Walker that day—they had planned to give the catcher's banged-up hands a rest—but they placed him in right field

*Welday Wilberforce Walker* (standing rear) *and his brother Moses Fleetwood Walker* (seated) *were both on Oberlin College's first varsity baseball team when it posed for this photograph in 1881. In 1884 they became the first two Afro-Americans to join a major league team but they were soon driven out—even though they were far better educated than most players of that day.*

after a representative from Chicago registered a pregame objection to playing against a team with a black.

Four years later, on July 14, 1887, Anson, whose policy of refusing to allow blacks on the same field with him had by then become well-known and generally accepted, refused to play against a Newark team that featured the temperamental George Stovey, considered by many to be the greatest black pitcher of all time. Fleet Walker, as it happened, was catching. When Stovey became aware of Anson's attitude, he walked off the field and refused to play the White Stockings.

Still, in 1887 it looked like blacks, already well established in the minors, would enter major league baseball's structure. The deleterious effects of "social Darwinian" ideologies had yet to set in. The rigid uniformity that would characterize race relations by the end of the century was only one of several options that apparently coexisted during what in retrospect appears to have been an experimental era when race relations varied widely from state to state and locality to locality. Such a climate encouraged John Montgomery Ward in 1887 to try to bring Stovey up to pitch for the major league New York Giants, but Anson, "the Grand Old Man of Baseball," who was as prestigious and popular as any player until Babe Ruth, mustered all of his tremendous influence to bring pressure against Ward. Declaring, "There's a law against that," he succeeded in preventing the signing and set a precedent. No blacks appeared in major league baseball after the 1880s, and shortly thereafter they became a rarity in organized baseball, disappearing completely by the turn of the century.

It would be an oversimplification to say that Anson was responsible for barring blacks from baseball; he clearly capitalized upon pre-existing prejudices and succeeded because the social climate was ripe. On the other hand, the motive for his racism is hard to fathom. It is interesting to note that in late July 1901 Anson, whose career as player and manager ended in 1898, umpired a game between an all-white Waseca, Minnesota, club and the Algona (Iowa) Brownies, half of whom were black. According to a contemporary account, during this series for independent clubs billed as the Iowa championship, "Anson made a good umpire. His decisions were impartial," and his participation was "clean, honest and good-natured." Although throughout his life his public pronouncements include numerous racial slurs of the grossest type, apparently once he was satisfied that blacks would have no place in organized baseball, Anson's racism relaxed. It is possible to conclude that his animosity toward blacks had a significant economic basis, for once they were excluded from his profession—at least to judge by this instance—he didn't much seem to care who or what they played.

*Baseball's Black Pioneer*   The twenty-five-year career of Bud Fowler neatly recapitulates black baseball history in the nineteenth century. Born John W. Jackson in 1854 to free blacks in Cooperstown, New York—and ironically the best player ever to emerge from the legendary town where baseball was not invented—Fowler learned the game around Hudson, New York, and began his career with the black Washington, D.C., Mutuals in 1869 (the same year the first all-professional white team was organized). In 1872 he became the first black professional ballplayer ever to play with a white team when he signed with the New Castle club of Pennsylvania. Three years later his name appeared in box scores as a pitcher (again the only black) for the Live Oaks of Lynn, Massachusetts, but after that records are sparse until he signed on with the Stillwater, Minnesota, club of the Northwestern League in 1884, where he was again the only black. Like most ballplayers of his era, he changed teams frequently, playing every position, wherever he could, although there is no doubt that it was at second base he made his mark.

Fowler was a great favorite at Stillwater in 1884, where the Stillwater *Sun* somewhat insensitively called him "our baseball mascot," a term usually reserved for batboys, black boys, albinos, and dwarves kept as good luck charms. When the Stillwaters disbanded he plied his father's trade and barbered before signing on with Keokuk of the Western League for 1885. When Keokuk disbanded late in July 1885 he moved to the St. Joseph, Missouri, club; and when St. Joseph disbanded he moved to the Pueblos of Colorado, where he was eventually "disengaged" because "his skin [was] against him."

Altogether, in eight years in the minors he played on at least twelve different teams in at least seven different leagues. He batted over .300 for Topeka, Kansas, of the Western League in 1886, one of many blacks who found work in organized ball during the expansion of the mid-1880s; and he signed on with the Binghamton, New York, International League club for 1887, where he had to play second base "with the lower part of his legs encased in wooden guards" to protect himself from the white players' spikes. He was a star in Binghamton, batting .350 and stealing over twenty bases in thirty-odd games until June 30, when he was released by the Bingos and forbidden to sign with any other league club two weeks before the International League formally barred blacks. Except for a few games with the Lansing club of the Michigan State League in 1895, his career with white teams was over.

Fowler then joined the leading black team of the day, the Cuban Giants, and thereafter resumed a peripatetic career that included organizing clubs such as the all-black Page Fence Giants (for the Page Woven Wire Fence Company of Adrian, Michigan), a crack squad that combined Harlem Globetrotter–like showmanship with demonstrations of athletic mastery. He had previously engaged in walking and running exhibitions; his baseball survival skills reached their zenith in 1899 when he organized the All-American Black Tourists, whom he made available for play attired in full-dress suits with silk umbrellas.

Having been reduced to becoming a clown in order to survive in a society that was rapidly institutionalizing racism, Fowler disappeared from view at the end of the century. He was known in his day for intelligent and exciting fielding, solid hitting, and great speed. *Sporting Life* and contemporary black players agreed that he was an outstanding athlete, one of the "best general players in the country," whose splendid abilities would certainly have secured him a post on "some good club had his color been white instead of black." In 1885 *Sporting Life* reported, "Those who know [him] say there is no better second baseman in the country."

Yet in view of the prejudices of the times, it is less remarkable that he was denied a chance to play in the majors than that he ever got a chance to play in the minors. In 1895 this undeniably dedicated athlete, the first black man ever to play in organized ball—and the first black man known to have played professional ball—wrote ruefully concerning his career, "If I had not been quite so black, I might have caught on as a Spaniard or something of that kind."

*Apartheid in the 1880s* The expansion of organized baseball in the 1880s saw an influx of talented black players, but despite some momentum to the contrary, growing segregation in baseball and in the nation as a whole made the use of black players on professional teams increasingly difficult. In May 1887 *Sporting Life* sneered, "How far will this mania for engaging colored players go? At the present rate of progress the International League may ere many moons change its name to 'Colored League.'" On the other hand, later in 1887 *The Sporting News* ran this response to a newspaper item that had referred to Fleet Walker as "the coon catcher of the Newarks": "It is a pretty small paper that will publish a paragraph of that kind about a member of a visiting club, and the man who wrote it is without doubt Walker's inferior in education, refinement, and manliness."

As it came down to the man on the field, reaction varied according to locale, fans, owners, and fellow players, many of whom must have felt that they had a professional interest in removing an entire race from competition. On occasion, teammates conspired to make a black player look bad, as was the case for southpaw Robert Higgins of the Syracuse Stars, whose teammates, including several Southerners, deliberately muffed plays and handed him a 28–8 defeat in his first International League game on May 25, 1887. "DISGRACEFUL BASEBALL" screamed the Toronto *World*. "THE SYRACUSE PLOTTERS," headlined *The Sporting News*, "The Star Team Broken Up By a Multitude of Cliques; The Southern Boys Refuse to Support the Colored Pitcher."

But it would be a mistake to believe that negative reaction to black players was limited to Southerners. One of the players who refused to sit for the 1887 team portrait with Higgins was from Utica, New York. And in July 1887, the Toronto *World* reported that spectators at an International League game with Syracuse confined themselves "to blowing their horns and shouting, 'Kill the nigger.'"

An unidentified white International League player told *The Sporting News* in 1889 that he pitied black players for the punishment they had to put up with, even though he himself was "prejudiced against playing in a team with a colored player." According to this account, Bud Fowler and outstanding second baseman Frank Grant on occasion left their bags on close plays or intentionally muffed balls in order to avoid contact with runners, and Grant eventually grew so weary of assaults from white baserunners that in the later part of 1888 he moved from second base to right field. Pitchers routinely

*Illustrations like this could be found frequently in newspapers and magazines in the late nineteenth century. Finding humor in just about everything Afro-Americans did, such illustrations may not have been hardcore racism but they contributed to the climate that allowed others to drive individual Afro-Americans out of organized baseball.*

threw at Grant's head, awarding the agile player an inordinate number of walks. In fact, black players were thrown at so often by white pitchers that balls thrown out of the strike zone came to be known as "nigger chasers."

The International League banned the further signing of blacks on July 14, 1887. Taking into consideration the underlying feelings of most whites of the era, the fact that blacks played professional baseball at all is testimony to the courage and determination of the individual athletes and to the relative lack of institutionalized segregation at the time. Still, the 1880s were a far cry from the more experimental 1870s, during which, according to former black player and historian Sol White, "colored players were accommodated in the best hotels in the country."

In 1908 former black major leaguer Fleet Walker wrote that he had seen race relations deteriorate over the past forty years while "a real caste spirit [developed] in the United States." To the extent that the national pastime in the late nineteenth century embodied the emerging American Way, it embodied racism; and as America hardened into a two-tiered caste system, baseball followed suit. After 1898 no black man played in organized baseball (unless he passed himself off as an Indian or a "Cuban") until Jackie Robinson.

*Charlie Tokohama*　It is no secret that many times after blacks had been unofficially but rigorously banned from the National League in 1887, managers and owners who cared less for the color of a man's skin than for what he could do for their team tried to sneak blacks onto their squads. One of the more bizarre attempts occurred in 1901, when John J. McGraw, then managing the Baltimore Orioles, happened to see a light-skinned black named Charlie Grant of the Chicago Columbia Giants playing when the Orioles were in training at Hot Springs, Arkansas. At the time Grant was employed at a local hotel. McGraw was so impressed with the young second baseman that he signed him to the Orioles. Knowing that he would be prevented from playing if word got out, McGraw selected the name *Tokohama* from a local map and tried to pass Grant off as Charlie Tokohama, a Cherokee Indian. On April 28, 1902, Grant left the Columbia Giants in Zanesville, Ohio, and joined the Orioles. Unfortunately, his cover was blown when some of his black friends ceremoniously congratulated him in public. Even more disastrous, Chicago White Sox owner Charlie Comiskey recognized Tokohama as a black he had seen playing on Chicago Negro teams and alerted the owners. American League officials demanded Grant's dismissal, and he never played a major league game.

A couple of decades down the line McGraw tried unsuccessfully to pass off black center fielder Oscar Charleston, considered by many to have been the greatest all-round Negro leagues player, as a white Cuban. McGraw had previously hired black pitching great Rube Foster as a pitching coach—some claim he worked extensively with Christy Mathewson—and had made it no secret that he would have liked to add him to his pitching staff. McGraw also spent considerable money in a campaign to transform pitcher José Mendez into an Indian after he saw the Kansas City Monarchs star pitch against white major leaguers in Cuba.

In fact, McGraw kept the names of black players he would have liked to sign on a list that his wife discovered and disclosed after his death. But in 1933 McGraw was the only one of six powerful baseball men polled by New York *Daily News* sportswriter Jimmy Powers at the baseball writers' dinner who openly objected to allowing blacks in the major leagues. Perhaps he was misunderstood, perhaps he was joking, perhaps he was concerned for the fate of the Negro leagues once white owners started raiding their players, or perhaps experience had taught him that it wouldn't work.

*The Written Law*   It is popular among baseball historians to repeat that organized baseball never had any *written* regulations barring blacks. What the historians and executives who protest baseball's egalitarianism may mean is that *major league* baseball never passed any written regulations barring blacks. It is a matter of record that the International League, which is part of organized baseball as well as America's oldest minor league, voted to exclude blacks on July 14, 1887. On that day Secretary White was directed to "approve of no more contracts with colored men." In October of 1887 the Tri-State League also prohibited black players.

The Tri-State League rescinded its prohibition in 1888, but the writing was on the wall, and apart from achieving its immediate goal, the barring of blacks in the minors sent an important signal; then as now, the traditional route to the majors was through the minors, and by voting to bar blacks the minors relieved the majors from having to formally prohibit blacks themselves. As the Chicago *Tribune*'s Westbrook Pegler wrote in 1931, "the magnates haven't the gall to put [it] on paper."

*The Gentlemen's Agreement*   Lest anyone still believe that the issue of blacks in major league baseball was not considered at the highest levels by baseball executives in the twentieth century, former Baseball Commissioner Happy Chandler confirmed in an interview on March 22, 1989, that a secret report on integration in baseball was prepared for the owners in 1946. Written by National League President Ford Frick, American League President William Harridge, Sam Breadon of the Cardinals, Phil Wrigley of the Cubs, Larry MacPhail of the Yankees, and Tom Yawkey of the Red Sox, the report urged that blacks be excluded from the major leagues.

According to Chandler, when the report was reviewed by all the owners, they deemed it too strong for public consumption and moved that all copies be collected and destroyed. There is no doubt, however, that the owners agreed with the conclusions of the report in substance: In January 1947, at a meeting at the Waldorf Astoria Hotel in New York, the owners voted 15–1 not to admit Jackie Robinson or any other black to the major leagues. After the meeting, Chandler assured Branch Rickey, the only dissenting voter, that he would not interfere if Rickey decided to bring Robinson up to the Dodgers. But the former commissioner would not confirm, in March 1989, that he had secretly preserved a copy of the 1946 report, as some sources maintain.

*The Yellow Kid*   Bert Jones, a hard-throwing southpaw with a reputation for being a character, holds the distinction of being the last black to play in organized baseball before Jackie Robinson. Known as the "Yellow Kid" after a comic strip character of the era, Jones pitched for Atchison, Kansas, in 1897 and was retained when Atchison became part of the Kansas State League in 1898. He won two league games in 1898 and played outfield in another before a white pitcher named Parvin made it clear that he would not play in a game or on a team with a "Cuban." Apparently Parvin got his way, for Jones next appeared on the mound for the Chicago Unions, a fine black team. Since the last black club in organized baseball had sputtered out a few weeks previous to Jones's release from Atchison, the Yellow Kid's position as the last black to play in organized baseball until 1946 seems secure. Claims have been made for black shortstop William Clarence Matthews, a letter winner who left Harvard in 1906 to turn professional with Burlington in the Vermont League; but the Vermont League was never part of organized baseball (and Matthews was condemned by his university associates for the ungentlemanly act of trying to make a living from a sport).

*Ty Cobb and Li'l Rastus*   Ty Cobb, one of baseball's immortal competitors, who even as an elderly man was banned from some California Bay Area golf courses because of his violent temper, was also one of baseball's legendary bigots. Along with other white players whose skill qualified them to play in the Caribbean Basin's integrated winter leagues, he was familiar with the quality of the best American black players. In November of 1910, while Cobb was playing against black catching great Bruce Petway in Havana, Petway threw him out on attempted steals three times in a row. On the third try Cobb saw that the throw had him beat and simply ran back to the dugout. Although usually not a consistent hitter, Petway also outhit Cobb .412 to .369 that day, and at the end of the game Cobb reportedly stomped off the field vowing never again to play against blacks.

At home the Georgia Peach had already distinguished himself by displaying a hostility toward blacks that surprised even his teammates. On several occasions he entered the stands to attack blacks who booed him, and in 1912 in New York he had to be pulled off a white spectator who called him a "half-nigger." In March of 1907, during spring training in Augusta, Georgia, Cobb became infuriated when a black groundskeeper known as Bungy tried to shake his hand. He chased the man to a shack on the edge of the field where he lived, and when Bungy's wife tried to intervene, threw her down and began choking her in full view of teammates and fans. Manager Hughie Jennings stopped the fight that ensued when teammate Charlie Schmidt pulled Cobb off the woman, but failed in his attempt to trade Cobb away because no one could give him a player of equal merit.

In July of 1907 Cobb was fined for attacking a black worker who objected to his walking on the asphalt he had just poured. In September of 1909 at the Euclid Hotel in Cleveland, Cobb severely knifed a black night watchman who asked him to identify himself and had to flee the city to avoid being jailed during a tight pennant race. The Tigers paid an enormous fee to the best lawyer in Cleveland to have the case settled. On another occasion Cobb, who was usually armed, was arrested and jailed after he hit a black butcher's assistant over the head with the butt of his revolver during a dispute with a white butcher over the bill.

The press generally ignored these incidents or treated them as amusing anecdotes, sharing in the ambivalence Cobb and many whites of the era displayed toward blacks, whom they at one and the same time considered inferior, appreciated most when they accepted their social inferiority, and endowed with supernatural powers. So it was that Cobb latched on to and eventually made a manservant of a homeless black boy known as Li'l Rastus, whose appearance at Bennett Park in July of 1908 coincided with the end of a team slump and earned him a reputation as a good-luck charm. Li'l Rastus's magic was enhanced when the Tigers went on the road without him and slumped again, and returned to winning when they came home to Bennett Park. Thereafter, with Cobb as his chief patron, Rastus accompanied the team on the road, often hiding under Cobb's bunk on trains and sneaking into his hotel room to circumvent Jim Crow laws designed to prevent just such racial commingling. Other players would touch his head before batting in order to benefit from his special powers. Back home in September, however, when the Tigers began losing and things began disappearing from the clubhouse, Rastus was released. The resourceful mascot went over to the Cubs when they arrived for the World Series with Detroit and, apparently as a result, the Tigers dropped four out of five and reinstated Rastus for the 1909 season.

Cobb took Li'l Rastus home at the end of that season to serve him in Georgia, where his duties included caddying for Cobb's golfing buddies, such as President Taft. Rastus wasn't entirely satisfactory as a domestic, however, and by 1911 Cobb, who always maintained that he was raised by a black mammy and got on well with colored folk, replaced him with one Alex Reeves, who stayed with him for many years, and was regarded by Cobb as "the best darky I ever saw."

*The First*   Jimmy Claxton, a well-known figure on the Pacific Northwest baseball scene for forty years, was the first black man to play in organized (white) baseball in the twentieth century. Claxton found his way from black baseball to white ball in 1916 when a part-Indian friend from Oklahoma introduced him as a fellow tribesman. He first pitched for the Oakland Oaks of the Pacific Coast League on May 28, 1916, and was released on June 3, 1916, when, according to Claxton, another "supposed friend" informed the Oakland officials that he was part Negro (Claxton was of white, Indian, and black ancestry).

By the time of his release, Claxton had already posed for the photographer working on the 1916 series of Zeenut baseball cards, the longest continuously published series of baseball cards (1911–39) before Topps, and thus became the first black player ever to appear on a baseball card. Claxton was elected to the Tacoma–Pierce County Hall of Fame in 1969 and was still pitching semipro ball once a week at the age of fifty-two; he reputedly won a two-hitter when he was sixty-one. How many other "black" men passed as Indians in organized ball is a mystery that may eventually yield to further research.

*Cubans*

I have always been convinced that Jackie Robinson was not the first black man in the modern major leagues. The Washington Senators in

*Jimmy Claxton just happened to be with the Oakland team in the Pacific Coast League in 1916 when the Zeenut Candy Company took the players' pictures for their baseball cards of that year. Claxton claims the distinction of being both the first Afro-American in organized white baseball in the twentieth century and the first to have his own baseball card.*

the mid-thirties and forties were loaded with Latin players of darker hue, who because they spoke Spanish got by with it.

— Art Rust, Jr., sports editor of the *Amsterdam News*

Before blacks were squeezed out of organized baseball in the last decade of the last century, writers outdid themselves in creating epithets for black players. Their prodigiousness in generating euphemisms, a reflection of the discomfort of a society grappling with the issue of free blacks, reached a great flowering in the 1880s, when circumlocutions commonly employed included: Cuban, Spanish, Indian, African, Arabian, mulatto, coon, choco-late, dusky, dusky-hued, snow flake, dark object, Ethiopian, simian, son of Africa, darky, colored, nigger, sable, simmenian, Senegambian, cimmenan, colored Ethiopian, Cherokee, Geronimo, gaucho, darkskin, and brunette. Black players were generally considered objects of curiosity, amusement, or derision by whites; and although research in this area is difficult because the minor leagues were not well organized before this century and usually did not get much coverage in the newspapers of the era, which tended to leave off first names, it is safe to say that in general, local papers refused to call local black players anything as explicit as *Negro* or *colored,* while papers of visiting teams did, creating conditions of excruciating confusion.

There are many well-documented instances of black Americans trying to pass as Indians in order to play ball. Apparently any foreigner was more acceptable than a former slave, but *Cuban* seems to have been the descriptive of choice. The great John McGraw, for instance, having failed to pass off Charlie Grant as an Indian, several years later tried to pass off outstanding black center fielder Oscar Charleston as a white Cuban. So many all-black teams called themselves Cuban, in fact, that by the beginning of the twentieth century *Cuban* meant black in baseball circles. Some black American teams took to spouting gibberish on the field in order to be taken as foreigners, capitalizing on a dialect that already may have caused some whites to think they were aliens. (In 1911 Booker T. Washington's *New York Age* suggested that "colored players could keep their mouths shut and pass for Cubans.") But the excellent all-black Cuban Giants could not have entertained much serious hope of being considered foreigners; their choice of name was in all probabil-ity an act of complicity as well as an expression of their desire to be taken more seriously and to find more work in exhibition games with white clubs. It may also have expressed respect and longing for a country where a black player was also a man.

Adding to the confusion, American blacks were sometimes hired to play on Cuban teams at home and abroad; and Cubans—at least light-skinned Cubans—were sometimes hired to play in America. Rafael Almeida and Armando Marsans of the Cuban Stars, the first Cubans in the majors, were signed by Cincinnati in 1911 (some observers thought they would serve as a wedge for integrating baseball). Mike Gonzalez began a seventeen-year career as a catcher in the National League in 1912, and Dolf Luque, "The Pride of Havana," began a distinguished National League pitching career in 1914. Many Spanish-speaking players signed with the Wash-ington Senators in the late 1930s and '40s. In fact, years later Branch Rickey, in response to former Washington owner Calvin Griffith's objections to integration, told Red Smith that Griffith had already hired blacks.

On occasion, white players who were suspected of being *too* Cuban, because of various physical characteristics, were hounded from white baseball. According to historian David Voigt, such was the case for Lou Nava in the 1880s and fine Orioles' outfielder George Treadway in the 1890s. Power hitter Cristobel Torrienti of the American Giants forfeited his chance at the majors in the '20s, supposedly because he had kinky hair. Black star Quincy Trouppe claims that a scout once told him he would have a good chance to play organized ball if he learned to speak Spanish. Conversely, such players as Luque, Gonzalez, Marsans, Tommy de la Cruz, and Mike Estallao were all claimed as black at one time or another by various black leaders (although it must be said that Americans have tended to consider any man with any black blood a black man).

The impression left on American culture by the confusing use of *Cuban* was so strong that as late as May 1987, when the major leagues were celebrating the fortieth anniversary of the breaking of the color line by Jackie Robinson, *The Sporting News* published a letter from a fan who said his father had always told him that Dolf Luque, and not Jackie Robinson, was the first black man to play in the major leagues in the twentieth century. *The Sporting News,* in an item called "Pure Castillian," set the record straight by responding that Luque was a Spanish Cuban.

*Josh Gibson: The Brown Bambino*   Joshua Gibson is generally considered one of the all-time great ballplayers of any color. From the time he made his debut in 1930 with the Homestead Grays, Pittsburgh's Negro American League team, until his decline during the war years, he was considered the finest slugger ever to play in the Negro leagues. According to Monte Irvin, "Gibson, without a doubt, was the greatest hitter I ever saw, black or white. He would have broken Ruth's record. The fans saw the Babe from the left side, they would have seen Josh from the right side."

But just how great a power hitter he was can never be known with certitude, because journalists, statisticians, and historians by and large ignored the Negro leagues. It is a sad commentary on race relations in America that when Gibson was elected to the Hall of Fame in 1972, his lifetime statistics read, "No statistics available." (The Negro Leagues Committee of the Society for American Baseball Research is attempting to rectify this situation by compiling statistics from box scores for the Negro leagues from 1920 to 1950.)

Negro league clubs played in every major league ballpark, and it is known that Gibson repeatedly hit tape-measure homers in Griffith Stadium, where black ball outdrew the Washington Senators by upwards of twenty-thousand per game; and he is the only man ever to hit a fair ball out of Yankee Stadium. In 1932 Gibson hit seventy-five home runs and averaged .380 in 123 games; during his years with the outstanding Pittsburgh Crawfords, when he caught for batterymate Satchel Paige, he sometimes guaranteed his fans two home runs per game; on one occasion he hit four fair balls into the Griffith Stadium seats. According to the *Guinness Sports Record Book,* estimates of his best season home run totals run as high as eighty-five. Clark Griffith, impressed by the huge crowds that turned out to see Gibson, toyed with the idea of signing him to the Senators in the '30s; Walter Johnson told Griffith that Gibson was worth $250,000.

In 1934, Gibson was among a group of black all-stars who beat a group of white all-stars headed by Dizzy Dean in seven out of nine exhibition games. Gibson hit well against Dean and the other major league pitchers. Satchel Paige, who with Gibson was the greatest draw in Negro league history, claimed that Gibson and Ted Williams were the toughest hitters he ever faced, but that Gibson hit more home runs. In 1945, Gibson led the Negro National League with a .393 average; Roy Campanella was fourth with .365.

In 1946, his last season, Gibson, by then ailing and plagued with a drinking problem, hit more homers (twenty-seven) into the Griffith Stadium bleachers than the entire white American League (thirteen). It is feats such as this, considered apocryphal by baseball officialdom because of the lack of official statistics, that cause numerous experts to believe that had Gibson been given the opportunity to play in the major leagues, he, and not Babe Ruth, would be considered the greatest power hitter of all time. Gibson died suddenly at the age of thirty-five on January 20, 1947, of a cerebral hemorrhage, a few months before blacks began to play in the majors.

*A Short Paige*   Dave Barnhill was a small man who weighed 130 pounds, but he threw so hard that his contemporaries considered him to be on a par with Satchel Paige. On one occasion when Barnhill and Paige were barnstorming with the Kansas City Monarchs, Paige kept the Toledo Mudhens, a white Triple-A club, scoreless for four innings, giving up only one hit while striking out ten. The manager of the Mudhens asked Kansas City manager Frank Duncan for a little mercy in the form of a lesser pitcher, since the Mudhens were a major league farm club and deserved some consideration. His request was not unusual, because black teams traditionally masked their skill in order to avoid winning by such margins that they would not be asked back.

The Monarch's manager, Duncan, pointing to Barnhill, asked if he would do, and the Mudhens' manager agreed that the little guy was exactly what he was looking for. Barnhill relieved Paige and stayed in for the last five innings, during which he kept the Mudhens hitless and struck out eleven. After the game, the Mudhens' manager confronted Duncan in the clubhouse. Duncan played dumb. The Mudhens' skipper finally exploded, asserting that Duncan hadn't kept his agreement to substitute a lesser pitcher for Paige—he'd just taken Paige out behind the dugout and sawed off his legs.

*Professional Courtesy* In the early 1930s, Judy Johnson played for the legendary Pittsburgh Crawfords. Five members of this team, which Bob Feller called "the Yankees of Negro baseball"—Johnson, Oscar Charleston, Josh Gibson, Satchel Paige, and Cool Papa Bell—eventually found their way into the Hall of Fame. On days when the Crawfords weren't playing, Johnson and his friends liked to attend white major league games to see what they could learn. "We never had to pay to see the A's or the Yankees," Johnson recalls. "The only park where we had to pay was St. Louis, and they [put] us in the Jim Crow section. Other than that, every big league park knew us."

Branch Rickey's legendary unwillingness to part with any pennies whatsoever may have been the reason black stars had to pay in St. Louis, but segregated seating arrangements preceded and outlasted his general managership. Gene Karst, who became the Cardinals' first publicity man in 1931, recalls with embarrassment, "One of my early calls on a newspaper editor was a visit to the St. Louis *Argus,* a Negro publication. It embarrassed me that while the passes I gave the black editor were the same as those I gave to white editors, the *Argus* editor could use his passes only for the bleachers."

*North of the Border* In July 1935 pitcher-outfielder Alfred Wilson became the first black on record to play in the Quebec Provincial League. Although the Provincial League was not part of organized baseball when he joined, it was part of organized baseball from 1921 to 1923, in 1940, and from 1950 to 1955, a fact that gives the loop at least as much legitimacy as any black U.S. league of the day. Wilson, who was born in Alabama in 1908, possibly in a Cajun district since he spoke some French, may very well not have been the first black in the league, because before the turn of the century Quebec included several teams from Missisquoi County, former northern terminus of the Underground Railroad, which had a substantial black population.

Quebec first experienced night baseball when Wilson's connections attracted black U.S. teams with portable lighting systems. In 1945, still one year before Jackie Robinson appeared in Montreal with the Royals, Wilson emerged from obscurity and reintegrated the Provincial League, which had become all-white during his absence. The Provincial League eventually became an entry league for players such as Vic Powers, Ed Charles, Dave Pope, Hector Lopez, and Ruben Gomez; and after the league left organized baseball again in 1955, it became an alternative for talented black players who preferred peaceful obscurity in Canada to riches in racist America. John Mentis, a native of Nova Scotia who twice topped .400 in thirteen seasons in the Provincial League, testifies, "I had offers to play American baseball. I wasn't ready for that, where someone else could walk on the sidewalk and you couldn't."

*How to Handle White Pitchers* Segregation was a fact of life in the States, but many of the better Negro leaguers played on integrated teams in Latin America during the winter months, teaming up with or against such immortals as Tris Speaker and Rogers Hornsby, especially in Cuba and Mexico, and even within the United States in the California winter leagues. But at a time when many white Americans who were not racist by profession still believed that blacks didn't have the mental equipment to play major league baseball, even knowledgeable baseball men such as Branch Rickey were apparently unaware that black players were used to performing in totally integrated environments. When Rickey, nervous about bringing Roy Campanella up to catch for the Dodgers, asked him how he would "handle" white pitchers, Campy replied with some amusement that he had already "handled" white pitchers in Mexico—and in Spanish—where black players routinely exercised authority over white players. In fact, American catchers of high caliber of any color were particularly sought after in the Latin leagues because of their understanding of the finer points of the game.

*Jake Powell Keeps in Shape* In a radio interview in Chicago on July 29, 1938, New York Yankees outfielder Jake Powell said that he kept in shape during the off-season by working as a policeman in Dayton, Ohio, and "cracking niggers over the head." Coming at a time when there was a groundswell

*As a young player with the Oakland club in the early 1930s, Joe DiMaggio was introduced to Biz Mackey, a player in the old Negro leagues whom some regard as the greatest of all Negro league catchers. (He is said to have taught Roy Campanella all he knew.) It was typical that white and black players got on fine on their own but that the major leagues simply couldn't find a way to integrate them.*

of liberal support for antidiscrimination legislation in America, his remark was met with protests across black America and a ten-day suspension from play by the commissioner of baseball.

The white press ignored the story after its initial reporting, in general downplaying Powell's comments as jocular despite continuing protests and numerous calls that Powell be banned from baseball for life. Meanwhile, the black press gave extensive coverage to the protests and to efforts by the Yankees to pacify opinion in the black community, including a trip by Powell to Harlem, where he toured bars, streets, and black newspapers issuing denials and seeking forgiveness. The white press checked in again only when Powell's return to the Yankees lineup was greeted with a shower of bottles.

Even so, Powell's radio comments for a while served to elevate the issue of blacks in baseball into national sports headlines, where white indifference was shaken by the New York *Post,* which accused Commissioner Landis of "smug hypocrisy"; and by barbs from the Chicago *Tribune*'s Westbrook Pegler, who wrote that the national pastime dealt with "Negroes as Adolf Hitler treats the Jews."

*Jim Crow in the Hall*   Admission to the Baseball Hall of Fame is popularly considered the dominant distinction in the game. Blacks who made their marks in the integrated major leagues are well-represented there, but controversy still rages over the treatment the Hall has accorded Negro leaguers, only eleven of whom have been enshrined at Cooperstown. Before Ted Williams was inducted into the Hall in 1966, little or no effort was made to include preintegration black stars. The famous slugger took advantage of the occasion of his induction to announce, "I hope that some day Satchel Paige and Josh Gibson will be voted into the Hall of Fame as symbols of the great Negro players who are not here only because they were not given the chance." In 1971 the Hall of Fame Committee on Negro Leagues was formed and, beginning with Satchel Paige, the committee elected nine men before it was disbanded in 1978.

In 1978 the preexisting Committee on Baseball Veterans was expanded to eighteen members, with three seats set aside for blacks, and given the power to select Negro leaguers as well; but in the past decade only two black veterans have been inducted compared to seventeen white veterans. Very few of the eighteen members have any real background in black baseball history. Since only four negative votes are necessary to defeat any candidate, only two veterans may be selected each year, and since most members are more familiar with white players, it seems unlikely that many more Negro leaguers will be inducted.

To those familiar with the quality of Negro leaguers it is clear that these players were among baseball's greatest athletes during one of baseball's greatest eras, and the omission from the Hall of Fame of players such as Smokey Joe Williams, Bullet Rogan, Willie Wells, Dick Redding, and Leon Day—to name but a few—is as glaring as the omission of Sandy Koufax or Joe DiMaggio would be. The recent availability of more comprehensive statistical data for Negro leaguers is one more reason for reconsideration and possible reinstitution of a Negro leagues committee by the Hall of Fame; it remains to be seen whether Negro league admissions to the Hall will be tokenism or long overdue recognition.

*A White Man's Memory Bank*   As historian John B. Holway points out, between 1887 and 1947 black baseball stars played white baseball stars over 400 times in exhibition games. The blacks won 269 games and the whites 169, but of the victorious black players, only 11 have been admitted to the Baseball Hall of Fame compared to over 140 white immortals from the pre–Jackie Robinson era. Monte Irvin recalls that during the mid-1930s, when blacks despaired of ever getting a chance to play in the majors because "the feeling of the country was so intense," black all-stars beat white all-stars consistently. Despite the quality of black players, Holway writes, "When the American Civil Liberties Union urged [then Commissioner of Baseball Bowie] Kuhn to open the doors of Cooperstown to blacks on a parity with whites, his legal counsel replied that Cooperstown is a private club that does not come under interstate commerce or the civil rights laws passed by the U.S. Congress."

*Black Meets White*   On September 18, 1869, the Pythians of Philadelphia became the first black team in recorded history to play a white team, beating the City Items, 27–17. But by the turn of the century, the prevailing view was that blacks should be relegated to a peripheral role in baseball. In 1906 the great black Philadelphia X-Giants, featuring Rube Foster, John Henry Lloyd, and Charlie "Chief Tokohama" Grant (whom John McGraw had previously tried to sign to the Orioles as an Indian), challenged the winner of the 1906 White Sox–Cubs World Series to a series to determine the championship of the United States. Their challenge was not accepted.

On Sunday, October 19, 1930, when the Baltimore Black Sox defeated an all-star team of major and minor league players for the fifth time in as many tries in the first game of the annual fall series played at the Black Sox' Maryland Baseball Park, Baltimore submariner Webster McDonald shut out Eddie Rommel of the world champion Philadelphia Athletics in a 1–0 pitching duel. Other pitchers who fell before the Black Sox included Lefty Grove, Howard Ehmke, George Earnshaw, Roy Sherid, and Jack Ogden. To save further embarrassment, in the mid-1930s organized baseball forbade more than three major leaguers per squad to compete against black teams. Commissioner Landis had previously forbidden players to wear major league uniforms in exhibition games against black clubs, apparently to prevent people from finding out that barnstorming major leaguers were losing to black clubs.

Although blacks won most of the semipro and exhibition games and series played between blacks and whites, one of the reasons whites gave for refusing to hire blacks in the majors was that blacks played an inferior brand of baseball. In all fairness, it must be noted that whites had been conditioned to relate to black ballplayers as roadshow clowns whose quality of play was far inferior to that of white players; but by no means everyone, even at the time, bought this rationale. (Decades later, Bob Feller was outspoken in his belief that blacks did not have the physical competence to compete in the big leagues.) Nowadays, of course, the prevailing view is that blacks are naturally gifted athletes.

In case anyone still has doubts, the statistics speak for themselves. In 1967, twenty-three blacks in the National League and seventeen blacks in the American League accounted for well over half of the base hits made that year. Black players continue to consistently outperform white players. In 1970, Bill Yancy, who was a shortstop for the New York Black Yankees, pointed out, "We had eleven out of the top twelve hitters in the National League last year and four out of the top five in the American. Hell, we've always had players of that caliber, only we never got any recognition."

*Under the Lights*   The Negro leagues were first on the playing field in more than just hits and runs. On July 25, 1930, the Kansas City Monarchs and the Pittsburgh Homestead Grays played the first night game ever played at Forbes Field, home of the Pittsburgh Pirates. Eighteen-year-old future super-star Josh Gibson got his start as a pro when the Grays' catcher, frustrated by inconsistencies in the Monarchs' portable lighting system, walked off the field, and manager Judy Johnson plucked Gibson from the stands on the strength of his local reputation. The first night game in the major leagues was played at Crosley Field on May 24, 1935.

*Fast Cool Papa*   Many stories have been told about how fast Cool Papa Bell really was. Satchel Paige, whose reputation as a storyteller equaled his skill as a pitcher, liked to tell about the time he was pitching to "Cool" and Bell drilled a ball through his legs. Paige claimed that the ball hit Cool Papa in the back as he slid into second. On another occasion, Bell got into a dispute with a catcher who believed he had tagged him out after he took off for first on a passed third strike. In reality, Bell had rounded the bases and was safe at home by the time the catcher tagged him.

One of Satchel Paige's more outrageous claims was that Bell was so fast he could turn out the light and jump into bed before it got dark. In 1981 at the Negro Baseball Reunion in Ashland, Kentucky, Bell revealed that during the 1937 winter season, when he and Paige roomed together in California,

*James "Cool Papa" Bell, one of the Hall of Famers from the old Negro leagues, here slides into third. Famed for his fast baserunning—he is said to have been able to score from first on a sacrifice bunt—Bell is one of many Afro-Americans who would have added much to the major leagues, but he was forced to spend his entire career (1922–46) in the Negro leagues, mostly with the Homestead Grays.*

he discovered that due to some anomaly of wiring there was a three-second delay between the time the wall switch was flicked and the time the light went out. Aware that Paige was telling tall stories about him, Bell told Paige that he was prepared to demonstrate just how fast he really was. "I turned off the light, jumped in bed, and pulled the covers all the way up to my chin. Then, the light went out. It was the only time I ever saw Satchel speechless."

*The Superstar as a Young Fan*   Monte Irvin recollects from his childhood, "There was an A&P store on 141st and Edgecomb Avenue where we did our grocery shopping. I remember having my mother buy all these boxes of Wheaties because they had pictures of the ballplayers on the back. I had Mel Ott, Carl Hubbell, Hal Schumacher, Danny McFayden, and Joe Medwick, among others, tacked up on my wall. Not a black ballplayer in the bunch. I do recall that occasionally to 'fill the void' I cut out pictures of black ballplayers that appeared in the *Amsterdam News* and the Pittsburgh *Courier* and put them up too."

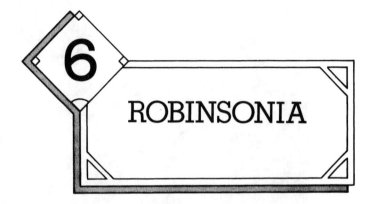

# 6

# ROBINSONIA

**I**n 1947 the Dead Sea Scrolls were discovered in Wadi Qumran, India and Pakistan became separate nations, *Kontiki* crossed the Pacific, and Jackie Robinson became the first black man to play baseball in the major leagues in the twentieth century. His debut was the most widely commented upon episode in American race relations of the century—in some ways even more explosive than the assassination of Martin Luther King, Jr., or the struggle for desegregation—for it marked a cooperative attempt to elevate the American creed of liberty, equality, and justice for all above the time-honored American tradition of social and economic discrimination. And it happened in baseball where, above all, Jackie Robinson's turn at the plate personified the hope that amidst the reality of inequality, the American Dream really could encompass everyone regardless of race.

As Ed Charles, third baseman with the 1969 championship Mets, remembers, when Jackie Robinson and the Dodgers came through his hometown of Daytona, Florida, to play in spring exhibition, "Everybody in our part of town wanted to see him. Old people and small children, invalids and town drunks all walked through the streets. Some people were on crutches, and some blind people clutched the arms of friends, walking slowly on parade to that ball park to sit in the segregated section. We watched him play that day and finally believed what we had read in the papers, that one of us was out there on the

*After being signed on to the Dodgers club in 1945, Jackie Robinson spent the 1946 season with their farm team, the Montreal Royals. While there, he received tips on how to play second base by an ex–major leaguer who was among the first to befriend him—Al Campanis.*

ball field. When the game was over, we kids followed Jackie as he walked with his teammates to the train station, and when the train pulled out, we ran down the tracks listening for the sounds as far as we could. And when we finally couldn't hear it any longer, we ran some more and finally put our ears on the tracks so we could feel the vibrations of that train carrying Jackie Robinson. We wanted to be part of him as long as we could."

Forty years after the fact nagging questions remain about the fulfillment of the promise of Jackie Robinson's debut. In retrospect it is clear that Jackie Robinson came to the majors under white terms, under rules created to make him more acceptable to whites, and that he was promoted as a special kind of black man, more intelligent, more moral, more disciplined, more deserving. Given this disingenuous approach and Robinson's level of skill before his elevation to the Dodgers, it is not clear that this was the best way. Indeed, after Branch Rickey was forced out of the Dodgers organization in the mid-1950s, he commented that perhaps Robinson had not been the ideal pioneer he had envisioned. Monte Irvin, himself a great Negro leagues player and a pioneer in the white majors, presented the issues in a 1985 interview with Stephen Garger: "In their selection Jackie [Robinson] was certainly the right guy to pick. He was not that good a ballplayer in the beginning but he made himself a good ballplayer. . . . He was very thrilling on the bases and a team leader—never say die. Plus he was highly intelligent, very vocal and the kind of guy we needed to break the color barrier. Now if they had started maybe ten, fifteen years sooner, they would have gotten the real stars. I'm talking about guys like Josh Gibson, Buck Leonard, Cool Papa Bell, Ray Dandridge, Leon Day, Raymond Brown, Willie Wells, Bill Wright—I mean these are guys who could really play. I *mean* could play, just had the natural talent. No telling how good they could have become if they had gotten the chance. But Jack did a good job and we're all grateful for that. He paved the way. . . . He got a chance and he did it. He made it better economically, financially, socially, everywhere."

Today black Americans are accepted as players, mostly for certain positions, but still not as managers; and not in executive positions in any substantial numbers. In fact, for these and other reasons, the number of blacks coming into baseball has declined steadily over the past decade. As New Yorker Ken Ferber pointed out in the December 27, 1987, *New York Times* sports letters column, "As we celebrate the 40th anniversary of Jackie Robinson's entry into baseball, we should be grateful to Al Campanis for reminding us of the continued prejudice and discrimination that permeates major league baseball."

Dr. Harry Edwards claims that former Dodgers general manager Al

Campanis, who enunciated on network TV the shared perspective of the baseball establishment that blacks don't have the intellectual "necessities" to be executives, "did more in ten minutes than we've done in twenty years. When a black says something, we're radicals, we've got a chip on our shoulder. When a white says something, people have to listen and evaluate and respond. . . . [Campanis] should have been nominated for the NAACP Man of the Year Award."

Jackie Robinson did not end discrimination in sports and society. In fact, after forty years and major "blunders" from spokesmen such as Campanis and Jimmy the Greek, who attributed black athletic superiority to the selective breeding blacks were allegedly subject to as slaves, white Americans are just getting around to acknowledging the racial reality that black Americans live with every day. As ceremonies at second base took place on opening days throughout both leagues in 1987 to commemorate Jackie Robinson's "integration" of American sport, Bill Comiskey evoked in *The Minneapolis Review of Baseball* how he first felt when Robinson came up to the Dodgers: "The natural order of things was . . . that baseball was white, all white. Baseball was the white people's game. The uniforms were white, the ball was white, the fans were white and all of the players were white. I was born into it. That's the way it was. Now, along comes this Negro to upset the natural order of things. And I resented it!"

Comiskey grew to accept the ballplayer, then the black, then the man, just as many Americans were moved by Jackie Robinson's performance upon the ultimate stage of ultraconservative American tradition to push beyond their usual suspicions of change and difference. Because of Jackie Robinson, some visible part of racism changed forever. But baseball is still the mirror of our nation, not its determining factor. Until racism is gone from American society its ugliness will continue to shine like a horrid beacon on and off the diamond.

*Rickey's Real Motives*    Many former Negro leaguers feel that Branch Rickey's principal reason for signing Jackie Robinson was to lure black fans into Ebbets Field. Robinson's older brother Mack recently commented, "That was business clear and simple. He wanted a black player because he thought it would help the Brooklyn club win and he thought it would bring people into the ballpark."

If Rickey truly regarded talent as the only criterion for evaluating an athlete, as he often said, he could have hired black players long before Robinson; if he wanted to act on deap-seated beliefs of racial equality and equal opportunity, he could have hired blacks to work in nonplaying baseball jobs, either before or after Jackie Robinson, and probably with much less fanfare. In all fairness, it is difficult to speculate from here on what might have been done then, and perhaps we should simply be grateful that Rickey had the courage to take the first step.

We do know that economics, that time-honored and effective method of motivation, was behind most of Rickey's moves, and that in the case of Jackie Robinson he was right on the money. Roger Kahn points out in his *Boys of Summer* that spring barnstorming trips through the South with the Robinson Dodgers stirred up so much excitement that the games invariably sold out, and Robinson annually earned his salary before the season began.

Likewise, the massive migration of blacks to Western and Northern cities during and after World War II held the promise of appealing revenues to any club that could tap this growing market. White baseball executives knew that black fans supported their own teams because they rented their stadiums to black leagues for a percentage of the gate, usually 10 to 20 percent in addition to concession rights; and Negro league games at the Polo Grounds and Yankee Stadium regularly drew crowds of twenty thousand to thirty thousand (Rickey, in fact, was shut out from this lucrative source of income because of various agreements among the other New York clubs). In the late '40s, attendance at black all-star games in Comiskey Park topped forty thousand.

Rickey first attempted to exploit this market by creating an all-black Dodgers club, the Brooklyn Brown Dodgers, which was to be one of five charter clubs in his projected United States League. While his authorized biographer and confidant, Arthur Mann, helped perpetuate the belief that Rickey created the Brown Dodgers solely as a screen to cover scouts searching for the ideal black man to join the white Brooklyn Dodgers, a growing body of evidence seems to indicate that his motive in this case was to establish an organization that would give him first pick from the best black baseball talent when and if integration occurred in the major leagues. Rickey, after all, had created the major league farm system, and was quite capable of conceiving and implementing such long-range planning. In any case, whether he signed Robinson to play for the Dodgers or, as some assert, to manage the Brown Dodgers, he stood ready to wrest control and profits from the black owners if his United States League venture succeeded; and to be the first with a black player in organized ball if it failed, a situation that also promised—and delivered—substantial financial benefits.

The rising tide of political and moral agitation against discrimination in baseball peaked two months after Rickey secretly signed Robinson, when New York's mayor, Fiorello La Guardia, requested permission from his special Mayor's Committee on Baseball to announce that the city's three major league teams would "shortly begin signing Negro players." Rickey, who didn't want his signing of Robinson to be perceived as a response to political pressure—which indeed it was not—persuaded La Guardia to postpone his announcement for a week, then sent Robinson to Montreal and arranged a press conference. Having amply prepared himself for any eventuality, he thus seized the moment and established himself as the initiator of the integration of baseball. By so doing, Rickey may also have realized a lifelong aspiration to be of greater cultural significance than he might otherwise have achieved in his capacity as baseball's greatest executive, a powerful but limited role. It is to his credit that in Robinson he chose a man equal to the task, at least as he saw it. Furthermore, his belief that the Dodgers would get an edge on other teams if they were the first to sign blacks was borne out when Brooklyn became the dominant team in the National League for a decade following Robinson's debut; and the National League, which was quicker to take advantage of the vast reservoir of black major league talent, gained a similar supremacy over the American League.

### Jackie Robinson: The Soul of the Pioneer

Everytime I look at my pocketbook I see Jackie Robinson.

—Willie Mays

Long held up as a model of restraint and decorum, Jack Roosevelt Robinson slowly revealed that it was not his innermost nature to turn the other cheek. A highly emotional, competitive, aggressive, and even militant man, when Branch Rickey revealed to him that his strategy for integrating baseball was for Robinson to demonstrate a combination of meekness and skill, Robinson replied, "Are you looking for a Negro who is afraid to fight back?" But he kept his mouth shut, at least until other teams and the American League also hired blacks.

In 1949, perhaps his best year as a player, when Robinson proved himself to be among the very best second basemen of all time, Rickey finally agreed that Robinson could be himself. Robinson first addressed himself to Ben Chapman, the Phillies manager who had led a vile stream of racial abuse from his bench during Robinson's first season, and had then issued the self-serving statement, "If Robinson has the stuff, he will be accepted in baseball the same as the Sullivans, the Lombardis, the Schultzes and the Grodzickis. All that I expect him to do is prove it." In 1949 Robinson told Chapman, "You SOB,

. . . if you open your mouth one more time, I'm gonna . . . kick the shit out of you." When a sportswriter advised Robinson to show gratitude if he expected to win the 1949 MVP award, Robinson replied, "If I have to thank *you* to win . . . I don't want the fucking thing." His talent was so undeniable that he got the MVP, and his fiery play helped spirit the Dodgers to six flags and a world title while his "black aggressiveness" continued to be a source of aggravation to those who felt he was too pushy and wanted too much too soon.

When he was traded to the Giants in 1957 at the age of thirty-eight (he had started in major league baseball when he was twenty-eight) Robinson shrewdly announced his retirement in a *Look* magazine article he got paid for, thereby angering the press, the Dodgers, and the Giants, negating the deal while demonstrating that he was very much his own man. Once out of baseball he became a major spokesman in the fight against racial discrimination. After he was elected to the Baseball Hall of Fame in 1962, he became particularly outspoken about the lack of blacks in executive positions in baseball.

Shortly before his early death at the age of fifty-three, the ailing pioneer, who suffered from diabetes and had had a heart attack in 1968, made a rare appearance to be honored at the 1972 World Series, where he threw out the first ball. Here the outspoken Robinson, who had become so angered by the lack of black coaches and managers that he usually avoided baseball gatherings, shocked his public by using almost his last breath to express his bitterness about baseball's lack of progress in integration off the field. "Someday," he told a capacity crowd and the national television audience, "I'd like to be able to look over at third base and see a black man managing the ball club. . . . I'd like to live to see a black manager." Nine days later he died of a heart attack in his Stamford, Connecticut, home. As former teammate Pee Wee Reese expressed it, "Jackie just seemed to get older faster than the rest of us. It had to be what he went through. I don't think Jack ever stopped carrying that burden. I'm no doctor but I'm sure it cut his life short." Three more years passed before major league baseball hired the first of the three black managers it has employed since 1947.

*Two Views of a Baseball Pioneer* Richie Ashburn, who retired after fifteen major league seasons with two batting titles and 2,574 hits, came from a small town in Nebraska and never saw a black man or a Catholic until he was eighteen years old and playing professional baseball. In 1948 he began playing for the Phillies under manager Ben Chapman. According to Ashburn, concerning Jackie Robinson, "We had been told to slide hard into him as often as we could. We wanted to put him out of the game, and we thought that his legs had taken a lot of punishment. I slid into him this one time and really cut him badly. The trainer rushed out to second base, and I could see he was bleeding the same color blood as me. I just stood there and felt ashamed of myself, like a real jerk. There was no reason for that. It wasn't part of baseball. The next game we played I walked over to him and apologized for cutting him and told him that it wouldn't happen again. It never did."

John Downey, a former ticket seller at Ebbets Field, recalls, "I started with the Dodgers in 1940 as a stile boy. Those are the kids who turn the stiles when people pay their way into the park. My salary was fifty cents a day and after the third inning I could go inside for free and watch the rest of the game. I always worked the bleachers. It was fifty-five cents and a dollar ten in later years. By that time I had become a ticket seller and there was always a lot of business and a lot of tickets sold when Jackie Robinson joined the club. We used to sell out most of the time in a big series against the Giants before he came, but we started selling out against the Cubs and Cards and Phillies and just about everybody after he came. I think Jackie Robinson had a lot to do with increasing the Dodger business. I don't know the figures because I was only interested in my own take."

### A Media Event

I do not care if half the league strikes. Those who do it will encounter quick retribution. They will be suspended, and I don't care if it wrecks the National League for five years. This is the United States of America, and one citizen has as much right to play as another.

—attributed to Ford Frick, May 1947

The widely circulated and generally believed story that the St. Louis Cardinals planned to go on strike rather than face a Dodgers team that included Jackie Robinson does not bear up under close scrutiny. In fact, the ringing and eloquent words that National League President Ford Frick supposedly used to condemn and abort the alleged strike were never said or written by him in the way they were reported. Similarly, the widely held belief that New York *Herald-Tribune* sports editor Stanley Woodward *averted* the strike by breaking the story doesn't make much sense; his version first appeared the day after the Dodgers and Cardinals completed their three-game series.

While there can be no doubt that certain Cardinals team members grumbled about playing with a black man—as certain members of the Dodgers also did—and may even have mentioned the word *strike* (the possibility of a strike among the Dodgers themselves was met head on by manager Leo Durocher during spring training), pioneering black sportswriter Wendell Smith wrote that the incident was greatly exaggerated and "made a better newspaper story than anything else." Nowadays the flap would be perceived as a "media event," that is, a nonevent that sells newspapers or improves TV ratings.

Apparently the story began when Cardinals owner Sam Breadon asked player representatives Terry Moore and Marty Marion if the team worried too much about a black man in the Dodgers' lineup; after winning the 1946 World Series and setting new club attendance records, the Cards had dropped eleven of their first thirteen games in 1947, and Breadon was concerned about anything that might affect team play. He also consulted with Frick when he heard rumors of an impending team strike. Frick made it clear that the National League was prepared to support Robinson's right to play and would suspend any players who might strike. Moore and Marion assured Breadon that there was no strike planned. Breadon assured Frick that the whole thing was "a tempest in a teapot." It is likely that the matter would have ended there if St. Louis team physician Robert F. Hyland hadn't expressed Breadon's concern to old friend Rud Rennie, baseball writer for the *Herald-Tribune.* Rennie took it to sports editor Woodward, Woodward spoke to Frick—who confirmed he would support Robinson's right to play—and then Woodward generated and copyrighted the story that contained the famous ultimatum that he later said Frick had "in effect" pronounced.

While precious little documentation exists to indicate that Cardinals locker-room chatter ever reached the level of mutiny, plenty of evidence indicates that Woodward's approach was opportunistic. Reports that Enos Slaughter and Stan Musial came to blows over the matter demonstrate how greatly stories of the strike were blown out of proportion: Musial points out that he was either in a Brooklyn hospital with an appendicitis attack at the time or otherwise too weak to be "worried about Robinson or Slaughter or anybody else."

The newspapers of the day might have made better use of their space to report that for seven years in St. Louis Robinson was barred from staying with the team at the Chase Park Plaza Hotel, which, when it finally did admit blacks, asked them to eat in their rooms, a color barrier that Robinson broke by simply sitting down in the dining room one day and asking to be served.

But in the end it is hard to condemn the overblown press response, for Frick's firm stance—however embellished, distorted, or exploited—coupled with the equally unequivocal position taken by Commissioner Chandler, demonstrated beyond the shadow of a doubt that public opinion was firmly behind integration on the diamond, and that those who thought otherwise were backing a lost cause.

*Indignities*   Racism in baseball has appeared in as many forms as there are expressions of hatred and ignorance. For the pioneer black players, discrimination off the field—on the team bus, in the restaurant, at the hotel—tended to be a greater problem than discrimination on the field. In the late 1960s, Jim Bouton reported the experience of black infielder Leon McFadden, who grew up in a mixed neighborhood in Los Angeles and had never had a racial encounter until his team bus stopped at a restaurant in Georgia. When the counterman asked him if he would like to eat in the kitchen, McFadden ingenuously replied that he was happy sitting where he was. He was told that he wouldn't be served because of the color of his skin. Hurt and angry, he returned to the bus, where he got angry again when his teammates brought him food. "McFadden said that incident marked him. For the first time in his life he began to view white people with anger and suspicion." Well-meaning but insensitive teammates added to his suspicions: "We'll be riding on the bus and we'll pass a couple of Negro girls on the street and one of the white players will say, 'Hey, Mac, there's a soul sister for you.' Now, why do I have to have any special interest in a black girl? And why can't *he* be just as interested in the black girl? And why can't I be interested in a white girl?''

Monte Irvin recalls that during his first spring training with the Giants organization, when the team bus stopped at a restaurant, he stayed aboard and white teammates brought him sandwiches; they stayed in air-conditioned hotels with private bathrooms, he stayed in a black rooming house with one toilet. Bathrooms were off limits to black players traveling in the South; Curt Flood recalls with bitterness how the bus used to stop along the highway so he could relieve himself. Hank Aaron recalls what happened when the bus reached its destination: "It was a silent kind of thing. The white players might have been joking and laughing when we drove into town, but when the unloading started it would get quiet." According to Piper Davis, this was the routine: "Go to the ballpark. Get in the bus and we go where we're going and we take them to their hotel and we take that great big old bus and drive me across over to the black hotel. In the evening . . . we drive that great old empty bus over to my hotel to pick me up . . . go back to the hotel where they're staying, and then go to the ballpark."

Young black players from the North tended to be confused by the mechanics of segregation. Frank Robinson couldn't figure out why he could do as he pleased in "California or Utah, but not South Carolina." White players from the North had to learn that they couldn't ask their black teammates to join them for dinner or the movies in some towns. White cab drivers transporting black players were sometimes reprimanded and ticketed by white cops. The unaccustomed social isolation black players were subjected to was sometimes intense. Black Puerto Rican player Vic Power recalls, "I was the first black player in Syracuse when the Yankees sent me there in 1951. There was no discrimination on the club, but in Kansas City the next year the city was bad. I could go to no movie, no restaurant, just play my games and there was no place for me to go, just home. And home was a hotel in the colored section. . . . Being a human being I never thought people were going to be like that, making me live alone, go nowhere and get poor pay."

Kansas City police stopped Power several times when he was driving with his wife, a light-complexioned Puerto Rican with red hair. They wanted to know what she was doing with a black man; on other occasions they wanted to know what she was doing in the colored section, which was the only place they could live. "In Kansas City every time I take my wife to the ball park and they see me with her they say, 'Oh, there's Vic Power with that white girl again.' And then the writers go all around the country saying, 'Power, he no good, he go after white girl.' " When Power went to City Hall to complain about being stopped while driving with his wife, he was told that he was being stopped because his car matched the description of a stolen vehicle.

There is not enough ink to list all the indignities suffered by black players. *The Sporting News* for June 8, 1987, reported that Oklahoma State senior center fielder Anthony Blackmon was suspended for two games in the College World Series after he mooned Mississippi fans who had been taunting him during the NCAA tournament. Blackmon, the Oklahoma Cowboys' only black player, who hit .397 in sixty-six games, had, according to coach Gary Ward, been "called a skillet . . . a nigger, a coon, and a buckwheat . . . a combination of profanity and racist statements that rained for six days."

As a white Texas Leaguer once commented to Chuck Harmon, "Hell, you don't know where you're gonna stay the next night; you don't know how you're gonna get to the ballpark; and you don't know where you're gonna eat. This game is hard enough." Many of the black players who withstood this hideous initiation to make good at baseball succeeded because the insults pushed them to play harder, and they took it out on the ball; Curt Flood claims he solved his problem by playing his guts out. But in addition to channeling frustrations into greater effort, humor was an important weapon. Vic Power, whose native Puerto Rican society is stratified along economic, not color, lines, once astonished a waitress in a Little Rock, Arkansas, restaurant who told him they didn't serve Negroes by replying, "That's all right, I don't eat them." On another occasion Power allegedly avoided a fine for jaywalking by successfully convincing a Southern judge that he thought the "Walk" and "Don't Walk" signs applied to whites only.

*The Stamford Bombers Make History*   In 1947, while the press crowed about the breaking of the color line in Brooklyn, the greatest number of blacks to play on any club in organized ball did so in Stamford, Connecticut, where a total of six blacks, more than a third of the sixteen blacks who played in minor league ball in 1946 and 1947, performed for the Class-B Colonial League Stamford Bombers. Stamford's proximity to New York compelled owners Lou Haneles and Stan Moor to scour college, minor, semipro, and black circuits for talent worthy of fans familiar with big-league play. Their efforts led to the signing of Johnny "Schoolboy" Haith on July 24, 1947, followed by the acquisition of five other black players, including Puerto Rican infielder Carlos Santiago, from the East Coast Negro leagues, and pitcher Fred Shepherd, formerly of the Atlanta Black Sox. In an August 18 exhibition game against the Newark Eagles, who had lost Larry Doby to the Cleveland Indians in July but still featured Monte Irvin, Johnny Davis, and Lennie Pearson, Shepherd and the Bombers shut down the 1946 Negro leagues champs 9–6. After finishing third in the league during the regular season, the Bombers captured the President's Cup and the 1947 Colonial League championship in postseason play. Neither the Bombers nor the Stamford fans reported any special problems for their integrated team.

*Jackie Robinson and the Watermelon*   After he broke the three-year silence he had guaranteed Branch Rickey, Jackie Robinson became the focus of locker-room reporters. The articulate, outspoken player soon learned that "as long as I appeared to ignore insult and injury, I was a martyred hero to a lot of people who had sympathy for the underdog. But the minute I began to sound-off—I became a swell-head, wise guy, an 'uppity' nigger." Robinson did get into as many scrapes with baseball executives as any spirited player, but in a climate of racial tension, almost anything can be taken as racist, and longtime Dodger broadcaster Vin Scully recalls one occasion when paranoia definitely got the better of Robinson.

In 1950 or 1951 at the conclusion of a game on a blistering hot day at Philadelphia's Shibe Park, an old fan took it upon himself to pass out huge slices of watermelon to all the Dodgers as they emerged from the clubhouse exit and boarded their bus. The tunnel-like nature of the exit prevented Robinson from seeing what had preceded him, and when he came out the fan smiled and handed him a piece of watermelon, too. Unfortunately, "gifts" of watermelons had by then become a standard ploy in bench-jockeying black players—not to mention the time-honored racist stereotype of pickaninny-with-watermelon—and Robinson lost no time in telling the kindly fan exactly what he thought of his behavior. His duty completed, he boarded the bus to find most of his teammates enjoying the refreshing fruit.

*Head-Hunting Negroes*   Larry Doby, who integrated the American League in 1947, relates, "I once checked statistics to find out whether there was any truth in the rumor that Negro players were being thrown at more than whites. The statistics prove it's true, no matter what some of us say. I was knocked down in many games. I was hit by more pitched balls than any player of equal power in the league. Jackie [Robinson], Campy [Roy Campanella] and Minnie Minoso were also hit repeatedly. We were hit 75 per cent more than Joe DiMaggio, Ted Williams or Stan Musial. If a guy wants to brush you back, that's baseball. But head-hunting Negroes isn't baseball."

During the 1949 season, when blacks first appeared in the minor leagues in significant numbers, a near epidemic of beanings resulted in the hospitalization of one out of four black nonpitchers in Triple-A ball. As historian Jules Tygiel points out in his incomparable study of the integration of baseball, *Baseball's Great Experiment,* there is no doubt that "black players, particularly those pioneering in a new league, faced greater danger than the average performer."

*The Great Equalizer*   On Valentine's Day 1978, political scientist and civil rights activist Richard Lapchick was working late in his office at Virginia Wesleyan College in Norfolk, Virginia. At 10:45 P.M. two men wearing stocking masks forced their way into his office, gagged him, beat him, carved the word *nigger* (misspelled "niger") on his stomach with his office scissors, and left him unconscious. Their repeated insistence that Lapchick had "no business in South Africa" (they also called him a "nigger lover" and asked him if he would continue doing what he had been doing *"now"*) left little doubt that their assault was connected with his role as National Chairperson of the American Coordinating Committee for Equality in Sport and Society, an organization that was at the time engaged in a successful campaign to end sports contact between the United States and apartheid South Africa.

Lapchick, son of Joe Lapchick, the former New York Knickerbockers coach who helped integrate pro basketball, soon found himself being accused by medical examiners of inflicting the markings on his stomach himself. Despite expert testimony that this would have been impossible and the wholly positive results of a polygraph test to which he submitted after initially refusing on the grounds that victims of crimes should not have to prove their veracity, Lapchick found little support from either the criminal justice system or the media. One UPI correspondent went so far as to ask Lapchick's mother if she thought he had cut himself; and TV's Walter Cronkite reported that "a Virginia state medical examiner has concluded that Lapchick apparently inflicted the stomach wounds on himself," and "refused to take a lie-detector test." Lapchick's case thus became a classic instance of what Karen Russell, daughter of black basketball great Bill Russell, has identified as society's presumption that racism no longer exists: "Given this myth, the person who complains about genuine harassment can expect to be seen as the source of the conflict."

In his own account of the incident, Lapchick wonders why "we boycott games to protest communism and do nothing in the face of racism or fascism." He describes his book *Broken Promises: Racism in American Sports* (New York: St. Martin's/Marek, 1984) as "the story of how little has changed since Jackie Robinson took that courageous first step." Pointing out that in 1983, 110 of the 123 major league coaches were white, he writes, "even considering the important exceptions, sports helps to mire most blacks in the quicksands of ignorance that only perpetuates their poverty." Although American society has fostered the idea that sport is a great racial equalizer, "sport free of racism can only exist in a society free of racism."

*Compare and Contrast*

If colored clubs were admitted, there would be in all probability some division of feeling, whereas, by excluding them no injury could result to anybody and the possibility of any rupture being created on political grounds would be avoided.

—The National Association of Base-Ball Players, on excluding blacks in 1867

### THE COLOR LINE DRAWN IN BASEBALL

The International League directors held a secret meeting at the Genesee House yesterday, and the question of colored players was freely discussed. Several representatives declared that many of the best players in the league are anxious to leave on account of the colored element, and the board finally directed Secretary White to approve of no more contracts with colored men.

> —The Newark *Daily Journal,* reporting the banning of blacks in the International League, July 15, 1887

Beyond the fundamental requirement that a major-league player must have unique ability and good character and habits, I do not recall one instance where baseball has allowed either race, creed or color to enter into its selection of players.

> —National League President John A. Heydler, 1933

There is no rule, nor to my knowledge, has there ever been, formal or informal, or any understanding, written or unwritten, subterranean or sub-anything, against the hiring of Negroes in the major leagues.

Each club is entirely free to employ Negro players to any and all extent it pleases. The matter is solely for each club's decision, without restriction whatsoever.

> —Commissioner of Baseball Judge Kenesaw Mountain Landis, 1943

I'd love to have you on my team and so would all the other big league managers. But it's not up to us. Get after Landis.

> —Chicago White Sox manager Jimmy Dykes, speaking to Jackie Robinson, quoted in the *Daily Worker,* May 26, 1942

I have been connected with the Red Sox for twelve years and during that time we have never had a single request for a tryout by a colored applicant. It is beyond my understanding how anyone can insinuate or believe that all ballplayers, regardless of race, color, or creed have not been treated in the American way as far as having an equal opportunity to play for the Red Sox.

> —Red Sox General Manager Eddie Collins, 1945

As it is, the field for the colored professional is limited to a very narrow scope in the base ball world. When he looks into the future he sees no place for him in the Chicago Americans or Nationals (champions); nor the Athletics (American), or New York (National, ex-champions), even were he superior to Lajoie, or Wagner, Waddell or Mathewson, Kling or Schreck. Consequently he loses interest. He knows that, so far shall I go, and no farther, and, as it is with the profession, so it is with his ability.

   —*Sol. White's Official Base Ball Guide, History of Colored Base Ball* (A *Spalding Guide*), 1907

Robinson was the wrong man, brought into major league baseball in the wrong way, for the wrong reasons, to the inevitable detriment of both the Negro Leagues and the majority of players whose careers and fortunes depended upon the leagues' survival in some legitimate guise.

   —Dr. Harry Edwards, *Journal of Sport and Social Issues,* 1983

For me, conventional team spirit was out of the question. My teammates despised me and rejected me as subhuman. I would gladly have sent them all to hell.

   —Player Curt Flood describing his season in the Carolina League

In essence, Jim Crow has evolved into the thoroughly modern "Mr. James Crow, Esquire." The "White Only" and "Colored Only" signs are gone but the fundamental reality . . . for the masses of Black people . . . is . . . subjugation within a two-tiered society predicated upon White superiority and Black subjugation . . . *sport inevitably recapitulates the structure and dynamics of human and institutional relationships both within and between societies and the ideological sentiments rationalizing those relationships.*

   . . . The bulk of the literature on the black athlete reflects the myth that a racist American society has succeeded somehow in producing and sustaining a substantially non-racist sports institution.

   —Dr. Harry Edwards, *Journal of Sport and Social Issues,* 1981

Our society has taken to the presumption that racism—and sexism—no longer exist, and that any confrontations are the work of a few bad actors.

   —Karen Russell on "the new racism," *The New York Times Magazine,* 1988

White racism in American society seems to be responsible for black athletic superiority to whites.
  —Dr. Harry Edwards, *The Black Scholar,* November 1971

Americans have always looked for the positive and tried to ignore the negative in sport. That is why each new scandal brings cries of anguish but rarely brings change or acknowledgement of root problems.
  —Richard Lapchick, *Broken Promises: Racism in American Sports,* 1984

*What Did He Say?*  The "question" of whether blacks can *play* baseball at the white major league level has long since become a nonquestion. Historically, the idea that blacks didn't have the competence to play major league ball, once voiced as a serious objection to integration, has given way to the belief that blacks are physically superior. The question now is whether blacks will ever be given a chance to work in baseball *off* the field: Having been granted superior physical endowment, blacks are still considered intellectually inferior by the baseball establishment. Assuming that Al Campanis and Jimmy the Greek represent the ideology of the power structure in professional sports—which is more reasonable than assuming that the ideas they expressed were aberrations—it is a question that may remain with us for some time. Possibly—as Reggie Jackson and many other black baseball men have suggested—until a black man purchases a franchise.

So much has been said about Al Campanis that it might be interesting to examine exactly what he said on Ted Koppel's long-running ABC-TV "Nightline" show, which, on the evening of April 6, 1987, was dedicated to commemorating and celebrating the fortieth anniversary of Jackie Robinson's integration of the major leagues. Al Campanis, Dodgers vice-president and general manager, considered a fair and decent man by everybody who knows him in baseball, was featured as a man who held special memories of Robinson. The seventy-year-old veteran of forty seasons in baseball had been a shortstop in Montreal in 1946, where he had befriended, defended, and tutored Jackie Robinson in the intricacies of his position at second base. As a Dodger executive, he was proud of his role in keeping Robinson's memory alive in the Dodgers organization.

Ted Koppel opened the show by remarking that forty years ago Jackie Robinson had "changed the face of baseball and the American social fabric forever." Rachel Robinson, Jackie Robinson's widow, lost no time in pointing out that in that forty-year period baseball "has not been able to integrate at any level other than the players' level." (All direct quotations are taken from the official transcript of the show unless otherwise indicated.) When Mr. Koppel asked Mr. Campanis if the reason for the lack of blacks in nonplaying positions might be prejudice, Campanis replied, "No, I don't believe it's prejudice. I truly believe that they may not have some of the necessities to be, let's say, a field manager, or perhaps a general manager." Asserting that blacks were not good swimmers because they lacked buoyancy, Campanis continued, "I think many of them [blacks] are highly intelligent, but they may not have the desire to be in the front office . . . they're outstanding athletes, very God-gifted, and they're very wonderful people, and that's all I can tell you about them." To which Ted Koppel replied, addressing another guest, noted baseball writer Roger Kahn, "I must say I'm flabbergasted. It seems to me we haven't made all that much progress, then, in forty years." Mr. Kahn agreed.

Campanis ended his participation on the show by claiming that blacks "are gifted with great musculature and various other things, they're fleet of foot, and this is why there are a lot of black major league baseball players. Now, as far as having the background to become club presidents, or presidents of a bank, I don't know."

Al Campanis's candor cost him his job; some observers thought he must have been drunk to speak that way on network TV. But the double edge of admiration and contempt for black athletes that he expressed was reprised and punctuated nine months later on the anniversary of the birth of Martin Luther King, Jr., when CBS-TV betting analyst and sports figure Jimmy the Greek Snyder was asked to assess the progress of blacks in sports. In a network outbreak of ignorance all the more remarkable because of the fresh lesson of Al Campanis's gaffe, Jimmy the Greek maintained that blacks were superior to whites in athletics because they had been bred by slave owners to be bigger, have bigger thighs, which explained their overrepresentation in sports relative to whites; and that if more blacks became coaches, "there's not going to be anything left for the white people. . . . All the players are black. The only thing that the whites control is the coaching jobs."

Although there is no doubt that he was also expressing what many whites in decision-making positions in sports believe, Jimmy the Greek lost his job, too. Neither he nor Campanis had previously been considered particularly racist, especially Campanis. And although they both did express racist attitudes, if they are guilty of anything it is of ignorance, of not challenging root assumptions thoroughly enough; of too easily accepting what they heard from others—probably men they respected and admired—and of thereby perpetuating the old-boy network that seemingly can always find another assign-ment for a white manager with a less-than-outstanding record but has little time for aspiring black managers.

Within a few months of his indiscretion, Al Campanis signed on to lecture in a Sports and Society class at the University of California at Berkeley given by black activist-sociologist Dr. Harry Edwards, who in the wake of Campanis's firing had been hired by Baseball Commissioner Peter Ueberroth to help resolve the reacknowledged racial inequality in baseball. Despite bold declarations from Ueberroth's office, by the end of 1987 minority representa-tion at baseball's three most spotlighted nonplaying slots—owner, general manager, and field manager—was at zero and in fact, with the loss of Indians manager Pat Corrales, had actually lost ground since Campanis appeared on the Ted Koppel show. As of November 29, 1987, nine teams had renamed a total of thirteen new managers, general managers, and presidents—all white. Former player Billy Sample reported in a June 7, 1987, *New York Times* article that there were seventeen members of minority groups among the 879 front-office employees in major league baseball.

The commissioner's office reported that 102 new minority hirings had occurred in baseball front offices and 78 on the field through 1987, but few of these remotely resembled decision-making positions. With the 1988 season well underway, only two minority third-base coaches existed in the major leagues and only two minority field managers were in place—Frank Robinson and Cookie Rojas, both of whom had been hired after the season began. There were still no black or minority general managers, owners, or club presidents. On May 11, 1987, the Cincinnati Reds, whose hometown is the site of baseball's first professional team and of many landmarks in baseball history, had one black front-office employee—in the ticket office.

*Happy Chandler*  In 1947 Albert "Happy" Chandler was commissioner of baseball. He recalls, "I don't understand—I have never understood—why Branch Rickey took the full credit for breaking the color line with Jackie Robinson. If I hadn't approved the contract transfer from Montreal, the Dodgers' farm, to Brooklyn, Robinson couldn't have played. No chance. In January 1947 in a meeting in the Waldorf-Astoria Hotel in New York, the major league owners had voted fifteen to one against it. . . . I read the votes one by one and all of them were no votes except that single yes vote in Rickey's hand. He was very angry, and he got up and walked out of the meeting room. . . . He said [a few days later], Negro people expected Robinson to be brought up. 'There will be riots in Harlem,' he said, if he didn't do it. He also expressed fear there would be fires in Ebbets Field and the Polo Grounds, and he also said his partners said there would be riots between blacks and whites in their parks if he did it. . . . Then he asked me what I would do about all this. I told him he could do what he wanted with his ballplayers, same as everybody else, and if he brought Jackie Robinson up, he would be treated the same as anybody else. I think that is all he wanted to hear.

"For 24 years Judge Landis, the former commissioner, had not let blacks into the majors. Suppose Landis had been commissioner in 1947 and Rickey had asked Landis to approve the transfer, what do you think Landis would have said? . . . Any time there was a hint of a black player being brought into the game, Landis had a standard answer, I've read the minutes of the meetings. Landis said, 'I've said everything that's going to be said on that subject. The answer is no.' Then he would move on to new business."

At the age of eighty-eight, Chandler explained, "It wasn't my job to decide who could play baseball and who couldn't. It was my job to see that the game was played fairly and that everybody had an equal chance. I think I did that, and I think I can face my Maker with a clean conscience." The following year, however, the eighty-nine-year-old former commissioner, governor, and U.S. senator was forced by Governor Wallace Wilkinson of Kentucky to apologize for a racist remark he made on April 6, 1988, while serving on the University of Kentucky board of trustees. According to Chandler, Governor Wilkinson, who had appointed him to a voting position on the board, "took me to the woodshed" and requested that he apologize to the board but not resign. Said Chandler, "I didn't intend to be offensive to anybody."

*Chicken Baron of Nashua*   In March of 1946 Roy Campanella received a telegram from Branch Rickey asking him to report to the Brooklyn Dodgers' office by March 10. Campy signed and was placed with the Dodgers' Class-B club in Nashua, New Hampshire—the Danville, Illinois, club turned him down—where he was joined by hurler Don Newcombe.

In New Hampshire, chicken farmer Jack Fallgren, following a long-standing tradition of local businessmen offering incentives to home teams, had a standing offer of one-hundred chickens for any Nashua team member who hit a home run. On the way to league MVP honors and a promotion to Triple-A ball in Montreal, Campanella hit thirteen home runs that year and sent most of the thirteen hundred chickens he collected home to Philadelphia. When Fallgren got out of the business, Campanella bought out his remaining stock of thirty-two hundred birds and, with his family, went into the chicken business.

### Death Threats

In those early days in Brooklyn I don't think we ever stopped worrying about him. He got so much hate mail and so many threats on his life. . . . One time in spring training he had to be snuck out of the ballpark with two Negro sportswriters, and when he called later he told us if they didn't get him out of there in time a gang was coming after him. "I might have been lynched," he said, and we just sat down and cried.
—Willa Mae Robinson Walker, Jackie Robinson's older sister

Among the many baseball records that Jackie Robinson holds, the least enviable is the one for receiving the greatest number of death threats. The pointed notice of imminent on-field execution he received on September 16, 1953, in St. Louis, in fact, marked the tenth *reported* death threat he had received in seven years. Although most of the threats were not taken very seriously, as Robinson's wife Rachel later remarked, the possibility of a crazy person shooting from the stands could never be ruled out, and for a while, as a protective measure, Robinson turned down all invitations to speak or be honored, including appearances for commercial endorsements.

In May of 1947 some creative members of the Phillies bench, capitalizing on recent death threats, according to Robinson, "pointed bats at me and made machine gun–like noises." In 1952 a death threat caused armed guards to be assigned to him during a stay in Cincinnati. On one occasion, when a death threat was read to the team in the clubhouse before the game so that Robinson's teammates could appreciate the pressure he was under, an alert player suggested that they might avert a shooting attempt if they all took to the field wearing Robinson's number 42.

*Robeson and Robinson*   By the end of the World War II the hypocrisy and absurdity involved in fighting a war against a country proclaiming a master race ideology while upholding racial discrimination at home had become obvious to many Americans. Paul Robeson, outstanding scholar, athlete, world-renowned actor and singer, undoubtedly spoke for a sizeable proportion of black America when he declared in Paris at the World Congress of the Partisans of Peace in 1949, "It is unthinkable that American Negroes would go to war on behalf of those who have oppressed us for generations against a country [the U.S.S.R.] which in one generation has raised our people to the full dignity of mankind." Robeson may well have overestimated the Soviet Union's commitment to nondiscrimination, but this expression of a widely held sentiment by a man who, with Jackie Robinson (and the much less articulate Joe Louis), was the most visible, successful, and respected black man of the age fed anticommunist fears and reawakened the nightmare of black insurrection among the white establishment.

Jackie Robinson, whom Jesse Jackson once described as believing "more in the American ideal than the people who held the franchise," was a rising star and the very image of the "right kind" of Negro. Asked by government officials to help destroy Robeson's status among Americans by denouncing him before the House Un-American Activities Committee, Robinson agreed. In the contemporary climate of anticommunist hysteria his testimony was so successful that for most Americans Robeson became a nonperson overnight. His concerts were canceled, his passport was revoked by the secretary of state, and his records were removed from stores; his income fell from over one hundred thousand dollars to about six thousand dollars in one year and his name was deleted from sports record books and halls of fame. By the '60s and '70s he was not widely remembered even among blacks.

Eight years later, in 1957, when Robinson announced his retirement from baseball, he evidently still felt the same way, for in his farewell article in *Life* magazine he thanked baseball for giving him the opportunity "to speak on behalf of Negro Americans before the House Un-American Activities Committee and rebuke Paul Robeson." But in his final years Robinson came to believe that he had been manipulated into destroying a man who like himself had put his life on the line in the fight for equality. Referring to his denunciation of Robeson he wrote, "I would reject such an invitation if offered now." In his 1972 autobiography, *I Never Had It Made* (G. P. Putnam's Sons), published in the last year of his life, Robinson's reprise was adamant: "As I write these words now I cannot stand and sing the national anthem. I have learned that I remain a black in a white world."

*A Note on Buoyancy*  What outraged many people about the network gaffes of Al Campanis and Jimmy the Greek was their use of alleged inherited characteristics to explain black superiority or inferiority. Al Campanis's remark that blacks were less buoyant than whites and hence not good swimmers fell on particularly sensitive ears. Many Americans had grown weary of racial theories of convenience such as the long-held belief that blacks were biologically engineered to be good sprinters but were useless at long distances—which had to be rewritten when Africans started to dominate long-distance events. They had come to share the understanding basketball great Bill Russell expressed when he said, "It's okay to be racist as long as you try to sound like a doctor."

This, apparently, was the text former white South African Olympic chief Frank Braun drew upon when he pronounced that swimming was among the sports the black Africans were not suited for, because "the water closes in on their pores so that they cannot get rid of carbon dioxide and they tire quickly." But buoyancy *is* a horse of another color, and Al Campanis was correct when he said that blacks were less buoyant than whites. As John C. Phillips summarized in his landmark "Toward an Explanation of Racial Variations in Top-Level Sports Participation," published in the *International Review of Sport Sociology:*

> The dearth of black swimmers has been attributed to their higher specific gravity (hence, less buoyancy). Cunningham (1973) reviewed the literature on this subject finding that blacks were considerably less buoyant than whites. This lack of buoyancy appears to make it more difficult for blacks to acquire elementary swimming skills, but it loses its importance in advanced swimming except, perhaps, long distance swimming [sound familiar?]. Indeed Faulkner (1970:14) found that college swimmers had *greater* body density than age-matched college students. Thus, it appears that the fairly large racial difference need not have the effects attributed to it.

It cannot go without saying that regardless of whether blacks are or are not less buoyant than whites, regardless of whether their buoyancy might affect them at competitive swimming levels, to be good swimmers, people, especially city dwellers, must have access to pools and to swimming coaches. In our society, this implies a social and economic status that has traditionally been denied to blacks (blacks are also underrepresented in the country-club sports of golf and tennis). Jackie Robinson, who excelled at several sports and was called by Branch Rickey the most competitive athlete since Ty Cobb, was permitted to swim only once a week in his city's swimming pool, hardly enough to develop the skill to become a swimming star. In the last analysis, the dearth of black swimmers is probably less attributable to buoyancy, density of flesh, or any other biological predisposition than to more clear-cut socioeconomic reasons.

*Genotype, Phenotype, Stereotype* Anyone who follows sports in America cannot escape the realization that compared to the percentage of blacks in American society at large, black athletes are grossly overrepresented in professional sports. Major league baseball, in which black Americans currently constitute about 25 percent of all players, is no exception. Furthermore, black American baseball players consistently outperform their white counterparts: At the beginning of the 1986 season, more than twice as many active black players as active white players had lifetime batting averages of greater than .280, and 40 percent of black pitchers compared to 11 percent of white pitchers had ERAs of less than 3.00 per nine innings.

Over half a century of anthropometric measurements leaves no doubt that there are indeed significant biological differences between blacks and whites. Bearing in mind that bodily proportions are only one aspect of the whole picture, and that placing emphasis on physical factors to explain *black* athletic success is a significant fact in itself, are there differences in build and function that give black baseball players an advantage over whites?

Compared to American whites, the average American black has greater weight, arm length, forearm length, hand length, elbow width, leg length, lower leg length, foot length and width, knee width, shoulder breadth, neck girth, and limb girth, all relative to height. In absolute terms, the average black is slightly shorter and weighs slightly more than the average white. The chest is shallower with 15 to 20 percent less breathing capacity than whites; and the black pelvis is smaller, which helps to explain the lighter birth weight, by about one pound, of full-term black babies compared to white. The differences in average limb length are on the order of a centimeter or two, that is, not very great; while the skeletons of black soldiers killed in the Korean War averaged 7 percent heavier than those of whites, or a few pounds. Black musculature is correspondingly heavier. Blacks have significantly less protective fat and denser flesh.

It might be tempting to suggest that the black man's average longer arm length (46.60 percent of his stature compared to 45.45 percent for the white man) makes him a better pitcher, but so far it has proven impossible to determine which physical factors or combination of physical factors cause success in any particular athletic event, if indeed the purely physical can ever be divorced from the complex of factors that lead to success in athletics. Likewise there seems to be no way to extrapolate between athletic success and average or normal physical variation between or within races. As John C. Phillips points out, "Like suicide, superior athletic performance is very rare. Hence, 'average man' theories are useless." Since superior athletes represent considerably less than 1 percent of the general population, the athlete may best be considered as a type by himself, having more in common with other professional athletes than with any "average" member of any race.

Black success explained on the basis of racially determined psychological characteristics in the end fares no better than theories of special black physical endowment, for both black and white athletes can be highly successful, and psychologists have been unable to agree which, if any, psychological traits are particularly associated with athletic superiority, let alone whether blacks possess them to a greater degree than whites. Major studies conducted by sociologists indicate that white youths value athletic excellence much more highly than academic excellence; so that if we were to ascribe a special emphasis on athletic skill to blacks, this would not place them at cultural variance with whites, at least on this matter. Much more persuasive is the economic corollary to the American two-tiered caste system, which Dr. Harry Edwards has expressed this way: "As long as sports provide the only visible, high-status occupational role model for the masses of black male youths, black superiority over whites shall go unchallenged." Jackie Robinson himself quit college to pursue a career in professional sports because he did not believe a degree would help a black man get a job.

The high standards established in organized baseball by the twentieth century's first black players, who were for the most part the cream of the black leagues, created a new stereotype of the black athlete as a species naturally gifted, with special advantages in speed and strength. This image was readily consumed by a white America that comforted itself for the alleged physical superiority of the black man by reserving superior reasoning for itself.

Statistically, if inborn physical advantages could be pinpointed, blacks would have to have them *three times* as frequently as whites to explain black overrepresentation in baseball (and sixty-six times as frequently to explain black sprinting success in the early '70s!). Another major problem with genetic explanations for black superiority is that observed differences in morphology do not always correspond to differences in performance. This was the case, for instance, when Africans began to dominate long-distance races in the face of expert opinion that their shallower chests would be "a handicap in events of long duration, such as distance running." And how to explain Roy Campanella? Was it his Italian father or his black mother who endowed him with the ability to be a superior catcher?

*Baseball's First Black Manager*   In 1975, Frank Robinson, the only man ever to be named Most Valuable Player in both leagues, became the first black manager in the major leagues when he was hired by the struggling

Cleveland Indians. Shortly before he was fired in 1977 after leading the Indians to their best two-season record in ten years, Robinson got into a well-publicized argument with Cleveland's white pitching star Gaylord Perry. The next day this sign was hung up at the ballpark for his benefit: "Sickle Cell Anemia: White Man's Hope." (Sickle cell is a hereditary anemia that primarily affects blacks.)

Hired at a time when blacks represented over 25 percent of all major league players, twenty-eight years after Jackie Robinson integrated baseball, Robinson is one of only three black major league managers in the history of baseball (he also managed the Giants from 1981 to 1984, and returned in 1988 to manage the hopelessly failing Orioles). At the winter baseball meetings in December 1987, when Commissioner Peter Ueberroth delivered a state-of-the-game address before seventy-eight major league executives citing the increase in the number of blacks in nonplaying jobs, Frank Robinson was the only black man there.

Superstars Larry Doby, who managed the Chicago White Sox for part of the 1978 season, and Maury Wills, who managed the Seattle Mariners for parts of the 1980 and 1981 seasons, are as of this writing the only other blacks ever to manage in the major leagues. All inherited weak teams.

*The View From Mr. October*   Looking back over the principal changes in his life in 1987, his last year as a player, Reggie Jackson remarked, "Between the ages of zero and fourteen, I was colored. Between the ages of fourteen and thirty, I was a Negro. And between the ages of thirty and the present, I'm black."

*Human Targets*   Pitcher Kirby Higbe says in his autobiography that he developed his strong arm by throwing rocks at Negroes. Satchel Paige says in his autobiography that he developed his arm by throwing rocks at white boys. Similar claims by pitchers who developed their skills on members of opposing races are not uncommon. Dizzy Dean got in some early childhood practice throwing rocks at blacks in Arkansas cotton fields, although it must be said that Grover Cleveland Alexander, who amazed his parents with his aim and reportedly could knock fowl out of the air, restricted himself to nonhuman targets.

Paige, one of the great pitchers of all time, packed ballparks both before and after he reached the white major leagues at the age of forty-two, and was already famous for hitting targets with rocks when he was eight. His claim that he crippled up some white boys pretty good probably holds water, particularly since he was a notoriously bad boy. At the age of fourteen he stole some small toys from a Mobile, Alabama, store and spent the next five and a half years in a reformatory. With characteristic resilience, Paige turned the time to good use, getting a sound education and playing baseball.

Willa Mae Robinson Walker, reminiscing about her baby brother Jackie Robinson and their life in a formerly all-white neighborhood in Pasadena, recalls, "People used to ask me how Jack got so good throwing a baseball and a football, and I said it was from throwing rocks at the other kids who were throwing rocks at him."

*The Quota System*  In the early years of reintegration in the major leagues there appears to have been an understanding among white club owners that no more than two black players would be brought up to any single club at a time. Sportswriters enjoyed speculating about a "saturation point," or limit, to the number of black players "permissible" on a club or in a lineup; but persistent discussion of "saturation" really applied only to the clubs with significant numbers of black players—the Dodgers and the Cleveland Indians. In 1953 the Indians' failure to repeat their 1948 pennant success was widely attributed to too many blacks in the lineup (they had five). But as Cleveland's general manager Hank Greenberg prophesied, when the Indians regained the American League pennant in 1954, interest in black saturation evaporated.

A quota system was universally believed to exist and accepted as a fact of life among black players waiting their turn for a chance in the big leagues. Like collusion among owners to ignore free agents, it was not the sort of arrangement that executives are ever likely to own up to, but the facts tend to speak for themselves. As Richard Lapchick has pointed out, "Ten years after the barriers fell in Brooklyn, the major leagues had only eighteen blacks," or slightly over one per team. This was accepted as the norm. When the Giants, despite the urging of Monte Irvin and Sal Maglie, failed to bring up Hall of Fame third baseman Ray Dandridge from their Minnesota farm team in 1950, Irvin maintained that Dandridge wasn't called because the quota system was still in effect and the positions for blacks on the Giants were already occupied by Hank Thompson and himself. According to historian John B. Holway, in 1950 "the quota system [was] still in effect on those few teams that had integrated." Holway maintains that when Willie Mays was called up to the Giants in 1951, "the Giants had to dismiss second baseman Artie Wilson, ironically Mays's old tutor with the Birmingham Black Barons, to maintain the quota."

Official claims of impartiality notwithstanding, in a study published in *Perceptual and Motor Skills,* author Martin Bloomberg attempts to explain the superiority of black over white hitters in 1970 by suggesting that a quota system rather than athletic superiority of black ballplayers may be responsible: "Fewer blacks are allowed into the big leagues and consequently those who arrive will tend to be more proficient than the average white at hitting." Bloomberg also points out that in 1970 white pitchers outnumbered black pitchers nine to one, although there was no significant difference in their performance (studies through 1985 document that black pitchers in fact perform significantly better than their white counterparts). Although there is now no apparent agreed-upon limit to the number of black players who may be on a team, there does seem to be some limit, however casual, governing the number of blacks who are permitted to play infield positions; and it is no secret that the number of blacks coming into baseball has dropped during the past decade.

Frank Cashen, general manager of the Mets, fielding questions about racism on the Mets in a March 1988 *New York Times* article, points out that "baseball's roots these days are in Little League, which is a product of middle class America. There are very few Little Leagues in the inner city in Baltimore, Harlem, Washington, Detroit." His comments lend fuel to the conclusion that the continued exclusion of blacks from "decision-making" field positions, combined with the growing disenchantment with baseball among blacks who have learned that there is no future for them in organized baseball after their playing careers are over—not to mention the growing climate of racism in contemporary America—have all contributed to creating a situation that may be more effective in excluding blacks from baseball than any quota system ever was.

*The Odds*  For blacks the reality of integration in sports may have been less an opportunity than an illusion. As Jack Olsen noted in his exhaustive 1968 *Sports Illustrated* series, "The Black Athlete," "At most, sports has led a few thousand Negroes into a better life while substituting a meaningless dream for hundreds and thousands of other Negroes. It has helped perpetuate an oppressive system."

In 1979 sociologist Harry Edwards, now with the baseball commissioner's office, expressed the chances for blacks to make a career in sports this way: "Less than 900 black athletes are earning a living in sports—and not more than 1,500 overall, including coaches and trainers. By comparison, there are perhaps 3 million black youths between [the ages of] 13 and 22 who dream of a career as an athlete. The odds are 20,000 to 1 or worse. Statistically, you have a better chance of getting hit by a meteorite in the next 10 years than getting work as an athlete." Including the six-hundred-odd jobs for players in major league baseball, the odds are about twelve thousand to one that *any* American youth will succeed in sports.

***Dollars and Quotas***   In his dissertation entitled "A Microeconomic Analysis of the Labor Market of Professional Baseball Players," which concentrates on the years 1961–73, Gary Lee Stone concludes that "nonwhites start their major league careers at a disadvantage to whites in terms of salaries," but that "the salaries of whites and nonwhites tend to converge over time, . . . as their careers advance." Currently this situation still holds true, although the starting disparity is less than it was, and there is no question that at the higher levels of achievement color has no effect on salary whatsoever, with one exception: If salary is plotted as a function of hits, white players receive slightly more per hit than nonwhites.

From the point of view of those who do the hiring, racism continues to make little sense. As evidence, the following finding concerning promotion from the minors to the majors is quoted from Stone's abstract (emphasis added): "Barriers to entry do exist against nonwhites. This is the case despite evidence that teams have an economic incentive to promote nonwhites from the minors since *those major league clubs which promoted the greatest number of nonwhite players tended to have the best winning percentages in the major leagues.*"

***Positional Segregation***   When Jackie Robinson died in 1972, there were no black officials in baseball, no field managers, no general managers, no scouting directors, no ticket managers, no public relations managers, no team presidents or assistants to presidents, and no black farm directors, with the lone exception of Bill Lucas, Hank Aaron's brother-in-law, who as Atlanta's farm director was the only black in baseball in a responsible executive position. At the same time, there were black players on every major league team. But the same prejudices on the part of management that have perpetuated the barring of blacks from baseball's hierarchy—the belief that blacks are lacking in sound judgment and decision-making ability—were also operational on the field then, as they are now, where they take two distinct forms of discrimination that sociologists call *marginality* and *centrality* (or "stacking").

*Marginality,* the tendency to exclude blacks of marginal or average ability in favor of whites of average ability, has tended to decrease over time, as it would have to when more blacks entered the game, but it is still obvious in baseball. As Jim Bouton observed, "There are a lot of Negro stars in the game. There aren't too many average Negro players. The obvious conclusion is that there is some kind of quota system. It stands to reason that if nineteen of the top thirty hitters in the major leagues are black, as they were in 1968, then almost two thirds of all the hitters should be black. Obviously, it's not that way." In 1988, a fierce dispute raged concerning alleged marginality in the Mets organization, which has frequently been accused of favoring marginal whites over black players of equal or superior skill.

*Centrality*, the tendency to exclude blacks from central positions, specifically the "thinking" positions of catcher, shortstop, and second baseman—the positions that traditionally provide most opportunity for postplaying careers in baseball organizations—has actually increased in recent decades. Even though there has been an increase in the proportions of blacks to whites at nearly all positions, stacking has remained such a remarkably consistent phenomenon that at the beginning of the 1986 season 70 percent of all American-born non-Hispanic blacks in the major leagues played in the outfield. Twelve percent played at first base, 10 percent at shortstop, 7 percent at second base, 5.7 percent were pitchers, and 4 percent played at third base (there were no black catchers). In 1980 there were only four black shortstops, two black catchers, and ten black second basemen in the major leagues, while seventy blacks and sixty-four whites played in the outfield. At least since 1983, over 80 percent of all black Americans in the big leagues have been outfielders or first basemen. In 1983, even though whites outnumbered blacks in the major leagues almost five to one, as they did in 1968, when more than half of all major league outfielders were black, there were seventy black outfielders and sixty-eight white outfielders. There are no blacks currently playing catcher, the most central and controlling of field positions, and black pitchers continue to lose ground. Since the late '60s, the proportion of blacks in the outfield has increased while the proportion of black catchers and pitchers has declined.

With the smallest percentage of blacks of the three major team sports and a declining influx of black players, baseball may indeed fulfill speculation that it is destined to become "whiter." This much is clear: Major league infields are not becoming darker. Taking into consideration the statistics and the remarkable stability of positional segregation since blacks entered the game in 1947, it is hard not to agree with those observers who maintain that management does not want to give certain field positions to blacks because they are associated with leadership and control. There may well be more blacks in the outfield because black players have learned that they have a better chance of making a career there than behind the plate—the complex phenomenon of discrimination by position has many tributaries and should not be oversimplified—but stacking had to start somewhere. And as Al Campanis recently reminded us, in the white world of sports, the whites reserve the brains for themselves.

*Bill White*  Under the pressure of a renewed public awareness of racism in baseball and the necessity of living up to their own promises of affirmative action, National League owners seized the opportunity of A. Bartlett Giamatti's ascension to the commissionership in 1989 and determined to fill the league presidency he vacated with a black man. Among those considered for the job were Louis L. Hoynes, legal counsel to the National League for nineteen years; Simon Gourdine, former National Basketball Association deputy commissioner; Gilroye Griffin, Jr., a Bristol-Meyers executive; and Joe Morgan, baseball broadcaster, businessman, and former superstar second baseman.

Simon Gourdine had been considered the leading candidate until February 2, when he was notified he was out of the race. On February 3, William DeKova White, a former all-star first baseman who served as the Yankees' broadcaster for eighteen years, and had been approached for the job only ten days previously, was informed that he had been unanimously elected by the National League owners. The choice of White, a universally respected baseball man, was warmly received at every level of baseball. The fifty-five-year-old White became not only baseball's top black executive, but the first black to head a major professional sports league in the United States. Except for John Tener, who served as National League president from 1914 through 1918, White is the only National League president to have been a former major leaguer.

According to Dodgers owner Peter O'Malley, chairman of the National League committee that selected White, "Bill was selected as the best man for the job. Race did not play a factor." White also downplayed the symbolic significance of his election: "To some people, I suppose this would be of symbolic importance." But it was lost on no one that O'Malley, who led the search for a qualified black league president, had been forced to fire his vice-president of player personnel, Al Campanis, two years previously, after Campanis announced on network TV that blacks weren't intelligent enough to be baseball executives. Race may not have played a part in White's selection, but Al Campanis certainly did.

The official protestations that race had nothing to do with White's selection were apparently deemed necessary to forestall speculation that White was chosen because he was the most qualified *black* man available. Indeed, it would have been hard to find any man more qualified for the job. White's acceptance of a job he neither solicited nor needed is perhaps best understood in the light that it meant his giving up a comfortable, ninety-day-a-year job for a rigorous nine-to-five that paid one hundred thousand dollars less than his three-hundred-thousand-dollar-a-year broadcasting salary. According to Phil Rizzuto, White's broadcasting partner for WPIX-TV, "He felt this was important for baseball, for himself, and for blacks in general."

White has never been known as a militant in the style of Jackie Robinson, but in 1961 he led Cardinals teammates Bob Gibson, Curt Flood, and George Crowe in a successful drive to end segregated housing in the Cardinals spring training quarters in St. Petersburg, Florida. The high regard in which he is held in the baseball world is based as much upon his straightforward, outspoken manner as it is upon his baseball savvy. Many felt that White could have been the first black major league manager, but he had a hard time during his year as a manager in Tulsa and decided not to pursue a career as a manager. Undoubtedly he has a first-hand understanding of racism in baseball, and no one believes he can be used as a token. One veteran sportswriter has described White as the kind of man who would probably resign rather than put up with too much, even though his years under George Steinbrenner as the only regular black broadcaster for a major league team must have ground him down.

What White's ascension from the broadcasting booth to the National League presidency means in terms of integration is another question. No one expects him to change his traditionalist stance against the designated hitter, batters who complain about brushback pitches, and umpires who are slow to walk away from arguments with players. No one doubts that he knows baseball, inside and out, and will find no surprises concerning baseball in his new office. And it is logical to expect that he will support the owners, his employers, in the approaching collective-bargaining negotiations, but he can't be the chief negotiator. In the end, although the job will be what he wants to make of it, the National League presidency is a figurehead position whose principal duties include signing baseballs and supervising National League umpires, and whose primary function is disciplinary, a fixer of fines and a court of last resort for his league's disputes. The real power in baseball is concentrated in the commissioner's hands. The actual hiring and firing of players and executives, the front line of racism, as it were, is done by club presidents, general managers, and field managers. As this book goes to press, there is still only one black field manager in baseball, Frank Robinson. Whatever else Bill White's National League presidency means, there are at present more black major league presidents in baseball than black major league catchers.

*Natural Gifts*   Blacks sing and play and we say they have natural rhythm. Blacks participate in athletics and we say they are naturally gifted. Who knows what other natural abilities we might discover among blacks if we let them participate in other areas of our culture? Will black doctors be discovered to be naturally diagnostic, and black judges naturally judicial? God forbid that blacks were to achieve excellence in any field through hard work, intelligence, and determination. Whites might then be forced to consider whether they have any claim to superiority at all.

Basketball immortal Bill Russell once countered the natural gifts explanation for the superiority of black athletes by stating, "I worked at basketball up to eight hours a day for twenty years—straining, learning, sweating, studying." Hank Aaron's complaint is that the gifted athlete attitude robbed him of the *thinking* he had to do to hit 755 home runs.

When the announcer at a sporting event speaks of a player as a hard-working or a thinking player, as a general rule the player in question is white; and when the player is described as naturally gifted, gifted, or naturally talented, he is black. Thurman Williams, a black man, explained in a letter to *The Sporting News* on February 29, 1988, "I'm . . . sick of hearing how black athletes can just roll out of bed and become professionals." But perhaps W. E. B. DuBois, writing in 1939 concerning the tradition on which our culture is based, expressed it best: "A largely unexpressed but central thesis of English rule is the conviction that ability, while inherent in the English ruling class, is, outside that class, largely accidental and a sport of nature."

*Assassination Aftermath*   In 1968 civil rights leader Reverend Martin Luther King, Jr., was assassinated in Memphis, Tennessee, one week before the opening of the major league season. Rioting and looting in many cities posed a threat to fans and their cars, and the opening games of the season were postponed. It isn't clear whether they were postponed solely as a gesture of respect for the martyred King, as baseball maintained, but this was without doubt the first and only time in the history of the national pastime that the opening games have ever been postponed.

*Attendance: A White Man's Game?*   So many brilliant black players moved into major league lineups after Jackie Robinson that baseball's expansion era stands out as the age of the black player. Record after record fell to black players, and by 1979, after discriminatory practices had paled, blacks were receiving better salaries, better publicity, and a bigger share of endorsements. Even so, there was still only one black umpire out of a major league staff of sixty, very few black coaches, and even fewer black managers.

Curiously, while by 1970 one out of four players was black, in 1979 only one out of five players was black (with the same proportional trend in the minors). Attendance at games by black fans shows even less participation: A survey taken in 1985 showed that blacks account for fewer than 5 percent of all fans in the major leagues. Former Commissioner Bowie Kuhn says that the figures he saw for black attendance between 1969 and 1984 were "very low, under 5 percent." A 1986 study of black attendance at professional sports showed baseball attendance by blacks to be 6.8 percent, a figure many feel is optimistic. (The same study showed NBA basketball attendance by blacks was 17 percent, with NFL football attendance by blacks 7.5 percent, rising to 12.5 percent during the playoffs. Blacks represent 11.7 percent of the American population.)

In 1986, during a racial controversy concerning the Red Sox, Hubie Jones, Dean of Boston University's School of Social Work, commented, "When I go to the ballpark, there are no other blacks there. It might as well be hockey." Boston fan Alan Shapiro remarked, "The absence of black employees, both on and off the field, is striking. . . . The impression, looking at a sea of 25,000 white faces at any given game, is that we could just as easily be in Johannesburg."

But according to American League President Bobby Brown, the dearth of black fans in Boston is nothing unusual. "Despite the fact that many of our greatest stars are black players, we simply do not enjoy support from the black community. . . . I have seen crowds of over 40,000 in Texas with only several hundred being black. The Chicago White Sox playing in Comiskey Park on the South Side of Chicago [a black neighborhood in a city that is 40 percent black] do not have a single black season-ticket holder." Don Newcombe, director of community relations for the Los Angeles Dodgers, estimated in 1987 that there were "25 or certainly no more than 50" blacks among the Dodgers' 27,000 season ticketholders. In 1982, only 6 percent of the New York Mets' fans were blacks in a city that is 25.2 percent black.

Brent Staples, an editor at *The New York Times,* asserts, "It is clear that black fans, after a romance with baseball that began at the turn of the century and flourished through the early 1950s, have abandoned the national pastime." Many believe that black attendance at major league games peaked in the late '40s and declined once black fans saw for themselves that black baseball players could compete successfully against whites. As former Minnesota Twins owner Calvin Griffith expressed it to the Waseca, Minnesota, Lions Club in 1978, his decision to move his club from the heavily black city of Washington, D.C., to Minnesota came about when he found out "you only had 15,000 blacks here . . . you've got good hard-working white people here . . . blacks don't go to ball games."

There are no easy answers to explain the fluctuations in black participation in organized baseball. Perhaps black Americans, who supported their own leagues with enthusiasm, even during the Depression, are less inclined, during an era of affirmative action, to lend their support to a sport in which they are allowed to participate—strictly speaking—only as performers. Perhaps the inertia generated by baseball having been exclusively white from 1898 to 1947 will take longer to overcome than anyone expected. Or perhaps blacks are more drawn—as attendance figures do seem to indicate—to sports with less of a tradition of apartheid, such as professional basketball or professional football. At any rate, it seems too early to speculate, as some have, that blacks, having been driven out of the major leagues in the last century, may now be abandoning the game after a brief heyday, and that major league baseball will again become the white man's game it was from 1898 to 1947.

*The Black Man in Baseball*

Black stars, who once played for black owners, now play for whites. The big effect of the Jackie Robinson revolution was not to get blacks into big league ball—they had always been playing big league caliber ball: It was to get the black owners out.

The role of the black man in baseball today has been reduced to that of an entertainer—albeit a very well-paid entertainer—of whites. Baseball is attended by whites, governed by whites, and its history is written by whites. . . . The Hall of Fame . . . may be called "a white man's memory bank." . . . The lily-white board and the almost lily-white vets' committee [of the Hall of Fame] keep baseball history firmly in their hands. . . . Is it any wonder that blacks feel alienated by baseball? Millions of potential black fans have turned their backs on the game they once loved.

—John B. Holway

## Hank Aaron Sets a Record

> Records are made to be broken. I'm hoping that some day some kid
> will come along and finally break my record. Who the hell cares?
> —Hank Aaron in a 1983 interview

Henry Louis Aaron hit more home runs in his career than Babe Ruth or any other major leaguer. When he retired in 1976 he ranked first in games played, at-bats, RBIs, and extra-base hits. He holds several Golden Glove fielding awards, and he was second only to Ty Cobb in hits and runs scored. Today, as vice-president and director of player development for the Atlanta Braves, the only black baseball executive other than National League President Bill White with significant power, Aaron makes it no secret that the years preceding his breaking of Babe Ruth's career home run record were a sad time in his career. During that time he received mountains of mail from those for whom it was simply unacceptable that a black man should surpass a white, and while he admits that some of it spurred him on in order "to make people eat their words," no single letter bothered him so much as just learning "how many people still thought that blacks had no business in baseball."

After his difficulties became known most of his mail expressed support for the dignified slugger; even so, death threats forced him to have body-guards at a time when "I should have been enjoying myself." Pointing out that it was nothing that Pete Rose ever had to deal with, Aaron recalls, "The last two years I had to have somebody with me all the time. In spring training. Everytime I walked out of the clubhouse, someone was with me. Every time I went to the bank. If I went to Cincinnati there was someone there with me. I could never travel by myself. The sad part about the whole thing for two and a half years was I never had a chance to join my teammates. They would stay in one part of the hotel and I had to stay in another part. I would be registered in one room and stay in another room. Just to decoy people off."

Forced to turn to TV, Aaron became a devotee of soap operas. Meanwhile, a fierce controversy, similar to what Roger Maris had experienced when he broke Babe Ruth's season home run record but with racist overtones, raged over the validity of Aaron's effort, for he was breaking Ruth's record in more lifetime at-bats than the Bambino had needed to set it. In the end, Commissioner of Baseball Bowie Kuhn didn't bother to attend the 1974 game in which Aaron hit his record-breaking home run, sending Monte Irvin in his stead to witness the historic event in the company of Governor Carter, Sammy Davis, Jr., and other celebrities.

The media attention Aaron received was likewise something of a back-handed compliment, for although for years he had been averaging thirty-five or forty home runs a season and scoring over one hundred runs, according to Aaron, "For fourteen years nobody interviewed Hank Aaron." In view of his remarkable achievements, he was underwhelmed with commercial opportunities, receiving and performing only one lucrative endorsement (for Magnavox). And once again there was talk of entering his record in the books with an asterisk, as had been done to Maris, although in his case more than one observer has pointed out that the asterisk should be on the other foot, and all records established before integration should be asterisked. In retrospect, however, Aaron doesn't consider it his problem: "I hit the home run, they got to figure out how they going to continue to snub it." He does feel he learned that fame and high salaries do not necessarily insulate black stars from discrimination. "Baseball has done a lot for me," he commented in 1983. "It has taught me that regardless of who you are and regardless of how much money you make, you are still a Negro."

# 7

# WOMEN AND
# THE GAME

**W**ould anyone seriously dispute the assertion that women now are much more a part of the organized sports world than ever before in history? Whether it is women's marathons or female fans cheering at NFL games in neighborhood bars or girls on Little League teams or the women who constantly break records at the Olympics or a woman on the Harlem Globetrotters, they have broken through many of the barriers. And the instances cited are merely the standouts, the headline-grabbers. Anyone who skims the sports section of the local newspaper must be aware of the sheer level of activity of schoolgirl sports—and if they aren't being reported, there is usually a letter to the editor pointing this out. The new age for women in sports has certainly dawned, if not peaked.

The reasons it has taken this long for women to begin to achieve parity in sports seem so obvious that, although they can no longer be defended, they don't need rehearsing. Given the history of mankind—the version, that is, in which men assumed the dominant role—it seems inevitable that women would be excluded from this realm of physical displays and competition. The exceptions are so few and special that they only confirm the generality: a dimly remembered female Olympics in ancient Greece, women in attendance at certain special nineteenth-century horse races or regattas, genteel tennis players in the late nineteenth century, some extraordinary swimmers and tennis players in the early decades of the twentieth century.

True, women began to compete in the modern Olympics as early as 1900, but this breakthrough only serves to sharpen the distinction between such contests and the great team sports of the modern era. In this arena, women seem to be still lagging. Although women now play soccer, volleyball, field hockey, softball, basketball, and several other team sports, and although they show up as fans at football games, hockey matches, and such contests, it still seems fair to describe professional team sports as a man's world.

Conspicuous in its absence from this account is any reference to baseball. Is this because baseball just falls in with "other team sports"? Or is it because baseball is a true exception? "Ladies Day" emerged as an adjunct of baseball clubs in the 1880s. Is this merely a marketing gimmick? The song that both captures the spirit of professional contests and provides the motto for American baseball fans, "Take Me Out to the Ball Game," is actually intended to be sung by a woman; it is Kitty Casey who in 1908 was expressing the sentiments of all who love the game—"I don't care if I never get back." Was this just a Tin Pan Alley convention? Or has there been something special going on between baseball and women?

*The First Fans*  Some of the earliest newspaper accounts of baseball games refer to the presence of women. In the *New York Times* of July 1, 1864, for instance, it is reported: "Yesterday afternoon the Capitoline Ball Grounds at Bedford, L.I., was visited by at least four thousand spectators, including a large number of ladies, to witness the important contest between [the Atlantics and the Empires]." The popular sporting journal of the day, *The Spirit of the Times,* on September 22, 1855, gave an account of a match between the Knickerbocker and Gotham clubs: "There were about 1000 spectators present, including many ladies, who manifested the utmost excitement, but kept an admirable order." The manner in which the presence of "ladies" is noted suggests that it is newsworthy to find them at public sporting events but not especially unusual to find them at baseball games. In the famous Currier & Ives print, evidently inspired by if not depicting a famous game played on August 3, 1865, women make up a fair proportion of the crowd at the far side of the field. The newspaper accounts of that game estimate that as many as twenty thousand people were in attendance but make no reference to how many were women; presumably many were.

There is no need, however, to overstate the case. Girls undoubtedly played in the childhood variants of the game. And ladyfriends of the players of the first amateur teams undoubtedly showed up for some of their high-spirited matches. But men clearly dominate most illustrations and accounts of

*Women, even though placed well back out of harm's way (and men's talk), were spectators at baseball from the earliest days. This illustration dates from 1866 and shows the women in the rear at a sort of fieldhouse.*

the game in the first couple of decades. One illustration of 1866 shows the men sitting close to home plate and first base while way off in the outfield are the women. But the point remains: The women are at a baseball game, not in a parlor.

*No Place for a Lady*  When the Cincinnati Red Stockings declared themselves a paid professional team in 1869, the character of baseball games was already changing. Wagering between friends was being replaced by organized gambling, paid admissions eliminated the casual spectator, enclosed ballparks created a special territory that men began to treat as a private club where they could drink, swear, and generally carry on like the male of the species. Many contemporary accounts of baseball from 1870 to 1900 describe the rowdy atmosphere of a typical major league game, both on and off the field.

Some ministers and moralists such as Henry Ward Beecher were only too glad to write off this new game as a wicked pastime that should have no appeal for women and children. What is more unexpected, though, is that not everyone was willing to abandon the new sport to the menfolk. As early as 1867 an editorial in *The Ballplayers Chronicle* had claimed that the presence of women at baseball games "purifies the moral atmosphere," and there were many who continued to feel that women could help "save" the game from its own self-destructive elements.

Newspapers and magazines editorialized against the environment that was making what should be "the national pastime" so unsuitable for women and families. As one editorial of the 1880s put it:

> Nothing is so well calculated to popularize the national game of the country among the best classes of the community as the encouragement of the presence of ladies at the matches. . . . To realize the advantage of the attendance of the fair sex at matches it is only necessary to contrast the behavior of a large crowd of spectators at a ball match during an exciting contest when no ladies are present with that of an assemblage in which are to be seen hundreds of bright-eyed fair ones. . . . At the former, profanity, ill feeling, partisan prejudice and other characteristics of "stag" gatherings are conspicuous features, while at the other the pride of gentlemen which curbs men's evil passions in the presence of ladies frowns upon all such exhibitions of partisan ill will, and order and decorum mark the presence of the civilizing influence of the fair sex.

Modern feminists may not appreciate the terms under which women are to be admitted to ballgames, but this was at least a start.

And women did continue to attend the major league games, as close study of contemporary drawings and photographs reveals. Or consider this account of the crowd at a game between New York and Chicago, the top contenders for the National League pennant, at the Polo Grounds in New York City on August 1, 1885:

> No portion of the populace is insensible to this craze. . . . The ladies are regular and numerous attendants at the grounds. The hundreds of them who stood on the seats and screamed and waved their handkerchiefs and brandished their fans in ecstasies of applause yesterday knew enough to come early and avoid the crush. How much they knew of the game, though none of them ever play it, was to be seen by the way they behaved. As they took their seats in the grand stand they brought out their score cards and pencils, argued

over the merits of the coming players, and consulted little diaries, in which they had entered records of past League games. The rough and blackened finger tips of some of them showed them to be working girls; others, by unmistakable signs, even when they had not their children with them, showed that they were housewives and mothers; others still, by their costly dresses and the carriages they came in, were seen to be well-to-do women and young girls; and a few were of the class of female gamblers and sporting women that has grown so considerable in this city of late.

Clearly women were part of the baseball scene in this era, yet it is also true that the "stag" atmosphere in many of the major league ballparks threatened to drive away many women and families. It was for this reason that some owners of major league teams began to try to attract women to the game by instituting "Ladies Day." The tradition actually can be traced to 1867 when none other than the Knickerbocker Base Ball Club formally decided to set aside the last Thursday every month as a day when members could invite their wives, daughters, or ladyfriends to the game; the club even appointed a committee to make sure that "suitable seats or settees" would be available to the women. Other amateur clubs seem to have adopted this practice, but it was 1883 before the Philadelphia Athletics and Baltimore Orioles became the first major league teams to institute Ladies Day. They also set Thursday aside, but the new twist was to admit ladies free only if accompanied by a man. Moreover, the free admission only allowed the lady to sit in the bleachers—so this put pressure on many a gentleman to buy a better seat for the lady as well as himself. In 1884 the Brooklyn club in the newly formed American Association adopted Ladies Day and one by one most of the major league teams followed. Some promised special facilities such as a women's entrance, protection "from distasteful spectacles," a women's restroom with a woman attendant, or a seating section where no smoking was permitted. Ladies Day proved so successful that soon men were complaining that the freeloading ladies were taking all the best seats.

Although it appears that baseball deserves credit as the first sporting event to introduce Ladies Day, it is interesting to note that the very idea and term were taken over from the world of men's clubs. The earliest recorded reference in America is an entry in a diary of 1787: "Dined with a Club. . . . The Gentlemen . . . met every Saturday . . . accompanied by the females every other Saturday. This was Ladies Day." The diarist? None other than George Washington—first in war, first in peace, and now first in the hearts of female baseball fans.

*This illustration from* Harper's Weekly *of August 31, 1889, is supposed to depict an intercollegiate game, which might explain the prominence given to so many stylish young ladies. But the artist is also having a bit of fun by portraying the one in the foreground with her binoculars aimed not at the game but at someone in the stands.*

Even Ladies Days were not enough to take baseball back from the gamblers and rowdies and this was one of the goals of Ban Johnson when he set about to establish a second major league. It is sometimes suggested that the American League was established to give baseball back to women and families, but this is far too simplistic; Johnson and his fellow team owners were first of all businessmen determined to get in on the profits being made in the large cities. And if Johnson was opposed to drunks and rowdies, it was more the ones on the field than those in the stands. Players were becoming increasingly unruly by the 1880s and 1890s, showing up drunk, fighting and cheating on the field, abusing the umpires, and all this only encouraged the crowds in disruptive behavior.

So it is true that Johnson realized that one of the ways to win over a public was to provide an alternative environment to that of the National League ballparks, an environment that among other benefits would be more hospitable to women and families. And thus did the American League come into being in 1901.


*Women Come to Bat*   Although women were beginning to feel uncomfortable in the ballparks overrun by gamblers, drinkers, swearers, and general rowdies during the last decades of the nineteenth century, some were finding other ways of taking up baseball. Women or girls began to play on teams that fell somewhere between fairground freakshows and amateur exhibitions. The earliest known such contests were played in 1875 in Springfield and Decatur, Illinois, when two all-girl teams, the "Blondes" and the "Brunettes," played several games. In New Orleans in 1879, it is reported, "a large crowd of miscellaneous people went to the Fair Grounds to watch a team of girls who refused to play until each received ten dollars." In the 1880s, one Harry H. Freeman organized a professional traveling "Female Base Ball Club," but they were soon denounced as little more than prostitutes: "The female has no place in base ball, except to the degradation of the game. For two seasons . . . [people] have been nauseated with the spectacle of these tramps." In 1883, Chester, Pennsylvania, had its "colored girl nine," known as the "Dolly Vardens" (after the high-spirited, independent heroine of Dickens's 1841 novel, *Barnaby Rudge*). The Dolly Vardens played in red-and-white calico dresses "of remarkable shortness," one man wrote. In 1900, the Boston Bloomer Girls were touring as far afield as Saskatchewan, Canada, and playing modified games against men's teams, while as late as the 1930s there was a touring team of women known as "Slapsie Maxies' Curvaceous Cuties."

None of these teams, of course, played regulation games. One women's team of this era played on a smaller diamond and against teams of five men, but even so had to be given a handicap. And some of these teams were no more than chorus-line vaudeville acts—never intended to play baseball but simply to dress up in a musical-comedy version of the game.

Short-lived novelties these female teams may have been, but they did not go entirely unnoticed. On August 19, 1883, *The New York Times* carried a story under the headline, "A Ridiculous Exhibition at a Philadelphia Park," describing a game between two teams of evidently inept young women; two days later a *Times* editorialist felt compelled to hold forth at greater length:

> The game of Base-ball recently played in Philadelphia by gorgeously dressed young women was confessedly a failure, and it established the fact that base-ball, unlike the modern drama, cannot be made

exclusively an exhibition of clothing. . . . The base-ball girls had undoubtedly been trained with great care. . . . When, however, the girls played in public . . . they did not cover themselves in glory—much as they stood in need of some glory. . . . The batter alone showed no signs of fear, for there was, of course, no probability that the balls aimed at her would come near her. The other players, whenever a ball came in their direction, would exclaim loudly, "Oh, my!" and would frantically dodge it. No casualties either among the girls or spectators occurred, for the reason no girl was able to throw the ball swiftly enough to inflict a severe blow. . . . Of course, the girls did not venture to catch the ball. They could not have caught it had they tried, for the simple reason they were standing on their feet and were without aprons. To expect a girl in such circumstances to catch a ball would be absurd.

About a month later (September 23, 1883) the *Times* was reporting a game between these same teams of young women in New York City. The headline read, "A Base-Ball Burlesque":

A crowd of about 1,500 people assembled . . . and laughed themselves hungry and thirsty watching a game of base-ball between two teams composed of girls. One side was composed of brunettes, whose costumes were of an irritating red; the other was of blondes who wore sympathetic blue. . . . These young ladies . . . were selected with tender solicitude from 200 applicants, variety actresses and ballet girls being positively barred. . . . They played baseball in a very sad and sorrowful sort of way, as if the vagaries of the ball had been too great for their struggling intellects. . . . Toward the end of the game the girls began to show symptoms of sadness and weariness, and doggedly refused to run from one base to another. . . . Often, when the fielders could not stop the ball in any other way they sat down on it. . . . When five innings had been played, and the back hair and brains of the girls appeared to be in a hopelessly demoralized condition, with a tendency on the part of their hose to follow suit, the game was called. . . . They play again tomorrow.

Echoes of the joc(k)ular chauvinism adopted by these writers when describing women playing games can still be heard among certain modern sportswriters, but the fact remains that females were playing baseball in public at a time when women were playing no other team sports. There is even the assumption that if only women would learn how to play the game proficiently it might be an acceptable pastime.

*The Old College Try*  If female baseball players on these nineteenth-century teams were regarded as something of a joke, there were women's teams that were definitely no laughing matter—the baseball teams at prominent women's colleges. As early as 1866, Vassar College (only founded in 1861) had its Laurel Baseball Club that played match games every Saturday afternoon. Some thirty years later, one Sophia Richardson said of this era at Vassar:

> About twenty years ago, when I was a freshman, seven or eight baseball clubs suddenly came into being, spontaneously as it seemed, but I think they owed their existence to a few quiet suggestions from a resident physician, wise beyond her generation. The public so far as it knew of our playing was shocked, but in our retired grounds . . . we continued to play in spite of a censurious public. One day a student, while running between bases, fell with an injured leg. We attended her to the infirmary, with the foreboding that this accident would end our play of baseball. Not so. Dr. Webster said that the public doubtless would condemn the game as too violent, but that if the student had hurt herself while dancing the public would not condemn dancing to extinction. . . . The interest in baseball did not increase; clubs were not formed by incoming classes. I think there was too much pressure against it from disapproving mothers.

All the bitter seeds of the women's liberation movement are present in such an account, but give baseball its due; it was this sport that these young women wanted to be a part of.

Vassar students were not alone. Baseball was being played informally by the young women at Smith College as early as 1879, introduced by Minnie Stephens, who would later declare: "It seemed to me that we ought to have some lively games in the way of wholesome exercise so I got a few friends together and we organized a base ball club." Soon they got other students to organize a second team so they could have true contests, but as Ms. Stephens described it, "We were told, however, that the game was too violent and also there was great danger in breaking windows in Hubbard House, so we were politely ordered to give it all up. No athletics for the Smith College Girls way back in Seventy Nine."

*Vassar College, in Poughkeepsie, New York, can evidently lay claim to being the first women's college to have anything like organized baseball teams. As early as 1866, there was a Laurel Base Ball Club; soon other teams were formed by different classes and games continued to be played on a fairly regular basis. By 1876, the Vassar Resolutes, pictured here, had become the first truly organized team. For all their fine caps and belts, it is hard to imagine these young ladies playing very strenuously in those heavy clothes.*

Some years later, though, baseball was reintroduced at Smith—it says a lot about the appeal of the game for women—and an alumna of 1899 would write:

> Someone remarked to [Smith's] President Seelye if he didn't think it "very unladylike for us to be playing baseball just like men."
> President Seelye asked the man if he had ever watched us play. The man said, No. "Then," said President Seelye, "you wouldn't say they played like men."

The president's one-liner has a familiar ring, but it was 1899, after all, and the fact is that Smith students continued to play intramural baseball for many years.

In those last decades of the nineteenth century, it was coming to be accepted that women could play lawn tennis or croquet, participate in archery or gymnastics, bicycle or ice-skate, but team sports had eluded them. Baseball seemed to be in a position to become the first modern team sport to be fully adopted by young women.

Then something happened. Or several things. For one, basketball came along in 1891, and as early as 1893 it was being played at Smith College with official support (and coached by, of all people, Bernard Berenson's sister). Presumably basketball was more acceptable as a proper young lady's sport because it was played indoors. Then along came field hockey about 1900; that was an outdoor sport and every bit as "unladylike" as baseball, yet it was promoted by women's colleges. Eventually women's colleges such as Smith promoted several team sports such as volleyball and lacrosse, but baseball lost its initial advantage and seems never to have been given full support by women's colleges. Almost certainly one of the things working against it was the reputation of professional baseball teams in the late nineteenth century— the roughness of many of the players, the crude language, the drinking and gambling that went with the contests. What is ironic is that women's colleges' rejection of baseball as "unladylike" came at just the time that the major leagues were working to make the major leagues more "family oriented."

What finally seems to have done in baseball as an acceptable sport for young ladies, though, was its own offspring—softball. This game appeared about the turn of the century when it was played under various rules and known by various names. One of the better-known versions was "indoor baseball," and as its name suggests, it was a form of baseball played in gymnasiums. All the variants used a larger and softer ball and a smaller diamond, plus numerous rule changes (in particular, underhand pitching) that

*The next women's college to take up baseball seems to have been Smith, in Northampton, Massachusetts—that was in 1879. Although they played only intramural games (or an annual game between students and faculty), the students kept this up until recent years. This picture shows the class of 1926 against the class of 1927 in the spring of 1927.*

made for a slightly easier form of baseball. By 1908, a variation of softball was being formally promoted as an outdoor alternative to baseball; by 1926 the name *softball* had pushed out the other names; and by 1933, the first world championships of softball were played (the women's champs came from Chicago). Sometime about 1940, Smith College's annual Field Day baseball game between faculty and student teams turned into a softball game.

Now softball has generally been adopted by females of all ages and throughout the world as an alternative to baseball. There are semipro women's softball teams with their own superstars, yet in Quincey Long's one-act play, *Something About Baseball,* produced in New York in July 1988, a woman who forces herself into a male baseball game becomes a symbol of the eternal war of the sexes. Whether that is really the issue is debatable, but baseball for grown women is now pretty much a lost cause. Unless an unexpected incident in March 1989 proves to be something other than an exception: One Julie Croteau became the first woman to play in an NCAA baseball game when she played first base for St. Mary's of Maryland; she handled her six chances perfectly, although she went 0 for 3 at the plate.

*Women Players*   The women who occasionally played baseball on exhibition, vaudeville, or college teams were amateurs in every sense of the word, but there have been women who played professional baseball teams—men's teams, that is. The first for whom there is recorded proof was allowed in an official minor league contest by none other than the pillar of Yankee propriety, Edward Grant Barrow. This was long before Barrow became the Yankees' respected head executive, 1898 to be exact, when Barrow was president of the Atlantic League. Barrow recounted it in *My Fifty Years in Baseball:*

> During those years, I used every device I could think of . . . to bring out the fans . . . many things I never would have done in later years or, for that matter, been allowed to do after baseball became well organized and regulated.
>
> Among other things, I dug up a girl pitcher. Her name was Lizzie Stroud. Someone told me that Jack Stivetts, the old Oriole, had taught her how to pitch, and I must say she wasn't too bad. Lizzie thought the name "Arlington" was more glamorous for professional purposes than Stroud, and it was as Lizzie Arlington that I booked her around the League. She made a number of appearances—in Paterson, Newark, Wilmington, Philadelphia, and Lancaster. After that, interest faded. So did Lizzie, I guess. But for a while it pepped up the gate.

Research conducted by SABR members does not totally corroborate Barrow's recollections. For one thing, Barrow did not really "dig up" Lizzie; she had been discovered by William J. O'Conner, an agent for sports and theatrical personalities, and she pitched in two semipro games before she came up to the Atlantic League. Her first game as a true minor leaguer was for the Reading team on July 5, 1898, and the local paper described the occasion as follows:

> With Lizzie Arlington heralded as the "most famous lady pitcher in the world," as a special attraction, over 1000 persons wended their way to the ball grounds Tuesday afternoon, including 200 ladies. But she was apparently brought there to show the audience what she

looks like and how she dresses, for she appeared only a few minutes in practice and twirled the last inning.

Lizzie was put in to pitch only in the ninth inning, when Reading had a five-run lead; she gave up two hits and a walk but got the side out without a run. Still, the Reading paper concluded: "Miss Arlington might do as a pitcher among amateurs, but the sluggers of the Atlantic League would soon put her out of the business. She, of course, hasn't the strength to get much speed on and has poor control. But, for a woman, she is a success." And that, according to the latest research, is the only game she actually played in the minors, despite the claims of Ed Barrow.

But Lizzie was not the only woman to play in a minor league game. On September 7, 1936, Frances "Sonny" Dunlap played right field for an entire game for the Fayetteville (Arkansas) Bears, in the Class-D Arkansas-Missouri League; although she did not hit safely, she connected with the ball on all of her three times at bat. That was her first and only appearance, however, and it also seems to have been the last time that a woman played in an officially recorded game of men's organized baseball.

There have been other attempts to sign women on in the minors. In April 1931, a nineteen-year-old girl, Vada Corbus, was reported as signing on for a tryout as a catcher with the Joplin (Missouri) Miners of the Class-C Western Association, but she never actually played in a regulation game. And in June 1952, the Harrisburg (Pennsylvania) Senators of the Class-B Inter-State League announced they were about to sign twenty-four-year-old Mrs. Eleanor Engle and she worked out as a shortstop in practice, but before she could play a game the president of the league prohibited signing women as players. Commissioner of Baseball Ford Frick supported this ruling, and *The Sporting News* reported, "Even President Bill Veeck of the Browns, who presented a midget in a game last year and tried many bizarre promotional stunts, declared it was going too far."

That effectively ends the history of women as players in men's organized or professional baseball. All the other reported episodes involve something less than official games. Babe Didrikson, probably the greatest all-round woman athlete, once pitched against the Cleveland Indians in New Orleans, but that was a spring season exhibition game. In July 1935, Paul "Daffy" Dean pitched to a Kitty Burke who had broken through the crowd on the field in Cincinnati and grabbed a bat; he lobbed her an easy one that she hit back to him, and he let her take first base before the umpire removed her.

One of the most oft-told tales is of the game on April 2, 1931, when a seventeen-year-old lefty, Jackie Mitchell, pitched for the Chattanooga Lookouts against the New York Yankees: Mitchell struck out Babe Ruth and Lou Gehrig and walked Tony Lazzeri and was then removed. Again, this was a preseason exhibition game and the whole thing was a publicity stunt arranged by the club's owner. The other most-recounted incident involves a game on August 14, 1922, between the Boston Red Sox and an All-Star team of American League players; Lizzie Murphy, who played with women's and mixed amateur teams in and around Providence, Rhode Island, was allowed to play first base for the Red Sox for one inning, and made one putout. Once again, though, this was an exhibition game, to raise money for the family of a recently deceased Red Sox player. And in another, less-noted exhibition, Joan Joyce, regarded by some as the best women's softball pitcher ever, struck out Ted Williams four times—but frankly this raises the question of whether Williams wasn't showing a bit of noblesse oblige.

There is another, still less-known footnote to this story of women playing baseball with and against men, and that involves the Negro leagues, before baseball was integrated. In 1912, J. L. "Wilkie" Wilkinson, a white minor league pitcher later to win renown as the owner of the Kansas City Monarchs, organized an All Nations team, a touring baseball team made up of American blacks, Indians, whites, Cubans, Mexicans, and even Japanese; on occasion, a woman called "Carrie Nation" played second base.

During the heyday of the Negro leagues, no women were on their teams. But after the majors were integrated, black teams became desperate to attract fans and became little more than touring show teams (in the manner of the Harlem Globetrotters). Marcenia "Tony" Stone had played with several such teams, including the famous House of David team (which Babe Didrikson also pitched for on occasion), and in 1953 Tony Stone was signed to play second base for the Indianapolis Clowns. In 1954, Stone went over to play for the Kansas City Monarchs, while the Clowns signed on two other women, Conni Morgan and Mamie "Peanut" Johnson. Tony Stone retired from the Negro majors with a .243 batting average.

It is clear that women were allowed into organized and professional baseball as something between freaks and teasers, to "pep up the gate," as Barrow put it. At least those days have gone, but there is no sign that women are going to break into the major leagues in the immediate future. For now the ones who have come closest are the heroines of two novels, Michael Bowen's *Can't Miss* (1987) and Barbara Gregorich's *She's on First* (1988), each imagining the first woman to play in the majors.

*The Professionals* Everything said about the failure of women to penetrate the world of serious professional baseball must have one asterisk, one exception: The All-American Girls Professional Baseball League (AAGPBL). This was a league of professional women baseball players formed in 1943 that ended in 1954. At its peak, it had ten teams (many managed by major leaguers) spread around the Midwest; the young women played as many as 120 games in a season at salaries up to $150 a week; some 500 women played during the twelve years and in 1948 the teams drew over a million fans; there were stats (pitching and batting records and the like), pennants, and championships, and even tours to Cuba and Nicaragua.

There is not much more to say about the AAGPBL that has not already been said in articles and books, including a 1976 master's degree thesis from the University of Massachusetts by Marie Fidler. There was even a TV documentary, "A League of Their Own," shown in 1987. (One of its producers was Kelly Candaele, son of Helen Callaghan, who played in the AAGPBL, and brother of Casey Candaele, second baseman with the Montreal Expos

*One of the stars of the first and only professional women's baseball league, the AAGPBL, was Helen Callaghan, shown (left) at bat in 1945. Note the feminine touch of the skirt—not really practical for playing baseball. At the 1986 reunion of these women, Helen Callaghan Candaele (mother of major leaguer Casey Candaele) shows she still has a lot on the ball.*

since 1986.) But there are several curious footnotes to this chapter in the history of professional baseball. The league, for instance, is now celebrated as an early example of "liberated women," when in fact the men behind it were less concerned with women's rights or abilities than with pleasing men.

The league was the idea of Philip K. Wrigley, owner of the Chicago Cubs and determined to do his bit for the war effort. (Cynics might also point out that since his Cubs were losing patrons and the majors were threatened with the possibility of shutting down for the duration, he was looking for a way to fill some seats.) He first proposed a women's softball league that would play in National League ballparks on off-dates, the goal being "patriotic service in building morale." When this initial plan failed to gain support (interestingly enough, about the only support within the league came from Branch Rickey, who would soon support another break with tradition), Wrigley changed his plan and set up a league that went into medium-sized cities in the Midwest, specifically cities with war industries. The idea was to provide a bit of sex appeal, so to speak, for the men stuck at home in factory jobs.

Then, as is typical of the times, having decided to dangle these women before the boys on the homefront, Wrigley and his people worked to make sure that they were sanitized sex objects. Actually, there were two images of women baseball players that had to be overcome: One was the old tradition of such women as "tramps" and the other was the tradition of such women as "tomboys." The former, of course, was a euphemism for prostitutes, the latter for lesbians. To counteract both images, chaperones were hired to be sort of "dorm mothers" for the teams, and none other than Helena Rubenstein was hired by the league to set up a "charm school" that prospective players were required to attend as part of their spring training. In these sessions they were taught everything from how to walk and talk and how to handle social situations such as eating in restaurants to how to dress properly and how to do their hair and makeup. They were also instructed in how to attract "the right kind of men." No tramps need apply.

The president of the AAGPBL, Ken Sells, put it bluntly: "Femininity is the keynote of our league; no pants-wearing, tough-talking female softballer will play on any of our four teams." Publicity photos and appearances invariably featured the most attractive women. The final giveaway of the ambivalent image that the team promised was the uniform Mrs. Wrigley designed: It had a short skirt that revealed a lot of thigh—but special satin shorts to hide everything else. Thus did these women assume the role of Betty Grable, who toured the battlefields in a swimsuit.

It is easy to snicker at all this now, but in its day it wasn't really that extreme. Feminists who today have latched on to this AAGPBL as proof that

North American women (for, by the way, there were many Canadian women in the AAGPBL) had begun to break down the sexual stereotypes in World War II, however, tend to ignore this aspect of the league. Boosters of the AAGPBL who contend that it was truly a "major league" also ignore the fact that in the first years the game these women engaged in was more like softball than baseball, including underhand pitching, a large ball, and a small diamond. Eventually the rules did change and the game became much like regulation baseball. But the boasting about the women's records cuts both ways: pitcher after pitcher with an ERA of 0.93, or 0.81, or 0.77—or the record for a season, 0.67; a pitcher who hurled two perfect games in two seasons; two pitchers who won thirty-three games in a season; a woman taking the batting championship with a .429 average; a woman stealing 201 bases—in 203 attempts. Such statistics are so far out of line when set alongside over one hundred years of men's baseball that it suggests a different level of play.

But the women themselves were serious about the game and took the "charm school" aspect with a grain of rosin. (Some participants and observers, in fact, argue that it helped many young women acquire some social graces they otherwise would never have had a chance at.) They should definitely not be confused with those nineteenth-century teams of "Blondes" and "Brunettes." The AAGPBL women played skillfully and they played to win. Individual players such as Dottie Schroeder and Dottie Kamenshek were top-level ballplayers. Kamenshek, in fact, was offered a contract by Fort Lauderdale of the regular minor leagues but she signed on with a semipro woman's softball team. So there is much to celebrate about this first and only true women's professional baseball league while keeping it in its true perspective. This was recognized in November 1988 when the Baseball Hall of Fame opened a permanent exhibit on women in baseball, most of it paying tribute to the AAGPBL.


*Little League*   Although adult women have generally given up playing baseball, there is one group of females who did not abandon the game or the fight. The Little League set. Nowadays, when girls show up on the roster of Little League teams competing for the world championship, it is easy to forget how recently the girls have attained this right—1974, in fact.

The circumstances that led to the "revolution of '74" can be fairly easily reconstructed, but what was overlooked then as now is the first battle in this revolution, in 1928. There was no Little League back then but there was American Legion Junior Baseball—also and obviously limited to boys. But Margaret Gisolo was accepted on a team in Blanford, Indiana, and contributed significantly to her team's moving on to the Mid-East regional tournament, in which they were beaten by a Chicago team. Protests were made from the time Gisolo and her team began to look like winners, but these were temporarily squelched when Commissioner of Baseball Kenesaw Mountain Landis himself supported her right to play. The Legion made sure this wouldn't happen again, however, by amending its by-laws to read that "boys only" could play on its teams, and there were no more girls in 1929 or any successive years.

That is where things stood for girls and youth baseball until 1974. Some years before that, a few Little League teams scattered throughout the United States allowed the occasional girl to play, but if the Little League's national headquarters got wind of it they took away the charter of the team. By the early '70s, some parents and their supporters were turning to the law on behalf of their daughters, but in Michigan and Massachusetts the courts upheld the Little League.

The breakthrough case arose in New Jersey in 1972. Twelve-year-old Maria Pepe was allowed on a Hoboken Little League team, but after she had played two games the national headquarters threatened to take away the team's charter. The local county chapter of the National Organization for Women decided to take up the fight and eventually the case went to the three-judge Appellate Division of Superior Court.

Little League Baseball, Inc., fought with all the arguments it could muster: Girls were too weak, their bones were too fragile; their reaction time was two thousandths of a second slower than that of boys; they would one day develop breast cancer if hit on the chest by a ball; there weren't separate toilets, and boys in any case often urinated on the field; the girls might be exposed to obscenities; there might be inadvertent touching of private parts in close plays; there was a rule that the manager must inspect to make sure the catcher was wearing a protective cup; and how about a coach who was used to patting his boys on the rear end or, the ultimate depravity, now would have to rub a girl's leg when she was injured. Essentially ignoring all such physical and psychological arguments, the judges ruled, two to one, in March 1974 that girls must be allowed on the teams, but the decision was based on the claim that Little League teams fell under the laws governing "public accommodations."

As the case made its way up through the New Jersey courts, however, the state's Little League teams and their communities found themselves embroiled in terrible disputes. Hundreds of teams voted to suspend play rather than accept girls, and communities were split as friends and neighbors found themselves arguing and demonstrating on opposite sides of the issue. The decision, however, inspired girls in other states to fight; one who received considerable publicity was Kimberly Green, daughter of Dallas Green, then directing the Phillies' scouting and farm system but more recently manager of the New York Yankees. Recognizing the inevitable, in June 1974 the Little League headquarters announced it would "defer to the changing climate" and permit girls. The federal charter it operates under, however, had to be amended, and this task was undertaken by Congresswoman Martha Griffiths of Michigan. On December 26, 1974, President Gerald Ford signed the bill, which had found an extremely simple solution to what seemed to be a thorny issue; wherever the word "boy" appeared, it was replaced by "young people."

That pretty much ended the struggle for young girls' right to play baseball with their peers. (Virtually all the men and teams who had quit when girls were going to be forced on them rejoined the league.) It didn't entirely end the controversy surrounding the issue, however. Many predicted that it would wipe out all-girls softball teams, but that has not come to pass. Others predicted that if no teams could be limited to one sex then boys would take over girls' sports such as field hockey. That has not happened. Nor have the other dire results predicted ever come to pass—incidents involving private parts and such.

Although some communities and teams undoubtedly are more hospitable to girls in Little League than others, the effect on the game itself has been all but unnoticed. Since most communities find space on their Little League teams for all young people who try out, girls usually "make the team"; any member of a team who shows up at a game must have at least two innings in the field and one at-bat, but any girl (or boy, for that matter) confined to this minimum can soon get discouraged and drop out. This often happens with the girls because, with some exceptions, they do not match the strength of boys in playing baseball.

One issue raised by the president of Little League Baseball, Inc., back in 1974, however, was never much publicized. "The great irony in this whole thing," he said, "is that the people who for so long attacked the Little League as being bad for boys, too competitive for them, are now precisely the people who are anxious for girls to share this awful traumatic experience." Presumably he was referring to the type of articulate middle-class people who would support such groups as NOW and the civil rights movement, the implication being that blue-collar families didn't object to gender-separate teams—any more than they objected to the macho-competitive element in Little League. He probably had a point, but if so it is just one of those passing ironies. The more enduring truth is that there have always been some girls and young women who want to play real baseball, and now they have that choice.

*Throwing Like a Girl* Hovering on the edge of any discussion of girls—or, for that matter, females of any age—playing baseball is the question, But can females really play the game like boys, do they have the physical "right stuff," let alone the psychological-emotional constitution? Presumably everyone can accept that the last-named factor, the psychological-emotional makeup, is by definition a matter of culture and conditioning. If a girl is made to feel she can play well, if she is trained and coached like a boy, if she is made to feel welcome on a team, her psychology and emotions, however different they may be, are quite adequate to playing team sports. Examples are everywhere, from Pony League softball teams to Olympic champion volleyball teams. On the other hand, it must also be admitted that if boys on Little League teams are going to harass a girl or in any way make her feel unwelcome, then many a girl is going to drop out of baseball before she really gets a chance to show her physical abilities.

But does a female's physical constitution "match up" to a male's when it comes to playing baseball? No one denies that women's physical development leaves them somewhat behind males when it comes to most athletic attainments; whether the general population is being compared or whether the best are being compared, women's times, distances, weights, what-have-you fall short of men's. True, the best female athletes can beat all but the best male athletes at their events, but there are definite physical explanations for why the fastest women do not run as fast as the fastest men in the one hundred meters, why the best women javelin throwers cannot attain the distances of the best male javelin throwers. This usually carries over right down to at least the level of high school competition, where the same differences hold true. At the younger ages, individual girls' somewhat faster maturation might well lead to situations in which the fastest person or best hitter in the sixth grade is a girl.

Let it be accepted, though, that there are certain physical explanations for why girls on the average are not going to be able to hit a baseball as far as boys on the average, why girls on the average cannot run to first base or to deep center as fast as boys on the average. That still leaves the one prevailing stereotype to deal with: Why must girls "throw like a girl"? Way back in 1883, that *New York Times* reporter described the way the young women playing at the Polo Grounds threw the ball: "Each one just raised her hand to the level of her ear and then sent it forward with a push from the elbow." So what's new?

Again, to clear the field for this pitchers' duel, it must be accepted that there are countless females of various ages, at least from high school on up, who can throw like males; that is, they use their body and arm to throw a ball overhand in the manner of the male thrower. But right there is where the question begins to become tricky. Do all males in fact always throw a ball overhand in this "male" manner? Is this not a manner used by some North American males and now passed on to males around the world who play baseball with some dedication? Do Taiwanese and Cuban and Korean boys start at any early age and instinctively throw a ball overhand like American boys? For that matter, do all American boys instinctively throw overhand in this "best" way?

The simple answer is that not all American boys do throw overhand in the approved manner. You have only to look around the neighborhood, if not in your own backyard, to see boys who "throw like a girl." A coach at Springfield College in Massachusetts, virtually all of whose students attend because they have a special interest in physical activities at some level, states flatly that many a male student "throws like a girl." Meanwhile you have only to go to a softball game between trained teams of girls or young women to realize that they can throw that ball "like boys."

Confronted with such exceptions—college boys who throw like girls, high school girls who throw like boys—even reasonable people will probably say that these are just that, exceptions to the general rule. Those males somehow failed to develop normally, those females were specially trained. Why, anyone can tell you: Put a ball in the hand of the average five-year-old boy and he throws it overhand like a major leaguer; place a ball in the hand of an average five-year-old girl and she throws "like a girl."

Again, this is where this law of nature begins to be tested. People want to believe that all little boys instinctively throw overhand in this manner, when in fact they don't. Rather, a lot of little boys in North America—and increasingly throughout the world, wherever baseball is played—have a lot of encouragement, the influence of role models, and instruction from their fathers and older brothers or neighborhood boys so that early on many little boys do start throwing overhand in the approved manner. Their training may may well begin with throwing objects other than balls—stones, for instance, or sticks—just as in societies in which soccer is the national pastime little boys are soon taught to emulate their older brothers and fathers by kicking objects and balls. Often as not this instruction is not deliberate or articulated, it is just the way things are done. Meanwhile, little girls in most societies are not being encouraged, by example or otherwise, to throw objects of any kind or in any manner. Certainly there has not been much reason until quite recent decades to encourage little girls to perfect their overarm throw. After all, who expects a girl to grow up to be a baseball player?

So, yes, many girls do end up throwing "like girls." And yes, girls do differ from boys in some of their anatomy and musculature. The bones in a female are set up with a slightly different lever system and the muscular mass is just different enough so that girls and women are not able to throw a ball quite as fast or as far as boys and men.

There is a doctoral dissertation well known to all experts in biomechanics or kinesiology or movement sciences, "Movement Characteristics of the Overarm Throw: A Kinematic Analysis of Men and Women Performers," by Anne Elizabeth Atwater (submitted at the University of Wisconsin in 1970). It's based on careful analysis of stop-action pictures of skilled college-age males and females throwing a softball overhand. And she did indeed discover differences between males and females as groups:

> Available data revealed that the velocity mean for men was considerably higher than the velocity mean for women, and superior performances by women barely surpassed average performances by men. . . . The average woman exhibited the least rapid body segment accelerations and decelerations of any group of subjects. By continuing to rotate the upper trunk forward at a relatively slow rate, these average women positioned the upper arm almost directly in front of the right shoulder so that the elbow extension just prior to release resulted in a "pushing" motion to project the ball. . . . The plane in which skilled men and women throwers move the forearm, hand, and ball forward just prior to release differs from the plane of action for women classified as average in throwing velocity.

But as damaging as this may sound to the conclusion that women throw "like girls" simply because they have not been trained from an early enough age to throw like boys, that is in fact the conclusion that the experts now draw from this and related studies. Your perception may, well be right: Many females do throw "like girls." But what this classic study had discovered is that inexperienced and less coordinated individuals of either sex had not mastered the complex movement patterns required for throwing a ball over-hand as major leaguers do. There is no known anatomical or physiological basis for limiting girls to throwing like girls. And if all males naturally threw overhand the same way, we would not even have the expression, "he throws like a girl."

*The Owneresses*    When John McNamara was abruptly dismissed as man-ager of the Red Sox after the All-Star break in 1988, it was soon made clear that the decisive force behind this move was Mrs. Jean Yawkey. True, she owned a large share of the club only because she had inherited it from her late husband, Tom Yawkey. But it was also true that this was not the first occasion on which she had acted forthrightly to maintain the club and team as she saw fit, even if it meant stepping on a few men's toes (and even over the occasional man's body). Many a woman inherits a business from her late husband but turns the operations over to some lawyer or surrogate. Yet here, as in so many other realms, baseball seems to defy convention when it comes to women: Baseball clubs have a long tradition of being owned and actively run by women.

The tradition may have begun at the turn of the century when the New York Giants were owned by the notorious Andrew Freedman. There is some question whether he or his wife was more detested and dreaded by the team; he only underpaid or fired them, but she is said to have sat at the Polo Grounds and occasionally called players or managers over and given them advice on how to win the game in progress. But the first woman who will come to most people's minds today is Marge Schott, prime owner of the Cincinnati Reds. Anyone who has any doubts about whether she has taken an active role in running that club need only speak with that other pillar of the contemporary Reds, Pete Rose. There have been many articles on Marge Schott and her ways of handling the Cincinnati club. But fading into memory's middle distance now is another wealthy and strong-willed woman who owned a ballclub, Joan Whitney Payson. Actually, Mrs. Payson stands alone in being the only woman effectively to found a major league ball club, the New York Mets.

Mrs. Payson, heir to the vast Whitney fortune, had been a baseball fan since her childhood, when her mother took her to see the Giants at the old Polo Grounds. By the 1950s, Mrs. Payson owned about a 10 percent share of the Giants, but that was not enough to stop the main owners from moving the franchise to San Francisco in 1957. When a few years later it was determined that New York could have another National League club, Mrs. Payson put up 85 percent of the funding, some $4 million.

Although she made some requests that were heeded—she was instrumental in getting Casey Stengel to come manage the team—she did not try to exercise the power commensurate with her share of ownership. (She wanted the team, for instance, to be called the Meadow Larks, but this was rejected.) She kept her own representative on the Mets' board, but over the years she never interfered in the day-to-day operations, let alone in the field play.

Instead, she was satisfied to be the Mets' number-one fan, attending as many games as she could fit into her busy schedule. Munching steadily on popcorn or candy as she sat in her choice box with her family or friends, Mrs. Payson was a familiar figure during the early years of the Mets' rise from the cellar to the pinnacle of the majors in 1969 and in the years that followed before she sold her share to Nelson Doubleday. An extremely supersitious fan, though: She crossed her fingers at crucial moments, turned her back when certain players came to bat, repeated whatever she was doing at the moment the Mets got hot, and forbade anyone in her box to change seats while the Mets were ahead. Always a jolly grande dame, good for a quotation for the next edition or a gesture for the evening newscast, Mrs. Payson probably thought she was starting a team as a tax loss, but it ended up a money-maker. To many New York baseball fans of those years, somehow the fabulously wealthy Joan Whitney Payson was the personification of the scrappy underdog Mets.

Yet even Mrs. Payson could not claim to have been the first woman president of a major league ball club. That distinction fell to another remarkable woman, Helene "Lady Bee" Britton, now all but faded in memory's far distance. In 1911, only thirty-two years old, as Mrs. Schuyler Britton, she inherited the St. Louis Cardinals from her uncle. (Her father had bought the team with this brother in 1898 and then left it to him on his death in 1905.)

At first she was reluctant to become involved in what was regarded as a "tricky" business at best, but the club's fortunes and profits rose and she became increasingly more engaged in details of running the club. Too engaged for the likes of Roger Bresnahan, who was managing the team: "No woman can tell me how to play a ball game!" he exploded after Lady Bee questioned his managing following a loss, and he quit the post. She promoted Ladies Day at the ballpark and she and her husband, whom she named president of the club in 1913, introduced a singer and band music to provide entertainment between innings. Eventually, though, her marriage deteriorated as her husband became more attached to the bottle than the ball team; in 1916, after one of his drunken nights, he left, never to return. Within hours she assumed the title of president of the Cardinals.

Back in 1914, the seven other owners of the National League clubs had tried to sell her franchise out from under Helene Britton, but she stood her ground and retained ownership. She drove some of those men up the wall by coming to every owners' meeting and sitting in the front row at all sessions as well as in the annual picture. (Imagine—a woman running a ball club in 1914!) Now, in 1916, with her husband gone and two children to raise, she decided to sell the Cardinals, and with that she vanished from the pages of baseball history. But for five years, this unusual young woman had owned and operated a major league ball club. Perhaps she and Mrs. Payson are even now sitting in some Great Ball Park in the Sky and watching their teams slug it out in the Eternal Pennant Race.

*The Negro Leagues*  Through the first half of the twentieth century, black Americans, of course, were segregated in baseball as in just about every other area of American society. Little wonder, then, that some differences developed in the world of the Negro teams, differences that inevitably involved the role of women in the culture of baseball. In black communities that did not have much else they could call their own, the Negro ball teams and their games were much closer to the social fabric. In this less professional, more homey world of Negro baseball, women were thus included in more informal ways than in the more organized world of white man's baseball.

In the earliest phase, back in the nineteenth century, local black baseball games were as much entertainment and social occasions as sports contests. Women, black historian William Carl Bolivar has said, "lent value by numbers and general attractiveness" on such occasions, and "there were picnics, dances, and lunches showered upon the players." Not surprisingly, this tradition survived even into the heyday of the Negro leagues, when attendance at games carried a sense of being at a glamorous social affair. In her history of the Kansas City Monarchs, Janet Bruce writes:

> Stepin Fetchit and Count Basie attended whenever they were in Kansas City. Basie explained that he went to Monarchs games on Sunday afternoons "because that was where everybody was going on a Sunday afternoon." Most fans did not attend in casual clothes. "They wore their finery!" asserted Buck O'Neil. "They'd have their fur stoles on and their hats on—just like they left church." Jesse Fisher . . . elaborated on the idea of the glamour of the game: "I tell you, women used to fry their hair. Used to get up early in the morning if the Monarchs were coming to town. . . . You could smell hair burning for a week—straightening that hair, getting ready for them Monarchs, with those great, big, pretty hats on.

Bruce goes on to tell how local merchants appealed to women to get dressed up for the games: "The Monarchs Are Here!" read an ad from a clothing store. "The opening game of the Monarchs is always a Fashion Parade and of course you will want to look your best." Ladies Day was a widely used promotion in the Negro leagues, for ladies could not only be ticket-buying "fannettes," they would attract male fans. "If you fannettes want to display new hats and dresses this summer, you can do so at an added expense of only $.15," was one appeal from the Kansas City Monarchs for women to buy box seats. The Negro leagues, like the white folks' majors, also hoped that the presence of women would make the men fans mind their language and behavior. That may or may not have worked, but both black players and black women from that era have testified that young black women definitely tried to attract them both during and after the games.

Among other promotional gimmicks that the Negro leagues came up with were bands with drum majorettes, booster clubs, and beauty contests. The Kansas City Monarchs, for example, had its own booster club, which began in the early 1920s as a true fans' club but became more like a prestigious civic organization with prominent white men taking over. In 1939 and 1940, the Kansas City Booster Club sponsored a "Miss Monarch" bathing beauty contest; one at a time, the contestants paraded from the dugout to home plate and stepped on a podium where they removed their beachrobes; the winner was determined by the volume of the crowd's applause as well as by a committee of judges (which, as is typical of the day, included white women). The plan was that the winner would represent Kansas City at a Miss Negro American League contest, but none of the other teams in the league ever got around to running contests.

When World War II came along, the bathing suit contest was dropped and in 1942 a sports editor for a black newspaper simply chose a young woman to represent "the spirit of Baseball"; she was no longer wearing a bathing suit but was pictured looking very solemn to "stress the seriousness" of the times. After the war ended and the Negro leagues were in decline, they tried to boost interest by picking a "queen" at some of the East-West games up through 1955 (this was the Negro leagues' equivalent of the All-Star Game) but by then even gorgeous young ladies, in finery or out of it, couldn't save the Negro leagues.

Not even Effa Manley could do that, and Effa was one of the more remarkable women to be involved with baseball, in any league and in any era. It was Effa's husband, Abe Manley, twenty years older than she and a streetwise black man, who during the 1930s built up the Newark Eagles as a Negro National League club by using his profits from the numbers racket. But everyone agreed that the day-to-day operations of the Eagles were left to Effa, whom Abe had met at the 1932 World Series, fittingly enough, since they both loved baseball.

With Abe supplying the money and scouting for new players, Effa took over virtually all the other operations of their team, and from all reports she excelled at all she undertook. The only time she seems to have been resented was when she interfered with managers in the details of the game. One of the tales told about her was that she would sit in the stands and cross and uncross her legs as signals to players to bunt, or hit and run, or whatever. Her legs were said to be quite attractive, and one day a batter watching them for the sign was hit on the head by a pitch because she had hesitated; when he returned to the lineup a week later he was wearing a hardhat he had picked up at a construction site—and thus did Effa Manley help invent the batting helmet.

Such stories were bound to arise when a woman as young and attractive as Effa was operating in what was essentially an all-male world. She could be tough but understanding with her players, and she could be tough but reasonable with other owners. As late as 1946, she and Abe proudly bought a new sixteen-thousand-dollar bus for their team to tour in, even as the Negro leagues saw the beginning of the end when the major league teams began to recruit their better players for their farm teams. Effa Manley did her best to save the all-black clubs, but she also recognized that ultimately integration was best for the black players so she worked to get her players the best terms she could.

Effa Manley fought for the rights of black people in more arenas than baseball parks. She was active with the New Jersey branch of the National Association for the Advancement of Colored People; in 1934 she picketed to help desegregate the employment policies in Harlem department stores; she had the usherettes in her ballpark wear sashes that read "Stop Lynching" when they collected money for that cause; and during World War II she organized special entertainments for the "colored" soldiers at Fort Dix. All this at a time before too many Americans in or out of baseball were taking such a public stand for equality.

Many years later, asked to describe Effa Manley, one of her former players said she was "a very light-skinned black woman," and that is how most of the people who knew her during her career with the Newark Eagles thought of her. In fact, this extraordinary woman was a white woman, the illegitimate daughter of a German-American woman from Philadelphia who had six other children by her two black husbands. Although Effa's father was white, she grew up with a black stepfather and mulatto siblings and evidently identified with black Americans. Whatever her motives or feelings, Effa Manley was a woman who contributed to connecting baseball to the broader patterns of American life.

*Sex and the Game*   At least since Jim Bouton pitched and told all in his controversial bestseller of 1970, *Ball Four,* Americans who care about such things have known that baseball players are just normal foulmouthed, dirty-

*One of the most extraordinary women to be involved with baseball was Effa Manley, who in the 1930s and 1940s served as general manager of the all-black Newark Eagles, owned by her husband; he was black and Effa was white, although she sort of "passed" as a light-skinned black. Manley antagonized some of her managers by interfering on many occasions but generally held the respect of all who dealt with her, including the owners of major league teams who eventually bought her star players and put the Eagles out of business.*

minded boys who have a thing about girls. Anyone who truly cared could have had a hint of this from an earlier (1960) pitch-and-tell book, *The Long Season,* by former National League pitcher Jim Brosnan. Brosnan was considerably more discreet in the language and incidents he chose to hang out on the line, but many aficionados of baseball books now tend to value his book above Bouton's. The interminable bravado, beaver, and blasphemies of Bouton's book now appear dated, and in any case it seems to have had little or no effect on the game of baseball as it is played and watched and revered. Its biggest effect, in fact, has been on encouraging a series of other books in which players, and now players' wives, insist on telling us about *their* sex lives. Why it should be and what it means is unclear, but neither ice hockey nor football nor basketball nor gymnastics nor any form of athletic endeavor except baseball seems to have need of this genre of sexual revelations.

Throughout the first century or more of baseball, there seems to have been little interest in and less written about the sexual activities, marital or otherwise, of baseball players. That a lot of them drank and brawled and wenched was taken for granted; that some of them got "involved" with women was also a vocational hazard. After all, here were all these athletic young men often on the road and with lots of time to hang around hotels and bars. And it did seem a fairly glamorous profession to many Americans. Perhaps it was best expressed by the manager of a hotel where black ballplayers stayed during the days of the Negro leagues: "Women follow a uniform— whether it's a soldier, musician, ballplayer."

That linking of the ballplayer with a musician showed great insight, for to this day the two professions share certain aspects, both allowing a freedom from ordinary routines that might translate into libertinism. Certainly if "musician" is broadened to include show business, the two careers share numerous elements, and just as "good" families didn't want their daughters to become actresses, "good" families didn't want their sons to become ballplayers.

The tradition of uniting the rowdy of baseball with the risqué of showbiz began with Rube Marquard and Blossom Seeley, but although they appeared together in vaudeville, no one pried into their sex lives. Babe Ruth was known to make time for the ladies, and his second wife, Claire Merritt Hodgson, although never a Ziegfield Follies girl as sometimes claimed, was a model and minor stage performer. In the next generation, much good copy was extracted from the marriage of Leo Durocher with the actress Laraine Day, but this was nothing compared to that generated by the marriage of Joe DiMaggio and Marilyn Monroe. That union of two Living Myths didn't work, but again, although there was some mild innuendo at the time, no one really pried into their sex lives.

Since then, it has been no holds barred, with everyone getting into bed with everyone else, and box scores issued daily. In 1972 there was the mild titillation when two Yankee pitchers, Fritz Peterson and Mike Kekich, "traded" wives (for no one even considered that two women would want to "trade" their ballplayer husbands); Peterson and the former Mrs. Kekich remain married as of 1988, but Kekich and the former Mrs. Peterson were divorced after less than a year. Aside from the occasional paternity suit or barroom brawl, there were no big scandals (unless one counts the divorces of such All-American Idols as Pete Rose and Steve Garvey) until the 1987 linking of Oakland A's players with teenage prostitutes in Minneapolis. Then 1988 produced the Wade Boggs scandal: Although his league-leading .366 BA seemed to lay to rest once and for all the age-old debate over whether sexual intercourse sapped an athlete's strength (serious thinkers long argued the pros and cons of this, but probably the only people to do so today are team managers) it did not deflect the public's interest in his affair, which all but threatened to spoil his career, if not the Red Sox.

Ballplayers today are virtually all presented as monogamous young men, whether single or married, more interested in the heft of a bat than the curve of a female. It is hard to imagine a *Sports Illustrated* article revealing that a player is as dedicated to bedding women as, say, Dwight Evans was shown to be to eating his wife's pesto. Yet it is also true that there exist the groupies, known as *Annies* or *Shirleys* or *bimbos* in various cities, so lustily portrayed in the movie *Bull Durham* yet so hastily ignored by sports reporters. Although one might have thought Jim Bouton let so much hang out that there is nothing more to shock and everyone can get on with the game, Margo Adams and Bob Guccione have shown that you shouldn't underestimate the public's need to be titillated.

*Female Fans*  Women were present at the birth of baseball and they remain among its biggest fans. Women make up 43 percent of the viewers of televised major league baseball games. Of the 55 million North Americans who pay to attend major league games each year now, some 35 percent are females of varying ages; an even higher percentage of those who attend minor league games are females. Down at the Little League level women are apt to make up well over half those in attendance; yes, they are there as proud or nervous mothers, but they are there.

Many women are active as managers and coaches of youth baseball teams, just as many women are dedicated fans of major league teams, and they are often very savvy when it comes to "inside" baseball. (Someone got a master's degree in physical education by showing that there is no significant difference in the degree of baseball knowledge of males and females who identify themselves as major league baseball fans.) In 1986 *Harper's Index* reported that 32 percent of men polled said their biggest sports thrill would be to get the winning hit in the World Series; of women asked the same question, 37 percent came up with the World Series game-winner. It can be said that this is because women know they have no chance to score the winning goal in the Stanley Cup or the winning touchdown in the Superbowl, but that's the point. Baseball is a sport that women can identify with.

Women also show up as sportscasters these days and talk knowingly and caringly about baseball, and women sports reporters have even won the right to enter the locker room along with male reporters. Like many such battles by the women's righters that at first seemed so controversial (women in men's bars, girls in Little League), once they are won, they vanish as an issue. Now there is a new generation of women who think and write about baseball with a level of sophistication that goes far beyond what is popularly referred to as "women's lib." There are creative writers such as Barbara Gregorich and academic critics such as Cordelia Candelaria who clearly know their baseball. Not all of these new women writing about baseball necessarily bring a feminist perspective to the subject, but some do, such as Sharon Roepke.

Not surprisingly, some of these feminists see a strong sexual element in baseball, although of a kind that eluded Jim Bouton. The psychoanalyst Adrienne E. Harris has published a fascinating article, "Women, Baseball and Words," in which she explores her own lifelong relationship to baseball with "a structural Marxist perspective" that leads her through an analysis of the ideology behind much of modern sport, the role of time peculiar to baseball, "baseball and desire: the sexual body," the excludingly male nature of baseball talk, and various other esoteric aspects of the game that all the millions of words written by men up to now have generally ignored.

Then there is the New York–based writer and video artist Vanalyne Green, who brings an ingenious imagination to focus on baseball. She has been working on a videotape she calls *Home-Run-Hero,* which examines "aesthetic, psychoanalytic, and historic aspects of how the game is played and represented," and uses various experimental visual techniques to illuminate hidden depths of the game. In her section called "Mortal Games," for instance, "the formal strategy is to compare the myth of the labyrinth—the journey of the hero through the maze (mythologically, the bowels of the mother, the dark land in which the hero must show courage or else perish) with the rules for playing major league baseball."

You can snicker or sneer at this sort of talk, but you cannot deny that women have as much right to baseball as do men.

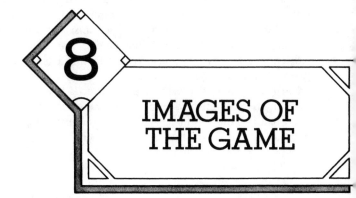

# IMAGES OF THE GAME

**I**t is now taken for granted that sports are an integral part of America's cultural patterns, that sports, athletics, games, and related activities both contribute to and reflect these broader forces. Whole books and university departments are devoted to this proposition, and any newsstand or sportscaster offers more immediate testimony to this phenomenon. It is customary, for instance, for host cities of the modern Olympic Games to mount exhibitions on "sports and the arts" or some similar theme. Countless magazines carry "artistic" photographs of athletes in action—pictures that elevate their exertions from sheer physical feats to "displays" or "performances."

Back in the 1950s, *Sports Illustrated* had a "Sport in Art" editor and occasional issues featured original works of art on sports themes. Thus, the June 13, 1955, issue had a portfolio called "Man Behind the Mask" featuring baseball paintings by one Thomas Meehan. The April 9, 1956, issue had a portfolio titled "An Artist's Ball Game," featuring the baseball paintings of Ralph Fasanella: *Sandlot in the Bronx, Polo Grounds,* and *Sunday Afternoon* (stickball in the street). Fasanella, a mechanic, was an untrained New York City "primitive" artist whose work gained him a considerable reputation. When a traveling exhibit, "Diamonds Are Forever: Artists and Writers on Baseball," appeared at Albany, New York, for its first stop on a nationwide tour (from fall 1987 to spring 1990), paintings by Meehan and Fasanella were featured along with delightful works by many other American artists. (One of the surprises of the exhibit is the lovely watercolor of Fenway Park by the French artist Raoul Dufy—possibly the only work on baseball by a truly foreign artist.) Most of the works in this exhibit are by modern artists—at least since World War II—and they include some wonderfully ingenious and whimsical visions of the game. During the summer of 1987, the Brooklyn Museum also had an art exhibit, "The Grand Game of Baseball—and the Brooklyn Dodgers," featuring fewer but more traditional works on baseball.

What most Americans are not aware of is how early in its history their national pastime began to enter the mainstream of American culture and how thoroughly baseball has lent itself to the arts. Nothing quite like this sudden yet persistent linking of a rather specialized activity and the world of the arts had ever occurred before. True, the ancient Greeks had their Olympics, with statues to winners and odes that elevated the competition to higher meanings; but during the next two thousand years only a few sports were recognized by artists, and these were not popular athletic competitions in the sense that baseball is.

The "sports in art" section in the usual library card catalogue still primarily lists books picturing such activities as hunting, fishing, sailing, and horse racing, traditional aristocratic "sporting" subjects that became increasingly less familiar to an American society that was rapidly becoming urban and middle class. How baseball made its way into the columns of the nineteenth-century sporting periodicals, which thought nothing of placing reports about chess matches alongside horse-race results, hunting stories, and theatrical reviews—because these were all "gentlemen's pursuits"—is itself a lesson in social history. As we showed in Chapter 2, baseball entered as an offshoot of cricket before it gained its own standing. But once baseball was accepted as a legitimate activity, it was quickly taken up by practicing artists.

*First Illustrations*   The history of the illustrations of baseball's forerunners was thoroughly documented by Robert Henderson in his *Baseball and Rounders* (The New York Public Library, 1939), which is also the account that definitively established the ancestry of the game. Among Henderson's more important finds was the 1744 London edition of *A Little Pretty Pocket-Book, intended for the instruction of Little Master Tommy and Pretty Miss Polly,* which contained a rhymed description and a woodcut captioned "base-ball." For

*This may well be the earliest known drawing of grown men playing what is clearly a game of baseball. It appeared in* Porter's Spirit of the Times, *September 12, 1857, and claims to depict a game being played at Hoboken's Elysian Fields in September between the Eagles and the Gothams, two of New York City's better-known teams.*

many years, American publishers tended to "borrow" drawings of baseball-like games from British books, but in 1839 the first truly American illustration of a game of baseball appeared in *The Boy's Book of Sports,* in which children are shown playing a version of the game on the Boston Common. There is a drawing thought to date from the mid-1830s showing young men of Philadelphia's Olympic Club playing a ballgame, but this is regarded as town ball, an earlier version of baseball.

So the first drawing of a true baseball game being played between teams of adults—or at least older youths—seems to be one that appeared in *Porter's Spirit of the Times* of September 12, 1857; it depicts a game played at Hoboken's Elysian Fields between two New York City teams, the Eagles and Gothams. The second such drawing appeared in *Harper's Weekly,* October 15, 1859, and is of a game between the Atlantics and Mutuals; interestingly, it shares the page with a picture of a cricket match, and the accompanying text compares the two games. It would be several years before other magazines

*As an example of how tricky it can be to rely on some of these early illustrations, here is one that appeared in* Frank Leslie's Illustrated Newspaper *on August 26, 1865, where it is captioned as depicting the big game between the Atlantics and Mutuals at the Elysian Fields on August 3, 1865. The crowds do seem to conform with the reports of the day, but no other illustration of the Eylsian Fields has any tree so close to the basepath.*

and newspapers began to carry drawings of baseball games, but by the mid-1860s they had become fairly common as illustrations.

*Currier & Ives* The early drawings of baseball games were hardly works of art; they were simply journalistic illustrations meant to convey some sense of the game to the sport's growing public. The first work that might deserve to be called at least an artful depiction of a baseball game—a work reproduced in many baseball, sports, and social histories—is a Currier & Ives print that is formally titled, "The American National Game of Baseball," with the subtitle, "Grand Match for the Championship at the Elysian Fields, Hoboken, N.J." Many quite reputable books, including the respected *World Book Encyclopedia,* identify the game being depicted as that famous "first game" between the Knickerbockers and the New Yorkers of June 19, 1846, a mistake that, once made, has apparently been passed on by uncritical caption-writers ever since.

The Currier & Ives print in question is clearly dated 1866, and although that doesn't preclude its depicting a game played twenty years before, it does raise questions. In fact, most authoritative books about Currier & Ives do date

*This is the frequently reproduced lithograph issued by Currier & Ives in 1866 and often identified as depicting the famous "first game" of June 19, 1846. This it certainly does not depict. Most likely the artist was not depicting any particular game, although he may have been inspired by a famous game played on August 3, 1865, between the Atlantics and the Mutuals; in any case, it does appear to portray individual members of those teams.*

the game in the 1860s; one says it was played in 1862 between the Atlantics and Eckfords, two Brooklyn teams; another says it depicts a game between the Brooklyn Atlantics and the New York Mutuals on August 26, 1865. But the truly knowledgeable now seem to agree that the game being depicted was in fact played on August 3, 1865, between the Atlantics and the Mutuals, one of the most famous games played up to that time. (Note the date: The Civil War had ended only a few months earlier, and Americans were in the mood to "play ball.")

This August 3 game was the first of a two-game "series" for what these New Yorkers even then presumed to call "the championship of the United States" (the second was played on August 14, over in Brooklyn; the Atlantics won them both). It was well reported in *The New York Times* and other periodicals of the day; so well reported, in fact, that it casts some doubt on whether the artist really was depicting this game. There were said to be twenty thousand spectators present that day, and even allowing for somewhat inflated estimates, there is no way that the Currier & Ives print depicts such a crowd. On the other hand, artistic license may have allowed the artist to eliminate the mass of people who crowded the field, for there is indeed some convincing evidence that the two teams depicted are the Atlantics and Mutuals. The issue is somewhat confused because Currier & Ives ran off these prints in black-and-white and then had them hand-colored, so that different copies sometimes show the teams in different-colored uniforms. Yet because the players' faces are detailed and realistic enough to be compared to existing photographs, a close examination of the team at bat clearly establishes that these are the actual Atlantics being portrayed. As of this writing, it has not been possible to compare the team in the field with a photograph of the Mutuals of that period, but there is good reason to believe that they were the opponents in this famous Currier & Ives print.

Assuming that this is the Atlantics, then it also seems clear that the man up at bat is none other than Dickey Pearce, a famed early player. It is interesting to note that in a book published in 1968, Red Smith, the equally famed sportswriter, said of the man at the plate: "He's got to be Dickey Pearce, star shortstop of the Atlantics, who devised the technique of tapping the ball gently in front of the plate and racing to first base before the defense could recover." Red Smith seems to have based his identification on the way the batter is depicted holding the bat rather than on facial characteristics, but he is probably correct. Smith, however, proceeds to commit his own incredible error: Discussing the print, he finds fault with the second baseman for being too far to the left. A closer look reveals that this player is clearly the shortstop; the basemen are all standing right on their bases.

In conclusion, the Currier & Ives print probably was *inspired* by that famous contest of August 3, 1865, but the artist chose not to clutter it up with thousands of spectators—and indeed, may not even have attended the actual game, for the realistic faces were obviously added in the comfort of a studio. But whatever the contest or teams or players being depicted, what really matters is that Currier & Ives, literally a household name in nineteenth-century America, chose as early as 1866 to include a baseball game in their popular series of prints. At that time, every well-decorated home had its colored lithographs depicting the everyday activities and customs of the land. Although Currier & Ives did reproduce scenes of such traditional sporting subjects as hunting, fishing, horse racing, and boating, they did not see fit to depict any team sport except baseball. Currier & Ives had an instinctive sense of what was acceptable when they allowed baseball into the parlor of respectable society.

It would be nice to leave Currier & Ives on this high plane, but their association with baseball does not end there. The firm published at least four other prints that draw on baseball, one of which is occasionally reproduced, and three others that have been totally, if conveniently, dropped from our national memory. The former is titled, "The National Game. Three 'Outs' and 'One Run': Abraham Winning the Ball," and is a straightforward political cartoon of the day; it was published late in 1860, right after Abraham Lincoln had defeated three other candidates for the presidency. All four men are shown in baseball uniforms and carry bats, and each has an appropriate statement in the "balloon" coming out of his mouth. Lincoln is saying, "Gentlemen, if any of you should ever take a hand in another match at this game,

### THE NATIONAL GAME. THREE "OUTS" AND ONE "RUN".
#### ABRAHAM WINNING THE BALL.

*Perhaps the first illustration that both took baseball for granted and then used it to make a point was this editorial cartoon issued by Currier & Ives after Lincoln's victory in November 1860, in which he had defeated three opponents—(left to right) John Bell, Stephen Douglas, and John Breckinridge. Already the slang of baseball was being used in ordinary speech.*

remember that you must have a 'good bat' and strike a 'fair ball' to make a 'clean score' and a 'home run.' " Nothing all that startling, except that this was only 1860, and although baseball had been around in this recognizable form for barely fifteen years, a political cartoon could rely on the viewers' "insider's" grasp of the game. (There are various tales associating Lincoln with baseball, recounted in Chapter 3, and one wonders if the cartoonist knew something that should make us consider whether these tales might be true.)

This cartoon, then, is a revealing bit of Americana. But what of the long-forgotten other Currier & Ives baseball prints, the ones that are never reproduced? During the 1880s and 1890s, the Currier & Ives firm issued a series of prints that gave vent to the emerging spirit of racism in America. These prints probably did not express any personal views of Currier or Ives but were simply issued to make a quick buck; numerous illustrations of this period make fun of American blacks playing baseball. The Currier & Ives "Darktown Series" depicts blacks in the accepted Little Black Sambo image and in all sorts of humorous situations that show them to be somewhere between children and buffoons. In the one called "A Base Hit," three black baseball players tumble in their effort to catch a ball that has just hit a portly white passerby in the stomach. As racist documents go, it is relatively tame, but coming when it did—as blacks were being forced out of organized baseball—it is a sad commentary on America's national pastime. Little wonder that later generations dropped such prints from the beloved Currier & Ives portfolio.

*First Baseball Art*  Thomas Eakins of Philadelphia, the first major American painter to apply his art to depicting baseball, has in recent years come to be regarded as not only the greatest American painter of his day but arguably of America's entire history. What makes his link with baseball all the more significant is that Eakins was known, indeed attacked during his lifetime, for pushing his art beyond the accepted limits. The same Eakins who shocked his contemporaries by painting live nudes or studying anatomy from dissections also analyzed the human body in motion by observing athletes. At some point, probably in the early 1870s, Eakins did a very careful perspective study in a pencil sketch of a baseball player at bat in an effort to firmly establish the position and stance. He later wrote to his friend, Earl Shinn, that "I think I will try [to] make a baseball picture some day in oil," but Eakins seems never to have gotten around to this.

However, in 1875 Eakins did do a watercolor that is called "Baseball Players Practicing," in which he depicts uniformed team players. In fact,

A BASE HIT.

*This is a bit of Currier & Ives Americana that has been conveniently forgotten: one of the firm's prints from the so-called Darktown Series, issued in the 1880s and 1890s and making fun of American blacks in all kinds of situations. The best that might be said in the firm's favor is that it was not alone in such an enterprise—that this was a common mode of behavior for most Americans in that era.*

Eakins wrote in that same letter to his friend Shinn that the players were members of the Philadelphia Athletics. (Not surprising, since Eakins spent most of his life in that city. Some years later, Eakins would go across the Delaware to visit with and paint the portrait of another baseball fan, and it is nice to think of Eakins talking baseball with his subject, one Walt Whitman.) After exhibiting this work in a show of watercolors, Eakins lent it to the famous Philadelphia Centennial Exposition of 1876. Amazing, really, to think that on such an early and significant occasion, baseball was made part of America's official family portrait. (Today Eakins's watercolor can be enjoyed at the Rhode Island School of Design.)

*The Inning Continues*   Eakins's pioneering work with baseball as a subject for serious art made hardly any impression on his contemporaries. Only his friend Earl Shinn was able to read much into it: "for American sporting life is the most Olympian, beautiful and genuine side of its civilization from the plastic point of view. . . . The forms of the youthful ball-players, indeed, exceed most Greek work we know of in their particular aim of expressing alert strength in a moment of tension."

Another painter of this era who happened to use the baseball motif was William Morris Hunt, no longer that well known but in his day more highly regarded and influential than Eakins. It is interesting that this same Hunt, who is credited with introducing the French approach to painting and with being the first American master-teacher to admit female students into his classes, also seems to have been the first painter to use oils to show men playing baseball. In 1877, after doing a charcoal study, Hunt executed an oil painting titled *The Ball Players* (now in the Detroit Institute of Art). It shows three men—one pitching, one at bat, and one in the field—who are clearly engaged in an informal activity; two of them, in fact, are attired in business suits. While hardly an "action-filled" work of art—Hunt based his work on an impromptu game outside his studio in Magnolia, Massachusetts—it does show that baseball was becoming accepted as part of the American scene and a legitimate subject for an artist.

*The Player as Artist*   After Eakins and Hunt ushered baseball into the "ballpark" of permissible serious art, the next well-known American painter to take on baseball was George Bellows (1882–1925). His career raises some interesting issues concerning the artist-as-athlete, a fairly well-recognized phenomenon in American cultural circles. Also known as the Hemingway syndrome, this desire or need by American artists to come across as jocks seems to be widespread: The classic case in recent times is Norman Mailer and his apparent need to see himself as a boxing champion. Less familiar is the reverse, the athlete-as-artist, in which an individual who started out as a serious athlete ends up as a practitioner of some art. A case in point is George Bellows.

Bellows's reputation as an artist is not what it once was, but it is still perfectly respectable; in particular, he is known for his paintings of boxers—his *Stag at Sharkey's* is probably the best known boxing picture of all time. Bellows also painted several other striking scenes of sports or at least youths at play, including swimming and a tennis game. But according to Mahonri Sharp Young, the author of a 1973 study of Bellows, "Bellows painted a lot of sports but not a single baseball picture, perhaps because the game is too spread out, except for the group at the plate. No artist has done much with baseball, with the crowd, the afternoon sun, and the score-cards, though it's still part of American life."

Whether this analysis is true or not, for now it is enough to focus on Bellows and the alleged lack of paintings of baseball. The reason that baseball is singled out by this authority on Bellows is that he knows Bellows had been a dedicated and expert baseball player as a youth. Bellows had been such a standout player at Ohio State, in fact, that he was able to play on semipro teams during his summers and was even approached by the Cincinnati Reds. When he went off to New York City to pursue a career as an artist, Bellows continued to play ball with a semipro team (the Brooklyn Howards) to earn some money; and even when he was making a decent living from his art, he continued to take great pleasure in playing in informal baseball games whenever he could. It was the pain he felt while playing baseball during the summer of 1924 that foreshadowed the appendicitis that killed him the next year.

Clearly, there's no question that baseball was an integral part of George Bellows's life. In 1965, Charles Morgan concluded his definitive biography: "If George Bellows at the age of twenty-two had elected a career as shortstop he would, in 1925, have left behind him a bust in Baseball's Hall of Fame and a scrapbook of yellow clippings. Instead he chose the artist's life."

In his thorough study of Bellows, Morgan (unlike Young) does not anywhere state that Bellows didn't paint "a single baseball picture," but he nowhere refers to such a painting. However, Morgan does claim that in the fall of 1906, "Remembering the whole long summer of throwing to first and sliding perilously to stolen bases on semiprofessional fields, [Bellows] sketched two versions of 'Kill the Umpire,' one in ink and the other in a combination of crayon and wash." The latter version eventually turned up in the collection of Arthur Magill (retitled *Take Him Out!*), but McGill traded it away in 1983 and it has at least temporarily disappeared. The first (ink) version apparently surfaced as a two-page spread in *Harper's Weekly* of May 2, 1914, where it was titled, *The Great American Game.* In another book, *The Drawings of George Bellows,* Morgan reproduces but doesn't date a lithographic crayon work that Bellows must have done at an early age, *Sweeney, the Idol of the Fans, Had Hit a Home Run* (now in Harvard's Fogg Art Museum).

That still leaves no mention of an oil painting of a baseball game in the authoritative texts on Bellows. But in the late-1980s touring exhibit, "Diamonds Are Forever," one of the first works that greets a visitor is a small oil

*This drawing by George Bellows appeared in* Harper's Weekly *for May 2, 1914, under the title* The Great American Game. *Its subject matter and subtitle, "All this excitement about an umpire," suggest that it was one that he did back in 1906 and called* Kill the Umpire.

by George Bellows, *The Baseball Game,* which has been owned since 1959 by the Muskegon (Michigan) Museum of Art. According to the museum, it was painted about 1908, the year that Bellows personally presented it as a wedding gift to Mrs. Grace Carter. Although it may not be the most dramatic of paintings, it catches the real atmosphere of an informal game of baseball, then as now. And this work, virtually unknown in the years since he painted it until it resurfaced in this new exhibition, adds an authentic dimension to this athlete-artist.

*Rockwell: Illustrated Baseball*   At the same time that Bellows was making his reputation as an artist, Norman Rockwell was making his own mark.

*This early work (in lithographic crayon) by George Bellows, titled* Sweeney, the Idol of the Fans, Had Hit a Home Run, *has been virtually forgotten in discussions of baseball in American art, yet it reveals Bellows's genuine feel for small-town baseball.*

And while Bellows's reputation has somewhat diminished, at least temporarily, Rockwell's reputation has greatly increased in recent years; indeed, his works are arguably *the* best-known and best-loved paintings and drawings of any American—ever.

Regardless of whether Rockwell is called an "artist" or his work "art," his work remains perennially popular and—unlike Bellows, the baseball player who for some reason avoided the subject for a major painting—he used baseball for many of his most popular illustrations. Few Americans will fail to recognize his *Saturday Evening Post* cover (April 23, 1949), *Game Called Because of Rain,* also known as *Tough Call.* Likewise his *Gramp at the Plate*

(August 5, 1916). Rockwell would do a baseball illustration for any occasion: When the *Post* decided to go along with the Abner Doubleday version of baseball's "invention," Rockwell drew a commemorative centennial cover (July 8, 1939). Furthermore, he was "bi-leagual": One cover, *The Dugout* (September 4, 1948), shows the Chicago Cubs; another, *The Locker Room* (March 2, 1957), portrays the Red Sox.

Rockwell's very first cover for *The Saturday Evening Post* (May 20, 1916) is titled *Boy With Baby Carriage.* It portrays a prissy little boy who is wheeling his infant sibling in the carriage, but the point is made that much more poignant by the two all-American boys walking by in the background in their baseball uniforms. Whatever future generations may have to say about his artistry, Norman Rockwell certainly knew his national pastimes.

*Artists at Bat*    After the impressive starts made by the likes of Eakins, Hunt, Bellows, and Rockwell, it would be nice and natural to expect that all American artists continued this affair with baseball. After all, there is a great tradition of painting sports and games and athletes; large books and major exhibits can be (and have been) arranged around this theme of art and sports, with many wonderful paintings using such subjects as swimming, boating, boxing, horses, or children's games. The very first drawing that Winslow Homer had published (1857) was of a football game at Harvard; in his Civil War drawings, Homer showed soldiers playing football and pitching horseshoes; later he painted lovely pictures of children playing snap-the-whip, of people playing croquet, ice-skating, boating, horse racing; but not one single drawing or painting of a baseball game is known from Homer's hand.

For some reason, artist after artist has ignored baseball as a subject. Glackens, Arthur Davies, John Sloan—the "ashcan school"—never even painted a sandlot game. Nor did Reginald Marsh, in all his drawings and paintings of youths playing on beaches. Nor did Grant Wood or Thomas Hart Benton in their Midwestern versions of the pastoral (although Benton did paint his son with a baseball bat, glove, and ball). Nor did Stuart Davis in his all-American icons, nor Edward Hopper in his cityscapes—in a full career as an illustrator, during which he depicted many sports, Hopper never depicted baseball. None of the Wyeths ever saw fit to reproduce a baseball player or game; neither did the "abstract expressionists" such as Pollack or de Kooning—baseball obviously didn't have enough *angst* for them. The next generation—Jasper Johns, Robert Indiana, James Rosenquist, Tom Wesselmann—may have been Pop artists, but they were apparently blind to the popularity of baseball. Romare Bearden, the superb African-American painter and collagist, pitched on his college baseball team and on an all-black team during the summers, but he never used a baseball motif in his work.

Sculptors do no better. It is understandable that the monumentalists such as Saint-Gaudens and French failed to appreciate the nature of baseball but less understandable that no John Rogers "group" captured baseball. He did do one of football players, and contemporary makers of similar sculptured "groups" such as John Deacon and Carl Muller turned out some baseball works, but they have vanished from the scene. And if Alexander Calder loved the pageantry and dynamics of baseball and did for the game what he did for the circus, it's not a matter of public record.

But making such a selective listing is a bit like throwing a spitball. Although few major American artists, so far as is known, chose to use baseball for their work, a number of important artists have. Ben Shahn has a fine drawing, *Out,* that shows an outfielder virtually horizontal as he snags a ball. Jacob Lawrence, a powerful black American artist, painted *Strike* in 1949; it is claimed "to commemorate the event" of Jackie Robinson's coming into the majors, but the crowd depicted seems to be all black. It is more likely that Lawrence was inspired by the events of 1949 to consider a black ballplayer as a fitting subject for one of his "freeze-frame" studies of figures in arrested motion.

Other modern artists have turned to baseball to make some comment on the contemporary scene. Red Grooms in 1968 made a mammoth painted-wood billboard for a temporary display in Chicago, a sort of summing up of familiar Chicago icons, including the Chicago Cubs team. In the same vein as Grooms's work is Claes Oldenburg's *Batcolumn,* erected in Chicago in 1977; this latticework iron rendering of a baseball bat weighs twenty tons and stands some one hundred feet high; anyone who thinks this sort of thing is "tossed off" by modern artists to make a quick buck should read what Oldenburg went through in conceiving and making this work. Contemporary American artists who at least approached baseball also include Andy Warhol, who did a screenprint of Pete Rose; Alex Katz, who painted *Baseball Figure;* and Elaine de Kooning, who did a lovely *Campy at the Plate.*

Baseball seems to have inspired its share of "oddball" art, quirky works that play with baseball and come up with surprises, often hilarious or insightful. Michael Langenstein, in a fairly well-known collage, borrows Michelangelo's hand of God giving life to Adam and places a baseball in it. Karl Wirsum's *Looking for a Curveball in Cuernavaca* depicts a ballplayer like some Mayan god. And Margaret Wharton's *Bat-e* twists a bat into a pretzel. It is hard to imagine any other sport inspiring such wit, inside jokes, and ironic views. And this tradition goes on. In 1987, *The Minneapolis Review of Baseball,* one of many little-known publications dedicated to promoting some attitude toward baseball, carried a clever series of drawings allegedly by Leonardo da Vinci and Albrecht Dürer depicting various artifacts and activities of baseball; of course he is credited there with inventing the game.

The roll call of American artists who have used baseball as a subject for their work, if not quite as distinguished as the roster of those who haven't, is certainly a reputable one. Recent exhibitions have managed to turn up most of the better works, but even they haven't exhausted the field. Paul Cadmus, perhaps a cult artist these days, did a study called *Two Heads* back in 1939; it depicts youths playing baseball in the background. Fletcher Martin, also a respected painter, did at least a couple of baseball paintings in the 1940s and 1950s. But the fact remains that for all the many American artists who *have* used baseball as a subject for individual works, the major American artists have *not* truly been taken by this sport.

Perhaps it was expressed best back in 1953 by, of all people, Ethel Barrymore, a distinguished actress and, according to *Look* magazine that year, "probably baseball's most distinguished rooter and connoisseur." In a note accompanying a portfolio of paintings of baseball subjects, Miss Barrymore wrote: "The inspiration to be found on a baseball field for great painting seems to be completely ignored. Think of the unconscious grace, the real poetry of motion of Hal Chase, the figure of Hans [*sic*] Wagner standing terrifyingly like the Rock of Gibraltar at shortstop, the ease and apparent unawareness of impossible plays by Joe DiMaggio or Terry Moore, and the speed-of-light achievements by Walter Johnson. Why was there no massive Degas to record them for us all?"

Allowing for a dash of theatrical rhetoric (and that reference to Terry Moore), she has a point. Why have American painters and sculptors not turned to baseball for any extended periods of time or bodies of work? The critic Mahonri Young speculated that Bellows, at least, had avoided the subject "because the game is too spread out, except for the group at the plate." But this is begging the question, as artists have been able to make art out of just about any subject and countless American artists *have* found ways to make artful individual works that draw on baseball. Why no major American artist has been inspired to devote any large body of work to baseball is a question that may go begging an answer until baseball does indeed find its Degas.

*Photography and Baseball* Baseball happened to come into being on the American scene at almost exactly the same time as the new medium of photography. The first photograph made by a camera (French, it must be said)

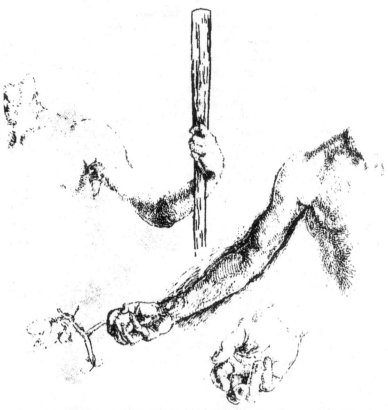

*One of the cleverest parodies inspired by baseball in recent years is by Wayne N. Farr of Minneapolis, who alleges to have discovered a cache of baseball-related drawings by Dürer and da Vinci—including such studies as these by Leonardo. The complete set was published in* The Minneapolis Review of Baseball *in 1987.*

dates from 1826—the very time that baseball was beginning to evolve from a children's game. Then in 1839—the same year, by coincidence, that people used to claim Abner Doubleday invented baseball—Daguerre, again a Frenchman, announced his new process for "fixing" an image on a plate; also in 1839, Talbot, an Englishman, announced he had developed a light-sensitive paper. The birth and maturation of baseball happen to overlap the birth and maturation of photography to a remarkable degree.

Aside from this historical coincidence, however, photography and baseball also share other elements. Both, for instance, have a strong basis in materials and techniques, both started out being social activities, and both have transcended their origins. Both involve the interaction between movement and stasis. Both require light, exposure, and viewers. And it seems fair to say that photography and baseball are at least cousins in the modern world's family of pursuits that set out to order time and movement.

Almost from the beginning of organized baseball teams, there were group photographs. At a time when most photographs tended to picture only stiffly posed individuals, a daguerreotype of the Knickerbocker Base Ball Club was taken. It shows several members posing with an informality and immediacy that makes these men jump right off the page—it is a truly extraordinary document for the history of both baseball *and* photography. (One of the men is even smoking a cigar, so relaxed and confident were these young bucks.) Its date has not been pinned down, but it must have been taken between 1845, when the club was organized, and March 1849, when Alexander Cartwright (who stands in the middle of the picture) went off to California to seek his fortune in the Gold Rush. This probably makes it the first known photograph of a baseball team. Another extraordinary photograph taken sometime in the mid-1850s shows the Knickerbockers and the Excelsiors standing in one long row; again, it is remarkable for the naturalness of the players' attitudes at a time when most people "froze" into mummylike poses when faced with a camera. It does seem to suggest that baseball and photography felt a natural kinship.

From the 1860s on, there exist increasing numbers of photographs of baseball teams, both the well-known clubs from the major cities and the now-forgotten ones of the provinces. But most of these are studio photographs, posed groups that, no matter how relaxed, were static. The earliest known photograph of a ballgame actually in progress is one taken sometime around 1861 at Princeton College and showing a game of baseball in the background. The next one dates from sometime during the Civil War and shows a game going on behind some troops of a New York regiment lined up at Fort Pulaski, Georgia. (Even though Mathew Brady was able to capture so many of the battles and activities of the war, and must have seen the game being played around the camps, he seems never to have taken a picture of a baseball game.)

As for the first photograph of two regular teams playing, that seems to be the one of a game on August 31, 1870, between the Troy Haymakers and the Philadelphia Athletics. The Haymakers–Athletics game is all but unrecognizable, so distant and dim are the players, but it is definitely a baseball game; the time required for an exposure in those days prevented a

*This is what the best-informed students of the subject at present regard as the earliest photograph of young men playing baseball: It was discovered in the Princeton College yearbook dated 1861–62, which means the game was almost certainly played before the game at Fort Pulaski (reproduced in Chapter 3).*

photographer from capturing the actual action of a game in a close-up. In the years that followed, however, relatively few photographers attempted to "capture" the action of baseball games. As late as September 10, 1886, when a photographer took pictures of the Chicago White Stockings and the Detroit Wolverines, such "action photos" were still regarded as worthy of comment.

In a sense, then, photography's relationship with baseball—despite starting out on such intimate terms—ended up taking much the same route as the more traditional arts. After a few individual innovators sought to capture the subject, most practitioners apparently were uninterested in pursuing the

*Long regarded the earliest photograph of a baseball game is this one of a game between the Troy Haymakers and the Philadelphia Athletics on August 31, 1870, in a field outside Troy, New York. The game itself is barely visible, but the crowd attests to the popularity of baseball at the time.*

game. Few of the early and great American photographers seem to have left any pictures of baseball. One rare exception is a 1909 photograph by Lewis Hine showing boys playing what is probably a game of stickball in an alley in Boston—and Hine was more concerned with showing the poor living conditions of these children than with celebrating the fun of the game.

Of course, as more and more people began to own cameras and as photojournalism began to need pictures, baseball games in all their diversity came to be a standard subject. There are any number of superb photographs of individual players and teams in action that appear in magazines such as *Sports Illustrated.* But the fact remains that relatively few serious *artists* with cameras seem to have been attracted to the game, nary a Steiglitz, a Bourke-White, a Smith, a Capa, or an Evans. As with the traditional fine arts, the question arises whether there is something inherent in the nature of the game or in the medium of photography that keeps artists from wanting to explore baseball.

*Baseball in Hollywood*   It was some time before photography advanced to the point where it could present moving pictures, but the movies were smart enough to take on baseball from the outset. The first baseball movie, and one of the very first movies ever made, was Thomas Edison's short, *Casey at the Bat*—made in 1899. Another version was made in 1916, with DeWolf Hopper, whose recitations had originally made the poem famous. In 1927 a movie was released with the same title (but a totally different plot) starring Wallace Beery. Between these two dates were several other baseball movies, some of which featured baseball stars of the day, including Hal Chase, "Home Run" Baker, Ty Cobb, and Babe Ruth. In 1928, Jean Arthur played opposite Richard Dix in *Warming Up;* that same year, none other than Babe Ruth appeared in a movie *(Speedy)* with Harold Lloyd. Hollywood has continued to turn out baseball movies, coming to a bumper crop in 1988 and 1989 with the release of *Bull Durham, Eight Men Out, Stealing Home, Field of Dreams,* and *Major League.*

Many people have tried to list all the movies that deal directly or indirectly with baseball, and everyone is invited to try. Zucker and Babbich, in their *Sports Films* (McFarland, 1987), have listed more than 120 feature films involving baseball. It is conventional wisdom that baseball movies don't do well at the box office, and in comparison with the blockbuster films, they don't. In fact, the few baseball movies that have done well—*Pride of the Yankees, The Natural, The Bad News Bears, Bull Durham*—probably did so because of their nonbaseball elements.

It is also conventional wisdom that the movies don't do well by baseball. This is also generally true. Whether it is something inherent in baseball or something intrinsic to Hollywood or both, they don't mix well. *New York Times* movie critic Janet Maslin wrote perceptively that when it comes to baseball movies, they have an "uncanny way of turning otherwise strong men into mush." Hollywood, for one thing, thinks nothing of casting inappropriate stars in players' roles, such as choosing lanky right-hander Gary Cooper for stocky left-hander Lou Gehrig. Likewise, Hollywood has no compunction about false touches to dramatize an incident, such as depicting the last game of the 1926 World Series as being decided by a strikeout, when in fact it ended with Babe Ruth's being tagged out trying to steal second.

Perhaps the most egregious example of such compromising is what Hollywood did to *The Natural,* which even as a book was far removed from the nitty-gritty of baseball. When it came to the story's ending—which showed the "selling out" of the American Dream—the movie ironically echoed this theme by selling out the true ending of the book. What makes this especially cynical is that the man who lent his box-office appeal to the success of this movie was a good college player who is said to have abandoned his try for a professional baseball career because of the sport's overemphasis on "winning": Robert Redford, star of *The Natural,* has tried to teach some worthy lessons through his movies, but he should be wary of setting up Hollywood against baseball when it comes to purity of motives.

Biographies are one obvious type of baseball movie, but there are many esoteric connections between baseball and moving images. For instance, movies and TV series in which characters were once baseball players include *Ironweed, Stealing Home,* "Cheers," and "Who's the Boss?" Many movies have characters who refer to baseball to make some point—usually in the nostalgic, "lost ideals of youth" vein—as when Jack Lemmon, in *Save the Tiger,* soliloquizes over the old Brooklyn Dodgers and later becomes wistful at the sight of some boys heading off to play baseball. There were two short-lived TV series built around baseball, "Ball Four" and "Bay City Blues." Movie and TV personalities who were one way or another associated with baseball include actor Dennis Morgan, who played semipro ball; Ron Shelton, a director-screenwriter *(Bull Durham)* who played minor league ball; former baseball announcers Ronald Reagan and John Forsythe; Robert Sterling, whose father, "Hub" Hart, caught for the Chicago White Sox; Kevin "Chuck" Connors, who played two years in the majors; and Bob Hope and Bing Crosby, who owned shares in major league teams. And of course Grover Cleveland Alexander was named after one American president and portrayed in the movies by another—Ronald Reagan.

*Baseball on Broadway*   Moving pictures were such a novel and wide-open medium that they were easily able to accommodate baseball. But at least since the last decades of the nineteenth century, baseball was being burlesqued in skits and farces in the popular theater. In one such revue, *The Black Hussar,* one character appeared as a catcher with a birdcage on his head and boxing gloves on his hands (in the original skit he was played by DeWolf Hopper, the comedian who made a career out of reciting "Casey at the Bat") while a woman swung a tiny baseball bat. The action took place while "One to Nothing" was being sung, and it "broke 'em up" at the time.

Charles Hoyt, a popular playwright of the late nineteenth century, wrote several farces using baseball players as characters. His most popular play was

*Testifying to the strong links between baseball and Hollywood, Bob Hope and Bing Crosby posed for this gag photo in the 1950s to promote their "Road" series of movies. But behind the gag was another bit of business promotion: Hope owned a share of the Cleveland Indians and Crosby owned a share of the Pittsburgh Pirates.*

*The Runaway Colt* (1895), in which a respectable family is shown as reluctant to entertain a big-league ballplayer in their home (no wonder, either, since the play also shows people openly betting on a game inside a Chicago ballpark). In this play the real player, Cap Anson, is portrayed as saying, "Don't leave me alone with her [a gushing woman] or I'll expel you from the league. Worse, I'll sell you to Louisville." Substitute a team of your choice and you have the makings for a joke as old as time.

With the exception of some now-forgotten minor characters or incidents in plays and musicals, baseball was largely ignored by creators of stage works during the first decades of the twentieth century. In 1955 there appeared the musical *Damn Yankees,* definitely all about baseball; but it was taken from a novel, so it can't truly claim to be a Broadway original. A quarter of a century passed before baseball appeared on Broadway again—Off-Broadway, actually, with a short-lived and little-noticed improvisatory work, *The Bleacher Bums.* But in the late '80s, there has been an acceleration of interest in baseball by theater folk. There was the aforementioned *First,* the play and then musical about Jackie Robinson, and in 1987 and 1988 alone there came *Out!,* a play about the White Sox scandal of 1919; a revue, *Diamonds;* and *The Single Season of Dummy Hoy,* a drama about a real baseball player, William "Dummy" Hoy. Hoy was at least partially deaf; legend has it that umpires first began to use hand signals to indicate the calls of strikes and balls because Dummy Hoy couldn't hear them. In any case, the play did not attract much of an audience.

The debut of perhaps the most ambitious baseball stagework ever, *Fences* by August Wilson, took place in 1987. It is an intense and moving study of a failed black man whose days as a baseball player in the old Negro leagues have come to symbolize the racism and discrimination that poisoned his life. (*New York Times* sportswriter George Vecsey claimed to find strong parallels between the life of Roy Dandridge and the drama's character, Troy Mason, but there are such parallels in far too many black men's lives.) At any rate, in *Fences,* baseball and theater made a winning battery: *Fences* won the Pulitzer, New York Drama Critics Circle, and Tony awards as the best play of 1987. The ballplayer was portrayed in the original production by James Earl Jones, who had previously played a catcher in *The Bingo Long Traveling All-Stars and Motor Kings,* a movie about the Negro leagues; the pitcher in that movie was played by Billy Dee Williams, who later replaced Jones in the lead in *Fences.* It is hard to imagine any other sport being so intertwined with the world of the theater, not to mention real life.

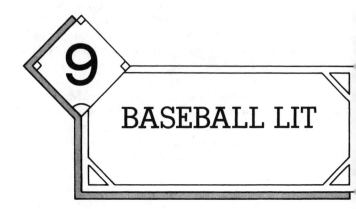

# 9

# BASEBALL LIT

**J** ust think who was writing in the years between 1845 and 1880—when baseball was being played throughout the Northeast and matured from a young gentleman's game to an organized league of professionals. How many know of the intricate short story by Edgar Allan Poe about a New York detective, investigating the death of a young woman found at the riverbank below Hoboken's Elysian Fields, who suspects a group of young men playing a mysterious game there? The reverie by Thoreau after he emerged from the woods to find a game underway in a field in Concord? The essay by Ralph Waldo Emerson about the transcendent Americanness of this new activity? What of the dark Hawthorne tale about the guilt that haunts a pitcher (descendant of an old New England family) who accidentally killed a Negro batter with a wild pitch? Who has read the encyclopedic novel by Melville that treats the competition between the old amateur teams and the emerging professional baseball teams as the struggle for the American soul? Even Henry James was writing by 1880; does anyone know his story about a young American who becomes involved with a beautiful, wealthy, aristocratic European but who is bothered by some vague feeling that she lacks something and finally realizes that he cannot marry her because she has no feeling for baseball?

Of course no such works exist. (Not quite: In a lecture on education, Emerson celebrates the natural genius of young boys by saying, "They make no mistakes, have no pedantry, but entire belief on experience. Their elections at baseball and cricket are founded on merit, and are right.") Although all these writers were setting down their versions of the American scene in those years, not one of them seems to have ever written so much as a passing observation of a baseball game. Aside from the now totally forgotten authors of the lyrics for the earliest baseball songs, American writers were surprisingly slow to see the possibilities of making literature out of the game. Certainly by 1880, baseball was making a great impact on society at large, and musicians and illustrators and journalists were trying to capture and convey the spirit of the game. Yet serious, imaginative writers of that time seemed to ignore the national pastime.

Today, hardly a week goes by that there is not another novel or short story with baseball at its core—works written, moreover, by authors who aspire to Hall-of-Fame status as well as by authorial utility players. Not to mention the poems that would fill a stadium, from box-seat sensitivity to bleacher doggerel. Whole magazines are now devoted to baseball writings, critical articles dissect and celebrate them, anthologies are made of the best of them, university courses are taught about them.

How did we get from there to here, from a time when few writers paid attention to baseball to an age when all writers rush to sign on? And is it in fact true that there is no baseball literature until Ring Lardner comes along? Is there anything more for writers to achieve after Malamud's *The Natural* or Mark Harris's *Bang the Drum Slowly?* A refresher course in baseball lit seems called for.


*The First Voices*   The most unlikely candidate as the first serious writer in the English language to take note of a game of baseball in an imaginative work would be someone like Jane Austen. Yet it was this epitome of English isolation from the hardy realities of contemporary life who seems to have been the first to do just this. In the opening chapter of *Northanger Abbey,* a novel completed by 1803, the heroine, Catherine Morland, is described as a young tomboy:

> And it was not very wonderful that Catherine, who had by nature nothing heroic about her, should prefer cricket, base ball, riding on horseback, and running about the country at the age of fourteen, to books.

Admittedly, this refers to a game played by children and it was undoubtedly far from the American game of baseball, but it was probably its true ancestor.

And since the description of Catherine's girlhood is almost certainly based on Jane Austen's own, this is probably an authentic allusion. Fortuitous fluke it may be, it is still fascinating to have an author such as Jane Austen in any way linked to baseball.

Over a century later, an American author did take on baseball as the subject of a highly idiomatic work of fiction, so original that not everyone knew what to make of Ring Lardner's *You Know Me Al.* And then if one were asked to say which writer in the English language was the first to articulate an appreciation for the indigenous nature of American baseball and Ring Lardner's embodiment of that, surely the most unlikely candidate would be someone like, say, Virginia Woolf. Yet here is what this epitome of British remove from the grubby realities of everyday life had to say about Lardner's achievement:

> When a crack player is in the middle of an exciting game of baseball, he does not stop to wonder whether the audience likes the color of his hair. All his mind is on the game. So Mr. Lardner does not waste a moment when he writes in thinking whether he is using American slang or Shakespeare's English . . . all his mind is on the story. Hence all our minds are on the story. Hence, incidentally, he writes the best prose that has come our way. . . . To what does [Lardner] owe his success? Besides his unconsciousness and the additional power which he is thus free to devote to his art, Mr. Lardner has talents of a remarkable order. With extraordinary ease and aptitude, with the quickest strokes, the surest touch, the sharpest touch, he lets Jack Keefe the baseball player cut out his own outline, fill in his own depths, until the figure of the foolish, boastful innocent athlete lives before us. . . .
>
> It is no coincidence that the best of Mr. Lardner's stories are about games, for one may guess that Mr. Lardner's interest in games has solved one of the most difficult problems of the American writer; it has given him a clue, a centre, a meeting place for the divers activities of people whom a vast continent isolates, whom no tradition controls. Games give him what society gives his English brother. Whatever the precise reason, Mr. Lardner at any rate provides something unique in its kind, something indigenous to the soil, which the traveller may carry off as a trophy to prove to the incredulous that he has actually been to America and found it a foreign land.

There it is—everything that could ever be said about Ring Lardner's baseball stories, about baseball in American fiction, and about baseball in

American life, essentially set down in 1915 by the most rarefied of British writers. The only thing stranger is the image of young Jane Austen as a baseball player.

*Cooperstown Revisited*    Most visitors to Cooperstown, New York, after taking in the Hall of Fame Museum, are content to stroll over to the ballpark, stopping on their way to smile at the statue of the rural lad intended to evoke Abner Doubleday. Some may stroll down to the lakefront where they are reminded by another statue that this is also the hometown of another American institution—James Fenimore Cooper, creator of *The Leatherstocking Tales.* (Although the statue's official name is simply *The Indian Hunter* and it is a replica of a statue in New York City's Central Park, some locals think of it as portraying one of the Indian characters in Cooper's works or even as *The Deerslayer*—another instance of the power of fictional lore.) Cooperstown, in fact, was founded by the novelist's father about 1785, and James spent his youth on these very fields and roads.

Surely many people who have wandered this far in Cooperstown must have had the thought: What if Cooper—creator of the archetypal American frontier hero—wrote about the early days of baseball? His dates are much earlier than Abner Doubleday's, but why could Cooper not have seen a still earlier version of the game and then included it in one of his many novels other than *The Leatherstocking Tales?* Yet none of the many accounts of baseball in American literature ever so much as mentioned James Fenimore Cooper.

Until, that is, Steven Gelber published his article, "Their Hands Are All Out Playing," in the *Journal of Sports History* of Spring 1984, and in the opening page referred to a ballgame being played by boys in one of Cooper's novels, *Home as Found.* Gelber makes no claim that this ballgame has anything directly to do with Abner Doubleday—and he even notes that the Cooper novel was published in 1838, one year before Doubleday was supposed to have "invented" baseball—but the notion is distinctly allowed to arise that Cooper did indeed describe a game of baseball.

Closer examination of this ballgame in the novel and of the novel in the context of Cooper's life reveals something both unexpected and relevant. Cooper had been in Europe for many years when in 1832 he decided to return to America and to take up residence in Cooperstown. After he bought back his father's great house, he found that the people of the area had taken to using a projection of land along Lake Otsego that actually belonged to the Cooper estate. Cooper decided to reclaim this land and posted No Trespassing signs on it. This so annoyed some of the locals that

*This is the drawing by a contemporary of James Fenimore Cooper to illustrate the "ballgame" played in Cooper's 1838 novel,* Home as Found. *Although it is tempting to want to find the characters playing baseball in the Cooperstown of that era, these youths are clearly playing some form of ball closer to field hockey.*

they called a protest meeting. It might have come to nothing except that their cause was taken up by a local newspaper editor, who was a Whig and thus opposed to Cooper, known to be a Democrat. Cooper then commenced a series of lawsuits over the paper's attacks on his conduct in the land dispute, lawsuits that cost Cooper both money and reputation. And it was to express his feelings and thoughts provoked by this encounter with his fellow Americans that Cooper wrote *Home as Found,* in which Mr. Effingham, a clearly autobiographical character, returns to his hometown and decides to restore his family's home.

One of the main themes of the novel is the contrast between the rude manners and customs of typical Americans and the more civil ways Cooper had experienced in Europe. One of the first incidents in the novel to make this point involves Effingham's looking out of his window and seeing some local youths playing "a game of ball" on his front lawn. He asks Mr. Bragg, a weaselly politician, to tell the youths to get off the lawn, but Bragg is afraid to challenge the players directly, so he ends up resorting to a trick: The man points out to the players that "it is very aristocratic to play ball among the roses and dahlias" and that, furthermore, the town trustees have forbidden ball playing in the street. That is all these youths need to hear—that they can defy the laws and authorities of the community—and they take their game out into the street.

Clearly, Cooper felt he was settling an old score over the trespassers on his land and at the same time making a satiric dig at his countrymen's lack of respect for the law and tradition. ("They are mistaking liberties for liberty, I fear," says Effingham of the trespassers on his lawn.) What is remarkable, though, is that he should settle on an innocent game of ball to make his point. Cooperstown may no longer insist that Abner Doubleday invented baseball there, but it certainly promotes its image as the home of the archetypal pastoral game, the all-American sport that represents all that is best about the country. And here is James Fenimore Cooper using a game of ball as an example of the natives' crude ways! In fact, the novel makes clear that the youths playing the game of ball are not farmboys (of the type depicted in the famous statue) but are apprentices, led by a "notorious street brawler." Cooper seems to have little liking for this "game of ball."

But does this make him, after all, the first to describe the game of baseball in a work of American fiction? Alas, no. It is clear from closer examination of the game being played that it is not baseball in any shape or form; there are no teams, no paths or bases, no pitching or batting; it seems, rather, to be a game that involves a lot of running around and chasing a ball. And at the end of the chapter, an illustration by a contemporary of Cooper's pretty much settles it: Several youths are shown holding curved sticks and all swiping at the ball at the same time. The earliest known "game of ball" in Cooperstown turns out to be a form of field hockey.

There remains one final consolation. The reception given *Home as Found* and the surrounding legal controversies over the land all but shattered Cooper's reputation and career. Just punishment for a man who would consider banishing a game of ball from a field in Cooperstown.

*The Great Gray Ballplayer*   On the list of the many great nineteenth-century writers who did *not* find baseball worthy of their attention, there are several names missing, the most notable being Walt Whitman. Yet even most serious students of American literature would not miss his name because they are not aware of how extensive and intense were Whitman's relations with baseball. When Whitman did anything, he did it wholeheartedly. As he once said of baseball:

> That's beautiful: the hurrah game! Well—it's our game; that's the chief fact in connection with it: America's game; has the snap, go, fling, of the American atmosphere; it belongs as much to our institutions, fits into them as significantly, as our constitution's laws; is just as important in the sum total of our historic life.

That we now know a fair amount about Whitman's lifelong and deep attachment to baseball is due mainly to Ed Folsom, a professor of American literature, who revealed his findings in an article that appeared in a rather obscure journal (*Arete,* Fall 1984), "The Manly and Healthy Game: Walt Whitman and the Development of American Baseball." Folsom traces Whitman's involvement from his boyhood days in the 1830s when he played the game (actually, one of its forerunners, such as town ball), and shows how he carried it over into his writings. By the time the Knickerbockers were playing that famous game on June 19, 1846, the twenty-seven-year-old Whitman was the editor of the *Brooklyn Daily Eagle,* and although there is no suggestion that he attended it, a month later he was writing in an editorial, "Brooklyn Young Men—Athletic Exercises":

> In our sun-down perambulations of late, through the outer parts of Brooklyn, we have observed several parties of youngsters playing "base," a certain game of ball. . . . Let us go forth awhile, and get better air in our lungs. Let us leave our close rooms. . . . The game of ball is glorious.

In the years that followed, baseball fever spread from Manhattan and Brooklyn throughout the Northeast, and by the late 1850s Whitman was writing accounts of ballgames, complete with box scores: yes, Walt Whitman, sports reporter. Although they are basically straightforward accounts, there are Whitmanesque touches here and there, as when he wrote of the Excelsiors, after they had lost a game, that they have "always reflected credit upon the manly and healthful game they practice."

Throughout his life, Whitman saw baseball as both a metaphor for and a reflection of what he regarded as essential American traits. It was in this way that it appears occasionally in his poetry, as in section 33 of "Songs of Myself"

(published in 1855 in *Leaves of Grass* ), where he lists various "manly" activities:

> Upon the race-course, or enjoying picnics or jigs
> or a good game of base-ball

It's too bad that more English teachers don't know about Whitman the sports reporter and baseball enthusiast when they try to introduce their students to the wonders of poetry.

When Whitman moved to Washington, D.C., during the Civil War and then took up a government job, he continued his active involvement in baseball, but after he suffered a stroke in 1873 and moved to Camden, New Jersey, he had to confine his interest to writing and talking about the game. Folsom shows how this interest manifested itself in numerous ways, such as his concern over the elimination of restrictions on pitchers, so that they were now allowed, for instance, to throw curves—a development that Whitman saw as mirroring the inequities and deceit creeping into American life (see Chapter 2). Folsom also reveals that a previously unidentified visitor of Whitman's on several occasions in the late 1880s, one Harry Wright, was almost certainly the very same Harry Wright who had founded the first professional baseball team and was now managing the Philadelphia Athletics, across the Delaware River from Whitman's home.

Another of those who called on Whitman during those years evokes a link with baseball that even Folsom seems unaware of. Between November 1887 and March 1888, Thomas Eakins, the great painter, came over from Philadelphia to paint Whitman's portrait, and it is fun to think of these two old hot-stove leaguers discussing baseball—for one thing, the Athletics had just missed taking first in the National League. Interesting, too, that such true American-original creative geniuses, Eakins and Whitman—and Charles Ives of the next generation—would be so quick to appreciate baseball. Whitman in his writings, moreover, anticipated two of the many "voices" that serious writers on the game would later adopt, the rhapsodic and the vernacular. But that's what being an artist is all about: recognizing the true thing when it comes across the plate.

*Mark Twain*   Another nineteenth-century American original who belongs on the list of those who did appreciate baseball was Mark Twain. His name surfaces elsewhere in this book: It is observed in Chapter 10 that he was scheduled to umpire a minor league game (but was unable to be present), and he did deliver a speech at the banquet honoring the round-the-world touring teams in 1889 (see Chapter 14). At the latter he was very much present, and in his speech, after a tribute to the Hawaiian islands, he returned to the theme of the triumphant baseball tour:

> They have carried the American name to the uttermost parts of the earth—and covered it with glory every time. That is a service to sentiment; but they did the general world a large practical service, also—a service to the great science of geography. . . . Why, when these boys started out you couldn't see the equator at all; you could walk right over it and never know it was there. . . . But that is all fixed now . . . and so I drink long life to the boys who ploughed a new equator round the globe stealing bases on their bellies!

Presumably this closing line "brought the house down," for it was vintage Twain in its mix of pretension puncturing and tall tale. It was also vintage Twain in that he was faking it a bit, for the fact is, although Twain seems to have had a genuine feel for the role of baseball in American life, he probably never stole a single base on his own belly. None of his biographers mention a single contact Twain made with a baseball, and none of his books about his own youth or that of his fictional counterparts growing up along the Mississippi ever describe such ballgames. (Twain was born in 1835, so early varieties of baseball were being played in some parts of the United States.) In fact, it is probably telling that Tom Sawyer and his friends did not play ballgames: Perhaps such games had not arrived that far west or "real" boys didn't engage in such artificial activities.

Yet Twain apparently was associated in some of his contemporaries' minds with baseball and he had some knowledge of and feel for the game. And it does finally surface in what was one of the first works of fiction by any writer to use baseball, *A Connecticut Yankee in King Arthur's Court* (1889), when his hero, Hank Morgan (now there's a ballplayer's name), introduces the kings and knights around the court to the game "to replace the tournament with something which might furnish an escape for the extra steam of chivalry, keep those bucks entertained and out of mischief, and at the same time preserve the best thing in them, which was their hardy spirit of emulation." The Connecticut Yankee continues:

> In order to give the thing vogue from the start, and place it out of the reach of criticism, I chose my nines by rank, not capacity. . . . Of course I couldn't get these people to leave off their armor; they

wouldn't do that when they bathed. . . . So, one of the teams wore chain-mail ulsters, and the other wore plate-armor made of my new Bessemer steel. . . . And when a man was running, and threw himself on his stomach to slide to his base, it was like an iron-clad coming into port.

The joke goes on in this vein, and with lots of heavy humor about umpires. In fact, we never really witness a game being played, suggesting once again that Twain did not have much actual experience with baseball. Admittedly it is no longer as hilarious as when baseball was still a newfangled phenomenon, but Twain deserves an assist for calling in baseball as a sign of Yankee ingenuity and the modern world.

*Crane and Garland*　By now it is fairly well known to those who care about such things that Stephen Crane, author of *The Red Badge of Courage,* had been a fairly serious baseball player in his youth and expressed a serious respect for the game. The details of his attachment to baseball are scattered through R. W. Stallman's definitive biography of Crane, but the best short summation was by Ed Burns in *Sports Illustrated* (April 14, 1986). Crane began playing pickup games as a young boy in New Jersey; played catcher for his prep school team in New York; spent so much time playing baseball during his first semester at Lafayette College in Pennsylvania that he flunked out; moved on to Syracuse University in New York (where his arrival was noted in the school paper with, "Crane, the old catcher of the Lafayette College team, has entered the university and will make a good addition to the team"); played catcher and shortstop so well that a local minor-league team showed some interest, but he left Syracuse after that one semester. Both during and after these years, Crane often spoke of himself as an athlete: He once wrote a friend that he wanted to become a professional ballplayer; he frankly admitted that "I did little work in school, but confined my abilities, such as they were, to the diamond"; and he claimed that he had learned about the psychology of men in combat from his experiences in athletic contests.

All this is a matter of record, but what is strange is that after Crane left Syracuse at the end of the spring semester in 1891 he never seems to have played in another game of baseball. Instead he plunged into New York City's demimonde and artistic bohemia and spent the few remaining years of his life as a writer and journalist mostly traveling about. Baseball requires a certain stability, and Crane never attained that, for all his fine writings.

And that is the other strange thing: Crane never wrote any fiction about

*If anyone doubts that Stephen Crane played baseball, here he is with the 1891 Syracuse University team. Crane is the rather neurasthenic young man with his chin on his hand—clearly he has placed himself at the center and then made sure he looks different. Crane found some of his happiest hours playing baseball.*

baseball. Only at his prep school did he write some articles on baseball for the paper that show his feel for the game's total dimensions:

> And here on the ball field one meets representatives of all classes, but however different their station in life, the one thought is displayed by all, namely, victory for their favorite. . . . And, too, the sedate President loses his sedateness and may be frequently seen to go through "very peculiar motions" with his plug hat on very slight pretext.

Years later, after he was becoming something of a celebrity due to his *Red Badge of Courage,* he wrote to his editor, "I see also that they are beginning to charge me with having played baseball. I am rather more proud of my baseball ability than of some other things." That he never found a way to work baseball into his adult years or his writings makes Crane's brief life seem all that much sadder.

The claim that Crane never played in a game of baseball after leaving Syracuse in 1891 deserves an asterisk, à la Henry Aaron: That very August, Crane was working as a reporter for the New York *Tribune,* for which he wrote an account of a lecture by Hamlin Garland, not yet the well-known writer he would become but merely a lecturer at a New Jersey summer resort where Crane was spending the summer. Garland liked the article enough to seek out Crane, and years later Garland described their meetings:

> We met occasionally thereafter to "pass ball," and to discuss the science of pitching, the various theories which accounted for "inshoots" and "outdrops," for he, like myself, had served as a pitcher and gloried in being able to confound the laws of astronomy by making a sphere alter its course in mid-air.

It sounds as though Crane promoted himself slightly by claiming to have been a pitcher, but aside from that, it is a fine image, those two young men, on the verge of becoming well-known writers, tossing a baseball back and forth on the Jersey shore as they discussed the finer points of the game. The question of whether and how a pitched baseball could be made to curve aroused strong feelings in those days, and it would be nice to think that Crane's expertise influenced Garland when in 1895 he lent Crane fifteen dollars to get his manuscript of *The Red Badge of Courage* out of hock from the typist. That book gave Crane an international reputation, but in five years he would be dead. At least Crane could look back at his youth and say, "But heaven was sunny blue and no rain fell on the diamond when I was playing baseball."

*Baseball Books for Boys*    Thus far in this search for baseball in the lives and works of serious American writers, one thing has been ignored: The first works of fiction involving baseball were those written for boys. The long family tree of juveniles' (and juvenile, too, by today's standards) baseball fiction is well documented and widely written about (most authoritatively by Michael Oriard in *Dreaming of Heroes: American Sports Fiction, 1868–1980*). But to keep the record straight here it should be noted that the first such work was *Changing Base* by William Everett, published in 1868; in 1870 Everett published *Double Play,* the second work of fiction to involve baseball.

*One of the earliest series of book illustrations of baseball was the one in* **Our Base Ball Club,** *a boys' novel by Noah Brooks, published in 1884. It was Brooks's second such novel—his first,* **The Fairport Nine,** *was published in 1880. Allowing for various changes in the game—such as the fact that the players still wore no gloves—this doesn't look too unlike a baseball game of a century later.*

But the big breakthrough came in 1896 with the appearance of the first Frank Merriwell stories; written by Gilbert William Patten—who had actually managed a semipro team in Camden, Maine, in 1890–91 (he is sometimes credited with having discovered Louis Sockalexis, the first American Indian to play in the majors)—these serial fictions were idealizations in the Horatio Alger tradition of the "All-American Boy" and his typical and not-so-typical adventures. Merriwell excelled at several sports but baseball played the major part in his life from his prep school days to his "Frank Merriwell finish" when he pitched and hit Yale to victory over Harvard. Patten, who published these stories under the name of Burt Standish, knew a good thing when he saw one, and would later write two more series involving baseball—the "Big-League Series" (beginning in 1914, with Lefty Locke as the hero) and the "College Life Series" (in the 1920s, with Roger Boltwood as the hero). Students of the genre claim that these latter two series are more realistic in every way than the Frank Merriwell books; Merriwell, for instance, could throw a "double-shoot," a pitch that curved in two different directions.

Noah Brooks and Gilbert Patten had some competition in the 1890s from another area, the so-called dime novels, cheap little paperbacks that were turned out by hack writers to meet the mass public's taste in popular genres. Such titles as *Muldoon's Baseball Club in Philadelphia* (1890) or *Yale Murphy, the Great Shortstop* (1892) were aimed at adults, even if they did not display much sophistication. Although the equivalent of dime novels have survived to our day, such baseball fictions are eminently forgettable.

Baseball fictions for boys, however, took on a life of their own. Edward Stratemeyer, author (or originator) of the Tom Swift books, the Rover Boy books, and still other series, wrote the "Baseball Joe" series under the pseudonym Lester Chadwick. Ralph Henry Barbour wrote a number of baseball books for boys, including *Wetherby's Inning* and *For the Honor of the School;* although bearing all the marks of such popular fiction of the first decades of this century, Barbour's books described baseball games with such crisp authority that he set a new standard for regular sports reporters. Then there were the works attributed to the popular pitcher Christy Mathewson but actually ghostwritten by John N. Wheeler—*Pitcher Plooock, First Base Faulkner,* and others.

The tradition of boys' baseball fiction was maintained by such authors as Duane Decker (with his "Blue Sox Series"), William Heylinger, and more recently John Tunis. At least one knowledgeable student (Ralph Graber), however, nominates as the best of the genre Owen Johnson's *The Humming-bird* of 1910. Johnson is best known for his Lawrenceville and Dink Stover fictions. By flatly stating, "In plot, characterization, and style, *The Humming-*

TIP TOP WEEKLY

"An ideal publication for the American Youth"

No. 232.                                        Price, Five Cents.

FRANK MERRIWELL'S DOUBLE-PLAY

OR

WINNING HIS OWN GAME

BY

BURT L. STANDISH

FRANK, CROUCHING BEHIND, CAUGHT THE BALL AS IT BOUNDED FROM BINE'S HANDS.

*Boys' sports fiction is a genre with a history of its own, but among the all-time favorites were the Frank Merriwell stories that began to appear in the magazine* Tip Top Weekly *in 1896 and would continue to appear into the 1920s. Merriwell participated in many activities and adventures, but he especially excelled in baseball while at Yale and, as this cover drawing and title suggest, he was capable of all kinds of heroics.*

*bird* is the best of the early baseball fiction," Graber moves the book up to the major league of baseball fiction.

*The Lardner Years*   In the first two decades of this century, baseball fiction for adults came of age, with Ring Lardner's *You Know Me Al* usually regarded as both the orphan and the granddaddy of it all. This began life in 1914 in *The Saturday Evening Post* as a series of short stories cast as letters from bush-leaguer Jack Keefe to Al, his friend back home. Published in 1916 as a novel of sorts, it was by no means hailed as a masterpiece by everyone, Virginia Woolf and H. L. Mencken being two notable exceptions. In fact, *You Know Me Al* had no real antecedents in baseball fiction but owes more to the folk and vernacular traditions that Twain exploited with such genius. Some of Lardner's other baseball stories—"Alibi Ike," "Harmony," "Horseshoes"—are at least as good, and in some ways no one has really surpassed Lardner when it comes to extracting human insights and essences from just plain baseball players, talk, and situations.

But it is misleading to assume that there was no serious baseball fiction between Lardner and the "expansion team" that includes Malamud and Harris. Over twenty years before Lardner's stories began to appear, in fact, Frank Norris—still famous for his novels *McTeague* and *The Octopus*—wrote a short story, "This Animal of a Buldy Jones," that is usually overlooked by baseball anthologizers. It tells of Buldy Jones, an American studying painting in Paris, who is challenged to a duel and, having been a pitcher at Yale, chooses baseballs as the weapon. The poor Frenchman naturally doesn't come close with his throw, but Jones pitches an "in-curve" that fools the Frenchman and dislocates his jaw.

Norris has great sport with the whole role of baseball in Americans' lives:

> In his studio—quite the swellest in the Quarter, by the way—he had a collection of balls that he had pitched in match games at different times, and he used to show them to us reverently, and if we were his especial friends, would allow us to handle them.

And when Jones's second comes up with baseballs as the weapon of choice, he describes what he will say to the challenger:

> He [Jones] comes from a strange country, near the Mississippi, from a place called Shee-ka-go, and there it is not considered etiquette to fight either with a sword or pistol; it is too common. However, when

it is necessary that balls should be exchanged in order to satisfy honour, a curious custom is resorted to. Balls are exchanged, but not from pistols. They are very terrible balls, large as an apple and of an adamantine hardness. "This Animal of a Buldy Jones," even now has a collection. No American gentleman of honour travels without them.

In a sense this is the same juxtaposition that Twain had fun with in his *Connecticut Yankee:* native American ingenuity versus rigid European tradition. In any case, Norris's story, if hardly a masterwork, has a certain colloquial confidence that slightly anticipates Lardner.

There were others in that era who were trying to make genuine American fiction out of baseball. Zane Grey, known today almost solely for his Westerns, had been a star baseball player at the University of Pennsylvania and even played on a minor-league team. His juvenile novel, *The Short Stop* (1909), is easily forgotten, but some of the short stories he eventually collected in *The Redheaded Outfield and Other Baseball Stories* (1915) are still anthologized. Now almost forgotten are journalists such as Gerald Beaumont (who also was an official scorer for the Pacific Coast League) and Charles E. Van Loan, both of whom turned out some respectable short stories about baseball. Even more forgotten is Philip Curtiss's 1915 novel, *The Ladder,* one of the first adult books to use baseball as part of the normal American working world. Still with a minor reputation as journalist-critic-columnist was Heywood Broun, whose 1923 work, *The Sun Field,* must rate as one of the first adult novels to use the baseball world as a microcosm of society at large.

So with all due respect and admiration for Lardner's contribution to baseball fiction, he was not entirely on his own. Ironically, in later years he claimed to detest his baseball stories in particular and sports in general.

*The Second Generation* By the 1930s and '40s, American writers had pretty much cut their ties to European traditions and were feeling free to write about anything in the American vein and vernacular. Baseball, it then follows, begins to show up in almost every half-serious writer's work—indeed, baseball begins to assume the role of validating the fictional world as authentically American. Sinclair Lewis, in *Babbitt,* treats the game in a bitter-satirical way, "an outlet for the homicidal and sides-taking instincts which Babbitt called 'patriotism' and 'love of sport.' " But Lewis remains a minority voice in this disappreciation of baseball; most authors have seen it in a far more favorable light.

Thomas Wolfe, for instance, wrote both rhapsodically and knowingly about baseball in three of his novels, *Of Time and the River, Look Homeward Angel,* and *You Can't Go Home Again.* For Wolfe, baseball represents much that is best about America:

> And is there anything that can tell more about an American summer than, say, the smell of the wooden bleachers in a small town baseball park.

There could be a whole anthology of Wolfe's tributes to baseball but the thing to be noted is that this was the baseball of small towns and minor leagues. He had a true feel for that world, as when Pearl Hines, in *Look Homeward Angel,* when considering marriage to a minor league player, concludes, "But she was in love with no one—she would never be—and caution told her that the life-risk on bush-league ball-players was very great." This is the world pictured in the popular film *Bull Durham,* only Wolfe was more realistic than romantic in these matters.

Virtually every writer of note of that era seems to have tried at least one baseball story, short or long, serious or comic. Robert Penn Warren, James Thurber, Damon Runyon, Nelson Algren, even P. G. Wodehouse—they all did their baseball "bits" that have, in turn, been duly analyzed by endless critics and anthologized by occasional editors.

James T. Farrell is an extreme instance of this, yet another American artist who played baseball as a boy and dreamed of becoming a major leaguer but who settled for writing about the game he loved. Baseball plays an important role in several of his characters' lives (particularly his Danny O'Neill), and Farrell always wrote of the game as a true insider. His most famous novel, *Studs Lonigan* (1935), includes a description of an actual no-hitter pitched on August 27, 1911, by Ed Walsh for the Chicago White Sox. In 1957 Farrell published *My Baseball Diary,* in which he puts down his thoughts about baseball, and near the end of his career Farrell could be found in the pages of *Sports Illustrated* more often than in the literary journals.

*Top of the Order*   Conspicuously absent from this roster of American writers of the 1920s, '30s, and '40s who took on baseball is the top of the batting order: Fitzgerald, Steinbeck, Faulkner, and Hemingway. Put another way, did the giants of Modern American Lit share a love of baseball as well as of booze?

Fitzgerald's sport was football; one of his biographers says he was "obsessed by football. . . . Throughout his life, football remained to Scott Fitzgerald a symbol of the unattainable . . . the last opportunity in an unheroic age for man to act heroically." This reminds us of George Carlin's classic routine about the difference between football and baseball ("football has the blitz . . . in baseball you run home") and if insecure males want to like football and war, then baseball fans wish them well. In fact, Fitzgerald seems to have had a positive dislike of baseball; when his friend Ring Lardner died, Fitzgerald went out of his way to put it down:

> Ring moved in the company of a few dozen illiterates playing a boy's game. A boy's game with no more possibilities than a boy could master, a game bounded by walls which kept out danger, change, or adventure. . . . However deeply Ring might cut into it, his cake had exactly the diameter of Frank Chance's diamond.

This from a man who was Lardner's old buddy.

Baseball's only appearance in Fitzgerald's work is equally negative: The Meyer Wolfsheim of *The Great Gatsby* is modeled on Arnold Rothstein, the gambler alleged to have been responsible for "fixing" the 1919 World Series; Wolfsheim is something of a "godfather" to Gatsby and it is hinted that Gatsby himself may have profited from the fix. This is often noted in articles on baseball in American lit, but often overlooked is the other side of that coin: the moment when Gatsby's father, to show that his son was a "self-made" man, produces a schedule that Gatsby made as a youth in which he set aside a half-hour a day for "Baseball and sports." The irony may be a little heavy-handed but the use of baseball in this way is a tribute to the game. In a novel about the ultimate disillusion that awaits the American Dream, baseball serves as its best symbol.

Steinbeck seems not to have had any affinity for baseball, although there may be passing allusions to the game in his work. He was on the basketball and track teams in high school, and his earnest moralism perhaps kept him from appreciating the "play element" in our culture.

Faulkner also seems not to have allowed baseball into his writing, so he is usually ignored in discussions of baseball and American literature. An exception is in *The Sound and the Fury* (1929) where Jason Compson, in a cigar store, says a few words against Babe Ruth—clearly intended to reveal "the most vicious character . . . I ever thought of," as Faulkner said. "To me [he] represented complete evil." But that was a fictional world, and it still comes as a bit of a surprise to discover that Faulkner did have time for baseball in his life. He played a lot of baseball as a boy—he usually pitched and usually made himself captain of his pickup teams—and in his adult years often took time out to attend Ole Miss games and even Little League games. One of his biographers attended some Little League games with Faulkner and flatly states: "His pleasure in sports seemed to increase in direct relation to their amateur nature, and though these pre-teenage boys had been elaborately outfitted and coached, there was a gusto and intensity about their play that he liked." Here again, the theme that occurs so often in American writings about baseball: Cooperstown's Pastoral Baseball is okay, Big City Organized Baseball is suspect. But Faulkner also seems to have liked the major league game; once in New York City he was recording a reading of his work and became "disgruntled because he was missing the World Series game between the New York Giants and the Cleveland Indians." And he shared another infatuation with many other Americans: One of his more pleasant occasions in New York came in 1951 when he met Joe DiMaggio as they both received a Page One Award from the Newspaper Guild of New York. So to the portrait of William Faulkner, tormented genius of Southern Gothic, we must add a touch of All-American Little Leaguer.

Hemingway was quite a different case. There are countless discussions of Hemingway's strong attachment to sports on many levels. Sports and sportsmen play prominent roles in his stories, he slipped comfortably into sports language when talking or writing, and both as a participant and as a spectator he spent much of his time with sports. One commentator on this aspect of Hemingway has even said that "by nature and temperament he was half-artist and half-sportsman." And whenever baseball and literature are being discussed, there is a reference to the appearance of Joe DiMaggio in *The Old Man and the Sea:* The old fisherman, Santiago, is close to surrendering his consciousness:

> But I must think, he thought. Because it is all I have left. That and baseball. I wonder how the great DiMaggio would have liked the way I hit him [the shark] in the brain.

But simply alluding to or admiring DiMaggio doesn't really prove that a person knows or cares that much about baseball. Hemingway, in particular, knew how to drop in all the right names—whether of wines or trout flies or great artists—to establish a feel for the best in life. Joe DiMaggio's name has come to be invoked in this way by numerous writers. He represents the ultimate in competence, cool, classiness, or as one critic observed of this invocation of baseball, "it is a touchstone of human perfection and possibility." (Although there may even be a touch of humor here: Joltin' Joe's father was a fisherman—maybe Santiago was alluding to him?)

The language of baseball shows up here and there in Hemingway's fictions, correspondence, and recorded talk—"I was always fast, too fast, since I was a boy, and I always tried to cut every infielder's legs off at the ankle." No one denies that Hemingway had an ear for authentic male talk. But when it comes to writing about baseball, he seems not to have ever taken it on directly—with one possible exception. George Monteiro, a student of Hemingway, pretty much established in 1982 that Hemingway wrote one baseball article during his seven-month stint with the Kansas City *Star*. The article deals with Grover Cleveland Alexander's holdout against the Chicago Cubs in the spring of 1918, and although some critics suggest that Hemingway honed his style on such journalistic writing, there is nothing intrinsically Hemingwayesque about this article.

The one fiction of Hemingway's in which baseball makes a significant appearance is "The Three-Day Blow," one of his early Nick Adams tales, in which Nick has gone on a hunting trip with his friend Bill; when a storm comes up they sit around drinking and exchanging "man-talk." Baseball is among the subjects they toss about, but a close reading shows that it is not exactly the hero that DiMaggio was. When they read in the paper that the Giants took a doubleheader from the Cards, Bill remarks, "As long as McGraw can buy every good ball player in the league there's nothing to it." A few minutes later, when Nick says he'd like to see a World Series, Bill observes, "Well, they're always in New York or Philadelphia now. . . . That doesn't do us any good." Finally, half drunk and talked out, they drink a toast to the one true thing they know—fishing.

> "It's better than baseball," Bill said.
> "There isn't any comparison," said Nick. "How did we ever get to talking about baseball?"
> "It was a mistake," Bill said. "Baseball is a game for louts."

The secret is out.

Hemingway knew a fair amount about baseball, knew how to talk a good game, and certainly admired the individual achievements of the great stars. But it's questionable if he was a true fan. His true loves were boxing, bullfighting, hunting, fishing, horse racing, auto racing. All involved bloodletting or at least the potential for some, all involved some physical violence or the risk of same. Also, they aren't team sports. Hemingway was not a good team player, he was not a city-dweller—not a civilized man but a lone stalker. That's why he could admire a DiMaggio, the lone huntsman of baseball. But when it came to organized baseball, the baseball of McGraw and the World Series,

Hemingway, like Fitzgerald, felt the "fix was in" on the American Dream. (In a sense, it's the reverse of Faulkner, who used the antibaseball remarks to underline a bad guy.) A writer could be forgiven for allowing a character to dismiss baseball as "a game for louts" but not for choosing to live so much of his life so far away from ballparks.

*A Man's Game*   Hemingway's appearance on a scene in real life tended to be provocative and this is equally true when it comes to teaming him with baseball. For one thing, Hemingway was one of the few writers who evoked baseball to image the elite. Once, for instance, asked by his old buddy Hotchner if he had considered retiring, Hemingway thundered:

> Retire? How the hell can a writer retire? DiMaggio put his records in the book, and so did Ted Williams, and then on a particular good day, with good days getting rarer, they hung up their shoes. So did Marciano. That's the way a champ should go out.

Hemingway had this thing about stepping onto the field with only the All-Stars, whereas most other creative Americans evoke baseball for the opposite effect. It assures the Great American Public that the writer/poet/painter/musician, although a sensitive artist, is also a man of the people. A love of baseball establishes one's democratic, even populist, roots.

No, Hemingway never cared to identify with "the louts" in the bleachers, but on the other hand he did want to make sure that everyone identified him as a man's man. His constant public displays as a sportsman worked to that effect; not for him the image of Henry James, whom Hemingway labeled "a little old lady writer." Hemingway was not the only creative American who used sports this way. The composer Charles Ives, one of his biographers claims, was especially worried about appearing to be effeminate (what he called "sissy"), and continued to play baseball through his adult years to counteract that image of the artist. On the other hand, American artists find it perfectly acceptable to connect baseball with one's youth, a boy's timeless summer day in the outfield, as opposed to the adult's time-structured days in an office.

The identification with baseball—actually having played it as a boy, playing it as an adult at least on occasion, certainly displaying a knowledge of the "inside" game, the seasons, the players, and all the rest—has long served still other functions for creative American males, such as disassociating them from any academic–ivory tower–hoity-toity world. Robert Frost, invited to cover the 1956 All-Star Game for *Sports Illustrated,* would boast of his qualifications to write about baseball:

> How do I know all this and with what authority do I speak? Have I not been written up as a pitcher in *The New Yorker* by the poet, Raymond Holden? . . . If I have shone at all in the all-star games at Breadloaf in Vermont it has been as a relief pitcher with a soft ball I despise like a picture window. Moreover, I once took an honorary degree at Williams College along with a very famous pitcher, Ed Lewis. . . .

Softball? That's for sissies! And who wants to share the podium with some ivory-tower academic? In fact, Frost was reported as playing softball in his later years, but he was a genuine lover of baseball from his boyhood on. How many teachers and students, however, pick up on this when reading one of his finest poems, "Birches":

> I should prefer to have some boy bend them
> As he went out and in to fetch the cows—
> Some boy too far from town to learn baseball,
> Whose only play was what he found himself,

There is a bit of ambivalence in that sentiment—the native American's distrust of city ways and group efforts associated with the Old World—but Frost's love of baseball remained. As a still struggling writer he said in a letter: "Nothing flatters me more than to have it assumed that I could write prose—unless it be to have it assumed that I once pitched baseball with distinction."

Old World artists might be intellectuals (read *bookworms*) or esthetes (read *sissies*) or elitist (read *snobs*) or mature (read *stuffy*), but American artists, at least since the end of the nineteenth century, have tended to cultivate the opposite image. Philip Roth has admitted that one of the reasons he took on baseball as the core of a major work was to defy the "official literary culture," and several other contemporaries attest to similar motives in writing about baseball. Walt Whitman provides the model: no college, no necktie, the consummate democrat, and loved baseball. That he was also a homosexual should not disturb the image.

That was a setup. For the fact is that American writers, for all their concern with avoiding the Old World image of the rarefied artist, have not been afraid to demonstrate sensitivity and pleasure in applying their thoughts and language to baseball. Thus in his article on the 1956 All-Star Game, Robert Frost wrote in a typically Frostian manner:

May I add to my self-citation that one of my unfulfilled promises on earth was to my fellow in art, Alfred Kreymborg, of an epic poem some day about a ball batted so hard by Babe Ruth that it never came back, but got to going round and round the world like a satellite. . . . I meant to begin something like this:

> It was nothing to nothing at the end of the tenth
> And the prospects good it would last to the nth.

It needs a lot of work on it before it can take rank with *Casey at the Bat.*

In other words, some baseball is the fate of us all. . . . As I say, I never feel more at home in America than at a ball game be it in park or sandlot. Beyond this I know not. And dare not.

Frost's little essay, the closer one reads it, and for all its horseplay, is one of the finest tributes to baseball around. He took the assignment seriously enough to get it in on time, "the first time I have met a deadline since I was a reporter on the *Lawrence American* in 1914."

Another writer of that era who was not afraid to write sensitively about baseball was William Saroyan. In his brief essay (also for *Sports Illustrated*), Saroyan came as close as anyone to capturing the essence of the game:

> Baseball is caring. Player and fan alike must care, or there is no game. If there's no game, there's no pennant race and no World Series. And for all any of us know there might be no nation at all.
>
> If the caring isn't for a team, . . . then for the game itself, the annual ritual, moving with time and the world, the carefully planned and accelerated approach to the great reward—the outcome, the answer, the revelation of the best, the winner.
>
> It is good to care—in any dimension. More Americans put their spare (and purest?) caring into baseball than into anything else I can think of.

Saroyan continues in this vein, typical Saroyan, typical American writer, typical prose-poem about baseball. A few writers did it before Saroyan and quite a few have done it since, but the ingredients are the same: the identification with the mass public, the "inside" knowledge of the game, the nostalgia for the greats of younger days, and a bit of manly hair showing at the open collar.

*The Self-Conscious Generation*    All this talk about baseball in American literature has brought us only into the 1950s, and not even a mention of Malamud. It is generally conceded that it was with the publication of *The Natural* in 1952 that the next generation of writers began to move into the ballpark. Malamud's novel was quickly followed by Mark Harris's Henry Wiggen trilogy, *The Southpaw* (1952), *Bang the Drum Slowly* (1956), and *A Ticket for Seamstitch* (1957). About this same time appeared Eliot Asinof's *Man on Spikes* (1955) and Charles Einstein's *The Only Game in Town* (1955). The literary turnstiles have not stopped since. The sheer numbers and diversity of baseball novels is mind-boggling; they far exceed the occasional Sunday-paper wrap-ups of "baseball in American fiction" or the college courses on sports fiction, all of which tend to go round and round the same well-worn basepaths.

The all-stars are now well credited—in addition to Malamud's and Harris's works, Philip Roth's *The Great American Novel* (1973); Irwin Shaw's *Voices of a Summer Day* (1965); Robert Coover's *The Universal Baseball Association, Inc., J. Henry Waugh, Prop.* (1968); Eric Greenberg's *The Celebrant* (1982); W. P. Kinsella's *Shoeless Joe* (1982). Those seem to be the ones that make all the quality reading lists. But baseball fiction readers could not be expected to agree on a few favorites any more than baseball fans agree on an all-time all-star team. So here follows a long list of personal candidates: Philip F. O'Connor's *Stealing Home* (1973); W. P. Kinsella's *Iowa Baseball Confederacy* (1986); Paul Hemphill's *Long Gone* (1979); Jerome Charyn's *The Seventh Babe* (1979); Harry Stein's *Hoopla* (1983); Martin Quigley's *Today's Game* (1965) and *The Original Colored House of David* (1981); Lamar Herrin's *The Rio Loja Ringmaster* (1977); Paul Quarrington's *Home Game* (1981); Donald Hays's *The Dixie Association* (1984); Steve Kluger's *Changing Pitches* (1984); John Alexander Graham's *Babe Ruth Caught in a Snowstorm* (1978); Peter Gethers's *Getting Blue* (1987); Jerry Klinkowitz's *Short Season* (1988); and on and on, a by-now probably never-ending list, since baseball fiction now comes out at such a rate that there will always be another to make it onto someone's recommended list. (Charles Einstein, who knows the literature as well as anyone, greatly admires a little-known short story, "The Spitter," by an unknown writer, Paul Fisher.)

Noticeably absent from anyone's list, however, is Norman Mailer who, except for some observations about Joe DiMaggio in his biographical essay on Marilyn Monroe, uncharacteristically seems to have had nothing to say about baseball and his fellow Americans. But then Mailer has a "thing" about boxing and Hemingway, so what can you expect.

There are book dealers that specialize in baseball fiction, and picking up at random a recent catalogue from one of these dealers, the Austin Book Shop, yields such entries as these:

· Ardizzone, Tony, *Heart of the Order* (1986). Novel of a split personality in the minors.

· Brady, Charles, *Seven Games in October* (1979). Novel of another Series' fix.

· Carkeet, David, *The Greatest Slump of All Time* (1984). Novel of a neurotic nine.

· Clifton, Merritt, *A Baseball Classic* (1978). Nice novel of a millhand grabbing for it.

· Craig, John, *All G.O.D.'S Children* (1975). Novel of "what happens when a Chinese restaurant tycoon buys a losing ballclub. . . ."

· Everett, Percival, *Suder* (1983). Bizarre novel about a third baseman with a taste for elephants and jazz.

These are only *some* of the baseball fictions from the early part of the alphabetical listing in one sports book dealer's catalogue. Such listings could go on and on—especially if fiction for young people were also to be included, for those titles run literally into the hundreds. And this is to say nothing of the hundreds of published short stories by serious writers who deal with baseball.

Some people have attempted to impose a bit of order on all these books and stories by placing them into different categories—as Cordelia Candelaria did in her 1976 doctoral dissertation, "Baseball in American Literature: From Ritual to Fiction." In it she divided the novels as "those in which baseball plays only a minor role as one of several competing organization metaphors, and those in which baseball is the controlling and dominant literary figure." (An example of the first would be Chaim Potok's *The Chosen;* an example of the latter would be Malamud's *The Natural.* )

Others focus on different groupings, such as women's baseball fiction or the many mystery stories built around baseball—so many, in fact, that people can draw up lists of the ten best baseball mysteries, sending many others to the showers. Or there is the whole tradition of tall-tale and fantasy baseball fictions, really launched by Twain in his *Connecticut Yankee* and to some extent picked up by Lardner. By the time one gets to Coover and Roth, it is serious fantasy indeed, but there is a subgenre of popular-humorous baseball fantasies: Valentine Davis's *It Happens Every Spring* (1945); H. Allen Smith's *Rhubarb* (1946); Douglas Wallop's *The Year the Yankees Lost the Pennant* (1954—this is the book that became the popular musical, *Damn Yankees*); Bud Nye's *Stay Loose* (1959); Paul Malloy's *A Pennant for the Kremlin* (1964); and so on to George Plimpton's *The Curious Case of Sidd Finch* (1987).

Of the making of baseball books there will be no end.

*The Jerusalem Giants*    Another special group of baseball fictions can be called the Jewish Baseball Genre. Numerous critics have been observing this phenomenon for some years now, none more clearsightedly than Eric Solomon in a 1984 article, "Jews, Baseball and the American Novel." Go back over the list of novelists singled out above, starting with Malamud, and it is striking how many are Jewish—Mark Harris, Eliot Asinof, Charles Einstein, Philip Roth, Irwin Shaw, Eric Greenberg, Jerome Charyn, Harry Stein, Chaim Potok. And this by no means exhausts the list of distinguished Jewish writers who have taken up baseball either as a significant element in some fictional work or as the dominant metaphor. Others include Jay Neugeboren, J. D. Salinger, Joseph Heller, Donald Honig, Isaac Rosenfeld, Paul Goodman, E. L. Doctorow, Sylvia Tennenbaum, and Robert Mayer. Some of these writers do not introduce anything explicitly Jewish into their fictions: Nothing in *The Natural* or Mark Harris's Henry Wiggen trilogy requires that the reader acknowledge the author's Jewishness. Some write about Jewish characters in baseball settings but extract no special significance out of this—it is simply the world they know. Others, however, inject a specifically Jewish significance into their characters' relations with baseball, usually showing some Jewish youth's desire to take up baseball as a badge of his Americanness.

Perhaps none of these Jewish-American writers has pushed the role of baseball to quite such an extreme as has Philip Roth, who has used baseball in many of his works, including his notorious *Portnoy's Complaint,* quite aside from his monumental tribute to baseball, *The Great American Novel.* Even in a novel that seems as far removed from baseball as possible, *The Counterlife,* Roth has a Jewish-American expatriate in Israel proclaim:

> That's the thing that's missing here. How can there be Jews without baseball? I ask Rabbi Greenspan but he don't comprendo. Not until there is baseball in Israel will Messiah come! Nathan, I want to play center field for the Jerusalem Giants!

With this, the ball has made the rounds: Jews who only eighty years before regarded baseball as an exotic and unattainable cultural rite have now appropriated it as their own Promised Land.

Well, a character in a Roth novel has, but some might feel that the utterly self-conscious literary imagination that Roth and some of his fellow Jewish-American writers bring to bear on baseball is a case of misplaced affection. Nowhere is this more evident than in Malamud's *The Natural;* routinely cited as the reversed grandfather of the baseball fictions of the last thirty-five years, this novel has a lot to answer for with its heavy use of symbolism, myth, and other gadgets from the literary tool kit. (Critics have been known to write

long analyses of *The Natural,* conclude that it is "one of the most brilliant
. . . novels in our literature"—and never once use the word *baseball.* ) Most
articles about baseball fiction tend to accept all this as a sign of the novel's
literary worthiness, but one critic has dared to speak out against it: Gerry
O'Connor in a 1986 article (in *Arete*) enumerates a disturbing number of
errors or at least "tin-ear" gaffes in *The Natural* and charges Malamud with
"total ignorance of the game, its rules, strategy, its players and its records, its
language and its culture." O'Connor's first and last words could not be more
clear: "Bernard Malamud's *The Natural* is, arguably, the worst baseball novel
ever written."

It may be rightfully objected that there is nothing intrinsically Jewish
about Malamud's achievements or failings in *The Natural.* Being ultra-literary
and infra-realistic are not monopolies of Jewish-American novelists. But it is
a fact that virtually all the rest of Malamud's literary output has a deliberately
Jewish edge to it, and it is arguable that only a Jewish-American intellectual
would have written *The Natural* in 1952.

As an antidote to Malamud's All-Star Literary Game and Roth's Shtick
Ball, readers should try the more natural baseball fictions of someone like Jay
Neugeboren. In short stories such as "The Zodiacs" or "Ebbets Field,"
without insisting on their Jewishness or raising the flag of symbolism, Neugeboren conveys just what baseball meant to young Jewish boys growing up in
Brooklyn in the 1950s. Gutsy Louie Hirshfield, "probably the worst athlete
in the history of our school," appoints himself manager of the Zodiacs and
gains them a citywide reputation by playing the national anthem on a Victrola
he hauls to every game. Or Eddie Gottlieb, who showed promise of becoming
an outstanding athlete until he is forced to quit because the doctor says he has
a bad heart, only to discover when he is drafted that his heart is perfectly
okay—that it was his mother who made up the story so that he would get out
of sports.

Neugeboren is also capable of taking imaginative leaps with baseball,
as in a long segment of his novel *Sam's Legacy,* "My Life and Death in the
Negro American Baseball League," an insinuating, almost breathtaking narrative by a light-skinned American Negro pitcher, Mason Tidewater, who
finds himself engaging in an extended duel with none other than Babe
Ruth, a duel that involves both sex and baseball and ultimately attains a true
mythic power as it interweaves the lore of baseball with the story of American race relations. Finally Tidewater decides that he is going to strike Babe
Ruth out of his life:

> I wanted to defeat him for ordinary reasons: because I had loved him
> and wanted now to destroy that love; because I had loved him and

not had that love returned; because I had been hurt and wanted him to be hurt. I wanted to defeat him because in so doing I must have believed I could thereby put on what I had thought I did not want—his power and his glory. I wanted—oh so dearly—to defeat him, not, that is, because he had what I wanted, but because he had what I hated myself for wanting.

He then proceeds to strike out Ruth three times in an exhibition game in Havana. But when Ruth taunts him—"a guy's got to have real brains, with an arm and a face like yours, to spend his life with a bunch of niggers"—Tidewater "slammed [his] fist into the pasty flesh of [Ruth's] dark face and struck him down." The narrator pays a terrible price for this, and it is Neugeboren's triumph that such a baseball tale can be both quietly and threateningly affecting, so imagined yet so real. Perhaps, too, only a Jewish-American writer could convey the ambivalent love-hate relationship that minorities may have with the national pastime.

*The Poetry of the Game*    If, as has been said, it is poetry that captures and expresses the true essence of a people, then it must be asked whether American poets—other than Whitman and Frost, already cited—have responded to this sport. The answer is a resounding Yes! Ever since the first *American* (for there were English verses at least as early as 1744) baseball poems began to appear in the 1850s as lyrics of songs, poets of varying talents have been inspired by baseball to compose poems of varying styles. One of the earliest baseball poems appeared in Cleveland in 1883 after an incident involving an attempted hoax by an umpire, George Burnham; entitled "The Ballad of Burnham," it recounted how Burnham was exposed as having bought a watch and then pretending it was presented to him with an inscription; the ballad concludes:

> But when the league turned Burnham out
> > It made the people roar
> To find that Burnham bought the watch
> > At a secondhand store.
>
> The moral is so obvious
> > That there the story ends
> Of Burnham and his little watch—
> > "The gift of Cleveland friends."

The history of baseball could probably be pieced together from such popular verse that little-known or anonymous poets set down to reflect the concerns of the day over the decades. The *Official Base Ball Record* of 1886, for instance, carried a poem that shows the impact baseball was having on people's working habits:

> "In court" says the card on the lawyer's door,
> "Back in ten minutes," on many more;
> "Gone to the hospital," on the doctor's slate
> [More examples of such excuses for absence]
> They were all too busy, a matter quite new,
> Very sorry was I, I had nothing to do.
> Then I hied me hence to the baseball ground
> And every man on the grand stand found.

This poem by Hubert R. Kotterman, written about 1910, reflects the emergence of the automobile:

> Some people think, absurdly, too,
>   That the horse's day is o'er;
> Fact is, the time is nearly due
>   When we'll need him more and more.
> . . . . . . . . . . . . . . . . . . . . . . . . . . . .
> We have ceased to be horse lovers,
>   As the term was once applied,
> But to make our baseball covers,
>   We've got to have his hide!

Such verses could fill a volume of their own, but one more demands quotation. It appeared in the 1893 edition of Reach's *Guide to Base Ball,* a parody of well-known lines (and others have tried it since):

> To sacrifice, or not to sacrifice, that is the question.
> Whether 'tis better in the average to suffer
> The absence and lack of base hits,
> Or take chances against a lot of fielders
> And by the slugging make them. . . .
> . . . To find—to fan—
> To fan! perchance to touch—ay, there's the rub. . . .

Such verses are fun and games, but it is questionable whether they are truly "poetry." The two most popular verses about baseball, however, earn their positions on the starting lineup by the sheer impact their rhythms and word-play have made on generations. One is Franklin P. Adams's little verse that appeared in the New York *World* in 1908, when the Chicago Cubs boasted a strong infield; it has its oft-quoted refrain:

> These are the saddest of possible words—
> Tinker to Evers to Chance.

Serious students of baseball records have since shown that this trio was not especially outstanding, but it is a tribute to the power of poetry that they remain synonymous with an overpowering infield. All three rode into baseball's Hall of Fame in the same year (1946)—an example of poetic license?

And then there is what some might argue is the greatest of all works inspired by baseball—"Casey at the Bat." Whole books have been written about this, the finest being Martin Gardner's *The Annotated Casey at the Bat,* and there is not much to add to a book that reveals that one of T. S. Eliot's cat-poems is clearly derived from "Casey." The poem has also spawned a whole subgenre of baseball ballads—countless imitations, parodies, variations (one book prints seventy-five such, and more came out in 1988, the centennial year of the poem's composition)—and has inspired numerous paintings and sculptures and even a fine little opera by William Schuman, *The Mighty Casey,* premiered in 1953. "Casey" passes most of the tests of great poetry—it relies on rhythm and words to make its effects, it resonates in ways that lie deeper than the surface text, it reaches people on many levels, it lends itself to various interpretations. All that it lacks is the polish and sophistication of high art.

It would be many years before sophisticated and polished American poets did dare to call their art to bat—always excepting Whitman and Frost, of course. And many fine poets never did seem to discover the game—Ezra Pound, Hart Crane, T. S. Eliot (despite Donald Barthelme and Martin Gardner)—or if they did it's buried somewhere in their many verses. But it is no coincidence that among the first of the serious baseball poets was another American original, Marianne Moore. By 1968 she was so well known as a fan that she was invited to toss out the first ball to open the season at Yankee Stadium. Her two best-known poems about baseball—"Hometown Piece for Messrs. Alston and Reese" and "Baseball and Writing"—date from 1956 and 1961, but her devotion to baseball far antedates those.

Moore was also famous for her wide-ranging knowledge and imperturbable manner. Alfred Kreymborg, the writer, tells how back about 1915 he decided to expose Moore to something he assumed she could know nothing about, so he took her to a Giants game at the Polo Grounds. To his astonishment, after observing only one pitch, she immediately identified the pitcher as Christy Mathewson. Kreymborg gasped and asked how she could know this, and Moore replied: "I've read his instructive book on the art of pitching . . . and it's a pleasure to note how unerringly his execution supports his theories." That sounds a bit too good to be true, but Moore definitely did know and love her baseball, and although some hardcore fans never forgave her for shifting her loyalties to the Yankees after the Dodgers moved to L.A., Pee Wee Reese did, because he kept a framed copy of her "Hometown Piece" on display in his house.

Marianne Moore's baseball poems are fairly easy to come by, as are so many of those by established poets: Rolfe Humphries's "Polo Grounds"; William Carlos Williams's "At the Ball Game"; Robert Wallace's "The Double Play"; Robert Francis's "Pitcher" and "The Base Stealer"; Richard Hugo's "From Altitude, The Diamonds"; Robert Creeley's "The Ball Game"; Donald Hall's "The Baseball Player"; Kenneth Patchen's "The Origin of Baseball." These are fine poems, on any terms, but they are only the better-known and anthologized poems by the more recognized poets. There are hundreds of other fine baseball poems that have not been so widely dispersed—some by well-known writers (such as Paul Goodman's "Don Larsen's Perfect Day," or Kenneth Koch's "Ko, or A Season on Earth"), some by lesser-known poets (Joel Oppenheimer, Tom Clark, Robert Gibb), some by all but unknown poets (Gene Fehler, Arthur Mann Kaye, Mike Shannon).

Everybody wants to get into this ballpark. Kids of all ages write baseball poems. Serious poets take any excuse to return to the subject: Rolfe Humphries, well known for his oft-anthologized "Polo Grounds," wrote "This Exhilarating Game" to commemorate the centennial of the first intercollegiate game, played in 1859 between Amherst and Williams. The range of manners, moods, and meanings employed by baseball poets is as infinite as poetry itself—doggerel to epic, elegiac to exultant, throw-away to profound. Among the wittiest are several poems by David L. Wee, "The English Professor Goes to the 1987 World Series," a medley of parodies of famous poems by English poets—"Ozzie" (for Shelley's "Ozymandias"), "Musée des Ball Parks" (for Auden's "Musée des Beaux Arts"), and "The Glove Song of Our Kirby Puckett" (for T.S. Eliot's "Love Song of J. Alfred Prufrock"). (Everyone seems determined to turn Eliot into a baseball fan. In fact, although he grew up in St. Louis, a real baseball town, he did not seem to have any interest in athletics and a congenital hernia prevented him from playing in games; some might argue he would have taken a less pessimistic view had he played a little baseball.)

These days, new baseball poems are apt to show up any place where poetry is printed, but there exist two magazines that are especially receptive to the more imaginative ones—*The Minneapolis Review of Baseball* and *Spitball* (this latter founded in 1981 solely to publish baseball poetry, although it has since made room for short stories, book reviews, interviews, and more). Baseball and poetry seem so ideally suited to each other that both should go on forever.

*Baseball Lit Wrap-up*   It should be apparent by now that there is more to baseball in American literature than Lardner and Malamud. Yet this has been only a superficial tour through the subject. There are still many authors to discuss and many different approaches to take. There are, for instance, countless novels and short stories in which baseball does not figure directly but in which it, and only it, gives the proper resonance to what is going on. William Kennedy's *Ironweed* (1983) is an example of this, with its lead character's grim life seen as the shadow side of his former career as a baseball player. Charles Baxter wrote a short story in which a young man seeks out a brother he has never met, and to help them feel comfortable he brings along a bat, a baseball, and two gloves. Such oblique fictions in some way are truer to baseball's role in Americans' lives than many of the overt baseball stories.

Then there are the curiosities of baseball writing, works that fall into no obvious categories. One such is Howard Senzel's strange hybrid, *Baseball and the Cold War* (1977), which one critic has classified as "a personalized historical fantasy." Senzel combines his lifelong fanship for his hometown minor league team, the Rochester Red Wings, with an account of baseball in Castro's Cuba, with his own hopes for using baseball to restore relations between the United States and Cuba, and throws in outright fantasies on these themes (Castro in the mountains before he seized power coming across the young Luis Tiant, Jr., practicing baseball; or Castro dumping a glass of water on a U.S. congressman, thereby spoiling the chances of reviving baseball between the two nations). There is much more to the book than this, and it is hard to imagine any other sport inspiring what is ultimately a serious inquiry into American history and the Cold War.

At the other extreme is a little-noted piece by experimental postmodern writer Donald Barthelme, "The Art of Baseball" (in *Spirit of Sport,* 1985). In this, Barthelme adopts a mock-solemn academic voice to claim that "a number of this century's most famous artists were also, at odd moments in their careers, baseball players." He goes on to reveal such overlooked gems as:

> What has been missed (in a series of misreadings so horrendous as to be without parallel in the annals of quality lit scholarship in this country) is that ["The Waste Land"] is essentially about the St. Louis Browns of 1922, a team for which Eliot, back from Britain in that year, briefly starred at short. . . . Item: The poem's very first line, "April is the cruellest month," was originally *"August* is the cruellest month." The allusion is to the dreadful set of games the Browns dropped to the Yanks . . . in August 1922, a setback that effectively removed them from serious league competition. . . . Item: The line . . . "Here is the man with three staves" is beyond cavil a foreshadowing of the movement toward the batter's box of the awesome Babe Ruth—one can almost see the Bambino twirling a trio of bats as he stumbles plateward.

Barthelme continues to play with his conceit, placing the critic-writer Susan Sontag, for instance, on the Chicago White Sox (forced to disguise herself as a man), or the painter Willem "Big Bill" de Kooning on the Brooklyn Dodgers, using baseball to skewer the idols and jargon of the artsy intellectual world. It all cries out for quotation, but must end here with Barthelme's own game-winning final strikeout:

> In 1977 the multi-talented Billy Martin exhibited, at the posh Pace Gallery on Manhattan's Fifty-seventh Street, a startling series of junked refrigerator doors smashed into the likenesses of his patron, George Steinbrenner. The critics gave Martin high marks for surface tension, structural integrity, originality in choice of materials, and use of the sledge, but most of all for passion, without which neither art nor baseball would signify at all.

No one has as yet compiled a complete and definitive bibliography of all the fictions involving baseball. There are two major bibliographies of baseball writings—Anton Grobani's *Guide to the Literature of Baseball* (1975) and Myron J. Smith, Jr.'s *Baseball: A Comprehensive Bibliography* (1986)—but neither even begins to attempt to list all the works of baseball fiction. (Even though Smith's work has 21,251 entries, immediately upon its appearance it was criticized by experts for its many omissions.) The closest thing to a bibliography of baseball fiction is due in 1990, when Peter Bjarkman, the reigning expert on baseball in literature, publishes his major critical study, *The Immortal Diamond: Baseball in American Literature and American Culture;* it will contain a more or less complete bibliography of baseball fiction since the 1950s (some one hundred novels since 1973 alone). Bjarkman, known as "the Baseball Professor," is one of the pioneers in the field of serious study of baseball fiction—teaching college-level courses, compiling annotated lists of doctoral dissertations on the subject, editing anthologies, and writing this encyclopedic survey of baseball writings.

By now, several anthologies by savvy baseball historians such as Charles Einstein or John Thorn have pretty much identified most of the good writing about baseball—the better poems, the short stories, excerpts from novels, and the sensitive nonfiction pieces such as Updike's "Hub Fans Bid Kid Adieu." There is, in fact, a whole genre of "fine writing" such as this piece by Updike, works that are nonfiction but rise to at least prose poems if not pure poetry— the writings of Donald Hall, Roger Angell, Roger Kahn, Tom Boswell, and such. (And this is not even to get involved with the "classics" of more straightforward nonfiction—Pat Jordan's *A False Spring,* Jim Bouton's *Ball Four,* or the one that insiders prize even more highly, Jim Brosnan's *The Long Season.* ) Book-reading baseball fans tend to know the canon and can play trivia with the best of them (Who was Holden Caulfield's favorite author aside from his brother?) and for those who cannot get enough from the regular media there are specialized journals such as *The SABR Review of Books: A Journal of Baseball Literary Opinion* or *The Minneapolis Review of Baseball.* An anthologist and writer of baseball fiction and poetry in a class by himself—namely, far out—is Richard Grossinger, who in 1976 published (with Kevin Kerrane) *Baseball, I Gave You the Best Years of My Life,* and has come out with several other collections since.

But the individuals and publications already cited are not alone in bringing serious and sensitive minds to this subject. Peter Bjarkman himself has discovered about a dozen Ph.D. dissertations that explore directly and in depth the subject of baseball in American literature (plus another ten or so Ph.D. dissertations that do the same for the role of baseball in broader areas of American culture and history). And these are serious works, with titles such as "The Interior Diamond: Baseball in Twentieth Century American Poetry and Fiction"; "Bernard Malamud's 'The Natural' and Other Oedipal Analogs in Baseball Fiction"; "Of Hobby-Horses, Baseball, and Narrative: Coover's *Universal Baseball Association";* "The Linguistic Accommodation of a Cultural Innovation as Illustrated by the Game of Baseball in the Spanish Language of Puerto Rico"; and "Take Me Out to the Ballgame: American Cultural Values as Reflected in the Architectural Evolution and Criticism of the Modern Baseball Stadiums."

Those are only the doctoral dissertations. There are scores of master's theses, and an increasing number of articles on baseball in American literature and culture that appear in all kinds of academic journals and "little magazines" outside the expected titles of sports history, publications such as *Arete* or *The Journal of Popular Culture* or *Journal of American Culture* or *Midwest Quarterly*. These articles bear such titles as "Shoeless Joe Jackson Meets J. D. Salinger: Baseball and the Literary Imagination"; "The Americanization of the Gods: Onomastics, Myth, and History in Philip Roth's *The Great American Novel*"; "Literary Fungoes—Allusions to Baseball in Significant American Fiction"; "Going from Rags to Riches With Baseball Joe, or Pitcher's Progress"; "The Intellectual Game: Baseball and the Life of the Mind"; "Wordsworth in the Bleachers—The Baseball Essays of Roger Angell"; and "Zip and Bump—Bliss in Left Field: An Achondroplastic Interpretation of Malamud's *The Natural.*" But whenever a ball fan meets "achondroplastic" interpretations of the game, it is time to quit.

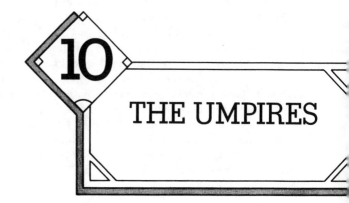

# 10

# THE UMPIRES

**E**ven the most dedicated baseball fans these days usually know little or nothing about the men who officiate at major league baseball games. Chances are that few fans could come up with the name of a National or American League umpire unless he had recently been involved in a major controversy. Yet this was not always the case. Far from it. There were many decades when a host of colorful individuals umpired games and were almost as well known as the great players. Some of these umpires were so individualistic—in their voices, their gestures, their behavior on the field—that they were instantly recognizable by any half-regular attendant. Ironically, now that TV brings dozens of baseball games into millions of homes week after week—and, what's more, provides closer views of umpires than most oldtime fans ever enjoyed—umpires have become practically indistinguishable.

They are usually listed by name and position at the outset of each game, by announcers at the stadiums and by sportscasters. Commentators will occasionally have something to say about an umpire when the camera happens to linger on him. Usually, though, umpires only come into focus when they are involved in some kind of controversial call or play. Any respectable newspaper still lists the umpires with the box scores, but the box score has never found a way of indicating the effect a particular call may have had on the outcome of the game. Instant replay on TV has given millions of viewers the opportunity to outsmart umpires but, with rare exceptions, the bad calls are almost instantly forgotten—along with the names of the umpires who made them. When umpires do get their names in the headlines, as in the 1988 fracas involving Billy Martin and what's-his-name or Pete Rose and whosamacallit, most serious students of the game suggest that the umpires should pull back, that they should become even less visible than they are.

The best book about umpires, Larry Gerlach's *The Men in Blue,* a compilation of first-person memoirs by a number of notable umpires, gives the impression that the game doesn't exist without them, that umpires are at the very heart and soul of the game. The fact is that umpires are inextricably involved with the game of baseball and have been from the very beginning. It is hard to think of another team sport where the umpires or referees play such a crucial role; if you are looking for an argument with sports fans, make that assertion and see what basketball or football fans have to say about it.

When Albert Spalding took his touring teams to England in 1889, one of the major reasons given by English sports commentators for the inferiority of baseball to other team sports was that it relied far too heavily on the judgment calls of umpires. Most fans today may not give this much thought, but the fact remains: Umpires are at the very heart of the game.


*The Famous First Umpire* No one really knows the name of the first umpire of even a fairly well-organized American baseball game. Games were being played throughout the Northeast during the 1820s and '30s and they undoubtedly had men who stood by as arbiters, but they were strictly volunteers and amateurs, most likely men who played the game themselves and were just taking time out to help fellow players. These first umpires did not have much effect on the game except in close calls at bases—strikes and balls were not called in those early years. By going back through the old local newspapers or personal journals it might be possible to come up with the names of some of these early local umpires, but no one has seen fit to undertake such a monumental task.

Instead, most histories of the game are content to settle on the famous "only acceptable date of baseball's beginning"—a game played on the Elysian Fields in Hoboken, New Jersey, on June 19, 1846—and then claim that this "first" game was umpired by Alexander Cartwright, who, it is further claimed, nine months before had set down the rules that were to govern this and all subsequent games of baseball. No statement about the history of baseball is repeated more often—and no statement about the history of baseball is full of more errors. It is tempting to think of Cartwright in this pivotal role, for he *seems* to have had a hand in drawing up the rules of the game as played in New York City in the nineteenth century, rules that gradually evolved into those followed by organized baseball; and he did serve as an umpire during many a game played by his Knickerbocker Club team as well as in games played all across America and even in Hawaii. Undeniably, Cartwright deserves his reputation as one of the earliest promoters of organized baseball games.

But the honor of being the first umpire in a recorded game seems to belong to one William R. Wheaton, a member of the same Knickerbocker Club to which Cartwright belonged. Like Cartwright, Wheaton alternated as player and umpire in the early years of that club's activity. In the same scorebook that recorded the famous "first game" of June 19, 1846—a game for which *no one* signed as umpire—Wheaton is recorded as umpiring a game played on October 6, 1845. This game has at least as much, if not more, right to be known as "the first recorded game of modern baseball" as the game of June 19, 1846. Furthermore, if Cartwright served as umpire of the June 19, 1846 game—and it is a possibility—he did not sign opposite the word *umpire* on either page, a practice that he and others generally had no trouble in maintaining, starting with the game of the previous October 6.

Although the best and most thoroughly researched biography of Cartwright, *The Man Who Invented Baseball* by Harold Peterson (Charles Scribner's Sons, 1973), flatly states that Cartwright umpired the game on June 19, it fails to offer any evidence for the claim. However, the author does reveal that Wheaton "was a young lawyer with offices on Beekman Place who lived fashionably on lower Broadway." There is some suspicion whether Peterson really knows that Wheaton lived "fashionably," or whether this isn't just part of the need by some writers to make these early Knickerbockers more patrician and prosperous than they really were. In any case, Wheaton deserves to be known as the first to have his name recorded as an umpire on an official scorecard.

Beyond that, Wheaton is one of only two men whose names appear as members of the committee on by-laws that drew up the famous Knickerbocker Club rules adopted on September 23, 1845. The other gentleman was William H. Tucker, not Alexander Cartwright. And to cap the case for Wheaton, Melvin Adelman, a professor of sports history at the University of Illinois, revealed in 1980 that the earliest known *newspaper* account of an organized baseball game, a match between the so-called New York Club and a Brooklyn club, appeared in the New York *Herald* on October 25, 1845. Although Adelman was not concerned with the question of umpires at that game, close reading of its simple box score reveals that among the three umpires at that game, all of whom belonged to the Knickerbocker Club, was none other than William Wheaton. As far as modern scholarship has yet taken us, then, credit for being the first rule-maker and umpire must go to Mr. Wheaton.

*The Early Years*  The gamebooks of the Knickerbocker Base Ball Club—formally founded in 1845—provide some interesting glimpses into the

*A page from the famous Knickerbocker Base Ball Club gamebook shows that the umpire had an especially busy day on April 26, 1847. Since Henderson was fined six pence "for saying s--t," we are left wondering what Henderson said to deserve six pence "for swearing." The impression remains, though, that such fines were levied in good spirits by umpires who were in fact friends and fellow players.*

early years of umpiring, at least in the rather restricted world of a few New York City amateur teams. Men moved back and forth from playing to umpiring, for example, and in some games both played and umpired; clearly they took a relaxed attitude toward it all. On the other hand, these umpires were not afraid to fine their fellow club members. Fines were levied for swearing, in particular, and for arguing over decisions; six cents was the basic fine, a considerable sum at a time when men worked long days at hard labor to earn just a hundred pennies. (Still heavier fines were eventually levied against those who used another player's uniform.) In all probability, these fines were levied more in good spirit than in an attempt to punish—a way, say, of raising some money for the club treasury to pay for drinks. Everything that comes through to us from these early years of the Knickerbocker Club suggests that high-spirited amateurism prevailed, and it is hard to imagine an adversarial relationship between men who umpired one game and then played alongside fellow club members in the next game.

But it is also clear that the umpire's presence and role was perceived as essential from the very outset of rules-governed baseball. The famous rules adopted by the Knickerbockers on September 23, 1845, which have little to do with the rules that now govern a baseball game—no mention of nine players or nine innings, of called strikes and balls—did make the role of the umpire perfectly clear: "All disputes and differences relative to the game, to be decided by the Umpire, from which there is no appeal." The amazing thing about this early (if not earliest) attempt at setting forth the procedures of baseball is that the codifiers realized that *whatever the rest of the rules said or didn't say,* there was a need for an absolute final authority.

*Evolution of the Profession*   The story of how the amateur umpires of the earliest years of baseball evolved into the essential, highly professional crew of today's games—even Little League games may be forfeited if "accredited" umpires aren't on hand—would require a book unto itself. But the general outline of this evolutionary process is clear. As it happens, some of the earliest "match games"—that is, those played between two formal teams and by agreed-upon rules—used three umpires, one provided by each team and the third a "neutral" individual. That was the case with the first game ever reported in a newspaper, the one written up in the New York *Herald* of October 25, 1845, at which William Wheaton was one of the three. At many of the games played by organized teams from the 1840s through the 1850s, three umpires continued to officiate, the third serving as a referee when the two partisan umpires disagreed. In 1858, however, the National Association of Ball Players decided that one umpire would do, and a single umpire would run major league ballgames for the next fifty or so years. (Up to as late as 1882, however, an umpire was allowed to ask spectators for advice on certain difficult calls.)

In the very early years of baseball, this single umpire sometimes stood far behind the catcher and batter, sometimes behind the pitcher, sometimes well off to one side (usually to the right of the first-base path); sometimes he didn't stand but sat on a chair or a high stool. Although these early umpires wore no special protective gear, at important match games they often wore high silk hats or broad-brimmed beaver hats and carried a cane. In any case, the umpire was strictly an unpaid amateur, often a former or at present inactive player, and the home team was required to provide him. All early accounts suggest that it was regarded as an honor to be asked to serve as an umpire.

The assigning of two umpires to a game actually started when the players formed their own breakaway league in 1890 and used an umpire in the field as well as one behind the plate; no one knew better than the players how important it was to have an umpire in on every close play. In the early years of the twentieth century, the use of two umpires gradually began to spread, although the majors did not adopt this as an official rule until 1911. Three umpires were not formally required during regular-season play in the majors until 1933, and four not until 1952, although four umpires had been working the World Series since 1909. Nowadays umpires work in crews of four, generally rotating from third base to second base to first base to home plate from game to game. Six umpires (the extra two in the outfield) are used in the playoffs and World Series.

As the baseball powers clamped down on verbal abuse and crowd violence in the early decades of this century, they began to formally recognize the crucial importance of having umpires' calls accepted as absolute and final. In one area, however, umpires lost one of their weapons: Since 1879 they had been empowered to levy fines on players or managers, but in 1950 this power was rescinded (and wisely so). Umpires now submit a report and the league president then decides on the fine. But by and large umpires have achieved the status and authority necessary to conduct the games in a manner that eliminates most of the earlier excesses and controversies. Special schools have existed since 1935 to train umpires in a truly professional way, and umpires have been unionized since the 1960s. While many fans greatly resent recent holdouts by umpires for better pay, their wage seems modest enough in comparison to that of many players: The maximum basic salary of an umpire in 1988 was $105,000; the average salary for major league players in 1988 was $433,000.

As proof that major league umpires are human and American, it was

1966 before the first black was allowed to come up to the majors. Emmett L. Ashford joined the American League that year, and a recent TV beer commercial to the contrary, there have been precious few blacks since. Women umpires, meanwhile, have yet to be allowed to work in the majors, although (as discussed later in this chapter) this claim may be overtaken by developments in the 1989 season.

*Enter the Villain*   How umpires came to be treated as paid professionals, how they came to be separated from their home-team ties, how their uniforms and gear developed, and how their mastery of the increasingly more detailed rules came to be crucial to the game is part of the standard histories of the game. Less known is the way the umpire developed into a kind of "villain"—like a stage character in a melodrama, a character whom the paying public felt they had a right, almost an obligation, to hiss and boo, the difference being that the umpire had to operate in a real world where public attacks went far beyond hissing and booing. David Q. Voigt, one of the premier historians of the game, has traced this development in his article "America's Manufactured Villain—The Baseball Umpire," but few of today's fans or even sportswriters realize what a long tradition of umpire-baiting lies behind contemporary "rhubarbs" involving umpires and managers such as Earl Weaver, Billy Martin, or Pete Rose. (The career record for ejections from games seems to be held by Earl Weaver—ninety-eight.) The distinguishing characteristic of these modern confrontations, in fact, is their tameness in comparison to the late-nineteenth-century treatment of umpires. Nothing that managers or players or owners or fans do or say these days comes anywhere close to the despicable treatment umpires were subjected to in the last decades of the nineteenth century.

The vilification began in the early 1870s and was directly related to the growing complexity and seriousness of the game, which in turn grew out of baseball's growing professionalism. When the Cincinnati Red Stockings openly declared themselves a paid professional team in 1869, other teams soon followed, and right on their heels came gamblers. A new kind of spectator began to dominate the big-city ballparks where professional teams were playing, spectators who came to bet on their favorites, to drink with their cronies, and generally to raise a bit of hell. They were not apt to have given much thought to the nature of the game, and the obvious focus for their ignorance and frustration was the umpire. Players were only too willing to exploit this blatant partisanship among the fans, especially at their home field, and some owners even encouraged it.

A HINT FOR THE NEW YORK NINE.—GIVE THE UMPIRE A CHANCE.

*This cartoon from a late-nineteenth-century issue of* **Puck** *magazine humorously conveys how umpires were treated by many players and fans, but it also is a plea for restraining such behavior, which many felt had gotten completely out of hand. Note that the umpire has been provided with a fan and a glass (of lemonade?) and looks far more delicate than any umpire then or since.*

So it was that, starting in the 1870s, there began a constant series of incidents involving umpires, confrontations that often led to violence and ultimately led to umpires' being cast as villains. Umpires were frequently assaulted both during and after games, by players as well as fans, and there are at least two references to killings of umpires in the minor leagues: Samuel White at Lowndesborough, Alabama, in 1889, and Ora Jennings at Farmersburg, Indiana, in 1891—both struck with bats by irate players. Sometimes games were tainted by gambling money riding on their outcome, enabling players to accuse umpires of being "bought"; conversely, umpires might accuse players of having "sold out." One notoriously feisty umpire, Bob Ferguson, accused a New York Mutuals player of holding back for the gamblers, and when the player called him a liar, Ferguson hit him with a bat. Ferguson had to be escorted off the field by the local police.

But Ferguson's assault was an exception to the usual situation. Accounts by umpires during this era are full of tales of flights from the field, fights with players and fans, police escorts out of town, and hiding in hotel rooms or under stands to escape the locals' wrath. Crowds turned into brute mobs and hurled dangerous missiles of all kinds, chasing umpires off the field both during and after games. Once an umpire named Johnstone was denied entrance to the Polo Grounds by the Giants management, which said the crowd was so unhappy with his calls of the previous day's game that there'd be a riot. Johnstone retaliated by declaring the game forfeited by the Giants. Understandably, umpires in this era were known to have carried and produced guns, although there is no case of their having shot anyone. (A Chicago judge in 1909 ruled that an umpire had no right to draw a gun even when confronted by an angry mob.)

Between 1870 and 1900, owners actually encouraged attacks against umpires, either through some naive notion that it was all "part of the game" or through a more calculated desire to attract spectators with a bit of violence. One of the ways owners contributed to this pervasive umpire-baiting was to refuse either to fine their players or to pay the fines levied against them for their attacks on umpires. Some of the most prominent and presumably respectable figures in baseball during these years participated in this guerrilla warfare against umpires. Even the great Albert Spalding, upholder of baseball as the American Ideal Incarnate, would claim that in attacking umpires the fans were simply demonstrating their democratic right to oppose tyrants. In 1887, National League President Nicholas Young told an umpire to give "the closest and most doubtful decisions to the home club" in order to avoid arousing the mob.

Baseball historian David Q. Voigt has documented the many headlines, poems, songs, and newspaper articles that openly whipped on the fans to

*This drawing appeared in Spalding's 1911 book,* America's National Game, *to illustrate his dislike of the professional gambling that threatened to undermine the integrity of the game in the years from 1870 to 1900. Yet through even the worst years, only one umpire was found guilty of taking a bribe to help throw a game—the only such instance in the long history of the game.*

dislike and assault umpires. The Chicago *Tribune* in 1886 printed a "humorous" poem typical of the era:

> Mother, may I slug the umpire
> May I slug him right away
> So he cannot be here, Mother,
> When the clubs begin to play?

Let me clasp his throat, dear mother,
In a dear, delightful grip
With one hand, and with the other
Bat him several in the lip.

The effect of such propaganda on the umpires themselves was understandably devastating. The rules for baseball were evolving, and no one had much experience with the subtleties that underlie close situations in a ballgame. Umpires were thus in an almost impossible situation as they tried their best to apply the new rules under the hateful glare of ballpark crowds.

One of the most touching expressions of the plight of umpires came in an article written for *Lippincott's Monthly Magazine* of October 1886 by one Joe J. Ellick, a former baseball player and manager who had retired to go into business but had accepted an invitation in July 1885 from the National League to serve as an umpire. His account of his brief career gives a sad glimpse into the state of baseball in that era: Within weeks he quit and went back to his business career, unable to stomach the conduct of players and fans and journalists. His parting advice says it all: "Some defensive armor for protecting the umpire against bad language and beer-glasses is imperatively called for."

Is all this a thing of the past? Not entirely. It is customary to say that the end of such atrocious treatment of umpires came with the establishment of the American League in 1901, for its founder and president, Ban Johnson, was a staunch defender of the inviolability of umpires. Indeed, when Johnson suspended a Baltimore pitcher for spitting in the face of an umpire that first year, team manager John McGraw was reportedly so furious that the incident contributed to his quitting the team and going over to the National League. (To even the score, though, it should be admitted that umpire Tim Hurst in 1909 spit in the face of Eddie Collins—and Johnson fired Hurst.) In 1907, umpire Bill Evans had his skull fractured by a bottle tossed from the stands. In 1917, John McGraw hit umpire Bill Byron in the jaw (and was fined five hundred dollars and suspended sixteen days).

Most fans today have no idea of how many umpires continue to leave the profession simply because they cannot take the abuse. (Dave Pallone's quitting in 1988 after his fracas with Rose seems to have been based on more complex matters.) Even the courts tend to sanction umpires' status as punching bags. As recently as August 1987, a New York State appeals court upheld George Steinbrenner's right to proclaim publicly that a particular American League umpire was "not a capable umpire. He doesn't measure up." The court's decision went on to say that "this action of defamation brings into play one of the most colorful American traditions—the razzing of the umpire.

. . . General Douglas MacArthur is reported to have said he was proud to protect American freedoms like the freedom to boo umpires."

*Guest Umpires*   One of the curious variations on the low esteem in which umpires were held in the late nineteenth century is reflected in the custom of inviting celebrities to umpire games. It was as though the owners and organizers of baseball were saying, "Who cares whether the umpire really knows the rules?" Or put another way, "Any fool can umpire a game." Major league teams did not allow such celebrity umpiring in scheduled games, but minor league teams went in for this as a way of attracting crowds. Thus, Mark Twain, as a celebrity summering at his wife's hometown of Elmira, New York, in July 1877, was scheduled to umpire at least part of a game between the Elmira team and the Binghamton Bingoes; in the end, he was unable to be present, but it says something that such a thing was even contemplated. Mark Twain did seem to have some appreciation for the game, but it is a remarkable inconsistency that fans who were prepared to kill a professional if he made a mistake would flock to see an untrained individual officiate.

Billy Sunday, the great evangelist of the early years of the twentieth century, appeared as a "guest umpire" at semipro games if he happened to be preaching in a city where a game was scheduled, although never on Sunday: He was adamantly opposed to playing games on the Sabbath. But Billy Sunday (his real name, by the way) had played professional baseball in an eight-year career (1883–90) and presumably knew something about the way the game should be played. In a lithograph depicting Sunday, the famous contemporary American artist George Bellows showed the preacher in a pose that looks like that of an umpire. (Bellows himself had been a semipro baseball player and had probably had his share of run-ins with umpires; he may have been having his own little humorous revenge.) During his years as America's most electrifying preacher, Sunday incorporated a wide array of baseball imagery and gestures in his sermons: He often called the devil "out" with an umpirish jerk of the thumb, and to emphasize the image of a sinner returning home in search of salvation, Sunday would actually throw himself on the floor in a headfirst slide and grope with his hand as though seeking home plate.

But of all the celebrities who were invited to umpire baseball games, the most popular were the great boxing champions of the day. Underlying this dubious practice was a perhaps unconscious linking of the "hated" villains of the game and the "dreaded" champions: Every ordinary man phantasized killing the umpire when he made one bad gesture with his hand, while the boxer could kill any ordinary man with one blow from his hand. Aside from such deep associations, there was the simple lure of show business. If baseball stars appeared on stage in vaudeville shows, why shouldn't boxing champs appear on the baseball diamond? The fun arose when a boxing champ made a "bad call"; who was going to dispute the heavyweight boxing champ of the world? (This sort of highjinks is carried out on TV these days: The champ appears on a talk show and the host or another guest is about to challenge him—then pulls back as everyone laughs.)

These boxing champions only appeared at minor league or semipro games, and often for only a few innings—cameo roles, so to speak—but their calls seem to have been allowed to stand for the record. John L. Sullivan, Jim Corbett, James Jeffries, and Bob Fitzsimmons—four of the greatest names in the early days of boxing—all appeared as umpires at one time or another. Corbett is perhaps a notable exception in that he actually played baseball for professional teams between 1895 and 1897—usually first base and with considerable success. His brother Joe was a professional pitcher (he won twenty-four games for the Baltimore Orioles in 1897) and Jim played with Joe in at least two minor-league games.

Edward Barrow, longtime general manager of the New York Yankees, signed up Sullivan, Corbett, and Jeffries during the 1890s when he ran a minor league. He signed up Jeffries immediately after he had defeated Bob Fitzsimmons at Coney Island for the heavyweight championship in 1899 on a Friday, and the very next Sunday Jeffries appeared at Paterson, New Jersey, where the players had been coached to protest Jeffries's decisions: "First one taunted him and then the other, while Jeffries kept backing away, trying to get away from them." Evidently this "broke up" the crowds in those days. Barrow goes on to describe how Jeffries wanted to quit umpiring after the seventh inning but Barrow wouldn't let him, as Jeffries was being paid 60 percent of the gate. Jeffries agreed to finish the game if he could smoke a cigar—and he umpired the last two innings from behind the pitcher doing just that!

The practice of inviting these guest stars stopped early in this century, although there are undoubtedly occasions when local celebrities have been allowed to umpire at least parts of minor league and semipro games. But the professionalism that took over the career of umpiring has effectively eliminated this curious practice.

*Tradition Versus Individualism*   Umpires have lots of rules and rituals that few fans are aware of. They take the gloss off new balls by applying a special mud taken from the banks of the Delaware River. ("Lena Blackburne Rubbing Mud," named for the player-manager who first employed it after the hit-happy season of 1930, is still gathered and sold by the same family.)

Umpires are not supposed to leave the field even to go to the toilet—in fact, they slip into a dugout toilet while the teams are changing positions. And they sweep off home plate always and only with their rear end to the outfield (although the whisk broom replaced a long-handled broom only in 1904).

There used to be two fairly distinctive "schools" of umpiring—the National League's and the American League's, with decided differences in gear (inside chest protector versus outside chest protector), position (to one side of catcher versus directly behind catcher), hand signals, and so forth. Most of these distinctions have vanished as umpires adopted similar ways, and some would say that the colorful individualism of umpires is also fading into a homogenized gray. Nowadays it would be hard to imagine an umpire such as Jack Sheridan, who took every possible occasion to boost his hometown by shouting after a batter had taken a called third strike, "Strike three! San Jose, California! The garden spot of America!" Ron Luciano may well have been one of the last of these "colorful" characters, with his extravagant gestures and operatic voice. Yet who really wants to return to the days of the autocratic characters like Bill Klem or brawlers like George Magerkurth? Fans today object when a Dave Pallone "follows" a player or manager too far and "provokes" an incident. But what would they make of some of the oldtime umpires who tried to dominate games by their very presence and personality, a practice that was both easier and more evident when there were only one or two umpires in a game.

It is traditional to pay tribute to Bill Klem as the greatest of umpires, and he undoubtedly did contribute greatly to the professionalism and respect umpires attained in this century. But the memoirs of umpires who worked alongside him convey the distinct impression that he was both egotistical and difficult—*overbearing* might be the nicest word applicable. He insisted, for instance, on always working home plate, refusing to rotate around the bases as all other umpires do.

And George Magerkurth may sound "colorful" when compared to today's gray, anonymous officials, but who really wants to see an umpire wrestling with fans on the field? Magerkurth has been described as "the most hated man in Brooklyn" because of his long-standing feud with the Dodgers. Does anyone *really* need to have an umpire that well known again?

In the end, umpires have generally become what they should be: consummate professionals, without whom the game couldn't be played and with whom the game proceeds largely independent of extreme personalities.

*Shop Talk*   Even when umpires are being their most professional and anonymous, there is far more individual personality and perception involved in a typical baseball game than most fans are ever aware of. Even TV close-ups fail to convey just how much conversation and other interaction go on between umpires and players, especially at home plate. Some players talk more than others, of course—many say nothing. And some catchers have little or nothing to do with the umpires. But during the course of a normal game, there is a fair amount of communicating: batters asking umpires why a particular pitch was called a strike, catchers complaining that the pitch wasn't called a strike. And there is a certain amount of just plain chit-chat that goes on, although contemporary players do not seem to go in for it as much as previous generations.

In *Ball Four,* Jim Bouton tells of an umpire who obliged a player who wanted to catch an early plane by ejecting him early in the game, and books about baseball tell many similar anecdotes that reveal a measure of "cooperation" between players and umpires. Umpires love to recount tales of witty exchanges between themselves and players—usually with batters or catchers, occasionally with someone playing or running the bases. Even allowing for the magnifying power of anecdotes, these tales suggest a side of baseball that few fans will ever experience.

*Bad Calls*  One of the constant themes running through the anecdotes and lore of umpiring involves bad calls. Umpires seem to have been taught that they make an average of 288 calls a game—at home plate, that is—although the figure is sometimes given as more, sometimes less. This figure does not include such calls as fouls down the line, "broken wrist" swings, or close plays at home. In any case, umpires all tend to boast that they make only three or four bad calls or errors in a game. The redoubtable Bill Klem is credited with saying that "I never made a bad call," although late in his life, perhaps expecting to confront the Greatest Umpire of Them All, he qualified this by tacking on, "at least in my heart." And that's the point: Umpires must be thought of as seldom, if not absolutely never, making a bad call, and certainly as never making a bad call for any other reason than human error. There can never be the slightest taint of favoritism or bias, let alone anything approaching bribery, in an umpire's decisions.

Only two umpires in the official history of major league baseball have ever been accused of taking a bribe to influence the outcome of games. In 1882 Richard Higham was banished by the National League after being accused of umpiring games to help gamblers; another umpire was accused and expelled but later readmitted to the league. One would be hard put to name any other profession in which such an infinitesimal percentage of its practitioners have been found guilty of corruption.

Errors, however, are another thing, and umpires, when they are truly "telling it as it is," will admit that they make occasional errors. Usually they insist that they dismiss such errors from their minds immediately, get on with the game, and don't carry mistakes over into some mental ledger that they try to adjust later on in the contest. But they also admit that, on occasion, they may be a bit harder on a pitcher or a baserunner if earlier in the game they gave him a "free ride" on a particular call, and vice versa.

Umpires also admit that they do harbor grudges against certain players if these players have consistently given them a hard time. Again, Jim Bouton states flatly: "Umpires do get even with people, even good umpires." (Tom Gorman, in his autobiography, actually admits he once called Johnny Bench out on strikes because Bench had refused to sign a baseball for him!) Certainly umpires are known to be, shall we say, especially sensitive to particular managers. Contrariwise, umpires admit that they find certain players "great gentlemen." Usually these turn out to be the heavy hitters, a Stan Musial, a Ted Williams; these men, it seems, seldom if ever questioned a call by an umpire. Since, by definition, great hitters must know something about pitches that other hitters don't, there may be some pressure on umpires to be influenced by what these heavy hitters refuse to strike at.

Meanwhile, umpires are entrusted with calling hundreds of pitches, and inevitably they must perceive things differently. A computerized analysis of all umpires during the 1986 season (made by Richard Kitchin and reported in *Sport Magazine* of June 1987) reveals there can be as much as 40 percentage points' difference in the batting average of major leaguers depending on the individual umpire. For one thing, the official strike zone differs from the umpires' strike zone, which differs from *each* umpire's strike zone; then there is the strike zone for every pitch as it is perceived by the umpire. Little wonder that there are many disputed calls. Yet strangely, fans who become livid with rage over some inconsequential call in the bottom of the fifth in a game that has no bearing on the standings love to trade tales of perfect games or no-hitters—where dozens of pitches were "called" by these same "blind" men. Those in the position to know best, for instance, agree that the final called strike in the ninth inning that gave Don Larsen his World Series perfect game was at best of dubious strike potential.

Base umpires' calls may not be so frequent as the calls on pitches, but they are often more likely to stand out. For a year or two, everyone in St. Louis could recount the mistaken call at first by umpire Don Denkinger in the 1985 World Series. Few fans were aware of the hate mail and phone calls he received during that first winter; and almost no one outside of St. Louis knew that someone made up a poster of the fateful wrong call—showing the base-runner clearly out at first. This poster sold well, but only in St. Louis and only for about a year.

For despite such occasional bad calls, and some that clearly do influence the outcome of a game or a Series, most true fans understand that bad calls are made every day but eventually even out. Few fans really want to get rid of the umpires. It should not be too much trouble for a modern tinkerer to come up with an electronic strike zone—something that would irrefutably indicate when a pitch went outside the perimeter of the zone. Yet no one has really ever tried to introduce such a device (although General Electric did once experiment with one at spring training). When *The New York Times* took a poll of the active players in the major leagues in 1983, some 75 percent said they preferred to stay with human umpires, for all their flaws, rather than to go over to instant replay on TV to decide close calls. That says as much as anything about the role—and standing—of umpires in the game today. The poor reception given George Steinbrenner in 1988 for his suggestion to institute TV instant replay only reinforces the feeling that people who can't accept the occasional "bad call" from an umpire don't understand what base-ball is all about.


*Female Umpires*   As the 1988 season approached, there was renewed publicity and controversy over the possibility of the appointment of the first woman to umpire in the majors. Pam Postema, who had been umpiring for years in the minors, was allowed to work the spring training games, but when the time came for the National League to fill out its roster, Postema did not get the call. (She had umpired spring training games for the American League from 1983 to 1985.) Most reports by knowledgeable individuals who had seen her work confirmed that she was a perfectly good umpire, and although there were vague excuses given that she needed a bit more "seasoning," it was not hard to perceive that the majors still weren't ready to allow a woman to join the Big Time. Few people in any league endorsed the Neanderthal remarks of pitcher Bob Knepper, but he was probably expressing the feelings of many fans when he said that a woman's place was not behind home plate. In 1989, Postema was to be given another chance and perhaps by the time this is published, she will have become the first female major league umpire.

The fact is, though, that as long ago as 1897 an editorial in Chicago's *Evening Post* suggested that the National League (then the only major league) employ women as umpires precisely because they were women. Turning Knepper's male chauvinism inside out, the editorial said that the feminine nature would act as a deterrent to the physical violence and verbal crudity so rampant in ballgames at that time. Home-plate umpires were the particular butt of this "rowdyism," and the idea was that the players would feel compelled to restrain themselves by the mere presence of a female umpire. Needless to say, the suggestion was never taken seriously by anyone in the major leagues.

But Postema was not the first woman to come to the edge of the majors as an umpire. In the 1970s there were two women who came close. Christine Wren worked from 1975 through 1977 in the minors and was well received, but "retired"—evidently because she could make more money elsewhere. Ms. Wren's career was uneventful and forgettable, but Mrs. Bernice Gera's career as a minor league umpire created little except headlines. A housewife from upstate New York, she had been umpiring at amateur and semipro games during the 1960s when she decided that she should be allowed to move up and work in the minors. When the minors wouldn't hire her—using as its principal reason that she didn't meet the physical requirements (she was only about five feet two inches and weighed 130 pounds)—Mrs. Gera went to court. For six years she fought her way up to the New York State Court of Appeals, which supported her charge that the physical requirements discriminated against women.

On June 24, 1972, Mrs. Gera took her place as a base umpire in the first game of a doubleheader between Geneva and Auburn (of the New York–Pennsylvania League). Whatever the reasons, her calls began to be protested. On the third dispute, she called an Auburn player safe at second and then reversed her own call; the Auburn manager protested vehemently, so Gera ejected him. She continued, but two more of her calls were disputed and when the game ended she walked to the home team's clubhouse and told the Geneva manager, "I've just resigned from baseball. I'm sorry, Joe." Then, in her blue uniform, she went over to some friends' car and drove off. "Witnesses said she had tears in her eyes," it was reported at the time. *The Sporting News* interviewed some major league umpires and their varied comments seemed fair and relevant, with nary a touch of chauvinism. Well, maybe a bit, as when Larry McCoy was quoted as saying: "There is no way [women] can take abuse the way a man can. A woman's feelings are different. You see it all the time. As soon as something goes wrong, a woman breaks out in tears. I hate to see it. It churns you up inside." Not bad, considering it was only 1972.

But none of the men seemed to consider why she had been driven to tears in the first place—that maybe, just maybe, all the men involved in that game were determined to give this woman a hard time. (Before we start congratulating ourselves that such crude machoism has vanished, realize that not too many years ago a minor league manager, when presenting his lineup card at home plate, kissed Pam Postema!) The fact remains that, as so often with early "test cases," Bernice Gera was probably the wrong woman to be used as the Pure Principle: She *was* too small and she lacked experience. Pam Postema is a totally different case, and it remains to be seen whether she will become the first woman to umpire in the majors.

Yet neither Bernice Gera nor Christine Wren rate as the first women to umpire in professional baseball. Although not much is known about this episode, Amanda Clement of Hudson, South Dakota, seems to have gained that honor way back in 1905. Having played baseball with young men as a college student, she served as an umpire in games between semipro teams in South Dakota and Iowa for about two years. It is interesting to note that she herself echoed the Chicago editorial of 1897 when she stated, "I believe I can do more for the game and the nation by uplifting the characters of professional players who do not know how to behave." That is not what baseball players want to hear, in 1905 or 1990, and Clement was soon back in college studying physical education.

Although there may have been earlier instances of women umpiring exhibition games in the semipro or minor leagues, Amanda Clement has gone into the history books as the first woman to umpire in organized baseball. What has been completely overlooked up to now is that the first woman on record to have umpired a game may well have done so for the seminal Knickerbocker Base Ball Club and in the very first year of its existence. On June 12, 1846, two teams composed of the familiar Knickerbocker names played a game that was recorded in the club's gamebook, but the score pages are unusual for at least two reasons. They are exceptionally messy, with several crossed-out or corrected names, outs recorded in wrong columns, runs canceled; it seems that whoever was recording the game was unfamiliar with the players' names and the method of recording outs and runs. And the handwriting is exceptionally florid, even for that period; it jumps off the page as the writing of someone who has cultivated an elegant penmanship. Or rather, "penwomanship." Because the signature of the umpire, which appears to be in the same handwriting as that listing the players, reads "Dolly Freres." No other name that appears in any record or account of the Knickerbockers or their competitors comes anywhere close to *Freres*.

That a young woman would be enlisted to umpire such a game is entirely

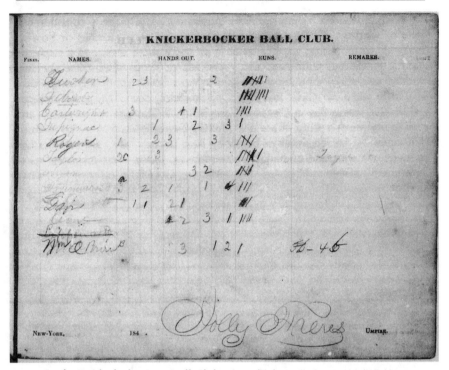

*In the Knickerbocker Base Ball Club's game book, on June 12, 1846, there is a game that was recorded and umpired in a manner that jumps right off the page. The unfamiliarity with the players' names, the constant corrections of outs and runs, the florid handwriting, the unidentified umpire who signs off: Was Dolly Freres the first woman umpire in the history of baseball?*

in keeping with the spirit of the Knickerbocker Base Ball Club, whose games were semisocial events and whose members were analogous to high-spirited twentieth-century Yuppies. And at a time when the choice of an umpire was somewhere between an honor and an afterthought, it must have tickled the members to draft Dolly, presumably a ladyfriend of one of the players. One can almost hear the hilarity as Dolly made ridiculous calls and recorded numbers in wrong columns. But she stayed with it and signed off with a grand flourish, thereby becoming the first woman to umpire a game in what became the national pastime.

*The Literature*   Umpires have generated or inspired a considerable body of writings. To begin with, there were the early manuals or how-to books about umpiring; starting as early as 1860, these remained a staple of various specialized publishers and sports-related firms. Then came the day when certain major umpires were asked to write books about umpiring—that is, a fairly technical guide. Bill Evans, for instance, one of the great umpires (1906–27), wrote *How to Umpire a Game* in 1920. These technical guides are now pretty much a thing of the past, having been replaced by video instruction tapes. As for the series of books by Ron Luciano, they are informative in their own way, and undeniably entertaining, but in their relentless spotlighting of Luciano and his gags they end up giving a false impression of what actually makes umpires so crucial to the game. There's room for one Ron Luciano each generation, but one's enough.

In recent years there have been two books that make something far more interesting out of this matter of how to officiate a game, books that take the reader through the complete rules of baseball and recount anecdotes, special conditions, actual situations, and just about anything else relevant to each rule. *The Rules and Lore of Baseball* by Rich Marazzi (Stein & Day, 1980) was followed by *Baseball by the Rules* by Glen Waggoner, Kathleen Moloney, and Hugh Howard (Taylor Publishing, 1987). Each is fascinating in its own way as, rule by rule, the reader is led to see all the possible combinations and permutations of how different rules work out in practice. Neither book is intended as a guide to umpiring, but they end up being just that.

Then there are histories of umpiring, of which only one complete book exists as of this writing. (Baseball historian Larry Gerlach is said to be working on a second.) This is a relatively obscure book, *The Umpire Story* by James M. Kahn, published in 1953 (G. P. Putnam's Sons). Kahn worked on at least one other book about baseball but is an otherwise unheralded sportswriter (and no relation, so far as is known, to Roger Kahn of *The Boys of Summer*). His book is decent enough, but it is neither definitive nor exhaustive. For a glimpse into the scholarly approach to a history of umpires, there is an article by noted baseball historian David Q. Voigt, "America's Manufactured Villain—The Baseball Umpire" (*The Journal of Popular Culture,* Vol. 4, No. 1), in which Voigt makes a run though the history of umpires in support of his theme.

But Gerlach's *Men in Blue* remains the best book about umpires. It's full of fabulous stories and human drama and is an authentic piece of American social history; it is hard to imagine a similar book by or about those who have umpired or refereed in other sports. Related to this compilation of umpires' reminiscences are a few memoirs or autobiographies such as Tom Gorman's

*Three and Two!* (Charles Scribner's Sons, 1979), a moving portrait of a man and the game and America all wrapped up in one career. Many other books about baseball, of course, refer to and pay tribute to umpires—Edward Barrow's *My Fifty Years in Baseball* (Coward-McCann, 1951), for instance, but perhaps that is because he wrote it with the help of James Kahn, who was obviously very aware of the role of umpires in the game. And everyone—players, managers, sportswriters, and all who write about the game—inevitably must pay some attention to umpires, favorable or otherwise.

But what of those *outside* the game who create fiction about the game? Do umpires figure in any of the canon of writings on baseball, the Ring Lardners and such? Not really. They might be mentioned in passing, but the only author who has seen fit to invent an umpire as a central character is John Hough, Jr., whose *The Conduct of the Game* (1986) tells of the trials of a young umpire. In the grandfather of all baseball literature, "Casey at the Bat," the umpire who plays such a fateful role isn't even given a name; interestingly enough, though, when William Schuman came to make an opera out of this poem, he or his librettist, J. Gury, did give the umpire a name—Buttenheiser. Since modern artists seldom do anything without being aware of it, one must assume the German-sounding name was deliberately chosen in contrast to the mostly Irish and Anglo names of the players.

No novels, then, about umpires, but what about shorter works? Well, there is one occasionally anthologized poem by Ogden Nash, "The Decline and Fall of a Roman Umpire," but it is not one of his wittiest gems; more amusing is a limerick Nash tossed off about the umpire whose "heart dictates my decision." There is so much poetry about baseball being composed these days that undoubtedly someone has written a fine poem about an umpire, but it hasn't surfaced yet.

What of the "classics" of our culture? They say "the devil can quote Scripture"—surely then he can locate an umpire there. But at least in its English translation, there is no umpire, referee, or arbitrator in the Bible. Probably someone has written at least a master's thesis on why the Christian faith has no need of an umpire, although when the great Mike Kelly—he of "Slide, Kelly, Slide!" fame—died in 1894, the obituary in a Boston newspaper said that Kelly had taken "the decision of the Great Umpire from which there is no appeal." Shakespeare used the image of an umpire or arbitrator on several occasions and in much the same way that the Boston obituary writer did. "The arbitrator of despairs,/ Just death, kind umpire of men's miseries," says a character in *Henry VI.* Says another character in *Troilus and Cressida,* "The end crowns all. /And that old common arbitrator, Time,/ Will one day end it." Here, finally, as so often when Shakespeare is called to witness, we see why the role of the umpire is so crucial and significant in the game of baseball: Baseball, like life, must be played out with some final arbitrator, capricious, error-prone, unfair, or whatever he may be.

Perhaps it was one of the classic writers who said it best, after all. In what is herewith revealed for the first time as the earliest account of a baseball game in the English language, John Milton in his *Paradise Lost* (1667) describes Satan looking on as the Gates of Hell are thrown open and seeing:

> . . . each his faction, in their several Clans
> Light-arm'd or heavy, sharp, smooth, swift or slow
> Swarm populous, unnumber'd as the Sands
> . . . . . . . . . . . . . . . . . . . . . . . . . . . .
> To whom these most adhere,
> He rules a moment; Chaos Umpire sits,
> And by decision more embroils the fray
> By which he reigns: next him high Arbiter
> Chance governs all.

Milton knew what the rules-makers of the Knickerbocker Base Ball Club knew some 150 years ago: There must be a knowledgeable and orderly "Umpire, from which there is no appeal," or else all is chaos.

# DEMON RUM
# AND THE OTHER
# SUBSTANCE

**B**aseball's mythmakers would have us believe that drugs are a problem new to baseball, but there may well have been more drug and alcohol abuse before World War I than at any time since. Homer documents the ingestion of mushrooms by Greek athletes to enhance performance, and Dio Chrysostom, the orator, writing in the first century A.D., describes the spectators at athletic events in Alexandria as behaving "as if under the influence of drugs." During the nineteenth century, the use among European athletes of caffeine, opium, alcohol, ethyl ether, and nitrogylcerin was widespread. "Smiling Mickey" Welch, one of the great pitchers on Jim Mutrie's Giants, used to chant in 1888 in support of his favorite intoxicant,

> Pure elixir of malt and hops
> Beats all the drugs and all the drops.

During the first forty-three years of professional baseball, almost every drug in the American pharmacopoeia was legal. Little old ladies bought tincture of laudanum—opium—over the counter to help themselves over the rough spots; cocaine and heroin were legal until the Harrison Narcotic Act of 1914, marijuana until 1937. After World War II, amphetamines and the similarly performance-enhancing anabolic steroids came into widespread use

*This illustration by Homer Davenport first appeared in A. G. Spalding's* America's National Game *in 1911. In the nineteenth century alcohol at times threatened baseball's very existence. Spalding claimed that whiskey was one of the three all-time evils baseball had to face in becoming established as the national game—the others were gambling and the owners of the 1890s.*

among professional athletes. And then there is cocaine, the drug of choice for children of the Permissive Society. As much as we might wish it were otherwise, drug use is a ubiquitous part of our culture. One writer, in an impassioned plea for the old vices, recently complained, "Baseball players who snort cocaine are neither lovable carousers like Babe Ruth and Paul Waner, nor corrupt in the sense that the 1919 Chicago Black Sox were corrupt."

Alcohol, of course, is a drug, and the pretense that it is not makes about as much sense as the pretense that baseball is not interstate business. Attitudes toward its use have ranged from banning alcohol altogether (from 1920 to 1933) to condoning its use as manly, but alcohol is still the overwhelming drug of choice among baseball players. When manager Leo Durocher prescribed a couple of fingers of brandy to quiet the pregame nerves of pitcher Tom Seats in 1945, he got excellent results, but Branch Rickey, outraged that his manager would use whiskey on a "man in uniform" and that Seats would agree, released Seats, who was 10–7 for the season, and threatened to fire Durocher as well.

In a society geared toward taking things to feel better—aspirin, antacid, vitamins—and ruled by commercial interests that insist we will be better off if we drink Coca-Cola and get a lift, eat a Snickers, take Sinutab; and which moreover is based upon the optimistic expectation of ever-increasing consumption and immediate gratification, should we be surprised that illegal drug use is epidemic? Drugs apotheosize the values of our commercial society, especially addictive substances. The buyer seeks out the seller, and the more the user buys, the more he needs. No advertising is necessary, although the media have lately supplied more free advertising than any presidential candidate ever got. For the consumer, the product is *pure* immediate gratification, stripped of all frills. For the seller the product is ideal—highly profitable, self-selling, and tax-free.

Now that everyone has gotten over how badly they were shocked to learn that baseball heroes also use drugs, some perspective has begun to replace the waves of denial and hysteria that rocked the late 1970s and early '80s. "Things have changed," NBA commissioner David Stern remarked in 1987. "The early revelations about drug use among athletes made it appear that sports was this culture that was tainted while the overall culture was not. Now the question is whether sports can remain pure while the culture around it is rotten." Commissioner Peter Ueberroth's comic pronouncement in 1986 that baseball was "virtually a drug-free sport" has given way to a more realistic appraisal; he now believes that baseball will probably always have "an occasional individual" with a drug problem.

The main concerns of baseball at any given time are the main concerns of American society at that time. Perhaps nowhere is this more clearly the case than with drugs, even though baseball confronts and deals with its problems in its own way, as any institution must. But criticism of the unequal way baseball treats its player-offenders, who in many cases are punished according to their current value as players, continues to mount. The rather skewed message baseball has thus far sent to the public concerning its sanctions against drug-using players is succinctly deciphered by columnist Mike Downey as, "Just say no to drugs, kids, unless you need a second baseman or a pitcher."

Above all, the hard fact remains that despite the most lurid exposés of drug use among athletes, attendance and interest in baseball has never been higher that it is today. In 1986 veteran sportswriter Leonard Koppett pointed out that "drug abuse, price inflation, labor strife, bad behavior and selfishness are not peculiar to baseball," and are in fact forces that operate "outside the baselines." By 1987 drugs tended to be considered another potential occupational hazard for athletes, like rotator-cuff injuries, torn ligaments, and broken bones; and baseball began to reflect changes in the way society perceives drug abusers, referring to addiction as "an insidious illness."

In a 1988 interview baseball writer Roger Angell remarked, "The drug issue has been diminished because people realize that when you have six hundred plus young men traveling around with a lot of money and not much experience, then drugs will be part of the scene. Drugs are an American problem and sports will have its degree of people with a drug problem." With its well-funded efforts targeted directly at specific groups, its fleets of medical specialists, and its high-ticket incentive to keep its athletes healthy, professional sports may well at this point be ahead of the rest of society in understanding and treating drug users.

*Testing*   In the late 1980s one of the pressing questions in baseball was who, what, when, where, how, and if there should be drug testing. Commissioner Ueberroth, anxious to assure the buying public that baseball was as pure as ever, at first tried to test all players, suspected or not, but was shot down by the Players Association. He then announced that all nonplaying personnel would be tested, which was ridiculous; then insulted the intelligence of all Americans by declaring in 1986 that baseball was drug-free; and in the end half-implemented an extraordinarily uneven "policy" of penalties and sanctions, which were generally not observed even for the most flagrant, self-confessed offenders. At bottom, of course, was the same cynical conflict of interest that permitted a superior player like Hal Chase to stay in the game until he helped engineer the fixing of the 1919 World Series, even though he was a known gambler.

Eighties' headlines may have concentrated on player-addicts, but in baseball the salient news was that revenues continued to soar consistently. The inability of the commissioner's office to avoid embarrasing itself on the drug issue was understood by many as just another indication that the powers that control baseball don't care about anything but their own clinking turnstiles. According to Lonnie Smith, outfielder and DH and recovered six-year cocaine addict, Commissioner Ueberroth did "nothing except go to the Little League World Series and say, 'Baseball is free of drugs.'"

314

When Smith spoke his piece in August 1987, *no* drug agreement existed at the major league level, although there was supposed to be constant testing in the minors. Smith, who played in the minors before being called up to the Kansas City Royals, reported that there was considerable drug use in the minors but little testing. He himself, who had been penalized by baseball after testifying under immunity at the 1985 Pittsburgh drugs trials, had been tested only twice since then, a lack of vigilance he considered "a joke." He also claimed that he had paid less than half of the $85,000 salary "contribution" he agreed to make in lieu of suspension, but that no one ever asked him about the rest; and that he had performed the one hundred hours of community service he had agreed to, but no one had ever asked him if he had done it. Referring to Dwight Gooden, who received no penalties from the commissioner's office when he was tested and found to be using cocaine, Smith remarked, ". . . he doesn't have to pay nothing. Where's the justice? Is it OK just because he's a Cy Young winner?"

Smith offered as final indictment of baseball's lackadaisical attitude the tale of his summons to the commissioner's office in January 1986. After he waited for three days in New York for the meeting, Ueberroth was late, had to leave early, and during their fifteen minutes together asked him only if he was still doing drugs and how he thought baseball could best rid itself of drugs. Two lawyers who were also present asked him one question each, "but they were so irrelevant, I don't even remember what they were."

Sports consultant Dr. Harry Edwards has pointed out that "for forty-nine dollars you can buy a six-pack of clean urine from a religious school and get your whole team through the drug tests." Different sports test for different substances anyway; several drugs not legal in the Olympics or in college are legal in professional sports. And the drug tests themselves, which have been known to register several over-the-counter cold remedies and commonly prescribed asthma medications as amphetamines or marijuana, are not notoriously accurate. Private labs now offer "pre-event" tests that will let the athlete know if he can make it safely through his conference or league tests.

The constitutional legality of mandatory drug testing, especially for athletes not suspected of illegal drug use, is another question altogether. Many observers consider testing tantamount to illegal search and seizure, while others suggest that it is all right to abrogate civil liberties in order to save the representations of our ideal selves, known as baseball heroes, from any meaningful brushes with contemporary social reality. Baseball itself has yet to uniformly decide whether illegal drug use is morally reprehensible or criminal—like fixing a World Series, for which any player could be expected to be expelled for life—or just a disease. At this point the only certainty is that baseball, true to form, has once again proved itself invaluable in highlighting a crucial issue in a society that often finds itself at odds both with its own technology and with its dual addiction to nostalgia and progress.


*Alcohol*    Albert Spalding observed in 1911 that drunkenness, with gambling and the destructive owners of the 1890s, was one of the three all-time obstacles major league baseball faced on the road to becoming the national pastime. In recent decades alcohol has not played quite the role in shaping the direction of the game or the lives of its players that it used to, perhaps because society has not chosen to wink at drinking as it has in the past. But despite flamboyant competition from today's fashionable intoxicants, there is no question that alcohol is still the drug of choice among America's athletes. When Ryne Duren drank himself out of baseball in the mid-'60s and became head of organized baseball's rehabilitation program, he estimated that 35 percent of ballplayers had a drinking problem. Today's players may be more health-conscious than ever before, but drinking by fans remains, as it always has, a threat to the peaceful continuation of the game, at least in some cities, and the presence in baseball of alcohol as a commercial power has grown, not diminished.

Roger Kahn recently remarked that "a history of hard-drinking ballplayers would make a very long book indeed." One reason this is true is that it would have to begin at the very beginning. In the 1840s and '50s, an important part of the ritual surrounding the matches played by the New York baseball clubs was the postgame banquet. Toasting and general imbibing on these occasions sometimes reached such gargantuan proportions that it became an object of public ridicule and a topic for debate at club meetings. Several of these early amateur clubs, which together created the basic outline of modern baseball, indeed had rules that prohibited any member who was clearly intoxicated from participating in games although, needless to say, this rule was not always rigorously enforced.

Harry Wright, a former professional cricketer who was hired to form the first professional baseball club in 1869, had considerable trouble with alcoholism and poor training habits on the very first championship team. His Red Stockings were overwhelmingly successful at demonstrating to business interests how potentially lucrative professional baseball could be, but within a decade of the beginning of professionalism, baseball players, in no small part because of their drinking habits and the practices of those who came to see them, acquired a distinctly unsavory reputation among certain portions of the public.

The difference baseball has always drawn between beer and other forms of alcohol likewise dates to the game's earliest days. In the 1850s, when cricket and baseball were both popular, cricketers and baseball players were advised to avoid "spirituous liquors" in hot weather, but that "to allay thirst and relieve exhaustion, lager beer answers every reasonable purpose." Since then beer has never left the clubhouse except, perhaps, during Prohibition. Currently it is part of most clubs' postgame rituals, during which it is both drunk and, in cases of victory, employed in baptisms and sprayings. Beer is still considered, if not good for athletes, at least not as bad as other forms of spirits, a distinction Jim Bouton found curiously observed when he pitched for Seattle. The club had a rule that players on airplane flights could only drink beer, with the result that "you could have 143 beers and get sloshed out of your skull, but you were not allowed to enjoy a cocktail before your meal." Likewise, players were forbidden to drink at hotel bars, although management was free to do so. Billy Martin and numerous sparring partners exemplify what can happen when players and managers drink together, but Casey Stengel simply explained, "You can't drink at the hotel bar because that's where *I* drink."

One of the great controversies in early professional ball was whether alcoholic beverages should be sold in the ballpark. Many well-known "lushers" played in the National Association of Base-Ball Players (1871–75), the first professional baseball league, and incidents of "drunkenness and riot," involving both players and fans, combined with gambling and scheduling difficulties to bring down the league after only five years. Some NAPBBP clubs sold liquor at games, a practice contributing directly to the deplorable conduct that made baseball realize that a bottom line of respectability and decorum was necessary to attract and keep customers.

The National League, founded in 1876 at the instigation of William A. Hulbert, was not instantly able to restore credibility to the game or to placate a hostile public, but it was founded upon the understanding that the integrity of baseball had to be established, and by 1880 Hulbert was successful enough and strong enough to get his league directors to agree to ban liquor sales and Sunday baseball. Cincinnati, unable to function without beer and Sunday games for its large German population, found itself forced out of the league. Hulbert died in 1882, just after ordering lifetime expulsions for ten of the National League's hardest-drinking players. In the same year, largely at the instigation of several outlawed teams that could not tolerate Hulbert's puritanical ways, the American Association began to compete with the National League. Promptly, and not without good reason, it was dubbed "The American Beerball League." Besides permitting the sale of alcohol in its parks, the new league also played games on Sunday, another great cause of the day, and charged only twenty-five cents admission—half of what the National League charged.

At the meeting in Cincinnati on November 1, 1881, that established the American Association of Base Ball Clubs, four beer-baron delegates—Chris Von der Ahe, John Park, John Hauck, and Harry Von der Horst—worked in concert to make the new league safe for "German tea" and Sunday games, a formula that was bound to expand their beer sales considerably. Their success was curiously offset by the inclusion of stiff penalties for drinking by players in the American Association constitution, which was a copy of the senior circuit's. But from its inception, the American Association gave official sanction to the sacred tradition of beer and baseball, and laid the foundations for the present beer-and-baseball cult. Its policies made the Beerball League such a success that by the beginning of the following season it was able to join with the National League in a new agreement that incorporated the reserve rule and paved the way for the first postseason World Series.

Most prominent among the beer barons who midwifed the American Association was Chris Von der Ahe, president of the St. Louis Browns. History has not been altogether kind to Von der Ahe, generally viewing him as a buffoon, but beer money has continued to be a powerful force in the game. Even if Von der Ahe only perceived the diamond as an extension of his successful beer garden, he had enough sense to hire Charles Comiskey to manage his team, and his winning formula of cheap Sunday baseball with horse races, fireworks, and beer sales significantly expanded baseball's commercial horizons. Today's amazing scoreboards and exotic promotional practices owe something to his trailblazing entrepreneurial mentality, which had much in common with the latter-day promotional visions of Larry MacPhail and Bill Veeck; all of their all-American innovations were widely criticized before they were universally adopted.

Von der Ahe had a statue made of himself and named apartment houses after his stars, but such self-aggrandizing commercial promotion hardly differs from that of beer baron August A. Busch, Jr., owner-emeritus of the St. Louis Cardinals, who rides out onto the field lashing his Clydesdale-driven beer wagon like some berserker urging the national TV audience on to ever greater heights of frenzied beer consumption. As it happens, both the colorful Von der Ahe and the American Association, the most serious nineteenth-century threat to National League baseball hegemony, were soon gobbled up by the senior circuit. But it is a lasting irony that the only other league ever to offer a serious challenge to National League monopoly was founded with the indispensable assistance of Charles Comiskey, Von der Ahe's former field manager, on the explicit platform of cleaning up the game and giving it a new image, particularly by discouraging the sale of liquor in ballparks. It was called the American League.

Von der Ahe and his cronies were by no means the only owners to bankroll baseball with beer money. The legendary Yankees teams of the 1920s, including such historic acquisitions as Babe Ruth, were financed by brewery tycoon Jacob Ruppert. August A. Busch, Jr., scion of the Anheuser-Busch billions, purchased the floundering St. Louis Cardinals in 1953, changed the name of Sportsman's Park to Busch Stadium to promote his product, and contributed $5 million toward the new municipal stadium that also bears his name; his son now runs the club. The Toronto Blue Jays are owned by a brewery; Seattle's Sicks' Stadium, now-defunct home of the now-defunct Raniers and Pilots, was named after beer baron Emile Sicks; the Milwaukee Brewers—named after guess what—are supported by fans who work for breweries; and in the old Negro leagues, the Indianapolis ABC's were named for the American Brewing Company, which owned them.

Because baseball has always been intimately associated with alcohol, its social and commercial ties with the industry are endless, including such subtle forms as air time for radio and TV broadcasts. Players, too, regardless of the fashions of the age, have always embraced alcohol both as consumers and as promoters. When the playing careers of today's stars are over we often see them again in a sort of frothy heaven, selling beer on the intimate medium of TV, which forbids advertising liquor, but still allows beer commercials.

*Alcohol and Integration*   In February 1947 Branch Rickey summoned a group of Brooklyn's black ministers and civic leaders to a dinner where they expected to hear him announce that Jackie Robinson was going to be brought up to the Dodgers. Instead, Rickey got straight to the point and announced that he wanted to discuss how the black community could further the "experiment." "If you parade and dine Robinson too much, you will make him fat and futile. . . . If you get drunk at the ball park and see Robinson as the conquest of one race over another, the experiment will fail." The black leaders understood Rickey's fears about alcohol, and spread the word throughout the black community: "When Robinson joins the Dodgers, leave your liquor outside the ball park. Don't ruin his chances."

### Drinking Today

When I came up to the majors at 23, I was the All-American boy. I didn't drink, I didn't smoke, I didn't chase girls, I didn't stay out late at night. I was a health food addict. I was with the Yankees one week and we were in Washington, D.C., and I got a call from one of the guys at 3 A.M. to come up on the roof of the hotel "to get drunk and look in the windows at women." That's when I realized I wasn't in shape for the big leagues.

—Jim Bouton, *Ball Four*

Cy Buynak, clubhouse attendant for the Cleveland Indians for twenty-three years, said in 1987 that players today drink more milk than beer, but *The Sporting News*—the first newsweekly in sports, founded in 1886—still lists the firm that handles their alcoholic beverage accounts on their masthead, in boldface. In the '50s, when the Yankees dominated the American League, home runs were announced by Mel Allen as "Ballantine Blasts," in honor of the Yankees' brewery sponsor, or sometimes as "White Owl Wallops," for the cigars. At Shea Stadium, home of the New York Mets, a seven-story Budweiser beer ad currently dominates the scoreboard. Miller Lite, often called the Gillette of the '80s, presents a check for one thousand dollars at the conclusion of the Game of the Week in the name of the Miller Lite Player of the Game to a charity designated by the player so chosen.

It's almost impossible to sit through a televised game without a former star popping open a cold one, as a reward for excellence, and admonishing the viewer to do the same; should a viewer respond literally to such ads, he would probably be unable to stand by the end of the game. As Ryne Duren points out, "Alcohol is tied in with masculinity—the more you drink, the better man you are. Alcohol is linked to sex, power, and fun things like beer commercials on TV." This image and this message, approved by sports heroes and sports heroes to be, and sanctified on TV, is as indelible in the mind of the fan as the image of a pitcher winding up. In basketball, the Big Ten Basketball Player of the Week, framed with the logo of a certain beer company on the televised Big Ten Game of the Week, is sometimes too young to drink.

Standard player contracts prevent active baseball players from appearing in alcohol endorsements, even though broadcasts of their games are often sponsored by breweries. But few former stars have either the resources or the convictions to pass on lucrative commercial appearances. In a 1987 attempt to counteract the wholesale, if tacit, endorsement of alcohol by America's national pastime, the San Diego Padres tried removing beer from the clubhouse, but faced player insurrection. Of course, most businesses don't traditionally supply beer at the end of the working day, but then most businesses don't pour beer or champagne over the heads of their successful colleagues. When the White Sox banned beer in their clubhouse, Carlton Fisk, threatening to ignore the rule and supply his own beer, maintained that "pizza with Sprite just doesn't make it."

Often the fans who complain the loudest about the substance abuse of some of today's players are the hardest drinkers, and a visit to most press boxes reveals sportswriters surrounded by stacks of empties before, during, and after the game. American drinking customs fall somewhat short of those found in the Latin Leagues, where rum companies like Bermudez and Don Q own and sponsor teams the way breweries do here, and liquor is sold right out of the bottle by vendors in the grandstands. In many winter league parks, press-box hospitality includes complimentary rum cocktails. Back in 1903, Brooklyn manager Ned Hanlon had the huge portrait of a whiskey bottle removed from right field because the colors of the ad made it difficult for right-handed batters to pick up curveballs; but it's been some time since North Americans felt comfortable, or were permitted, to drink spirits stronger than beer in their ball parks.

No one speaks as eloquently for the enduring tradition of baseball drink-ing as Jim Bouton does in *Ball Four*. Before one game, according to Bouton, former manager Joe Schultz exhorted the team, "Let's keep our minds on the game. And let's remember we're the same as everybody else. Let's go out there, kick the shit out of them and come back in and enjoy the beer." After one win: "Attaway to stomp 'em. Stomp the piss out of 'em. Stomp 'em when they're down. Kick 'em and stomp 'em. . . . Pound that ol' Budweiser into you and go get them tomorrow." After another game: "Attaway to stomp on 'em, men. Pound that Budweiser into you and go get 'em tomorrow." Then, writes Bouton, Schultz spotted Gelnar sucking out of a pop bottle. "For crissakes, Gelnar," Joe Schultz said. "You'll never get them out drinking Dr Pepper."


*Alcohol Anecdotes*   As representative archetypes of an ultraconservative body of folklore, baseball alcohol anecdotes are endless and identical. We are told that Rube Waddell, the great half-mad pitcher of the early twentieth century, had to be carefully watched because he might pocket a baseball, which, after leaving the park, he would swap in any bar for a couple of drinks, swearing it was the same ball he had used in a legendary strikeout of one famous batter or another. The only problem with this story is that, adapted to different decades, it is told about Grover Cleveland Alexander, Don New-combe, and dozens of other hard-drinking pitchers.

Of course, trading on celebrity by using a baseball is a stratagem that *could* have been arrived at independently by any number of desperate pitchers, but this explanation is less likely in the case of the Hack Wilson anecdote. The story goes that the legendary slugger, head lowered and eyes almost shut from the effects of an awful hangover, was playing right field one day in 1934 when Dodgers manager Casey Stengel removed pitcher "Boom-Boom" Beck from the mound. Acting in justifiable frustration, Boom Boom threw the ball at the right-field wall. Wilson heard the ball hit the wall, raced over, picked it up, and threw to second base before realizing that there had been no batter. This same story, with the names changed, is used to illustrate the drinking habits of Jimmie Foxx, Babe Ruth, and God knows how many other outfielders.

So is this one: Mickey Mantle, laid low by injuries, certain he won't be in the next day's lineup, partakes of spirituous liquors with even more abandon than usual. But the next day, at a crucial moment in the game, he is unexpectedly called upon to pinch-hit. Barely able to walk to the plate, he nevertheless blasts a scorching home run, makes his way painfully around the bases, and after acknowledging a standing ovation from the crowd, squints in the direction of the stands and pronounces, "Those people don't know how tough that really was." According to a reliable source, this really happened. It probably did, but if this book's writers had a nickel for every slugger this anecdote has been told about, they wouldn't have to be writing this book.

Tales of the pitcher-kidnaped-and-made-drunk date from the nineteenth century. One of the best examples features hard-drinking pitcher Flint Rhem, who led the National League in wins in 1926 while pitching for St. Louis. Sometime around 1930, Rhem disappeared for a few days without notice. When he finally showed up again, worn and bedraggled, he explained to Cardinals manager Gabby Street that he had been kidnaped by gangsters, presumably to influence the outcome of a game, and forced at gunpoint to drink vast quantities of alcohol. He had just escaped from the room in which he had been held prisoner. This story, often told about Rube Waddell, also crops up concerning nonpitchers whose presence at a certain game was considered crucial.

Perhaps the most famous alcohol anecdote of all concerns Grover Cleveland Alexander, who allegedly staggered to the mound in the seventh game of the dramatic 1926 Cardinals–Yankees World Series, either actively drunk or horribly hung over, and despite having pitched the day before, saved the day and won the Series by striking out Tony Lazzeri with the bases loaded. This story has several interesting angles, not the least of which is that it took place during Prohibition, which is to say that alcohol was an illegal substance, just as cocaine is now, and presumably morally reprehensible. Alexander himself insisted that he was neither drunk nor hung over, and that he had consciously moderated his celebration of the previous day's victory in order to be prepared if his services were needed. At any rate, his drinking, although genuine, was partly a mask for his epilepsy, much as rock singer Janis Joplin hid her heroin addiction behind her bottle of Southern Comfort. But apparently, one epileptic striking out another epileptic—Lazzeri suffered from the same disease—doesn't make as good a story.

Such a good drinking story did it turn out to be that after Alexander left baseball, he for a time eked out a living by reciting the tale of the Lazzeri strikeout at a Times Square flea market and at various circus sideshows. Thus it became sort of an anecdote's anecdote. Of course, everyone knew that "Ol' Pete" always pitched better with a hangover; in a culture in which drinking is manliness, how could it be otherwise?

Some players, perhaps hoping to claim Alexander's greatness, still believe that they play better when hung over. Bouton quotes one player as saying, "I found I can't play if I feel good. I've got to have a little bit of a hangover to get the best out of me." But fashions change, even in major league baseball. What was once condoned is now, for better or for worse, understood as a "problem," at least when it is out of control. Don Newcombe, pitching in the majors from 1949 to 1960, recalls, "As long as I could pitch a little, nobody cared that I was getting drunk." Some players, of course, weren't so lucky, and Newcombe, who is black, was subject to different standards of behavior, according to the peculiar racism of baseball, which figures that most black players are dogging it or abusing themselves in some way anyway.

Until the 1970s, when baseball alcoholics began receiving sympathetic treatment, baseball considered drinking a problem only to the extent that it was bringing bad publicity, which meant that some players were likely to be traded and treated like outcasts even when effective on the field. But as the '80s progressed, alcoholism began to be understood as something more than material for new legends, and some players who might have been passed around like hot potatoes—Bob Welch is a prime example—instead found themselves receiving treatment and support from their organizations. Today alcoholism has pretty much lost both its moral stigma and its heroic connotations, and is considered less the stuff of myth than just another disease, like epilepsy.

*Tobacco* When the rules for what became modern baseball began to take shape in the 1840s, chewing tobacco was very popular. Players chewed to keep their mouths from becoming too dry in dusty parks, and when gloves came into common use, chewing provided a ready supply of saliva to soften leather. Later on, tobacco juice was used to create spitballs, which were legal until 1920. When it was discovered at the turn of the century that tuberculosis was transmitted through expectoration, chewing and spitting became socially unacceptable and in some places illegal, but the baseball park, always a universe of its own, continued to be a haven for tobacco users. The majority of players chewed well into the '40s; a survey conducted in 1987 disclosed that more than half of today's major league players have used some form of smokeless tobacco and that over one-third do now.

Snuff, a form of powdered leaf taken intranasally or applied directly to the gums, was also used by early players—obviously one of the benefits of smokeless tobacco is that it leaves the hands free. Players who smoked tended to use pipes or more usually cigars. Until the early 1920s, when cigarettes replaced smokeless tobacco in the general population, cigarettes were considered effeminate by most Americans, and especially by baseball. Trainers in the 1890s linked cigarettes with batting slumps and failures of endurance; one manager, keeping alive the belief that cigarettes killed King Kelly's batting eye, pleaded with his men to smoke cigars if they had to smoke anything. Pirates President Barney Dreyfuss, an implacable foe of tobacco in any form, had Tris Speaker scouted in Texas but passed on him because he smoked cigarettes; Dreyfuss also passed on Walter Johnson because the man who recommended him was a cigar salesman.

Needless to say, tobacco has been opposed on and off the diamond since earliest times, not only as a filthy habit, but because its effects were presumed to be debilitating. Honus Wagner, who hated the stuff, refused to let his portrait be used on baseball cards that advertised cigarettes; baseball pioneer Harry Wright, who played for the New York Knickerbockers, advised aspiring professionals to abstain from tobacco at least as early as 1874; and Babe Ruth, who chewed, smoked, snorted, and dipped, died at fifty-two from an oropharyngeal tumor occasioned by heavy tobacco use in association with alcohol.

By the 1950s baseball had caught up with mainstream America and chewing and dipping had been largely replaced by cigarette smoking. Practitioners of the national pastime did a great deal to spread the almost universal use of cigarettes through appearances in TV and magazine advertisements. But by the late '70s documentation of the disastrous effects of smoking all but ended the practice among baseball players, who are athletes, and smokeless tobacco regained its ascendency. Implementing this shift was an aggressive marketing program by the tobacco industry, which represented chewing tobacco and snuff as safe alternatives to cigarettes. Famous baseball players were again recruited to advertise smokeless tobacco, as they had been for cigarettes, and were remarkably successful. Between 1978 and 1985, sales of snuff, now commonly packaged in tiny tea bag–like pouches, increased 55 percent while cigarette sales declined nationally. In 1985, 40 percent of male college baseball players used smokeless tobacco regularly; only 3 percent smoked cigarettes.

The average chewing or dipping habit delivers about as much addicting nicotine to the bloodstream of the user as the average smoking habit, or more. By 1988, when the Minnesota Twins purchased a machine to clean tobacco stains from their artificial turf, it was abundantly clear that smokeless tobacco was addictive and causally related to oral cancer and a host of other oral and dental disorders. A growing number of teams stopped making free samples of chewing tobacco and snuff available to their players, and Commissioner Ueberroth's "campaign against the risks in using smokeless tobacco" included dental examinations at spring training camps. Nevertheless, over one third of major league players continued to use smokeless tobacco.

Not one former or current user surveyed in 1987 claimed that smokeless tobacco enhanced his game or sharpened his reflexes. This is in accord with recent clinical findings that indicate that smokeless tobacco increases an addict's heart rate and blood pressure but does nothing helpful for an athlete; any perceived relaxation is primarily a relief from the craving associated with nicotine withdrawal. But as so many players have expressed, tobacco use, like alcohol, is part of the game. For the majority of players who chew or dip more during the playing season than during the off-season, the most legitimate use of chewing tobacco and snuff is ritualistic or superstitious. One manager always takes a chaw to signal he is about to replace a pitcher; a batter in a slump may take a "hit dip" before coming to the plate. It is possible that chewing gum and sunflower seeds could replace smokeless tobacco in releasing tension, filling dead time, or working magic, or that new rituals could be developed. But Todd Welborn, who after one game last year put his clothes on backwards and announced that he had left his brains in his locker, may already have the answer. Although he grew up on a tobacco farm, Welborn dips dirt, especially the clay-laced infield at Jackson, Mississippi, where he pitches relief for the Mets' Class-AA farm club. "I don't like tobacco because it causes diseases," says Welborn, but "dirt is free and nobody ever bums it off you."

*Greenies*  Since World War II, dextroamphetamine sulfate—known throughout the baseball world as *greenies*—has been the most widely used controlled substance in baseball, with the possible exception of alcohol. One reason those baseball players are always chewing something is that many of them are speeding their brains out. During the famous 1985 Pittsburgh drug trials, where former all-stars testified to doing cocaine with current All-Stars, testimony was also heard from Dave Parker and Dale Berra that former Pirates captain Bill Madlock and superstar Willie Stargell were reliable sources of pregame amphetamines. And John Milner even implicated the immortal Willie Mays, testifying that Mays had routinely used a potent form of liquid speed referred to as "red juice." In August 1986 Lonnie Smith, confessed long-time cocaine user, revealed in a *Sporting News* interview that some of the guys he had recently played against were "taking greenies and smoking pot." Cocaine gets the press because it is fashionable and exotic, but amphetamines are undoubtedly the most widely used drug in the major leagues, and also the most effective.

As Jim Bouton described the situation in the late 1960s, "Some of the guys have to take one just to get their hearts to start beating . . . and a lot of baseball players couldn't function without them." "How many major league ballplayers do you think take greenies?" he asked a fellow player. "Hell," came the reply, "a lot more than half. Just about the whole Baltimore team takes them. Most of the Tigers. Most of the guys on this club. And that's just what I know for sure." Somewhat later he muses on their availability: "We've been running short of greenies. We don't get them from the trainer, because greenies are against club policy. So we get them from players on other teams who have friends who are doctors, or friends who know where to get greenies. One of our lads is going to have a bunch of greenies mailed to him by some of the guys on the Red Sox." Echoing rumors that not all of Pete Rose's celebrated hustle was 100 percent organic, Bouton writes, "We were kidding in the bullpen about how many greenies the Reds must have been taking during this pennant race and just then there was a ball hit into short right that Pete Rose made a great diving run at and caught on a short hop. 'Five more milligrams and he'd have had it,' Tom Griffin said."

Greenies can lift a road-weary ballplayer out of the doldrums or a hangover, get him "up" for the game—they are also called *ups*—and ready to play. Younger players are generally introduced to greenies by veterans when the need arises. Their use is so pervasive that players are generally reluctant to talk about them, because if *they* aren't using them, one of their friends or teammates is; and anyway, since they are a legal prescription drug they are regarded as utilitarian, and therefore escape the stigma attached to glamorous cocaine, which is associated with fun and decadence.

While amphetamines may increase a player's power output and performance, they also increase susceptibility to injury, and the long-term effects, not excluding premature death, are disastrous indeed. But as Bouton points out, if a pill existed that could guarantee a pitcher twenty wins a season, few major league pitchers would think twice before taking it, even if it took five years off their lives. Not until the '70s did baseball acknowledge the common-place use of greenies and begin to issue warnings to players about potentially hazardous effects, especially on the heart. But like most Americans, baseball players took little heed, and the use of greenies has continued relatively unabated.

Former Chicago Cubs team physician Jacob R. Suker, M.D., had this to say about greenies in an article in the *Illinois Medical Journal:* "There is evidence that amphetamines can drive trained athletes to increased perfor-mance in situations that involve sustained effort. . . . With the protracted travel schedules and rare 'off days' there is a great temptation for professional baseball players to resort to amphetamines. The almost universal availability of these drugs does little to minimize this problem. Our medical staff recog-nizes that there are definite medical indications for the use of amphetamines. Fortunately, we have not encountered any of these indications while treating members of our team."

*Marijuana*   Marijuana, not being a performance-related drug, has not been a particular problem in major league baseball, although the herb, which has become sort of the beer of the drug pantheon, is undoubtedly used from time to time by many ballplayers, as it is by one third of all Americans. Like LSD-25, mescaline, certain mushrooms, and other psychedelic drugs, pot's power as a symbol of pervasive drug abuse and alleged moral degradation has far outstripped any influence it ever had on the playing field. It is worth noting that Dock Ellis, who pitched in the majors for twelve years, claims that when he was with Pittsburgh in the early 1970s he pitched a no-hitter while he was tripping on LSD.

A more recent cultural artifact concerns the case of Ferris Fain, who was arrested for marijuana cultivation and sale in 1985 and again on March 17, 1988. Fain, a major leaguer who played with distinction for the Philadelphia Athletics of the late '40s and early '50s, took back-to-back American League batting titles in 1951 and 1952 with .344 and .327 averages, and was a defensive first baseman of the first rank. After retiring because of failing legs at the age of thirty-four, he moved to Georgetown, in northern California, where he worked as a carpenter until arthritis ended that career. Fain pleaded poor health and poverty—his maximum baseball pension is $8,200—when he was first busted, and was placed on probation. When he was busted again in 1988, at the age of sixty-seven, his marijuana operation had expanded to include sophisticated artificial lighting and irrigation, and power supplied via bypasses around Pacific Gas and Electric's meters. The police estimated the value of his crop at $1 million.

Those who recall Fain from his playing days may remember the famous Connie Mack anecdote he played straight man for: After he threw the ball into the grandstand twice in one week while trying to catch runners going from second to third on a bunt, Fain was admonished by manager Mack, then eighty-four years old, who suggested, "Perhaps you should just pick up the ball and hold it." Fain replied, "What in the hell do you want me to do with the ball, stick it up my ass?" "Well, Ferris," replied Mack, "you'll have to admit it would be safer there."


*The Cocaine Decade*    Comedian Richard Pryor once said that cocaine was God's way of letting you know you were making too much money. For millionaire baseball players, cocaine comes with the territory. According to Eric Davis, "The temptation is always there with drugs. . . . A lot of people you meet are involved in drugs, and there's a lot of guys I grew up with who are involved in it. . . . If I was the type of guy who wanted to go out and party all the time, there would be easy access, because everybody has drugs."

Not until the well-publicized 1985 Pittsburgh baseball drug trials was widespread public reaction to drug use among baseball players focused enough to be gauged. High up on the list of horrified outcries was reference to the fixed 1919 Black Sox World Series, baseball's biggest known scandal. But the only real point of correspondence between the two events was that Commissioner Landis wasn't able to rid baseball of gambling, and Commissioner Ueberroth wasn't able to rid baseball of drugs. Dave Parker and Keith Hernandez, two of the most significant players to implicate themselves in use of cocaine in Pittsburgh, were neither imprisoned nor barred from playing, and as Eric Davis so eloquently pointed out two years later, drugs are still everywhere.

Cocaine, of course, is the drug of the '80s. Even a partial list of the players known to have used it would be long and boring; some players claim they only use coke for recreation, others because they think it might help their game. As a performance-related drug, it is sort of like super greenies, and in the short run—the very short run, because the long-term effects of cocaine are extremely debilitating—it can provide an extra spurt of energy in a competitive situation.

One of the most sensational cocaine cases of the '80s was that of superstar prodigy pitcher Dwight Gooden of the New York Mets. Caught with traces of cocaine in a test he could have avoided—he had paradoxically insisted on having a testing clause in his contract—the twenty-two-year-old tearfully admitted to having used cocaine and entered the Smithers Institute in Manhattan just before the start of the 1987 season. The media tore him apart; one fan wrote to *The New York Times,* "I wasn't sure if Gooden was a mass murderer, a key witness in the Iran-Contra Affair, or a celebrated AIDS patient. . . . The only thing [the journalists] enjoy more than building up a potential superstar is tearing him down and kicking dirt in his once-proud face."

Doctor K, or Doc, as Gooden is affectionately known, insisted that his cocaine use was slight and recreational, and that he never used drugs during the season. When he had completed his drug rehabilitation, during which he missed about eleven starts, he returned to the Mets in June and won 15 games while losing 7 for the 1987 season, a slight decline from his 17–6 of 1986. Gooden received no further punishment, but baseball heroes are used to special privileges, and baseball is used to protecting its superstars. In 1920, Charles Comiskey, whose penurious policies were largely responsible for driving his White Sox to cheat in the first place, hired the best lawyers in Chicago to defend his valuable players, whom he paid the lowest salaries in both leagues.

In 1988 Gooden had to sit still for a $100,000 pay cut from his $1.5 million 1987 salary, a reduction that engendered grumbles from players' agents. Other players involved with cocaine, including Hernandez, Joaquin Andujar, and Parker, were given the option by Commissioner Ueberroth of being suspended or performing fifty or two hundred hours of community service and donating 5 or 10 percent of their 1986 salaries to drug-abuse prevention facilities and programs; a few players were suspended. In 1987, for the first time since coming up to the majors in 1984, Gooden was not named to the National League All-Star team.

In May of 1987 the Dwight Gooden Special was deleted from the menu at the Stage Delicatessen in New York. (A spokesman for the deli said that the deletion of the grilled salami, melted cheese, and hot sauerkraut affair had been planned before its namesake entered Smithers for rehabilitation.) Even more distressing, Gooden's rookie baseball card, which was originally worth about 3 cents and shot up to $120 in 1984, plunged to $30 in 1987 before climbing slowly back to $60; as of March 2, 1989, it was quoted at $70.

Opinion polls taken at mid-decade revealed that due to drug use, almost half of all Americans felt athletes were worse role models than they used to be. Seven out of ten people polled pinpointed drugs as their biggest source of disgust and the biggest problem in sports; over half felt that athletes charged with drug violations received preferential treatment; and only one out of six said his interest in sports had diminished. When Gooden emerged from Smithers to pitch for the Mets in June 1987, the most significant fact of his victorious comeback was that the publicity surrounding his drug problem helped create the largest regular-season crowd at Shea Stadium in a year and a half. When Doc stepped to the mound, 51,402 fans rose to their feet in a standing ovation. Here and there, of course, a fan grumbled that if he weren't an athlete, he'd probably be doing time.

*Breakfast of Champions*   For thirty years the medical establishment insisted that anabolic steroids didn't work, but athletes working with black-market steroids and underground handbooks demonstrated conclusively that at least for some people, anabolic steroids can significantly enhance bulk, power, and endurance. By the mid-1980s athletes and sports medicine experts agreed that almost all power-lifters use them, 80 to 95 percent of competitive body builders use them, and at least 30 to 50 percent of professional football players use them. Smaller but growing percentages of other professional, college, and Olympic athletes also use them; Edwin Moses, twice the Olympic four-hundred-meter hurdles champion and now a United States Olympic Committee official, recently estimated that up to 80 percent of all athletes use drugs, with steroids heading the list.

Anabolic steroids were probably first given to Nazi SS troops about fifty years ago, when they were initially developed. Even then it was understood that anabolic steroids, which are derived from the male sex hormone testosterone, tend to cultivate aggressive behavior and a sense of invincibility; in short, all the social graces of an attack dog. (It has been pointed out that Adolf Hitler himself displayed all the characteristics of a modern body builder on steroids.) While the psychiatric effects of anabolic steroids have not been well documented, even the users and their opponents perceive that they make users more aggressive, hostile, and able to train harder and recuperate more quickly, and may be helpful in training and competition.

In 1984 the ten-thousand-member American College of Sports Medicine broke with the medical establishment's know-nothing attitude when it acknowledged that steroids "seem to enhance performance." On October 22, 1988, the *British Medical Journal* reported an astounding experiment that showed that stanozolol, the anabolic steroid found in Ben Johnson's urine after he set a new hundred-meter dash Olympic world record, actually increased the size of endurance, or Type I, muscle fibers, without training. It is worth noting that Johnson's alleged use of the steroid resulted in his expulsion from the Olympics, but as of this writing, steroid use is not illegal in major league baseball or in any other professional sport.

Especially when combined with disciplined training, anabolic steroids, which enhance all normal processes, can enhance athletic performance. Sheer bulk and ruthlessness are not as prized in baseball as they are in football, but speed and power are, and the implications of finely tuned applications of anabolic steroids stagger the imagination. Steroids, now known in baseball as a "Canseco shake," after Oakland's José Canseco, achieved wide notoriety in the baseball world in 1988 when Canseco became the first human in the major leagues ever to hit forty home runs *and* steal forty bases in one season. He deeply resented allegations that he used steroids to achieve an elevated level of play, and threatened to sue Washington *Post* columnist Thomas Boswell for announcing on network TV that Canseco was "the most conspicuous example of a player who made himself great with steroids." When fans at Fenway Park chanted "ster-oids" at Canseco during the 1988 American League Championship Series, he flashed his teeth and flexed his muscles.

Sports consultant Dr. Harry Edwards, who has indicated that 75 percent of professional football players currently use steroids, believes coaching staffs are supportive of steroid use. "If the club doesn't actually hand out the drugs, it lets the players know where they can get them. In an already drug-infested society, it helps create a climate for drug use in sports. After all, if you can take anabolic steroids to get up for the game, why not take coke to get over the game?" Any real dangers connected with anabolic steroid use are undocumented, and principally brandished by a medical establishment that has thoroughly discredited itself on the issue. Increasingly, athletes feel that they have to take steroids to remain competitive; one of the greatest dangers of steroids may be that their use by professional athletes will create a sports mentality geared to doing whatever is biochemically "necessary" to win. High school and junior high athletes have already begun using steroids as a pathway to college sports' scholarships and professional careers.

Now that steroids have joined the arsenal of analgesic, ergogenic, and tranquilizing agents so commonly used in professional sports, it is possible that in time they may be seen as having revolutionized sports as thoroughly as nuclear weapons revolutionized warfare. Street-smart athletes, already miles ahead of the medical establishment, are now into human growth hormone harvested from the pituitary glands of cadavers, which at two hundred dollars a shot builds muscle mass without any of the annoying side effects of steroids, which can include increased body hair, acne, and feminized breasts. While it is impossible to predict what marvel will next issue from the pharmacopoeia of modern technology, it appears that real potential now exists for engineered baseball players more specialized than anything Aldous Huxley ever dreamed of, and closer to any superman than Hitler ever envisioned.


*Fans*   "Real big league baseball beer here, sanctioned by the commissioner of baseball. Look for his signature at the bottom of the cup," bellows Wally the Beerman at the Metrodome. Neither the commissioner nor the league presidents actually sign Wally's cups, but the tacit sanction of alcohol—especially beer—by baseball comes almost as close to an official endorsement as Wally's famous cry implies. Baseball leagues and franchises have risen and fallen on their alcohol policies, and despite its disastrous effects on some of the game's finest players, baseball condones alcohol, because history has proven that it is an essential ingredient to commercial success, and the fans expect it.

Something happens when people gather in large numbers, especially when they become intoxicated. On June 4, 1974, at Cleveland's infamous Beer Night, fans could buy all the beer they wanted at ten cents a cup (umpire Joe Brinkman remembers it as "nickel-beer night"). In the ninth inning two fans ran up to Texas Ranger right fielder Jeff Burroughs with the apparent intention of stealing his cap; all action stopped while Burroughs tried to defend himself. Players from both teams rushed to his support and were soon battling over fifty spectators. The game, which was tied, 5–5, with two Indians on, two out, never got under control again, and was awarded to the Rangers, 9–0, according to a rule established at the inception of the National League, which requires that home teams maintain order. Brinkman recalls, "Every inning it got worse, until finally, there were five thousand people on the field fighting with chains and broken bottles. There was this one pile and I picked up somebody who had blood pouring from his head . . . [it was] the scariest I've ever seen"

An editorial entitled "Swill and Spill" in the June 21, 1987, *New York Times* encouraged stadium operators to control "The beer slobs . . . those grinning rowdies who get sloshed in the stadium and slosh beer on others." General Manager Al Rosen of the San Francisco Giants announced in May of 1987 that new security measures were being instituted to curb fights, public drunkenness, and profanity in the stands: Concessions would have to limit their sale of beer to two fourteen-ounce cups per customer instead of limitless twenty-four-ounce cups. According to Rosen, "In 90 percent of the disturbances at the ballpark, alcohol is the main contributing factor." Of course such disturbances by spectators are not new. In first-century Alexandria, Dio Chrysostom's description of spectators at an athletic event went this way: "When they enter the stadium, they behave as if under the influence of drugs; they forget everything they have ever learned, and say and do the first thing that comes into their heads. . . . Who could describe the yelling and uproar, the frenzy, the change of color and look on [their] faces, not to mention the foul language?"

In 1987 Commissioner of Baseball Peter Ueberroth announced the implementation of a program called Techniques for Effective Alcohol Management (TEAM) to help "maintain a family atmosphere in all our ballparks." His action was partly in response to renewed pleas that sections of each major league ballpark be set aside for alcohol-free seating. A 1988 *Sporting News* article described tightened security in Philadelphia as part of "a nationwide trend to combat underage drinking at sports events." But despite such pronouncements, baseball continued to send a mixed message about drinking. As Mets fan Jonathan A. Judd argued in a letter published in *The New York Times* in 1988:

> It is the epitome of hypocrisy that fans are instructed to curb their beer intake, as well as that of their friends, through a program known as Techniques for Effective Alcohol Management, while cries of "Beer here!" and "Budweiser Man!" permeate the stadium. This is exacerbated by the fact that the team has made little or no effort to institute an alcohol-free seating area.

Beginning in the 1960s, a new intoxicating element has begun to permeate some stadiums. As described by Lesley Hazleton, an Englishwoman, who first saw a baseball diamond (Yankee Stadium) in 1979, "The combined smell of hot dogs and marijuana [drifted] over the stands." For her this aroma remains an indelible part of her first impression of baseball; and while it remains to be seen whether pot smoke will ever take its place as one of the traditional scents of summer, marijuana does go very well with beer, and its use is still commonplace in the stands in a number of parks around the country.

Baseball is of course itself a drug, as is any spectator sport, as far as the viewer is concerned. It takes the spectator out of time and place to a separate, ritualized reality, safe from worldly concerns. The effect is enhanced on TV, which is itself a narcotic, although there's nothing like being there. To the spectator, baseball is a vacation from life, a removal to be facilitated by alcohol, the accepted intoxicant of a society in which baseball is the national pastime; and for business, which is after all the business of America, it is an opportunity to make sure there is plenty of beer available.

# TRAGIC ENDINGS

**T**his chapter attempts to be as little morbid as possible in detailing some of the game's harsher realities, recognizing that injuries, cracking under pressure, lives and careers ruined by the press, accidental death, suicide, and dying in obscurity and poverty are part of baseball, too. Here are some of the better-known and lesser-known stories of some of those who made it to the top; of some of those who didn't; of some who didn't make it all the way but could have, or who couldn't handle it when they did; and of those who disappeared from public view when they left baseball. In a sport in which pressure and injury are king, it is amazing how many endings are *not* tragic.

*Pressure, Crackups, Breakdowns, and Flipouts*   There are fashions in illnesses. Epilepsy, for instance, which for centuries was stigmatized as demonic possession, has in more recent times been promoted from a spiritual disease to a psychiatric disorder, and is now considered an electrical problem of the brain. Grover Cleveland Alexander, however, had to mask his epilepsy with alcoholism, which in his time was more socially acceptable than epilepsy. Ty Cobb's extreme psychotic behavior, which today might get him banned from baseball, was tolerated during his career because he was so successful.

On one occasion, after he was suspended for entering the stands and viciously attacking a spectator, his entire team went out on strike until he was reinstated.

Baseball is a conservative sport that has always been reluctant to acknowledge emotional problems of any kind among its participants. Players would sooner surrender themselves to the surgeon's knife than to the psychiatrist's questions; and since "nervous breakdowns" have traditionally been disguised in a genteel way that broken ankles have not, the impact on the game of broken hearts and minds will probably never be fully understood. The strange persistence in our culture of prejudice against mental illness is the source of many logical inconsistencies. Much is said in baseball of "the mental game," but it is the rare major league team that employs a full-time psychologist; the White Sox, A's, Rangers, Orioles, Padres, and Astros are among the handful of clubs to even keep a psychologist or psychiatrist on retainer. Players, owners, and union agree that pressure is part of competition, but players still tend to view the "shrinks" as spies for the management, while managers fear that witch doctors will undermine their leadership. Contemporary experts agree that "the capacity for enduring stress is intrinsic for success in the game," but the St. Louis Cardinals, the first major league club to openly employ even a part-time *team* psychologist, did not do so until 1982.

Phrenologists were still in vogue when the great Rube Waddell was pitching. Perhaps their analysis of the bumps on his head could have told us something; from this distance in time it is difficult to know if his problems were emotional or whether he was simply retarded. Rube Waddell stories aside, the big, eccentric, unpredictable left-hander had a blazing fastball and the finest curve of his day. He was the greatest draw in the early years of the American League, which he led in strikeouts for six straight years, from 1902 through 1907, averaging 263 Ks per season with a high of 349 in 1904. Once he directed his outfield to sit down behind his infield while he retired the side. Connie Mack called him "the best left-hander I ever saw," and many felt he could have been as great a pitcher as Walter Johnson.

Waddell was fascinated by firefighters and fire engines and was known to drop everything in the middle of a game if he heard fire bells; on days he was going to pitch, a teammate was assigned to him to make sure he didn't become enthralled by fire bells on the way to the park. He wrestled alligators professionally during the off-season and might wander off without notice to go fishing in the middle of a pennant race. Opponents learned that they could distract him with displays of children's toys or pets. Managers learned that it was best to dole five or ten dollars out to him at a time; a salary was an invitation to disaster, and twenty-five dollars might mean he disappeared for a week. Eventually even Connie Mack couldn't manage him and traded him to the Browns after his outstanding 1907 season. Waddell drank himself out of baseball in a few years and died of tuberculosis in 1914 at the age of thirty-seven.

Johnny Evers of "Tinkers-to-Evers-to-Chance" suffered a nervous breakdown before the Cubs' 1911 season and played only forty-four games that year, when he was otherwise at the height of his career. This rather significant development in the Hall of Famer's career is rarely mentioned in conventional histories. But the pressures of the game being what they are, strange statistics and unexplained absences lead the serious student to surmise that there may have been many more breakdowns in major league baseball than teams, families, and "histories" allow.

Charlie Hollocher's sad story is no secret. Unless what ailed him was some rare disease unknown to medical science, his tragic career is a classic case of psychosomatic self-sabotage. In his rookie year with the Cubs in 1918, Hollocher led the league in at-bats, hits, and total bases, and placed third in steals and fourth in batting; in 1921 his .965 fielding percentage led the league; and in 1922 he led again with a .965 fielding percentage while hitting for the highest batting average by a shortstop since Honus Wagner. But the talented shortstop's career had already been interrupted by a stomach complaint that limited him to eighty games in 1920.

Just as he was on the brink of superstardom, his ailment, with which he had apparently struggled most of his life, resurfaced. Hollocher didn't get into a game until May 11, 1923. After sixty-six appearances, in which he hit .342, he disappeared from the lineup on July 26, one week later jumping the team, leaving manager Bill Killefer with a note that read in part, "Feeling pretty rotten so made up my mind to go home and take a rest and forget about baseball for the rest of the year. No hard feelings, just didn't feel like playing anymore."

Stomach X rays found nothing organically wrong with Hollocher. He returned to the Cubs for seventy-six games in 1924, this time receiving permission to return home to regain his health. But despite announcements through 1930 that he intended a comeback, he never donned a baseball uniform again. On August 14, 1940, at the age of forty-four, Hollocher killed himself with a shotgun blast to the throat in the driveway of a house in a St. Louis suburb. His widow stated that he had been complaining of severe abdominal pains.

Rube Foster, perhaps driven mad by overwork, left black baseball and was committed to a state mental institution in Kankakee, Illinois, in 1926.

According to his wife, he had a recurring delusion that he was needed to pitch in a World Series game; his son Earl recalls that he wasn't dangerous, but that his hold on reality was too weak for him to live at home.

Foster, who had received the nickname "Rube" because his skill was equal to Rube Waddell's, was called by Honus Wagner, who faced white major league pitchers for twenty-one years, "one of the greatest pitchers of all time . . . the smartest pitcher I have ever seen in all my years of baseball." He was a consummate manager whose legendary grasp of strategy still survives in major league ball; his considerable executive skills enabled him in 1920 to found the Negro National League, an organization that served as a model for black baseball organizations to come. His vision encompassed self-reliance and integrity for the institutions of black Americans with the ultimate goal of integration as equals.

At the time his reason deserted him Foster was negotiating an agreement with John McGraw and Ban Johnson that would have enabled his club, the American Giants, to play any white major league club that had an off-day in Chicago. In testimony to his standing in the black community, thousands of Chicagoans attended the funeral following his death on December 9, 1930. The floral arrangements from those who honored his passing included a two-hundred-pound white chrysanthemum baseball with roses for seams.

Jimmy Piersall's well-publicized on-field crackup in 1952 is one of the most famous mental breakdowns in the history of organized baseball. The outstanding Red Sox center fielder was booed and jeered when he ran the bases backward or came to the plate without a bat, but his behavior was symptomatic of an impending mental collapse that after fifty-six games in 1952 saw him enter a mental hospital. He returned in the 1953 season to begin fifteen more years of successful major league baseball, but found the fans less willing to welcome a player back from psychological problems than from an operation or a broken leg. "After I got back from the sanatorium, people in the stands started calling me 'nutsy' or 'wacko,'" Piersall recalls. "They would blow sirens at me. Even today . . . people . . . want to know if I'm really crazy. You have to face all that. You've got to be tough to survive in sports."

Ryne Duren, pitching hero of the 1958 World Series and the 1960 All-Star Game, came to grief upon the perennial shoals of drink. A sometimes formidable reliever but infamous for his crazy antics, Duren was traded like a hot potato during his ten-year career. After a particularly humiliating drunken performance for the Senators in 1965 he attempted to jump off a bridge. But he came to terms with his alcoholism and eventually became head of baseball's alcohol rehabilitation program.

Denny McLain, the last thirty-game winner in the major leagues, met his nemesis in the fashionable world of drugs. McLain was only twenty-four years old when he won thirty-one games in 1968. In 1970, after two consecutive Cy Youngs, his record plummeted to 3–5; his twenty-two losses led the American League in 1971, and he was suspended for gambling, attacking sportswriters, and carrying a gun. He was out of the majors after 1972 and soon behind bars for cocaine trafficking, loan-sharking, possession of cocaine, extortion, and bookmaking. Out on probation in 1989, he was still trying to put his life back together. Self-destruction due to intoxicants is really only possible if there is a flaw to magnify; Duren's drinking was admittedly a response to stress, while Denny McLain's arrogance was abetted by the pressure to perform and the perverse emotional cost our culture exacts for success.

When Jim Eisenreich came up to the Minnesota Twins in 1982, the twenty-three-year-old was touted as the best player ever to pass through the club's farm system. Former club president Calvin Griffith predicted he would be "a superstar and a millionaire in three years." But by the end of April, with Eisenreich batting .310, the tics he had experienced since grade school became so extreme that his fielding was severely affected, and late in a game with Milwaukee he became unable to expel air from his lungs. He called time, but was unable to return to the lineup. At intimate Fenway Park, abusive Boston fans picked up on his strange, involuntary movements and vocalizations and accelerated his rush from the field to the fourth inning. The next day their heckling drove him off the field in the third inning. Eisenreich scratched himself from the starting lineup the following day.

Although he played only thirty-four games for the Twins in 1982, Eisenreich strenuously resisted psychological treatment for his inability to stay on the field, insisting that his problem was purely physical and related to his tics. In 1983 and 1984, perhaps because the outfields in the minors are not enclosed by bleachers, he played well in the Grapefruit League, but his comeback to the Twins lasted a two-year total of only fourteen games.

Psychiatric hospitalization resulted in the diagnosis of performance anxiety or agoraphobia, but he rejected the use of inderal, a drug commonly used to combat "stage fright"; the Twins felt that the use of Klonopin, which controls panic attacks, left him drowsy and at risk from fastballs at the plate. When they discovered that Eisenreich had secretly been taking medication for Tourette's Syndrome, a physical disorder that causes tics and vocalizations, they gave him an ultimatum to accept treatment for agoraphobia or return to the minors; Eisenreich opted to retire with a year's wages at the end of 1984. In 1987 he accepted a minor-league contract from the Kansas City Royals, who paid the Twins one dollar for his waiver.

In 1984 the Yankees signed a $4.5 million, five-year contract with pitcher Ed Whitson, only to discover that he had a mental block against pitching in Yankee Stadium. Except for beating Billy Martin in a memorable late-night boxing match, Whitson showed none of the aggressive style that he had displayed on the pennant-winning 1984 Padres. Yankees fans were outraged at the size of his salary, and Whitson's critical comments about New York didn't help. As he grew increasingly embittered, his lackluster performance on the mound was further aggravated by fears for his family, whom disenchanted fans had threatened with reprisals. A friend relates that he dreaded each day he was with the Yankees in 1986. Whitson was traded back to the Padres in July of 1986; by July 1987 he was back in form, having hurled two shutouts with an 8–6 record on a club that was then 23–48. According to Whitson, "This game is 85 to 90 percent mental. When your mind is right, you're right, and I didn't have that feeling in New York."

Whitson's inability to shine in New York was less a clearcut matter of emotional illness than a clash of pressure, attitude, and situation; the chemistry just wasn't right, and the fans, who expect perfection in their athletes, ran him out of town. The recent case of Butch Wynegar, who in his fifth year of catching for the Yankees bolted the club on a road trip between Milwaukee and Cleveland, is clearly one of emotional distress. His teammates believed that he had deserted them, but Wynegar, who was suffering from a deep depression that eventually needed medication, had convinced himself that the team would be better off without him. He makes no bones that it was pressure, especially the pressure of New York, that brought on his breakdown: "For the first three years, I handled the pressure pretty good. . . . It just reached a point where I didn't want to see a ball or a bat . . . [or] talk baseball. . . . When it started to affect my family life, I knew something was wrong."

There may be no name for what ails Cesar Cedeno, but his responses to being alive on and off the field have not always fallen within the normal range. Cedeno, who was for fifteen years a major league outfielder, batting .320 with twenty-five home runs and fifty-six steals in 1973, was awaiting trial for smashing a glass into a man's face at a Nassau Bay nightclub when he was arrested in 1988 on charges of assault, causing bodily injury, and resisting arrest. Three years before he had been fined $400 plus $7,000 restitution for driving while intoxicated after his car struck a tree. In 1981 he attacked a heckler in the stands and was fined $5,000 by the Astros. And in 1974 he was convicted of involuntary manslaughter in Santo Domingo and fined $100. His most recent arrest, for attacking his girlfriend, taking their baby, and battling several policemen, took place in Webster, Texas. The thirty-seven-year-old native of the Dominican Republic, who had failed to sign with a major league club, was reported to be playing in a Mexican league, although he told the police he was unemployed.

Problems associated with pressure are not limited to the major leagues. In *Clinical Sports Medicine* (November 1982), Dr. R. S. Brown reported that he had treated "a 10-year-old Little League player with a generalized anxiety disorder; a 7-year-old Pony League outfielder terrified over the possibility of being hit in the head with a baseball; and a 9-year-old with peptic ulcer associated with a Little League all-star selection." Dr. Brown suggested—pleaded—that in the interests of mental hygiene sports should be encouraged for pleasure rather than glory.

*Murders and Assaults*  Major leaguers used to come from social strata where violent ends were presumably more likely to be met, but the vastly increased glare of the media and pressure from fans and owners on highly paid athletes to compete have more than compensated for any social leavening that may have occurred in the sport. Risk-taking on the field is rewarded, but risk-taking off the field can be costly. During the first seventy-five years of the National League, *twenty-seven* times as many major leaguers were murdered as American males of the general populace. For a group of men whose lives have always tended toward the fast lane in any era, it should not be surprising that a high proportion do not go gently into that good night.

Such was the case for pitcher Ed Morris, who at the age of thirty-two was about to begin spring training for his fifth season with the Boston Red Sox when he became embroiled in a dispute with service station operator Joe White. Stabbed twice, Morris died three days later on March 3, 1932, in Century, Florida.

Outfielder Len Koeneke hit .320 in 123 games for the Brooklyn Dodgers in 1934 and was batting .283 through 100 games in 1935 when manager Casey Stengel gave him an unconditional release for repeatedly breaking training rules. Koeneke boarded a commercial flight for Chicago but was put off in Detroit for being drunk and disorderly. He chartered a small plane to take him to Buffalo, but apparently attempted to wrest control of the aircraft, sinking his teeth into the pilot's arm and imperiling the flight. Copilot Irwin Davis tried to subdue Koeneke. The fifteen-minute battle that ensued ended when pilot William Mulqueeney bludgeoned the thirty-one-year-old baseball player to death with a fire extinguisher. Both pilot and copilot were exonerated for the killing on the grounds of self-defense.

Gordon McNaughton, who pitched for the Red Sox in 1932, was shot to death by a jealous husband in a Chicago hotel in 1942.

Lyman Bostock, outfielder for the California Angels and one of the highest-paid players in baseball at the time of his death, was killed on September 23, 1978, when the husband of the woman he was sitting next to opened fire with a shotgun.

The strange attempt on the life of talented Phillies first baseman Eddie Waitkus graphically illustrates the perils of notoriety. On June 15, 1949, Waitkus received a note at 12:40 A.M. from one Ruth Ann Steinhagen, who was likewise a guest at Chicago's Edgewater Beach Hotel. "It's extremely urgent that I see you as soon as possible," she wrote. Responding gallantly to this desperate call from a damsel in distress, Waitkus found his way to her room, but when he opened the door the nineteen-year-old Steinhagen, whom he had never met, shot him in the chest with a .22-caliber rifle. Steinhagen, whose obsession with the ballplayer was so great that she had threatened to move from Chicago to Philadelphia when Waitkus was traded by the Cubs to the Phillies, had previously been told by a psychiatrist that her intense feelings for Waitkus were not grounds for treatment. Waitkus, who was batting .306 for fifty-four games at the time of the shooting, played no more that year, although he eventually recovered to play six more seasons. Miss Steinhagen was committed for psychiatric therapy.

Hi Bithorn died under mysterious circumstances in El Mante, Mexico, on January 1, 1952. The hot-tempered, bilingual pitcher, who won eighteen games for the Cubs in 1943, was allegedly on his way to visit his mother when a Mexican policeman who later claimed Bithorn was planning to sell his expensive car for $350 asked him to show documents proving ownership. According to the policeman, Bithorn failed to produce any documents, assaulted him, and tried to escape; the policeman shot him in the stomach. Bithorn, who had two thousand dollars on his person and was not desperate for money, died a few hours later. The policeman's story that he was attempting to sell his car did not sit well with anyone. Another story has it that Bithorn was a member of a communist cell on an important mission, but it has proved of no more use in explaining his death.

Murder, often the product of a moment of passion, does not tend to be particularly explainable, and those who live on the competitive edge appear to be particularly susceptible. The most recent murders of former major leaguers ended the lives of Dave Short, who played with the White Sox, in 1983; and Luis Marquez, who played with the Boston Braves, was shot during a family quarrel in 1988.

*Suicides* Seven times as many major league ballplayers died by their own hands during the first seventy-five years of the National League as American males of the general populace, but few professional baseball players at any level kill themselves during the season. Suicide is rare in June, July, August, and September; November, December, January, and March seem to be the favored months. Only one active major leaguer has ever killed himself during the regular season, but all sorts in baseball—from a National League president to established major league stars, writers, and those who never made the big leagues—have tried their hand and occasionally succeeded.

Boston National League catcher Marty Bergen led off this century's baseball suicides by slashing his wrists (some say throat) after murdering his wife and two small children with an axe on January 19, 1900; but the most sensational baseball suicide of the era was that of Boston's Chick Stahl, popular player-manager of the Red Sox, who left the world with a .307 lifetime batting average after imbibing four ounces of carbolic acid at the Bosox spring training camp in West Baden, Indiana, on March 28, 1907.

Stahl's previous season—his first as player-manager—had seen his team settle into the American League basement. While he understandably deplored this result, he seems to have dealt with his disappointment in an adult way. Stahl resigned as manager on March 15, 1907, complaining of pressure, but was persuaded to retain the team captaincy. He sent his bride of less than a year a letter in which he claimed he was sleeping well again and looking forward to the new season: "I am all right now and able to play the game of my life." Certain insiders have theorized that Stahl took his life rather than risk disclosure of a relationship with a certain baseball groupie, but little evidence has been offered to support this claim. The unusual death of his widow a year and a half later suggests another explanation for his suicide as well as for the cryptic words he gasped to his mates as he writhed in his final agony: "Boys, I couldn't help it. It drove me to it."

On November 16, 1908, Mrs. Stahl—young, attractive, and according to *Sporting Life*, "fully and richly dressed," but denuded of two thousand dollars worth of jewelry—was found dead in the doorway of a South Boston slum. The cause of death was determined to be "exhaustion brought on by the use of drugs and alcohol"; nowadays we would say she died of an overdose. The first decade of this century was an era of drug abuse unparalleled until modern times, and the fact that Mrs. Stahl went to her rendezvous wearing her wealth of jewelry when it was her habit to wear only the wedding ring that was found on her body suggests that she was either off to make a major buy or to pay a major debt. In any case, the "it" that drove Chick Stahl to take his life may well have been his or his wife's addiction. Both of their deaths were comfortably written off as "mysterious" by the press, reflecting either the discretion or the naiveté of a less rigorous age.

Sportswriter Randolph Blanch of Johnstown, Pennsylvania, shot himself at the age of thirty on November 29, 1911, and White Sox outfielder Johnny Mostil, who led the American League in walks, stolen bases, and runs scored in 1925, slit his wrists, neck, and chest in a failed suicide attempt on March 9, 1927. Especially prominent among the over twenty baseball suicides of the first quarter of this century, however, was the tragic death of National League president Harry Clay Pulliam. On July 28, 1909, Pulliam, head of the league since the beginning of the 1903 season, "broken in health from overwork in his long fight to maintain a high standard of baseball," took his dinner as usual at the New York Athletic Club, returned to his room, lay down on a sofa, and shot himself through the head. According to *The Philadelphia Inquirer* (also quoted above), "The ball entered the right temple fracturing the frontal bone, tore out the right eye and passed out at the right temple. He was found lying near the telephone by a club servant who was sent to find out who was trying a telephone connection. 'I think he struggled on the floor for two hours,' said Dr. T. Hamilton Burch, 'and that he was so overcome with the intense pain that he tried to get to the telephone to send for me. He probably got the receiver off the hook and then lost his strength entirely.'"

Pulliam, an honest, overly conscientious man whose nervous temperament may have rendered him unsuitable for the rigors of the job, had become convinced, not entirely without reason, that the club owners were conspiring against him. He had been under constant pressure since ruling in favor of the umpires in the Merkle Affair the summer before, and he broke down at the February 1909 banquet for National League club owners, announcing, "My days as a baseball man are numbered. The National League doesn't want me as president any more. It longs to go back to the days of dealing from the bottom of the deck, hiding the cards under the table, and to the days when the trademark was the gumshoe." After an enforced leave of absence that failed to revive his spirits, the forty-year-old bachelor resumed his duties in June, then took his life. On hearing of Pulliam's suicide, John McGraw reportedly commented, "I didn't think a bullet to the head could hurt him."

The next baseball suicide of note was Willard Hershberger, twenty-nine-year-old back-up catcher for the Cincinnati Reds, who became the only active major leaguer ever to kill himself during the regular season when he slashed his throat at the Copley Plaza Hotel in Boston on August 3, 1940. At the time of his death Hershberger had taken over the starting position from injured regular catcher Ernie Lombardi and was batting .309 (.316 lifetime) for a club that was on its way to its second consecutive flag and a Series win over Detroit, but had become despondent over a self-judged "bad call" on a pitch that Harry Danning had hit for a game-winning home run at the Polo Grounds.

Talented and well liked, Hershberger had descended into a deep melancholia including insomnia, extended periods of depression, headaches, brooding over team losses, and fears that his teammates disliked him; he even told Reds manager Bill McKechnie that he was going to kill himself. McKechnie became alarmed the next day when Hershberger failed to turn up as promised between games of a doubleheader with the Boston Bees, and dispatched businessman Dan Cohen, who was traveling with the team, to see what had become of him. Cohen discovered that Hershberger had spread towels on the bathroom floor, removed his shirt, and slit his throat as neatly as possible into the bathtub.

Except to baseball men preoccupied with the pennant race, his suicide came as no great surprise to anyone. Hershberger's father had killed himself in a considerably bloodier fashion with a shotgun in the family bathroom when his son was eighteen years old and, as the psychologists say, young Willard probably felt responsible for a death he did not understand. His response—the development of a morbid fear of disappointing people, which helps explain his vow never to marry while his mother was alive—was manifest in an abnormal sense of responsibility that left him unable to forgive himself once he determined that he had let his teammates down. He even tried to mitigate the mess he knew his death would make by spreading towels on the bathroom floor. (Mr. Cohen, the man who discovered his body, later committed suicide, too.)

At least nine former major leaguers committed suicide in the 1940s; between eight and ten former major leaguers have died by their own hand in most decades of this century, fewer in the '70s and '80s. The case of Bruce Gardner, who wasn't a major leaguer but could have been, attracted considerable attention in 1971, perhaps because it is such an all-American story.

Gardner was NCAA All-American Player of the Year in 1960. Handsome, seemingly universally talented, he was a model son, superior scholar, actor, musician, and gallant hero to the neighborhood kids. He had already received his first invitation to the majors three years before, when he was offered the then princely bonus of $66,500 to sign with the White Sox in 1957. But he was only eighteen years old, and needed his mother's consent; influenced by USC baseball coach Rod Dedeaux, she opted instead for the security of a college education. Gardner was unhappy, but dutifully and successfully finished college. He signed with the Dodgers for a twelve-thousand-dollar bonus in 1960, won twenty games in the minors in 1961, hurt his arm, and was out of professional baseball by 1964 at the age of twenty-five. When asked what he remembered most about Gardner, former Dodger general manager Al Campanis, whose son had been Gardner's roommate, replied, "He didn't win." Gardner's lifelong dream was shattered, and despite the continued admiration of friends and family, he was never able to forgive his mother or his USC coach.

Shortly before dawn on June 7, 1971, Gardner drove to Bovard Athletic Field on the USC campus, scaled the fence, and walked to the site of his former glories. He placed a bitter, eloquent typewritten suicide note, which he had carefully taped to a board, on the grass at the edge of the pitcher's circle, and walked about halfway to second base. Then he lay down and, cradling his USC diploma and his All-American plaque in his right arm, shot himself in the temple with his pitching hand.

Although Gardner departed from the norm of baseball suicides by taking his life in June, his use of a pistol places him in the mainstream in terms of method. Pitcher Don Wilson, who in nine years with Houston chalked up two no-hitters, once struck out eighteen men in one game, and still threatened to become a star pitcher when he took his life on January 5, 1975, was one of four players who chose carbon monoxide. However, gunshot wounds are the cause of death in over four times as many baseball suicides as its nearest competitor, the razor. Major league suicides also include one drowning, some jumping, and considerable ingestion of acids, drugs, and poisons. John Henry Mohardt severed his femoral artery in 1961. But Danny Thomas, who performed briefly as an outfielder and designated hitter for Milwaukee in 1976 and 1977, is one of only two former major leaguers to hang himself. His death at age twenty-nine on June 12, 1980, also places him among the 7 percent of former major league suicides who took themselves out of the game during the sixth month, when the best of the promise of summer was still ahead.


*Injuries on the Field*    Baseball players make their livings by pushing their bodies beyond the limits for which they were designed. Sports injuries—and the amounts clubs have invested in their players—have in recent years given rise to the exotic industry of sports medicine, an entire discipline with its own equipment, procedures, clinics, and institutes. In the *American Journal of Sports Medicine, Clinical Sports Medicine,* the *Canadian Journal of Applied Sports Sciences,* and *Physician and Sports Medicine* specialists contemplate arcane prophylactic and remedial strategies for ballplayers in articles such as "Valgus Extension Overload in the Pitching Elbow," "Digital Ischemia in Baseball Players," and "The Biomechanics of Head-First Versus Feet-First Sliding." The Macmillan Publishing Company, best known in the baseball community for its *Baseball Encyclopedia,* publishes an *Encyclopedia of Sports Sciences and Medicine.*

"Injuries and Infection Have Unraveled White Sox," trumpeted *The Sporting News* for June 15, 1987. "Stars on the Sideline" reports *The New York Times* for April 19, 1987; "A series of devastating injuries . . . have struck the Cardinals since the start of the season." These stories and headlines sound so familiar that they may have been learned as formulas in journalism school. Columnists and scouts analyze a team's injuries like its bullpen, and not without reason. After football players, baseball players are the most injury-prone of athletes. Rivers of ink flowed when the New York Yankees, who many predicted would meet the Mets in a Subway Series, fell behind in the 1988 American League race because their pitchers couldn't stay healthy; and rivers of tears were shed by players, fans, and investors alike. In baseball, the human condition is black-and-white: You win or you lose.

The New York Mets spend about five thousand dollars each year for tape to wrap backstop Gary Carter. While it's clear that catchers get more injuries than players at other positions, they don't get the attention other injured players do. According to Bob Brenly, "If another player gets hit on the shoulder with a ball traveling 100 mph, chances are they'd take him out of the game. But for a catcher, they don't even send the damn trainer out there. They just expect you to spit on it and go about your business."

Superstar catcher Johnny Bench got out of bed at his hotel one morning for a trip to the bathroom and fell flat on his face. He had been hit in the foot with a foul tip the day before but hadn't thought much about it until his legs wouldn't work. Bench says that the X rays revealed "I had broken bones in other places besides my foot." But true to his profession, he was back in the lineup in a few days.

In thirteen years of catching Bench sustained a broken right ankle, six broken bones in his left foot, five broken bones in his right foot, and one broken finger on his left hand. He had cartilage surgically removed from his left shoulder and would have needed surgery on his right elbow if he had continued catching; flirted with death during lung surgery in 1972; and ruined his knees and back. He also broke seven athletic protective cups. To save his throwing hand, Bench pioneered a technique of one-handed catching using a hinged glove to trap the ball that enabled him to keep his free hand out of the way of foul tips. He was the first catcher to wear a batting helmet instead of a baseball cap, adding a new element to catching equipment, which, in baseball, is known collectively as "the tools of ignorance," presumably because only the ignorant would catch. Bench retreated to the infield for the last three years of his outstanding seventeen-year career.

The only active major leaguer ever to commit suicide during the regular season—perhaps because of the responsibility that comes with the position—was a catcher.

Most fans think of injuries to pitchers as injuries to their throwing arms, but the balls they throw at ninety to one hundred miles per hour sometimes come back to them going even faster. Hank Greenberg once beaned pitcher Jim Wilson with a line drive, fracturing his skull; on another occasion Wilson's leg was broken by a liner. Bob Gibson was out for months when his leg was fractured by a liner. Wilbur Wood had his kneecap shattered. And in 1957 Gil McDougald nailed promising young Herb Score in the eye. Score lost the season, failed at several comebacks, and became a legendary never-was when he retired in 1962 at the age of twenty-nine. McDougald, hounded by fans, perhaps retired earlier than he otherwise might have.

Dizzy Dean's demise also began with an injury from a batter, when Earl Averill hit him in the toe with a liner in the 1937 All-Star game. Dean could have healed completely, but it was his misfortune to be the greatest draw in baseball since Babe Ruth. Encouraged by the Cardinals management and his own eagerness, he returned to the mound with his toe in a splint, altered his delivery to favor his sore foot, and destroyed his arm. Before 1937 he had averaged twenty-five wins per season for the preceding four seasons; after 1937 he averaged fewer than four wins per season.

Given the current state of medical expertise, such treatment of a pitcher is less excusable now than it was then; but it's axiomatic in baseball that those who play when they're injured get paid the most, and superstars are simply too valuable to be kept out of the lineup. Aggravating the situation are the team physicians, who are paid by the club management, and who sometimes find themselves telling athletes to play with injuries for which they should recommend bed rest.

Such apparently was the case for J. R. Richard, Houston's star pitcher of 1980, whom team physicians diagnosed as having a blood clot in his neck. They told him to play out the season, but during his first workout after the diagnosis, Richard had a stroke and nearly died. As Richard's attorney, Tom Reich, put it, "The question is why they let him go back and pitch once they publicly diagnosed the clot. . . . Normally, a person with that kind of clot wouldn't have been permitted to do anything. . . . I am not casting aspersions at team doctors generally . . . but there is no denying the fact that there is a major conflict of interest."

The list of pitchers with debilitating arm problems is nearly endless. Major league pitching is an unnatural activity and, as Sandy Koufax has pointed out, "After you've pitched for any length of time, the X rays show spurs and a general irregularity brought on by the accumulation of minor injuries to the protective cartilage covering the [elbow] joint—all the nicks and chips and pulls and tears from the thousands upon thousands of times that the hinge has snapped, the sheer wear and tear of pitching."

Koufax awoke after his nineteenth victory in 1964 to find his arm swollen like a log from his shoulder to his wrist. His elbow was as big as his knee, and when he exercised the little movement that remained in the arm, he could hear liquid squishing around like a wet sponge. Koufax and the Dodgers' team physician, Dr. Robert K. Kerlan, had been monitoring the arthritic deterioration of his arm for several years, and the pitcher reluctantly ended his brilliant career after his 1966 season rather than risk losing all use of his arm in the future.

X rays can't tell us what happened to Smokey Joe Wood's arm but, at least for a moment, he was one of the greatest pitchers the game has ever seen. Walter Johnson once declared, "Mister, no man alive can throw a baseball harder than Joe Wood." In 1912 Wood was 34–5, including 16 straight wins, 10 shutouts, 258 strikeouts, an ERA of 1.91, a batting average of .290, and a winning percentage of .872. After he injured his arm in spring training in 1913, he became an average pitcher for three years before his pitching arm deserted him completely and he moved to the Cleveland outfield.

At the other end of the spectrum, in 1987 Cardinals rookie lefthander Joe Magrane, disabled with a sore elbow, remarked, "I've had so many X rays that my pitches might take on a subtle glow."

Nowadays, of course, pitchers' arms can sometimes be rebuilt. On July 17, 1974, Tommy John was looking for his fourteenth win of the season when he ruptured a ligament in his left elbow. Dr. Frank Jobe broke new medical ground by transplanting a tendon from John's right forearm to his left elbow; John was expected to recover, but not to pitch. After warming up with ten wins in 1976, John turned in a terrific 20–7 in 1977. The forty-five-year-old southpaw, who first pitched in the majors in 1963, was starting pitcher for the New York Yankees on Opening Day 1989. His 4–2 victory made him the oldest pitcher ever to start and win an opener, and his appearance in his twenty-sixth major league season established a modern record for longevity. Before the game the Hall of Fame asked him to autograph a baseball to commemorate the occasion.

*Beanings and HBPs*   Of all the injuries in baseball, beanings are the most dramatic. In some horrible way they fulfill the worst expectations of the mythological confrontation between pitcher and batter, and when severe, they wreak the most indelible damage.

Ray Chapman, the only major league player actually killed on the field, was beaned at the plate. Apart from his personal tragedy, the death of this superior, tremendously popular player, who was probably destined for the Hall of Fame had he continued playing, was an event of enormous historical significance. Coming within a month of the breaking of the Black Sox scandal, which itself led to the establishment of the baseball commissionership, Chapman's death was a major factor in initiating the substitution of a new ball whenever the one in play became scuffed or dirtied. This innovation, combined with the rules changes forbidding trick pitches and the introduction of the lively ball, completed the process of turning the game in the direction of the batters that Babe Ruth had begun with his home runs. Batting averages in the new game rose as much as fifty points above what they had been during most of Chapman's career. Ray Chapman was dead, but so was the old baseball.

It is questionable whether Chapman would have continued playing after 1920. His wife, Kathleen Daly, was the daughter of the president of the East Ohio Gas Company, and Chapman had made his intention clear to quit baseball for a career in business after he helped Cleveland capture its first pennant; his club indeed did win its first pennant ever in 1920. It is a curious footnote that of the twenty-two men who played in Chapman's last game, the last to die, ninety-one-year-old Sammy Vick, passed away on August 17, 1986, exactly sixty-six years to the day after Chapman.

Of course, the roll of those beaned is legion. Mickey Cochrane, one of the greatest catchers of all time, stands out among players who have been permanently affected. After he was beaned at the plate in 1937, Cochrane hovered unconscious and close to death for ten days, his skull fractured in three places. He gradually recovered and became a successful manager, but his career as a player was over.

Joe Medwick, one of the strongest right-handed batters in the National League during the 1930s, was beaned by former teammate Bob Bowman in his first at-bat after being traded by the Cardinals to the Dodgers in 1940. His power was permanently attenuated.

Don Zimmer, a respected baseball man who began his fourth stint as a major league manager at the helm of the Chicago Cubs in 1988, was a hot prospect in the Dodgers minors before he got beaned. The Dodgers let him suit up and stay on the bench even though he couldn't talk; his promising career as a major league infielder was reduced to one that was merely average.

In 1967, sensational Red Sox outfielder Tony Conigliaro, who hit twenty-four home runs as nineteen-year-old Rookie of the Year in 1964, was beaned by a ball—probably an illegal spitter—that fractured his cheekbone and left his vision permanently impaired. His promise of baseball immortality went unfulfilled.

Like Conigliaro, Dickie Thon was such a hot young prospect that he was being heralded as "one of the five best players in the game," a shortstop equal to Phil Rizzuto and Pee Wee Reese. But also like Conigliaro, after he was beaned at the plate in 1984, his vision was impaired. He has struggled ever since.

The confrontation between pitcher and batter is essentially a territorial struggle for possession of the strike zone. According to Conigliaro, getting thrown at is "part of baseball"; Dickie Thon has likewise consistently absolved pitcher Mike Torrez of having thrown at him. But recently batters have indulged in the almost obligatory macho move of charging the mound when they get hit.

In 1987 National League President A. Bartlett Giamatti, in response to several incidents of bench clearing and retaliation by opposing pitchers, issued an edict that proscribed "acts clearly intended to maim or injure another player" and directed that a warning may be issued by the umpire, after which any pitcher in a game is subject to ejection if he is deemed to be throwing at batters. Oldtimers dislike both current behavioral trends and the warning rule: Eighty-seven-year-old Hall of Fame umpire Jocko Conlan recalls that batters in earlier, prehelmet eras considered it a weakness to let pitchers know they were bothered by brushbacks. Hall of Fame pitcher Don Drysdale asserts that contemporary pitchers don't know how to throw a brushback, batters don't know how to get out of the way, and umpires don't know how to call them, a situation that the National League's warning rule promises to make even worse by giving batters a false sense of security.

Not every player hit by a pitcher is beaned, of course. Apparently, in the nineteenth century, getting hit by a pitch was much more common than it is today. Hugh Jennings holds the season record with 51 HBPs in 1896, and Tommy Tucker holds the career record with approximately 270. In this century, Ron Hunt was, by his own assessment, "stupid enough to be hit by pitches 50 times" in 1971. Hunt led the National League in HBPs for seven consecutive years on the way to a modern career high of 243, and became so well known for his ability to get on base by being hit that the Expos' press guide once remarked, "He gets good flesh on the ball." His most serious modern competition is Don Baylor, who could set a new lifetime HBP record by the end of his career if he stays healthy.

*Other Injuries*  Jim Creighton, the first professional baseball player, was the first man to die from a baseball-related injury. During an 1862 game against the Unions of Morrisania, New York, Creighton, the star pitcher for the Brooklyn Excelsiors, swung hard at a pitch and "sustained an internal injury occasioned by strain," probably a ruptured bladder, and died a few days later. A gaudy granite monument to his memory was erected by his fans in Brooklyn's Greenwood Cemetery. It is topped by a giant baseball and chiseled with crossed bats, a base, a baseball cap, a scorebook, and oak leaves.

The remarkable career of Pete Reiser is a catalog of baseball injuries. During his brief period of playing greatness he broke his ankle twice, tore

*James Creighton was one of the most popular of the early New York ballplayers when he died prematurely in 1862 of an injury sustained in a game. The monument on his tomb, in Brooklyn's Greenwood Cemetery, has a bat, base, cap, and scorebook carved on the column, which is topped by a baseball.*

cartilage in his left knee, tore muscles in his left leg, suffered countless concussions, broke a bone in his right elbow, and accumulated numerous knicks and scrapes. So talented that he was scouted by the Cardinals when he was only twelve years old, called by Branch Rickey the greatest young player he had ever seen, Reiser began his major league career by winning the National League batting title with a .343 average in his first full season. He also got beaned twice, and was following through with a .381 average in July 1942 when he ran into a cement wall chasing a fly ball. Although the outfielder fractured his skull and suffered a deep concussion, according to the macho style of the day he pinch-hit two days later; Reiser collapsed after knocking in the winning run and was ordered to sit out the season by the doctors, but returned to the lineup three weeks later to play out the season through fuzzy vision, headaches, and dizziness.

He returned to the game after three years of wartime service to steal home a record seven times, rack up an impressive list of beanings and minor injuries, and break his ankle in an attempted steal while running with a badly pulled hamstring. In 1947 he again ran into the center-field wall, spent ten days paralyzed, returned to help Brooklyn take the pennant, and broke his ankle in the Series against the Yankees. By 1948 his injuries had begun to take their toll. The Dodgers traded him to the Boston Braves in 1949, and Reiser played parts of four more seasons before leaving the big time for good. According to the dauntless outfielder, "I was only twenty-nine when traded, but the fun and the pure joy of it were gone." During his ten playing years he averaged only eighty-six games a year and never played a full season.

With a .314 career batting average as of 1987 that would rank him fifth among post–World War II inductees, All-Star third baseman George Brett of Kansas City once seemed to be an automatic entry into the Hall of Fame, but Brett has lost the equivalent of two full seasons to injuries, and may not be able to come up with the three thousand career hits that are believed necessary to qualify him for serious consideration. A dedicated player who has been sidelined with injuries twenty-six times in his career, Brett remarked after he suffered a cartilage separation of his right ribcage while batting in a game against the Yankees: "I really hate this crap. I can't believe all of the time I've missed . . . there are guys in this game that don't really like it and play just for the money. But they seem to be the same guys who don't even catch a cough."

*Three Fatalities*   At least three fatalities that were not strictly speaking baseball casualties have occurred on baseball fields. The following story from a 1907 newspaper is reproduced in its entirety.

### SINGULAR FATALITY
*A BASE BALL PLAYER CHOKED*
*TO DEATH BY A GUMDROP*

Montezuma, Ia., April 21.—Choked to death by a piece of candy was the fate of Orrie McWilliams to-day, while he was playing ball. An exciting game was in progress, and McWilliams was catching. He had a gumdrop in his mouth. The ball was thrown to him to shut out a run home by a man on third. McWilliams caught the ball, but fell to the ground in a violent fit of strangulation. A doctor was summoned, but the boy was dead before he arrived. The gumdrop was found lodged in his windpipe.

Even a timely Heimlich maneuver could not have saved James Phelps, who in 1909 was playing outfield for Rayville in a game at Monroe, Louisiana, when he was bitten by a large snake. Phelps, one of Rayville's star players, was determined to stay in the game and did not disclose his injury until after the ninth inning. Two hours later he was dead.

A few years later a baseball player named O'Hara also gave his life for his team, but went on to score the tying run; it is perfectly legal for one runner to assist another, even if one of them is dead. According to *Baseball Magazine,* here's how it happened:

Chatham was leading 2–0 and there were two outs in the bottom of the ninth when O'Hara, a weak hitter, doubled to left. He was followed by Robidoux, "a scrappy young Arcadian," who hit a long ball over the center fielder's head. As O'Hara reached third base, he collapsed and died. Robidoux, rounding third, picked O'Hara up and carried him down the base line, touching home plate first with O'Hara and then stepping on the plate himself. The game was tied 2–2.

*Fans, Umps, Birds, and Bees*   In the old days when wooden stands were common, fire was a particular hazard to spectators. In May 1894, for instance, John McGraw of the Orioles got into a fight with the Boston third baseman, the benches emptied, the fighting spread to the stands, the stands were set on fire, and the entire ballpark burned to the ground along with 170 other Boston buildings.

On August 8, 1903, the Phillies were playing a doubleheader in their home park against Boston when the overhanging gallery in the left-field bleachers collapsed, killing 12 spectators and injuring 282. On the Fourth of July, 1950, spectator Bernard Boyle, one of almost fifty thousand fans gathered at the Polo Grounds for a Dodgers–Giants doubleheader, suddenly slumped forward, killed by a bullet to the head. Although his death made front-page news, no one knew where the shot had come from. In a similar incident at Sportsman's Park in St. Louis in June 1947, a spectator named Morris was shot in the leg during a flurry of ninth-inning scoring excitement. Again, no one knew where the bullet had come from.

While watching a baseball game at the Astrodome in 1978, young Karen Bernstein of Houston, Texas, was struck in the face by a foul ball off the bat of the Astros' Enos Cabell. Jurors awarded the girl and her father $125,000 damages, but the trial judge threw out the award. The First Court of Appeals in Houston upheld that decision, and in 1987 the Texas Supreme Court ruled that the Houston Sports Association did not have to pay damages to the girl's family. But in 1988, a Rochester, New York, court upheld a $50,000 award for plaintiffs Deborah Schirtz, who suffered a broken nose, and Dorothy Matteson, whose dental plate was broken, when a bat hurled by Cleveland's Cory Snyder struck them during a game on May 26, 1986. Snyder testified that the bat he was attempting to throw toward the dugout stuck to pine tar on his batting glove and flew into the stands.

Perhaps the most bizarre baseball injury sustained by a fan occurred to a forty-nine-year-old man who arrived at the Letterman Army Medical Center Emergency Room in San Francisco in great discomfort. According to a paper published in *Diseases of the Colon and Rectum* (January–February 1977), a firm, round object was found lodged high in his rectum. "The patient then reluctantly described his recent activity. He and his sexual partner had celebrated a World Series victory of the Oakland Athletics by placing a baseball (hardball) in his rectum because, as he put it, 'I'm oversexed.' " X rays confirmed the presence of the baseball. Attempts to remove it the way it had come in proved fruitless, so the doctors made an incision through the abdomen to expose the baseball, which they skewered with a corkscrew instrument. By applying enough force "to raise the patient off the table, the ball was delivered through the colotomy." The patient recovered completely.

Stanton Walker was not so lucky. Walker was keeping score at a game in Morristown, Ohio, in 1902 when he discovered that his pencil needed sharpening. The man next to him lent him a knife, and Walker had just begun to put a new point on his pencil when a foul ball struck his hand and drove the knife blade into his heart.

Umpires, of course, have taken their share of lumps, too. John A. Heydler, who was an umpire in the 1890s and later a president of the

National League, summed up his experiences with the famous Orioles teams of the late nineteenth century this way: "They were mean, vicious, ready at any time to maim a rival player or an umpire if it helped their cause. The things they would say to an umpire were unbelievably vile, and they broke the spirits of some very fine men. I've seen umpires bathe their feet by the hour after McGraw and others spiked them through their shoes. The club never was a constructive force in the game . . . and I feel the lot of the umpire was never worse than in the years when the Orioles were flying high."

Several accounts have it that at least two umpires have actually been killed by ballplayers. In 1899 an umpire named Samuel White was allegedly officiating at Lowndesborough, Alabama, when he became exasperated and knocked down a player who had been abusing him for several innings, whereupon the player jumped up with a bat and dealt him a fatal blow to the head. Two years later, an umpire named Ora Jennings was allegedly killed at Farmersburg, Indiana, in much the same way. In 1911, former major league player Ed Cermak was killed when he was hit in the throat by a baseball while umpiring in the Cotton States League.

Chickens, cows, and other barnyard animals used to be frequent sights on the diamond in earlier, more bucolic days, and on occasion they ran afoul of baserunners and baseballs, to their mutual detriment. According to the Elias Sports Bureau and the Audubon Society, however, the first wild bird to have been struck by a batted ball in major league history was a dove that was killed by a fly ball on April 12, 1987, at Shea Stadium. Dion James of the Braves, the batter, was awarded a ground-rule double for what otherwise would have been a routine fly out. Shortstop Rafael Santana fielded the bird and handed it to the ball girl; and pitcher Bob Ojeda, who looked up after his pitch to see feathers and a bird falling, momentarily thought he had lost his mind. A similar incident occurred in organized ball in 1981, when Eric Davis, later with Cincinnati, hit and killed a bird with a fly ball in Oregon. A more questionable incident occurred on August 4, 1983, when Dave Winfield of the Yankees killed a seagull in Toronto with a warmup toss between innings. Winfield was arrested by Toronto police and charged with cruelty to animals, but the charges were dropped the next day.

Bees invaded Cincinnati's Riverfront Stadium on May 10, 1987, for the third time in eleven years. Three beekeepers were summoned to break up the swarm, but one of the bees that eluded their nets stung Reds pitcher Ted Power on the index finger of his pitching hand. While more bees were removed from the field, Power received treatment; he struck out a career high eleven batters that day. The first attack at Riverfront had occurred on April 17, 1976, when bees in the visitors' dugout caused a thirty-five-minute delay; on May 26, 1980, a swarm attached itself to the backstop screen but was not disturbed.

Interestingly enough, not all ballplayers perceive bees as a menace. According to a 1939 report in the *Fargo Forum,* when former Yankee pitcher Wes Farrell was once playing a round of golf, "He caught honey bees from flowers and held them to his arms until they stung him. When Farrell finished the round his arm was swollen to almost twice normal size. 'It is the only way you can get that arthritis out of your arm when it's sore,' Farrell replied when asked for an explanation."

*Tragic Endings*   Baseball players are subject to the same illnesses and accidents as ordinary mortals, but because their aspirations are so much higher than those of ordinary mortals, when a baseball player is stopped short by injury, illness, or accident, his fate seems that much more tragic. If he has already attained baseball immortality, his premature or unseemly demise is that much more poignant. Hall of Fame outfielder Al Kaline once observed, "I guess the saddest things I've ever seen in baseball are the guys that are cut down in midcareer by freak accidents, and injuries. You may not know them personally, but as an athlete you can identify with them. Like a Roberto Clemente, who at the time of his death was playing the best game of baseball I'd ever seen, or a Harry Agganis or a Herb Score. Or a Mark Fidrych . . . all the poor kid had was just that one great season."

Charlie Bennett, a major league catcher with Boston for twelve years, was run down by a train in 1893 and lost both his legs. Several ballplayers are known to have come to grief on the tracks, including one who died when his train was engulfed in the Jamestown Flood, but a survey conducted in 1911 determined that since none of these mishaps could properly be called a train wreck, there was no evidence to contradict the widespread belief that if members of a baseball club were aboard, a train would never get in a wreck. In days when trains were the predominant mode of rapid transportation, such a topic was of no idle interest. The report concluded: "Traveling men, when they learn that they are to ride on a train bearing a ball club, do not take out accident policies for the trip."

Baseball writers have taken pains to enshroud the ridiculous death of Ed Delahanty in mystery, although there is nothing particularly mysterious about it. In June 1903 the great slugger was batting .338 when he was suspended by manager Tom Lofton in Detroit, probably for drunkenness. He was put off the train he was returning home on at Niagara, Ontario, for being drunk and disorderly, just as it was about to cross the International Bridge. According to Canadian law, he should have been turned over to a constable, but the conductor didn't bother. Delahanty wandered off, circumvented a guard, ignored a bridge tender who tried to tell him the bridge was open, fell into the river, and was swept over Niagara Falls. The story that his twisted and mangled body was found by honeymooners one week later is a ghoulish embellishment best left to those who invented his "mysterious death" in the fist place.

Louis Sockalexis, who began a sensational career when he came up to the Cleveland Spiders in 1897, has been racially stereotyped as a "dumb Indian" who came to grief when his teammates introduced him to whiskey, for which, like all members of his race, he supposedly had an overwhelming weakness. In fact, Sockalexis was no stranger to strong drink, and his demise came about following a foot injury sustained when "The Red Romeo" made a rapid exit from the second story of a sporting house on the Fourth of July, 1897. When he was playing every day, Sockalexis was apparently able to keep his drinking under control, but the foot injury forced him out of the lineup, and his enforced inactivity pushed him over the edge. After 1897, Sockalexis played only twenty-eight more games before he was released and his major league career came to an end.

At least twenty of the 230-odd major leaguers who have died in accidents met their ends in train mishaps. By the third decade of this century our nation had made considerable technological progress, and the automobile became the main engine of destruction. At least ninety-seven former major league players have died in automotive accidents, beginning with second baseman Heinie Reitz, who began his career with Baltimore in 1893 and was struck and killed by an auto on November 10, 1914. Tony Boeckel, regular third baseman for the Braves, died in 1924 after his sixth season when his car collided with a truck. Walt Lerian, age twenty-six, was a promising catcher with the Phillies when a truck leaped a curb and pinned him to a wall in Baltimore. Al Montgomery, who had debuted with the Braves in 1941, was on his way from spring training to open the season when he was killed in an automobile crash in West Virginia in 1942.

Bobo Newsom skidded in a car before his debut with the Cubs in 1932 and fell 225 feet down an embankment; he walked away with a broken leg. A few days later Newsom left the hospital to attend a mule sale, where one of the beasts kicked him and broke his leg all over again. During his years in the majors he broke another leg, fractured a kneecap, fractured his skull, fractured his jaw and assorted other bones, and accumulated more than his share of a pitcher's arm injuries.

Among those seriously injured, Roy Campanella, one of the great power-hitting catchers of all time, was paralyzed when his car skidded on ice in 1958, just before he was due to depart with the Dodgers for Los Angeles. Campy has been confined to a wheelchair ever since. Babe Ruth, of course, was famous for fast driving and crackups. Although he avoided serious consequences himself, on one occasion when he discovered that his automobile was indeed too wide to slip between two streetcars, the young woman accompanying him (who was not his wife) needed hospitalization. Fred Newman, who pitched for the Dodgers and the Athletics, and Jim Brewer, who pitched in the bigs for seventeen years, both died in car accidents in 1987.

While the automobile has continued to be a popular vehicle in which to be maimed or killed, the airplane has given it some stiff competition. Marv Goodwin, a major league pitcher for seven years, became the first major league player to die in an airplane when he crashed in a military plane near Houston in 1925. Tommy Gastall, who received forty thousand dollars to sign with Baltimore in 1955, drowned after the plane he was piloting plunged into Chesapeake Bay on September 20, 1956. Charlie Peete, who would probably have been the first black regular in the Cardinals organization, died when his plane crashed while he was en route to play winter ball on November 27, 1956.

The incomparable Roberto Clemente met his death a few months after logging his three thousandth hit when the plane in which he was accompanying aid to earthquake-stricken Nicaragua crashed into the sea shortly after takeoff from Puerto Rico. Clemente, who helped organize the relief effort for Managua, chose to deliver the aid personally because it was feared that Nicaraguan dictator Anastasio Somoza, who apparently pocketed the $30 million the United States sent for the earthquake victims, would abscond with his contribution. The possibility cannot be ruled out that Somoza seized upon the unscheduled flight as an opportunity to silence Clemente, who was one of the Caribbean's most beloved heroes and an outspoken critic of his oppressive regime.

"Ah, hell, Lou, there's no need to worry," said thirty-two-year-old Thurman Munson to Lou Piniella as he sat at the controls of his sleek new jet. Two days later, on August 2, 1979, team captain and first-string catcher Munson, the only Yankee ever named both Rookie of the Year and Most

Valuable Player, was killed when his plane crashed short of the runway near Canton, Ohio.

So far no major leaguers have died from injuries sustained on the golf links, but six have died from accidental shootings, three of those while hunting. And of the twenty-seven major leaguers who have drowned, eight did so while fishing. In 1938 pitcher Monty Stratton of the White Sox, aged twenty-six, ended his promising career when a hunting accident cost him a leg. Cardinals shortstop Charlie Gilbert hurt his foot hunting in 1942, missed most of the next two seasons, and never regained top form.

Several major leaguers have died in battle. Christy Mathewson was finished with his pitching career when he went overseas, but his lungs were severely damaged by poison gas in World War I, leaving him susceptible to tuberculosis. He coached the Giants for three years between visits to Saranac Lake sanatorium, and was president of the Boston Braves when his death at the age of forty-five on the first day of the 1925 World Series cut short a career as a baseball executive that promised to be as exciting as his career as a pitcher.

Grover Cleveland Alexander, drafted and sent to France in 1919, endured shelling that caused a loss of hearing in one ear and brought on the first attacks of the epilepsy that would plague him for the rest of his life. Following his stint in the service the formerly good-natured Alexander began drinking heavily, in part to mask his epilepsy. He won twenty-seven games in 1920 and remained an effective pitcher throughout the '20s, but never regained his former heights. After baseball he worked as a sideshow attraction, retelling some of his pitching feats. Bouts with epilepsy, alcohol, and cancer, for which Alexander had an ear amputated, left him down and out, and at the end of his life he subsisted chiefly on small pensions from the government and the Cardinals. He died in 1950 at the age of sixty-three in a rented room in St. Paul, Nebraska, a few miles from the farm he had been born on.

Illness has interrupted or ended the careers of a surprising number of fine players. The Hall of Fame bent its rule that a man must play in ten seasons to be eligible for induction in order to admit Addie Joss, whose credits include a 1.88 lifetime ERA and a perfect game. Although Joss's effectiveness waned in his last two seasons, he kept pitching until he collapsed during an exhibition game in 1911; one week later he died of tubercular meningitis at the age of thirty-one.

A look at the decade of the '20s demonstrates how much influence illness can have on the game. When .300-hitting Cardinals outfielder Austin

*Christy Mathewson, who as much as any single player helped to make baseball respectable early in the twentieth century, was gassed in a training exercise while in the service in World War I and never pitched again. Here he is in the early 1920s before his early death at the age of forty-five.*

McHenry began to have trouble following the flight of fly balls in 1922, fans jeered but manager Branch Rickey sent the player to a doctor. McHenry died following an unsuccessful operation for a brain tumor on November 27, 1922. George Sisler, who twice hit .400 and struck out only 347 times in fifteen seasons, sat out the entire 1923 season when he developed a case of poisonous sinusitis that gave him double vision. Despite his .340 lifetime batting average, Sisler claimed he was never the same batter again.

The most dynamic figure in baseball history—and with George Washington and Abraham Lincoln one of the three most famous Americans in the world—Babe Ruth came down with a monumental stomachache at the height of his career during a 1925 exhibition junket. "The Bellyache Heard 'Round the World," resulting in surgery, served to limit his playing appearances and effectiveness for that season, and was a major contributor to the Yankees' seventh-place finish and weak gate receipts. Ruth came back for several more record-breaking seasons, although his high living, marked by heavy consumption of tobacco, undoubtedly contributed to his death from throat cancer, in comfortable circumstances, at the early age of fifty-three on August 16, 1948.

Ross Youngs, famous for nonstop hustle long before Pete Rose graced a diamond, was diagnosed as suffering from Bright's disease in 1926, left baseball before the end of the season, and died of the kidney disorder on October 22, 1927, at the age of thirty with a .322 lifetime batting average. His picture and a portrait of Christy Mathewson were the only photographs ever to grace the office of his manager, John McGraw.

Urban Shocker, after one of his best years ever on one of the greatest teams in baseball history, the 1927 Yankees, appeared to be ill at spring training in 1928 and pitched in only one game before heart disease forced him to retire. He died that September at the age of thirty-eight.

Miller Huggins, whose accomplishments in twelve years as manager of the Yankees included the purchase of Babe Ruth and winning six pennants, relinquished his field command in September 1929 to get checked out at the hospital. He told his coaches he would be back the next day. Less than one week later, on September 25, he was dead at the age of fifty from a combination of influenza and erysipelas. The first monument at center field in Yankee Stadium was dedicated to his memory.

Perhaps saddest of all tragic endings in Yankees history was the incomprehensible demise of baseball's "Iron Horse," Lou Gehrig, who still holds the major league record for appearing in 2,130 consecutive games. This magnificent player who built his reputation on stamina and dependability slowly declined from the muscle-wasting amyotrophic lateral sclerosis until, when his teammates praised him for successfully executing a routine play in the eighth game of the 1939 season, he realized how ineffective he had become and took himself out of the lineup. Manager Joe McCarthy had been unable to bring himself to scratch his team captain even though he feared his reflexes were so shot that he might get beaned at the plate. Gehrig never played a game after May 1, 1939; two years later he was dead, two weeks short of his thirty-eighth birthday.

Few Yankees fans might be prepared to admit that Joe DiMaggio was mortal, too, but the Yankee Clipper played his sensational 1948 season in great pain because of a bone spur in his right heel. A postseason operation sidelined him until June 1949; and despite a great comeback and a salary offer of one hundred thousand dollars, DiMaggio chose to retire at the age of thirty-six after the 1951 season rather than continue to perform his godlike chores in an imperfect body.

Not so his successor in the Yankee pantheon, Mickey Mantle, who followed up a ligament-tearing injury at the end of his rookie year with a career played through continuous pain and injury. Mantle's performance was so effective despite his injuries that teammates such as Elston Howard reckoned he would have hit seventy homers if he had been able to stay healthy for an entire season. In addition to his baseball injuries, Mantle dislocated a shoulder playing touch football with his family, reinjured a knee playing basketball, injured his hand so badly in a 1966 wrestling match that he couldn't hold a bat, and burned his flame brightly in a number of New York City night spots. But he agrees with those who say there is no telling what he could have achieved if he'd remained even normally healthy: "I know that I could have set a lot of records that I didn't get a chance to because of my legs."

Moving from the legion of players like Don Drysdale and Sandy Koufax who left the game because of illness or injury after successful careers and those like Mickey Mantle and Willie Mays who perhaps remained on stage too long, it is important to remember that for baseball players life is not a snapshot of the playing years; it may be difficult for fans to comprehend, but baseball players have a life before baseball, and for most baseball players, the end of their career is not the end of their life. Some live happily after baseball, but even great glory accrued during a career of playing is no guarantee of a glorious end. Joe Tinker, Johnny Evers, and Frank Chance of "Tinker-to-Evers-to-Chance" fame died like all men; their careers may be immortal, but their ends are representative of the mortality that the ritual of baseball goes so far to disguise.

With good reason, this immortal trio was inducted into the Hall of Fame together. Tinker, Evers, and Chance weren't the greatest double-play combination of the era, but they were close to the best. During the eight years they played together on the Cubs, 1903–1910, their club established the best five-year won-lost record of this century, including, in 1906, the best one-year won-lost record of the century. Tinker and Evers had a falling out that erupted into a fistfight during a game in 1905 and barely spoke. Chance, who used to say he wished Evers was an outfielder so he wouldn't have to listen to him, had little time for Tinker.

Frank Chance was an excellent batter but tended to crowd the plate and was beaned frequently; headaches and impaired hearing eventually led him to brain surgery and an early death in 1924 at the age of forty-seven. Evers, aptly called "the Crab," was both hated and loved for his intensity. He was probably wrapped too tight and missed most of one season after he suffered a nervous breakdown, but he brought fire to his teams. After several years in a wheelchair he died of a stroke in 1947 at the age of sixty-six. Tinker—broke, one leg amputated, and suffering from diabetes and a respiratory ailment—died one year later at the age of sixty-eight. Thus they died in reverse order to the way they are remembered, Chance-to-Evers-to-Tinker.

Eddie Gaedel, the subject of baseball's most famous trivia question, also came to a sad end. By all accounts, Gaedel, the midget who had one famous at-bat for Bill Veeck's Browns on August 19, 1951, was dealt a hard hand by fate. After his brief big-league career he made lucrative TV appearances on the Ed Sullivan and Bing Crosby shows, and also got into trouble on a Cincinnati street corner for screaming obscenities and trying to convince a cop he was a major league ballplayer. He worked as a Buster Brown shoe man, appeared in the Ringling Brothers Circus, worked in promotions for Mercury and reappeared in the ballpark in 1961 when Veeck, by then owner of the White Sox, responded to complaints about vendors blocking the view by hiring Gaedel and seven other midgets to service the boxes on Opening Day.

Less than two months later, on June 18, 1961, Gaedel was mugged and beaten on a Chicago street corner for eleven dollars. He somehow made his way home and died in bed of a heart attack at the age of thirty-six. Bob Cain, the Detroit pitcher who faced Gaedel on that fateful day in 1951, heard about Gaedel's death in the news and "felt obligated to go" to his funeral even though he had never met him. No other baseball people attended. According to Gaedel's mother, Helen, a man claiming to represent the Hall of Fame swindled her out of her son's bats and Browns uniform.

# THE MUSIC
# OF THE GAME

**I**n one artistic medium, at least, baseball was adopted quickly and fondly. Why musicians and music-lovers have always found baseball such an attraction and inspiration might yield to analysis, but perhaps we should just be grateful for what we have. It's hard to believe, for instance, that musicians know more about baseball or have seen more games than other artists. It is reliably claimed that neither Jack Norworth nor Albert von Tilzer, the lyricist and composer who came up with "Take Me Out to the Ball Game," had ever seen a baseball game before they wrote the best-loved baseball song of all. And until more recent decades, when ballpark organists cropped up, there has not been anything obviously "musical" about the game.

Yet there must be something going on between baseball and music, for musicians have taken to baseball and baseball players have taken to music. The results of their unions may not all be art, but they are usually great fun.

*Early Popular Music*  The first published baseball song seems to be "Baseball Polka," composed by J. R. Blodgett for the Niagra Base Ball Club of Buffalo, New York, in 1858. (To appreciate how quickly baseball became part of the popular culture, consider that the first popular American song

*In the early years of this century, vaudeville and nickelodeon houses showed slides illustrating the words to popular songs as the audience sang along. These slides were especially photographed and hand colored. This one is from the set for "Take Me Out to the Ball Game" and illustrates the words "buy me some peanuts and crackerjack."*

about *any* sport seems to have been Stephen Foster's "Camptown Races" of 1850—and horse racing had been around a lot longer than baseball.) "The Live Oak Polka" (1860) launched a special tradition in baseball music of "team songs." It was followed by numerous other songs in the 1860s such as "Home Run Quick Step" (1861), "Home Run Galop" (1867), and "The Base Ball Quadrille" (1867). As their titles indicate, most of this music had no words, having been composed chiefly to satisfy the market for another craze of the day—the piano in everyone's home. But there were other songs that had quite entrancing lyrics, such as "The Base Ball Fever" of 1867, with its complaint:

> Our merchants have to close their stores,
> Their clerks away are staying,
> Contractors, too, can do no work,
> Their hands are all out playing.

Or from "Catch It on the Fly," also of 1867:

> Come, jolly comrade, here's the game that's played
>   in open air,
> Where clerks and all indoor men can profit by a share.
> 'Twill make the weak man strong again,
> 'Twill brighten every eye,
> And all who need such exercise should catch it on the "Fly."

Or how about these words from "Hurrah for Our National Game" of 1869:

> The Gamester may boast of pleasures of play,
> The billiardist brag of his cue,
> The Horse jockey gabble of next racing day,
> The Yachtsman discourse of the Blue.
> The patrons of Racket may feast on its joys,
> Whilst Cricket its lover inflame,
> Croquet's very well for young ladies and boys,
> But give us the National Game!

Then there was "Tally One for Me" of 1877, where the player boasted:

> I'm the pride and pet of all the girls,
> That come out to the park,
> My ev'ry play out in the field,
> You bet they're sure to mark!
> And when you see them smiling and
> Their hands go pit-a-pat,
> Just mark it down, for number one
> Is going to the bat. Oh,
> For when I take the bat in hand
> My style is sure and free,
> Just put your money on my side,
> And tally one for me.

The entire social history of America begins to emerge from such songs—the nation's exuberance after the grim years of the Civil War, the emphasis on baseball as a form of healthy exercise for sedentary types, the response of the old puritan work ethic to men who abandon jobs for play, and the chauvinism (national and male) that early on found a home in baseball. No wonder that baseball quickly caught the fancy of American music composers and enjoyers.

And it never really lost that fancy. The sheer number of baseball-related popular songs is impressive. Richard H. Miller, a professor at Brooklyn College who knows as much about early baseball music as anyone, estimates there are over three hundred such published or recorded songs (and that's not counting hundreds more written by amateurs) and more are undoubtedly being written even as we write. The variety of these songs—both in their subject matter and their sources—is also revealing. Miller has described the various types, or genres, and the curious backgrounds to many of the songs; but most Americans, baseball fans or otherwise, still have little notion of how truly pervasive these baseball songs have been. "Take Me Out to the Ball Game," written in 1908 (and 1908's number-one hit record, sung by Billy Murray), remains the all-time favorite, and deservedly so. Along with "Happy Birthday," it must be one of the few songs that *all* Americans of every persuasion can join in singing. Not to be forgotten, either, is that baseball, as much as any single element in our national life, has kept alive our impossible-to-sing national anthem, "The Star-Spangled Banner."

*Team Songs*   Much of the baseball music of the 1860s and '70s (including several of the titles already cited) was written expressly for particular teams—mostly amateur and minor league teams, but sometimes for the majors. In 1869 "The Red Stockings March" was written for the best-known team of the day, the Cincinnati club. (There was another song that year, "The Red Stockings Polka," dedicated "to the Ladies of Cincinnati.") This tradition of composing songs for particular teams faded as teams went professional, until today, if New York Yankees fans were asked what "the team song" is they'd probably all answer, " 'New York, New York' sung by Frank Sinatra."

In fact, although the tradition faded, it did not completely die, and in recent years it has been revived—so much so that there has probably never been a time when so many teams were promoting so many songs. These contemporary team songs come in several forms. One, like the Yankees' "New York, New York," includes hits or popular songs that, for one reason or another, get adopted by the local fans. In the case of "New York, New York," it's fairly obvious why, but with other teams there's no particular rationale. The Chicago White Sox fans, for instance, adopted "Na, Na, Hey, Hey, Kiss Him Goodbye" (a hit by Steam in 1969–70) one night in 1977, although the stadium organist had been playing it for a long time; it has remained an unofficial team song. Meanwhile, Orioles fans adopted John

*After the great success of "Take Me Out to the Ball Game," there were numerous imitations, one of the more blatant being "I Want to Go to the Ball Game." This is one of the song slides that, no matter how imaginative, couldn't help to save that song from oblivion.*

Denver's "Thank God I'm a Country Boy" one night in 1974 when it was played during the seventh-inning stretch, and it became the Baltimore fans' traditional seventh-inning stretch favorite. A variation on these adopted popular hits are the ones that last only a season or two and are taken up because the team is having an especially winning time. In 1967 Boston Red Sox fans adopted "The Impossible Dream" (from *Man of La Mancha*), while in 1979 the Pirates took up "We Are Family." Oakland A's fans adopted the Kool and the Gang hit "Celebration" in 1981, but the next year shifted to a Coasters hit, "Charlie Brown"; and in 1983 they converted to "Soul Man." But it must be said that these songs were actually "pushed" onto the fans from the Oakland team's front office. Not only that, the team commissioned new words for the two last-named songs—"Charlie Brown" became "Billy Ball" (in honor of that year's manager, Billy Martin), while "Soul Man" was turned into "I'm an A's Fan." Not quite the same thing as spontaneously adopting a song, but not that far from the tradition of someone writing a special song for a team.

Many teams now do just that—commission special words *and* music for a team song. Most of these have a brief shelf life and seldom make it out of their home field, but some have provided work for songwriters such as Walt Woodward, who sprang to fame when he wrote a song in 1977 for the Cleveland team, "Indian Fever." When the team's fortunes gave the fans more of a headache than a fever, Woodward's song-writing firm had to come up with a new song, "Indian Country"; after that one, there had to be at least another. In recent years, teams have frequently changed words or music or

*Uniformed marching bands were often hired by clubs to provide music at major league games in the late nineteenth and early twentieth centuries. This one is playing at the Boston Red Sox stadium in the 1903 World Series. Standing beside the band are some of the famous "Royal Rooters," what would be called a "boosters club" today, famous for singing a popular song of the day, "Tessie." Their serenading so unnerved the Pirates that the Sox won the Series.*

both, so that in the end there is no true "team song"—just more attempts at marketing a product.

This is nothing like the old days when the Boston Red Sox, for instance, had a phenomenally dedicated bunch of fans who called themselves "The Royal Rooters." During a crucial moment of the fifth game of the first World Series in 1903, these fans began to sing a popular song of the day, "Tessie" (from a musical, *Silver Slipper*), and so unnerved the favored Pirates that the Sox went on to win the championship. From that moment on, "Tessie" became the favorite song of the Royal Rooters and Red Sox fans. The words seem far removed from baseball, but that was evidently what unsettled the Red Sox' opponents:

> Tessie, you make me feel so badly
> Why don't you turn around?
> Tessie, you know I love you madly,
> Babe, my heart weighs about a pound.
> Don't blame me if I ever doubt you.
> You know I couldn't live without you,
> Tessie, you are my only, only, only.

The point is that it was the fans themselves who made this a true "team song," while more recent attempts by front offices to impose team songs seem doomed from the start. The Astros, for instance, in 1970 commissioned a team song called "Who Says It's Only a Game?" but who's ever heard of it? Jim Bouton, however, in *Ball Four,* tells of a song he and his teammates on the Astros sang lustily and readily, a raunchy version of Tom Lehrer's "It Makes a Fellow Proud to Be a Soldier."

> Now, Harry Walker is the one that manages this
> crew,
> He doesn't like it when we drink and fight and
> smoke and screw,
> But when we win our games each day,
> Then what the fuck can Harry say?
> It makes a fellow proud to be an Astro.

Now *that* was a team song.

*Songs of the Heroes*   Another basic type of baseball song with a long pedigree is the one that celebrates a contemporary "superstar" of the diamond. The first such song seems to have been "Slide, Kelly, Slide!" composed in 1889 by a vaudeville monologuist, John W. Kelly, in honor of his friend, Michael Joseph "King" Kelly; both title and refrain came from the chant that Kelly's adoring fans used during his games. This King Kelly was—and remains—one of the best-known baseball players of his day; he also was one of the more outrageous types ever to play the game. His kind of showmanship would probably not work too well these days, but in the 1880s and '90s his exuberance seemed to express the very spirit of baseball. When phonograph cylinders first came on the market in 1892, one of the top hits that year was "Slide, Kelly, Slide!" Sung by a silver-voiced Irish-American tenor, George Gaskin, its jaunty lyrics work even today:

> Slide, Kelly, slide!
> Your running's a disgrace!
> Slide, Kelly, slide!
> Stay there, hold your base!
> If some one doesn't steal you,
> And your batting doesn't fail you,
> They'll take you to Australia!
> Slide, Kelly, slide!

"Slide, Kelly, Slide!" is now well established in the histories of baseball, but what is not generally known is that Kelly also inspired a second popular song. When he was sold by the Chicago Nationals to the Boston team in 1887, Kelly's Chicago fans took up a song to the tune of the then-popular song, "Climbing Up the Golden Stairs":

> Arab Kelly's gone and left us,
>   Of his presence he's bereft us—
> Kelly of the diamond bold.
>   He's deserted us for Boston.

As special as Kelly was to his contemporaries, he cannot claim the distinction of having inspired the most songs. No one need work very hard at guessing who holds that honor. The first was in 1921, "Babe Ruth," by George Graff, Jr. (who wrote the words to "When Irish Eyes Are Smiling"); in 1926, an Irving Berlin song of 1914, "Along Came Ruth," was adopted with new words—"There's a new star who is bringing / Fame to our national game"; in 1947, Ruth inspired "Babe" by Peter DeRose; and when he died in 1948 someone wrote yet another tribute to Ruth ("the mighty Babe is coming home"). Nor should it be too hard to guess who the next player was *after* Ruth to inspire a song (although it may be hard to accept that both Ty Cobb and Honus Wagner had earlier inspired songs): "Joltin' Joe Di-Maggio," as the hit of 1941 was titled. DiMaggio should also be credited with at least an assist for the Simon and Garfunkel hit, "Mrs. Robinson," with its nostalgic evocation of this paragon of integrity: "Where have you gone, Joe DiMaggio?"

The next ballplayer to inspire a song was none other than Jackie Robinson. "Did You See Jackie Robinson Hit That Ball!" by Buddy Johnson, was recorded in 1949 by both the Johnson and Count Basie bands. It's a really swinging tribute to American blacks' new pride in their baseball stars. "Play Ball!" it starts out, and proceeds with such lines as:

> Jackie is a real gone guy!
> Satchel Paige is mellow, so is Campanella
> Newcombe and Doby, too
>
> . . . . . . . . . . . . . . . . . .
>
> But it's a natural fact,
> When Jackie comes to bat,
> The other team is through!

Jackie Robinson, by the way, can claim a distinction that even eluded the Babe: He also inspired a serious drama in 1981, *First*. It was later turned into a musical, but neither play nor musical enjoyed much success.

The Doby referred to in the Jackie Robinson song was, of course, Larry Doby, the first black to play in the American League, and he got his own song in the early '50s ("The Doby Boogie"). The emergence of black players in the late 1940s also inspired several baseball songs by noted bluesman Brownie McGhee—titles such as "Baseball Boogie" and "New Baseball Boogie."

Some of these songs or subjects will come as little surprise, even if most fans no longer remember them. But how many realize that Willie Mays not only inspired two songs but actually sang along on one of them? On the 1954 recording of "Say Hey, Willie" with the Treniers, Willie can be heard repeating the title as part of the refrain. (The King Odum Quartet recorded "The Amazing Willie Mays" in 1954. And in 1962 Willie recorded two non-baseball songs that left him in the outfield.) Not to be outdone, Mickey Mantle joined in on Teresa Brewer's 1956 recording, "I Love Mickey":

> The one who drives me batty every spring,
> I wish that I could catch him
> And pitch a little woo.

Mickey can be heard repeating "Mickey who?" in the refrain. As Hank Aaron moved in on Ruth's home-run record in 1973, Bill Slayback, the Tigers pitcher, recorded "Move Over Babe (Here Comes Henry)," music by Slayback and words by Tigers announcer Ernie Harwell. Reggie Jackson may be the only ballplayer to have inspired a candy bar, but Pete Rose was the last individual player known to have inspired a song.

Umpires have also inspired songs, although not as actual individuals. Thus "Finnegan the Umpire" of 1890 was an all-purpose umpire. And while virtually all other baseball songs are positive, a song came out in 1909 titled "Let's Get the Umpire's Goat." (It was composed by Nora Bayes with words by Jack Norworth, the husband-wife team who also wrote "Shine On, Harvest Moon." He, of course, wrote the lyrics to "Take Me Out to the Ballgame.") And there was "The Umpire," a kiddies' novelty song recorded in the 1950s by a quartet composed of Tommy Henrich, Ralph Branca, Roy Campanella, and Phil Rizzuto.

As for baseball managers, if you had to name the one least likely to have inspired a song, it would probably be Connie Mack, the stiff-suited autocrat of the old Philadelphia Athletics. Yet none other than George M. Cohan honored him with "The Connie Mack Song," and when Mack retired in 1950, someone in Philadelphia composed "The Grand Old Man of Baseball." Even Casey Stengel can't claim that distinction.

*Serious Music*  The connections between baseball and popular music, given the grass roots they share, should not seem nearly so surprising as those between baseball and more serious music. Charles Ives (1874–1954), for instance, who juggled a career as an insurance executive with that as the great original of American classical music, loved baseball; he pitched at Yale, once boasted of having taught a young boy how to pitch properly, and even went to a baseball game on his honeymoon. What a delight, then, to discover that about 1909 Ives composed a short but virtuoso left-hand piano piece, "Some Southpaw Pitching." Also in the early years of this century, Ives composed what he called three "cartoons" or "takeoffs" with titles that clearly announce his attachment to baseball and his defiance of the conventional proprieties of his day: "Mike Donlin—Johnny Evers," "Willy Keeler at Bat," and "Rube Marquard trying to walk 2 to 3." Clearly, the man loved baseball.

The most ambitious musical composition centered on baseball is William Schuman's opera, *The Mighty Casey,* which had its world premiere on May 4, 1953, in Hartford, Connecticut (Charles Ives's home city). Inspired by Thayer's poem "Casey at the Bat," this short opera expands on the situation but retains the basic "plot" of the poem. It is highly sophisticated music, but all in good fun; the opera is revived occasionally (and, naturally, has been performed in Japan), but in an effort to make it easier to perform, Schuman also made a cantata out of the work in 1976.

Less known is "The Brooklyn Baseball Cantata" by contemporary American composer George Kleinsinger; composed in 1949, it calls for soloists and a chorus, and as might be expected has a lot of fun at the expense of the Dodgers and their fans. A more recent musical joke on baseball is the work of Peter Schickele, who has made a hugely successful career as the parodist-composer P. D. Q. Bach. In his baseball piece, an orchestra plays Beethoven's Fifth Symphony while two sports commentators talk as though the conductor were a baseball manager and what we are experiencing is a baseball game ("Next week they'll be facing Toscanini . . ."). The joke, as in the Kleinsinger piece, depends on the juxtaposition of High Art with pop culture.

This idea was first worked out in a famous episode in the Marx Brothers' brilliant movie *A Night at the Opera,* which ridicules the pretensions of grand opera. One of the funniest moments comes after Harpo has slipped a sheet of music into the orchestra's scores for Verdi's *Il Trovatore;* at one point in the opera, all the members turn their pages—and go straight into "Take Me Out to the Ballgame"! The ultimate American pastime thus deflates the great balloon of Old World Culture.

Perhaps, though, opera had already had its revenge. Sid Farrar, a first baseman for the Philadelphia Phillies from 1883 to 1889, had a daughter who had a fine voice but needed expensive lessons. Ballplayers not being that well paid in those days, and used tinfoil having some resale value, his teammates began to save tinfoil from wrappers. Soon other teams and then people outside baseball began to contribute tinfoil, and Geraldine Farrar got the lessons she needed to become one of America's first great opera singers.

*Crossover Artists*   Baseball players have from the earliest times crossed over into the world of popular culture. Everyone vaguely remembers that Denny McLain, in his happier days, recorded himself playing the organ: "The Detroit Superstar Swings with Today's Hits" proclaimed the record jacket, and swing away he did on such novelties as "Extra Innings." (On the back of the jacket, McLain was quoted as saying, "When it's all said and done, some day in the future, I hope they will remember Denny McLain as a professional musician.'') But as early as 1877—only one year after the founding of the National League—professional baseball teams had begun to make paid appearances at vaudeville theaters, much as players now appear as guests on TV shows. A handbill of that year announces the visit to the Adelphi Theatre in Chicago of "the crack Base Ball Clubs—The Boston Nine and the Chicago Nine." At first it was enough for a team just to show up and be gawked at and applauded. But soon the stars were asked to appear on stage and say a few words, and in the 1880s and '90s such superstars as "King" Kelly and Cap Anson and journeymen such as Arlie Latham and Tony Mullane put in postseason or postcareer appearances on the vaudeville stage, where they occasionally sang or participated in a comic skit.

In the twentieth century, the stakes were upped and players were expected to actually show some talent, singing perhaps, even dancing a few steps, or at least telling some anecdotes if not acting in skits. The salaries of most players were low and this was as easy a way as any to make some money over the winter. The first baseball act paired National League outfielder "Turkey Mike" Donlin with a singing comedienne, Mabel Hite; they eventually got married, but by 1908 they were performing a skit known as "Stealing Home." (Most of these skits, in the best traditions of vaudeville, involved some kind of sexual innuendo.) Donlin, a well-known player of the era, continued his career in vaudeville after retiring from baseball; for some years he and a Boston Red Sox player, Marty McHale, played vaudeville with a mildly off-color skit, "Right Off the Bat," and then Donlin went on to play bit parts in Hollywood. McHale had his own reputation as "The Baseball Caruso" and for years balanced his baseball career with his singing and vaudeville career.

Another player who performed in vaudeville and ended up marrying his partner was the famed pitcher Rube Marquard. He made his first appearance in 1911 at New York's Hammerstein Theater, then the most popular showplace for the baseball players, and in 1912 joined a popular star of the day, Blossom Seeley, in a new skit, "Breaking the Record." They got married and collaborated on the music and lyrics for two songs, "Those Ragtime Melodies" and "The Marquard Glide." In 1913 they came out with a skit called "The Suffragette Pitcher," which required Marquard to get into a woman's dress in order to pitch for Blossom's all-woman team.

Once the gate was opened about 1910, a host of players began to turn up in vaudeville and in the movies. Some highly unlikely stars of baseball took their turn over the next couple of decades—Joe Tinker, Johnny Kling, Chief Meyers, Germany Schaffer, Hank Gowdy, Vernon "Lefty" Gomez, Mickey

Cochrane, Hughie Jennings, Rabbit Maranville, and Chief Bender, among others, sang and joked and shuffled their way across the stage. There were several baseball quartets over the years. The Boston Red Sox Quartette made its debut in 1910 with Hugh Bradley, Marty McHale, Tom O'Brien, and Larry Gardner, who was later replaced by Bill Lyons (McHale later claimed Lyons couldn't play that well but Boston signed him just to keep the quartet going; tell that to George Steinbrenner). In 1912 came another quartet featuring two major league ex-pitchers, Frank Browning of Detroit and George Crable of Brooklyn; this quartet reappeared in vaudeville in the mid-'20s. During the 1920s, Waite Hoyt, whose father had been in show business, sang at that mecca of vaudeville, New York's Palace; in 1989, Mae Questel, who supplied the voices of Betty Boop and Olive Oyl, reminisced how she appeared at the Palace with Hoyt and his pianist, Fred Coots, in their vaudeville act.

Even Christy Mathewson and Lou Gehrig, who were possibly too polite to refuse, took to the stage, but so did those "bad boys" of baseball, Cap Anson and Ty Cobb. Anson first appeared in 1913 and returned in 1921 in a skit with his two daughters—it had been written for them by Ring Lardner. (Lardner had earlier written the words to "Gee! It's a Wonderful Game," music by Guy Harris "Doc" White, a former National League pitcher who won twenty-seven games for the Cubs in 1907.) Even the ferocious John J. McGraw worked up a monologue, "Inside Baseball," but he saved it for sedate after-dinner occasions.

Starting in 1921 with a well-known singer-comedian, Wellington Cross, Babe Ruth appeared regularly in vaudeville, where he sang a song especially composed for him, "Little by Little and Bit by Bit, I am Making a Vaudeville Hit." Although he was said to have a fairly decent singing voice, Ruth never drew the crowds in vaudeville that might have been expected, given his status as a superstar.

Moving from vaudeville to the recording studio, Dizzy Dean "and his Country Cousins" recorded "The Wabash Cannonball." Dean's effort was a one-time novelty record, but Tony Conigliaro made a serious attempt to launch himself as a singer in the 1960s with a half-dozen recordings including "Playing the Field." Perhaps the most unusual case was that of Lee Maye, who had a respectable major league career from 1959 to 1973. Before professional baseball he had been Arthur Lee Maye, a fine "doo-wop" singer who, with the Crowns, recorded several songs. A more recent case is that of Lenny Randle, who, although best known for having slugged his manager, went over to Italy to play baseball; he has also made a new career for himself there as a singer.

There is also a special group of singers who started out in the minors or were signed by the majors but who went on to make careers in country music: Bob Luman, Conway Twitty, Jim Reeves, Charley Pride, and Roy Acuff are only the most prominent ones. There's no telling how many baseball players considered careers as rock musicians, of course, or how many still go home after the season and perform as local celebrities. After all those showers, some ballplayers might be expected to have developed their voices to some degree.

A special variation on this theme of baseball players as singers began to emerge in the late 1950s (although Babe Ruth and Lou Gehrig are said to have made records in the 1920s), undoubtedly due to the new spotlight cast on players by television: Heroes of the most recent World Series were often called on to make a recording to capitalize on their new celebrity. Mickey Mantle, Whitey Ford, and Yogi Berra recorded a song (if that's the word for the gruff sounds that resulted) after their triumphs; Lew Burdette, Bob Gibson, and Don Larsen all made records after their great years; Don Drysdale recorded "Give Him Love" in 1963. After his record-setting year as a base stealer, Maury Wills recorded "The Ballad of Maury Wills" (1964) and even appeared at a Vegas nightclub playing the banjo. When the Miraculous Mets won in 1969, the whole team made a record. Beneath its veneer of novelty, this trend is simply a return to the days when the hottest stars appeared on vaudeville stages. The tradition is maintained by television: The very day after the Dodgers won the 1988 World Series, star pitcher Orel Hershiser appeared on the Johnny Carson Show and when the talk came around to Hershiser's habit of singing hymns to calm himself on the mound, he sang a hymn for the national audience. By now perhaps a record of Hershiser singing hymns is in the stores.

Another offshoot of vaudeville and baseball was nurtured by the new phonograph recording industry. The song "Slide, Kelly, Slide!" as mentioned, was one of the very first cylinders made for the home market in 1892. In 1893, Russell Hunting, a popular comedian of the day, made a recording of "Casey at the Bat." (DeWolf Hopper, who made the poem and himself famous with over ten thousand public recitations, did not record it till 1903; he recorded it again in 1926.) The Casey poem, of course, has inspired a whole family of variations, including a 1909 recording by Digby Bell, "The Man Who Fanned Casey," and Joe Laurie, Jr.'s, 1940 monologue, "Casey's Revenge." In 1907, Cal Stewart, a popular vaudeville monologuist as the old New England character, Uncle Josh, recorded "Uncle Josh at a Baseball Game." Famed vaudeville duo Weber and Fields recorded "The Baseball Game" in 1917. And there were many other early recordings by vaudeville stars: Miss Ray Cox's "The Baseball Girl" (1909); Elsie Janis singing "That Fascinating Baseball Slide" (1912); Arthur Collins doing "That Baseball Rag" and Eddie Morton's "They're All Good American Names" (both from the 1910–15 era). This tradition was still alive as late as 1962, when Danny Kaye released a novelty record, pairing "Myti Kaysi at the Bat" with his inimitable patter-style "Dodgers Song":

> Them bums, them bums, they may be bums
> But they're our bums. . . .
> Down in the dugout, Alston glowers. . . .
> Bottom of the ninth, 4 to nuttin. . . .

After vaudeville faded away in the 1930s, most of the routines involving baseball also faded. But one survived to become perhaps the best-known comic baseball routine of all time and is now enshrined at the Cooperstown Hall of Fame: Abbott and Costello's "Who's On First."

*The March King and Baseball*   John Philip Sousa wrote more than one hundred marches, including many for specific occasions and institutions, and it should not come as a surprise to learn that he wrote a baseball march. Now all but forgotten, "The National Game" was finished in 1925 in time for the fiftieth anniversary of the National League, and was recorded that year in Camden, New Jersey. Behind the march, however, lie several other links between Sousa and baseball.

Sousa had formed his own concert band in 1892 and for some thirty-five years toured the United States and Europe (and the world in 1910–11). For all the work involved in rehearsals and concerts, his band found time to form a baseball team, and they soon began to play local teams as well as those of other bands. Sousa's team had their own uniforms, and Sousa himself sometimes pitched. On the Fourth of July, 1900, finding themselves on tour in Paris, France, they played the first game of American baseball in that city since Spalding's tour of 1889.

The Sousa band baseball team eventually stopped playing outside teams (for reasons never made clear), but they continued with "intramural" games—usually the woodwinds pitted against the brasses. At some point early in the 1920s the band was touring in Havana, Cuba, and there Sousa met the new commissioner of baseball, Judge Kenesaw Mountain Landis. When Landis learned of Sousa's long-time enthusiasm for the game, he commissioned him to write a march to commemorate the National League.

Commissioner Landis could hardly have known that Sousa had already had an earlier "brush" with the national game. Sometime in 1888 a Washington journalist had come up with the plot and words for a comic operetta involving an umpire who had evil designs on both the heroine and the Giants' star pitcher. Sousa got as far as writing the music for such songs as "An Umpire I, Who Ne'er Say Die" and "He Stands in the Box With the Ball in His Hands," but the operetta never was seen or heard of since.

Sousa deserves one final word on baseball. The following is taken from one of several novels he tried his restless fingers on, *Pipetown Sandy* of 1905:

Our national game! What an enemy to nepotism, or any other "ism" that thrives on the favor of influence!

Oh, base-ball! thou art truly the embodiment of purest democracy; like love, thou dost level all ranks.

Of what avail is distinguished ancestry, pre-Adamite origin, cerulean blood or stainless escutcheon, when one is at bat and strikes out! Intellectual superiority, physical perfection, social status, wealth or poverty count for nothing, if you fail to bring in the winning run.

Albert Spalding could not have said it better.

*Bands and Ballclubs*  John Philip Sousa was not the last band leader to have a thing about baseball. In the 1930s, when the Negro leagues were going strong with their public, Louis Armstrong sponsored a baseball team for a while, Armstrong's Secret Nine. Cab Calloway also supported a ball team for a while; unlike Armstrong, he actually played for his. Perhaps it is all the touring they do, or the hanging around hotels and bars in strange cities, or the waiting for the few hours of performance, but there must be something about the life of a bandsman and a ballplayer that allows these two institutions to fit so well.

The most extraordinary union of bandsmen and ballplayers, however, came about with the group known as Bill Monroe and His Blue Grass Boys. Bill Monroe is revered as virtually the founder of bluegrass music, but the story of his devotion to baseball is not well known. By the mid-'40s, Monroe's band was playing various ballparks before local teams (semipro or minors) played their games. Monroe and some of his band members began to hang around to watch the game, and soon got to wishing they could play, too. So in 1945, Monroe formed a team called the Bluegrass All-Stars, made up of some men who doubled as musicians and others who were only ballplayers.

Some of the latter had played in the minors or semipro leagues and allowed the team to more than hold its own, but many of the players were basically musicians who played for the love of the game—Bill Monroe himself, Clyde Moody, Charlie Cline, Chubby Wise, Cedric Rainwater, Don Reno, Jackie Phelps, "Stringbean," and others well known to country music fans. Usually their games were played after the band had given its concert.

As Monroe's band became better known, he had to spend more time either in Nashville or traveling to distant parts of the United States, so he formed a new team, the Bluegrass Ballclub, which played only in Nashville. By the early 1950s, even that team was disbanded. Monroe may never make the Hall of Fame at Cooperstown, but as an honored member of the Country Music Hall of Fame he deserves at least a footnote in the history of music's long affair with baseball.

*Modern Pop Baseball*  Baseball is surprisingly alive and well in recent popular music. Frank Sinatra's version of Joe Raposo's "There Used to Be a Ballpark" might be set aside as an oldtimer's song (1973), but there is a definite contemporary feel to Dave Frishberg's 1969 song, "Van Lingle Mungo," with its nostalgic roll call. In 1968 the soul group the Intruders had a hit with "Love Is Like a Baseball Game." Prominent among recent releases is John Fogerty's "Centerfield" (1985): "Look at me/I can play/Centerfield," pleads the benchwarmer to his coach, while Fogerty pays tribute to Chuck Berry's 1956 classic, "Brown-eyed Handsome Man":

> Three-two count, no one on
> He hit a high fly into the stands.
> Rounding third, he was heading home,
> He was a brown-eyed handsome man.

In Fogerty's song, this line returns as: "Three-two count/It's a home run/ Brown-eyed handsome man." And then there's Bruce Springsteen's "Glory Days" (1984): "He could throw that speed ball by you. . . . Saw him the other night at this roadside bar . . . all he could talk about was glory days." Not so well known, but no less touching, is Steve Goodman's 1981 recording of his own actual situation, "A Dying Cub Fan's Last Request."

Some aficionados maintain that the best of the recent baseball songs has been Terry Cashman's 1981 hit, "Talkin' Baseball," sometimes known as "Willie, Mickey, and the Duke" in reference to its incantation of those great players' names. Cashman enjoyed such success at the time with this song that he began to adapt its lyrics to whatever baseball town he was in—intoning the names of local favorites—and for several years he updated these local versions to accommodate roster changes! "Talkin' Baseball" also led Cashman to commissions for a number of team and special-event songs, including one for Pete Rose, when he broke Cobb's record; one for Johnny Bench Night ("One Stop Along the Way"); and one for Earl Weaver's retirement game ("The Earl of Baltimore"). It couldn't have happened to a more deserving guy: Cashman pitched well enough at City College of New York to be signed by the Tigers organization, but after a season in the minors (he lacked control), he left organized baseball. Obviously, though, baseball has been good to him.

Almost all of the songs of the present generation differ from those of previous generations in their way of treating baseball. The first wave of nineteenth-century songs reflect a need to justify baseball somehow—it could be fun but it also had to mean something. Then in the early decades of this century, baseball was just plain celebrated in its immediate, fun-giving sense. More recently, songwriters *use* baseball in a more self-conscious, self-referring manner, usually to invoke some "purer," more idyllic age: In the 1980s, baseball has become nostalgia and metaphor.

# 14

# THE
# INTERNATIONAL
# GAME

**T**he standard version of how baseball stacks up as a team sport around the world can be expressed quite succinctly: Baseball may be the national pastime of the United States, but it just doesn't count on the international scene. The exceptions can easily be ticked off. The Japanese take the game seriously and people seem to play a fair amount of baseball in some Latin American countries, including Cuba and the Dominican Republic. As for Mexico and Canada, they're neighbors, so naturally they have picked up baseball from their gigantic cousin. To be sure, the Olympics have now accepted baseball as an official competition, and come to think of it, some kids in Korea and Taiwan must play a fair amount of baseball because they're always beating our Little League teams.

But none of this really qualifies baseball as a serious adult sport on the scale of, say, soccer. Now there's the international sport! Its televised World Cup games engage more people than any other single event in the history of this earth. Basketball and volleyball have been Olympic competitions for many years, so Americans should settle for having introduced two sports to the world. Baseball is just too . . . too . . . too American to appeal to masses of people in other societies.

With this received wisdom in mind, a round-the-world tour with bat and ball in hand should not require that many words.

*The Canadians* Canadians not only can lay claim to a long history of playing baseball, at many levels and in many leagues, but they have even laid claim to inventing the game. Not quite "inventing," perhaps, but certainly a strong case has been made for Canadians having played some of the earliest recorded games of baseball. Three of these games are placed in the 1830s, others in the early 1840s, but the problem with all of them as historical "firsts" is that they were not recorded in writing until many years later. The strongest candidate is a game played on June 4, 1838, in Beachville, Province of Ontario, a game between local villagers and farmers to celebrate the birthday of King George IV. Even the dimensions of the diamond have been provided—sixty-three feet between bases, fifty-four feet from the pitcher's mound to home plate—but the problem is that none of this appeared in writing until 1886, in the *Philadelphia Sporting Life.* The other candidates are even less solidly based in time and details.

If the Beachville game is authentic, of course, it would predate the mythical game in Cooperstown in 1839, but the real point is that neither of these were "the first baseball game" any more than was the Knickerbockers' game of June 19, 1846, or any other single game. There were so many young men throughout North America playing so many different forms of baseball by the 1830s that no one team or city can really claim to have invented the game.

Canadians, rather, should be proud of their many other connections with and contributions to baseball. From the early games in Ontario, baseball spread both to the eastern and western regions; most of these games were strictly amateur and occasional affairs, with teams made up of men in different occupations, particularly from the railroads. By 1874, games were being reported in a Winnipeg newspaper; by the 1880s there were professional teams and leagues; and by 1904 there was an international (amateur) series for the championship of the Northwest between Canada's Whitehorse team and Alaska's Skagway team—the Canadians won the first two games and the series.

Throughout the twentieth century, baseball in Canada has developed pretty much like baseball in the United States—with professional and minor league teams, semipros, amateurs, youth teams. Some of these teams are affiliated with baseball organizations in the United States, but many others are strictly Canadian affairs. Players of Canadian birth move back and forth freely now in the majors and have ever since William Phillips from New Brunswick joined the Cleveland Spiders in 1879. There have been some 150 Canadian-born players in the majors, including such standouts as Ferguson Jenkins, Jeff Heath, Jack Graney, James "Tip" O'Neill, and many others. So baseball is very much alive and well in Canada, with its own roots and its own offshoots. Its history, somewhat independent of (and wilder and woolier than) baseball in the United States, has been told in a number of books and articles, the most notable by one Bill Humber.

And in one department, Canadians can claim precedence. Everyone who thinks about it must realize that it was actually the Montreal Royals, then a Dodgers farm team, that first fielded Jackie Robinson in 1946 and thus reintegrated organized baseball. But well before that, in July 1935, an Alabama-born black pitcher, Alfred "Freddy" Wilson, had joined the Granby Red Sox of the Quebec Provincial League. At that time, that league did not belong to U.S. organized baseball, but it was part of Canadian professional baseball, and Wilson racked up a fine record. So successful was Wilson, in fact, that in 1936 and 1937 the Provincial League added a new team, the Black Panthers, made up mostly of young blacks from the American South. By 1940 the Provincial League was all-white again (although Wilson returned to it in 1945), but after Robinson opened the gate, this Canadian league started many black and Hispanic players on their way to the majors. So Canadians can lay claim, if not to inventing baseball, to taking the lead in getting minorities into the majors. Many might regard that as the true beginning of modern baseball.


*Baseball Russian Style*  In July 1987, Americans were astonished to hear that, just as Mikhail Gorbachev was relaxing many of the old tensions between the United States and U.S.S.R., the official newspaper *Izvestia* was announcing that baseball was actually a Russian invention. The Russian original, called *lapta,* had been played for centuries in villages throughout the land, and in the eighteenth century, said the *Izvestia* writer, it had been introduced to North Americans by Russian settlers on the West Coast. What was little noted by the American press, however, was that this *Izvestia* article contradicted another one urging Russians to reject baseball because it was an American game. No matter, because whether it was Americans' new sophistication or chauvinism, they took all this in good humor, perhaps emboldened by the premonition that American-style baseball was about to take over Russia in a big way.

What also went unremarked in 1987 was that the Russians had tried this same stunt at least once before, only then it was back at the height of the Cold War and it was handled much differently. It was in September 1952 when another Russian publication, *Smena,* suddenly proclaimed not only that the traditional Russian village game *lapta* was the source of "beisbol," but that in the hands of the capitalist Americans, it had become "a beastly battle, a bloody fight with mayhem and murder." The article cited the names of some of the teams, such as the Tigers and Pirates, as proof of the violent nature of the game, referred to capitalist businessmen who "intensively implanted" the sport in young boys, and implied that players and spectators were constantly being wounded, even killed, by the action. The players were in a "situation of slaves . . . bought and sold and thrown out the door when they become unnecessary"; after six or seven years, a typical player, "with ruined health and often also crippled, increases the army of American unemployed." Newspapers such as *The New York Times* attacked this article in editorial columns, and the U.S. government denounced it as an example of the "Hate America" campaign the Russians were waging to turn their people against Americans. When the new Soviet ambassador to the United States arrived at just this time, one of the first questions he was asked was whether he would go to see a baseball game. (He assured everyone he would.) The storm soon subsided, the Russians went back to playing *lapta,* the Americans returned to playing baseball.

The fact is that, although little noted either in 1987 or 1952, back on February 17, 1935, *The New York Times* carried a small item on its sports pages:

## SOVIET UNION SPONSORS
## NATIONAL BASEBALL PLAN

Moscow—The Soviet Government decided today to sponsor a program for introducing baseball throughout the Soviet Union as a national sport.

A special baseball section was ordered to be organized as part of the Supreme Council of Physical Culture, to superintend the spread of the game.

That was all, and for whatever reasons, nothing seems to have come of it. Presumably more pressing demands, such as increasing iron production and hydroelectric power, took precedence over introducing baseball, and then World War II came along and there was not time for such frivolities. By the time the official *Great Soviet Encyclopedia* was published in 1950, the entry on "Beisbol" opened: "A sport that somewhat resembles Russian *lapta.*" After explaining the way the game is played, the article concludes: "Baseball demands great agility, speed, and coordinated action among all members of the team. With highly developed techniques the game becomes a genuinely athletic physical exercise. In the U.S.S.R. baseball is not very widespread."

But now the Russians seem intent on changing all that. Perhaps the initial impetus comes from the adoption by the Olympics of baseball as a medal competition, but it seems obvious, too, that it is related to Gorbachev's new policy of *glasnost*—"openness." Nothing promotes openness between people so much as good healthy sports rivalries, and there is every reason to believe that the Russians want to challenge all the baseball-playing societies. (It was only some eight years after the Russians began to play serious ice hockey that they took the gold medal in the Olympics.) As it turns out, Russians have already been playing more baseball for some years than the outside world realized. There are reportedly at least thirty teams in the U.S.S.R., most being what Americans would regard as semipros in that the players have to hold other jobs but are undoubtedly rewarded for their game playing; the most powerful team is the Tashkent Subway Builders.

The big "opening to the West" came in 1988. In February and March that year, two Soviet baseball coaches toured American baseball spring training and softball training sites to study training techniques and playing facilities. This was only the first of what promises to be increasing contacts between Russian and American baseball interests; increasing numbers of players, coaches, and administrators from various levels of American baseball and other nations' baseball organizations (Cubans, Japanese, Nicaraguans) are appearing in the U.S.S.R. to provide help in various ways. The Little League in 1988 also began negotiating with Russia to start Little League teams there, while the umbrella organization that promotes baseball on every level, the International Baseball Association, accepted the U.S.S.R. as its sixty-fifth member. Perhaps the most extraordinary development, however, is the announcement that the Russians are building their first real ballpark (think about it—no playing fields in Russia have ever had a pitcher's mound), complete with artificial turf, in a section of Moscow; novel enough, but beyond this, it is being paid for by Japanese, who are also providing a lot of equipment. Baseball has truly become international when the Japanese pay for Astroturf in Moscow. And anyone who still has doubts should read Steve Wulf's article in *Sports Illustrated* (July 28, 1988); by the time you're through learning about such pivotal figures as Richard Spooner and Victor Starfin and Vadim "Carter" Kulakov, you'll realize that Soviets and baseball are a battery history has been waiting for.

*Baseball and the English* All who write about the early history of baseball acknowledge that the first deliberate attempt at "internationalizing" the game was the 1874 visit to England of the Boston and Philadelphia teams.

*Except for the scoreboard, there is little to suggest that this is a baseball game between Czechoslovakian and Russian teams in Moscow in 1987. (The Czech National Team is at bat.) Baseball has begun to catch on big in Eastern Europe and the U.S.S.R., and each year sees more teams, games, and international matches in these countries.*

The details of that famous trip have been pretty much set forth by now: how Harry Wright, English-born former cricketer but now a leader in American baseball, sent Albert Spalding, then a twenty-three-year-old pitcher for Boston, to England to line up the support of the British cricket establishment as sponsors; how Wright and Spalding misrepresented the American baseball teams' ability to play cricket; how during July and August the teams played a series of cricket matches in which, to everyone's surprise, the Americans more than held their own against the English (albeit by being allowed to field larger teams and by using techniques that were decidedly "not cricket"); and how they also played fourteen demonstration baseball games that failed to win over the English. (Actually, one of those games was in Dublin: Harry Wright felt a game in Ireland was a good idea because of "all our Mc's and O'Rs.")

*Harper's* Weekly *(September 5, 1874) carried this picture of an exhibition game between the two American teams in London, England, earlier that summer. Note that there were a few women present among the stylishly dressed English who turned out to see this exotic game played by their American cousins. Most likely this is the cricket grounds of the famed Marylebone Cricket Club.*

Crowds were small and financially the trip was a disaster, although its three American promoters—Harry Wright, Henry Chadwick, and Spalding— never quite admitted this. Wright simply cut the salaries of his Boston team, while Chadwick wrote snidely about the American ballplayers having "manlier" physiques and being "more abstemious in habits." Near the end of the tour, *The Field,* England's leading sporting magazine, dismissed baseball in these terms:

> The verdict of the spectators is almost universally against it as a competitor with our national game; and in our own individual judgment, it has so many inherent defects that it has not the slightest pretensions to be considered superior to, even if it is the equal with, our own juvenile amusement "rounders," on the basis of which it has been modelled.

That was a double swipe at the Americans—the game was defective, and in any case it was stolen from the English—and for a variety of reasons, the English did not show any interest in taking up baseball after this first exposure to the game.

Some have speculated that Spalding was so stung by such criticism of this early effort that, when he had the opportunity thirty years later, he took revenge by promoting the notion that baseball had been invented by Doubleday, totally independent of any English games. This doesn't seem to hold up, because in 1889 Spalding was back in England at the culmination of his world tour and was still trying to convert the English to baseball. Again, the English looked on with bemusement at their boisterous American cousins but again they did not embrace the game. Spalding, however, never backward when it came to promoting baseball (especially since he was now in the business of making baseball equipment), donated a fair sum of his own money in 1890 to help British soccer clubs organize baseball teams; he also supported the setting up of a Baseball Association of Great Britain and Ireland as well as a National League of Professional Base Ball Clubs of Great Britain. After one season, though, there were only four teams and the league effectively went under.

And that would be pretty much the story of attempts to get baseball established in Britain over the next fifty years—on again, off again, teams and leagues, amateurs and semipros, Americans and British, here and there, no consistent or persistent establishment. On the other hand, it is probably fair to say that not a year passed from 1890 on that there weren't a few games of baseball played somewhere in Great Britain. Much of the impetus for keeping the game alive came from Americans, one of the more curious instances of this being Newton Crane, at one time United States Consul in Manchester, England, who as "President of the National Baseball League of Great Britain" in 1891 got a London publisher to bring out a booklet, *Baseball,* in which he both explains some of the essentials of the game and presents arguments as to why the game should be adopted by the English. Among the latter is his observation that whereas large crowds of Britishers turn out to see soccer games in even the worst of weather, cricket attracts relatively few even in pleasant weather, so there is obviously a need for a fine-weather sport such as baseball. It is all reminiscent of Louis Armstrong's words about rhythm: If you gotta have it explained, you'll never have it.

There was another brief flurry of interest in 1906 when Nelson P. Cook, an American from Vermont, and James McWeeny, a journalist, took the lead in organizing two leagues, and there was even a "championship" match played that summer. Some correspondent for *The New York Times* got so carried away that on June 24, 1906, an article appeared under the headline:

## BASEBALL IS POPULAR WITH THE BRITISHERS

### England's National Sport Threatened by American Game

But all this was premature, and although a number of English teams did continue over the years, much of the baseball played and much of the interest depended on Americans in England for one reason or another (crews of ships, entertainers, YMCA, university students, businessmen, and the like).

One of the more surprising British boosters of the game, however, was Sir Arthur Conan Doyle, the creator of Sherlock Holmes. In 1922, on a visit to the United States, Doyle heartily encouraged his countrymen to take up baseball: "Baseball is a noble game. I enjoy watching it immensely and have even played it. I was once a member of an impromptu team of Englishmen and played against an impromptu team of Americans, all in Switzerland at the time. Our side won. . . . I was shortstop on that occasion. . . . I know baseball is the game England needs. . . . It would not displace cricket . . . as that is an old man's game." The thought of Sherlock Holmes and Dr. Watson warming up must have been too much for the British, because they failed to heed Doyle's advice.

Baseball got its second wind in Britain, though, after World War II, when several teams were organized in large English cities and the clubs also began to play teams from the Continent. In 1967, the National Baseball League of the United Kingdom competed in its first European Championships and since then Britain has been quite active in European and international baseball competition at the amateur level (although it is predicted that there will soon be professional teams). There are about fifty senior teams divided into five leagues, and there are a variety of support activities—junior teams, coaching clinics, and all the rest. Private corporations are beginning to invest large sums in supporting teams, and final testament to British conversion is that one of their television networks now carries the U.S. World Series. (The 1986 World Series drew 30 percent of the British TV audience.) Baseball has by no means replaced either cricket or soccer, but Albert Spalding can finally relax knowing that the English have stepped up to the plate.

***Baseball's Manifest Destiny*** Albert Goodwill Spalding's attempt to introduce baseball into England in 1874 may not have succeeded, but never

*Americans never did quite give up hoping that their English cousins would someday see the error of their ways and take up baseball. When the duke of Windsor visited New York in May 1953, he posed with Yankees manager Casey Stengel, Mickey Mantle (left), and Phil Rizzuto (right) before one of their games, but there is no record that his patronage influenced the English to drop cricket.*

daunted, some years later he took on something far more ambitious: He organized a trip around the world with two American baseball teams. In the fall of 1888, the two teams—the Chicago White Stockings, captained by Cap Anson, and an All-Star team mainly from the other National League teams, captained by John Montgomery Ward—accompanied by some of their wives, Spalding, various baseball officials, a half dozen reporters, "Professor" Bartholomew, the hot-air balloonist, and Clarence Duval, the White Stockings' black-American mascot, set sail on what one journalist of the time called "a mission of instruction," namely, to introduce the world to baseball. The first stop was Hawaii; unfortunately, the ship's schedule allowed only for a Sunday game, and as this was forbidden (by the Americans, that is, then "looking after the moral welfare of the natives," as Spalding put it), the American teams had to sail on without showing the state of the art to these isolated islanders.

Although Spalding makes no mention of it, he must have met one of the islands' most prosperous and prominent residents, Alexander Cartwright. Yes, the very same Cartwright who had been so instrumental in founding the Knickerbocker Base Ball Club in New York City back in 1845. After leaving for California in the great gold rush of '49, he moved on to Hawaii (with a baseball and a copy of the Knickerbocker baseball rules), where he would spend the rest of his life. Within a few years of his arrival, he was laying out baseball diamonds and organizing teams, so that by 1888 baseball was already a popular sport in many parts of the islands. Spalding indicates his awareness that Cartwright lived on Hawaii and that he had been a founder of the Knickerbockers, but we can only speculate why this had no effect on Spalding's later promotion of the Doubleday version of baseball. Had Spalding truly listened to Cartwright on that Sunday in Honolulu, Hoboken instead of Cooperstown might well be the goal of all baseball enthusiasts.

This was not to be, and Spalding's ship sailed on to New Zealand, where during a brief stop the teams played an exhibition game. They they sailed to Australia, where from December 1888 to January 1889 the American teams played twelve exhibition games in some of the major cities of Australia—Adelaide, Ballarat, Melbourne, and Sydney. Then the teams went on to Ceylon (now Sri Lanka), where they left the natives mystified by this strange game, and up to Egypt (where they played a game near the great pyramids). From Egypt they went on to Italy (where Spalding's attempt at playing a game in the Coliseum was sternly rejected, but they did play in Naples "under the shadow of Vesuvius," on the grounds of the Villa Borghese in Rome, and another game in Florence) and France (where they played in Paris), ending up with a tour of England, Scotland, and Ireland.

For Spalding and most of his entourage, it was a generally successful and pleasant expedition. For one thing, he had opened up new markets for his line of sporting goods and sports books, including his series of baseball guides. He had a special edition of the latter printed for Australia in 1889 and in it called the Australians' attention to baseball as embodying "all those essentials of manliness, courage, nerve, pluck and endurance, characteristic of the Anglo-Saxon race." No one knows how Clarence Duval, the black mascot, felt about such Anglo-Saxon virtues when some of the players made him put on a catcher's mask and gloves, tied him to a rope, and then dragged him around the railroad station in Cairo as if he were an animal. This was the behavior of crude, uneducated ballplayers, of course; one of the more literate journalists with the tour took a broader perspective when he reported that "a disciple of Darwin . . . would have bounded with delightful visions of the missing

*On their round-the-world tour in 1888–89, Spalding's teams made their way through the Suez Canal to Egypt where they went ashore and played a game in front of the Great Sphinx. No one ever thought to ask the local Egyptians what they thought of such highjinks.*

link.'' Spalding conveniently forgot to mention that Duval (and the balloonist) were part of the world tour.

On their arrival back in New York, the teams were treated like conquering heroes. At a famous dinner in their honor at Delmonico's, Mark Twain typically put his finger right on the subject when he slyly complimented Spalding on exporting baseball, "the very symbol, the outward and visible expression of the drive and push and rush and struggle of the raging, tearing, booming nineteenth century," to places "of profound repose and soft indolence and dreamy solitude" such as Hawaii.

For that was the point about this whole tour, at least in Spalding's mind if not in all those who made it: He viewed baseball as an object of veneration somewhere between the Stars and Stripes and the Bible, and he felt it should be America's mission to bring the benefits of baseball to the whole world (and if this meant that it opened up the world as a market for his equipment, so

AMERICA'S NATIONAL GAME

*This drawing appeared facing the opening chapter of Spalding's 1911 classic,* America's National Game. *It clearly was intended to express all that Spalding thought was best about baseball and America, but to some it looks suspiciously like Teddy Roosevelt's neoimperialist bully, the Uncle Sam of "speak softly and carry a big stick."*

much the better). Perhaps no one articulated this role of baseball so explicitly as did Spalding, but this image of the game was implicit in various happenings at the turn of the century. Baseball clearly seemed to be "following the flag" and it also seemed to be part of the Christian missionary's kit. Undoubtedly it is just a coincidence but Theodore Roosevelt, less than twenty years after he had hailed Spalding's round-the-world tour, would send the "Great White Fleet" on a similar tour. But it is no coincidence that in the New York Public Library's Spalding Baseball Picture Collection there is a series of musty old photographs from the turn of the century showing baseball teams at various missionary outposts and resource-rich underdeveloped countries. These teams were made up of either the native residents or Americans temporarily assigned to these locales, suggesting that baseball was being introduced as a sort of "colonial" pastime—more or less just what happened with cricket throughout the British Empire.

In fact, one need not be a Marxist to notice that baseball (with a few exceptions, the most notable being Japan) seems to have become most popular in those countries that fell under the American "sphere of influence" at the end of the nineteenth century and in the early years of the twentieth century: Hawaii, Cuba, Puerto Rico, the Philippines, Guam, Mexico, Nicaragua, Panama, Venezuela, and the Dominican Republic. Hawaii was annexed by the United States in 1898 as the result of what was effectively a coup by American commercial interests. Then it was in the wake of the Spanish-American War that the United States for the first time in its history found itself taking on what looked suspiciously like a colonial empire—Puerto Rico, the Philippines, and Guam; Cuba was granted its freedom but the United States remained a force there until Castro took over in 1959. Meanwhile, the United States was extending the Monroe Doctrine to cover not only the United States' right to keep Europeans out of the Americas but also its own right to intrude. Increasingly the United States was inserting itself into the countries of the Caribbean and Central America, and where the U.S. troops went, baseball also went.

Indeed, the spread of baseball around the world would ultimately depend at least as much on the influence of American military units as on Spalding's deliberate proselytizing. In 1922, for instance, *The New York Times* could carry an account of some baseball games at Rio de Janeiro, Brazil:

> If a nation's interest in a pastime is measured by popular knowledge of the game, it may now be said that South America has been made safe for the democracy of baseball. The people of Brazil have at last mastered the lingo of the bleachers and made the Yankee game an institution of their own. For this conversion, credit must be given to

the sailors of the United States Battleship *Nevada*. . . . The enlisted men decided that in the matter of international friendships, sailors have their duties no less than diplomats. In the fulfillment of their obligation, the sailors proceeded to spread their message of baseball by teaching Brazil the fine points of its language.

This is all being written with some humor, but it reveals how many Americans felt about carrying baseball around the world.

The result is that a roll call of the countries where baseball is most popular

*By the early years of the twentieth century, American missionaries, teachers, and businessmen had introduced baseball into most of the far-flung corners of the world. These pictures of that era show local teams in Macao (upper left), Burma (upper right), Korea (bottom left), and Egypt (bottom right).*

today sounds suspiciously like a roll call of those countries where the United States has maintained a strong military, business, or political presence since the late nineteenth century. (Even Japan was effectively forced to open itself to Western influences by the U.S. Navy's expedition under Perry. Baseball may not have been on the U.S. government's list of demands, but it followed shortly thereafter.) It is no coincidence that the same writer who called Spalding's round-the-world tour a "mission of instruction" also referred to his 1874 attempt to introduce baseball into England as "an invasion of foreign territory." Ring Lardner was being funny but honest when he wrote of yet another "missionary expedition" (in 1914) by American baseball teams that it was to show "to the foreign element that baseball is a better game than cricket, roulette, hopscotch, baccarat, parchesi, or any other sports in vogue abroad." The plain fact is that the United States was in a chauvinist mood and expansionist mode during the years 1880 to 1920, and along with the confidence that they had the one true religion and the one true economic system, Americans believed that they had the one true sport—baseball.

Gradually this Christian-capitalist-chauvinist element in Americans' enthusiasm for baseball became less explicit, but it has never entirely vanished. This self-righteous chauvinism can take many forms, as when Branch Rickey, commenting on his decision to sign Jackie Robinson, said: "I couldn't face my God much longer knowing that His black creatures are held separate and distinct from His white creatures in the game that has given me all I own." And there have always been ballplayers and managers who speak of their performances as though the Christian God is giving the signals. Jules Tygiel, in *Baseball's Great Experiment,* his fine study of Robinson and the issue of integration in sports, writes:

> In subsequent years [after 1949] other people attempted to use baseball integration as a pro-American, anti-Communist propaganda message. Reports from the Gold Coast of Africa related that copies of *The Sporting News* with pictures of black players "have done much to make the missionary work of the Catholic missions easier."

Tygiel goes on to tell of a plan in 1952 to organize a world tour of the Brooklyn Dodgers and Cleveland Indians specifically to show off Robinson and Doby "as living evidence of the opportunity to reach the top which America's No. 1 sport gives all participants regardless of race."

Today, things are a bit more subtle, but not that much more so when one pays attention to all the words and messages and images that emanate from the national pastime. From the singing of "The Star-Spangled Banner" at the outset of every game (including the "World Series"), to players and managers who speak of "God's help," to George Steinbrenner's belief that his million-dollar contracts give him certain rights over his players, traces survive of the days when baseball was regarded as an integral part of a superior civilization's gift to the poor benighted heathens.

If anyone thinks this is an exaggeration, consider pitcher Orel Hershiser's words after he had negotiated his contract with the Dodgers in 1989: "I believe it is my responsibility to God to do the very best I can in everything I do, whether it's playing baseball or negotiating a contract."

*Baseball Down Under*   Of all the countries visited by Albert Spalding in his efforts to win foreigners over to baseball, the one on which he seems to have had the greatest effect is Australia. Although there are reports that people were playing baseball there as early as 1857, and although there was an Australian-born player, Joe Quinn, in the majors as early as 1884, baseball did not really catch on in Australia until after the visit of the American teams on their world tour of 1888–89. The Chicago White Stockings and the National League All-Stars played twelve exhibition games in Australia, and unlike the reception they received in most countries, including England, they drew thousands of spectators—twelve thousand at one game. True, Australian males were prepared for the game by their familiarity with cricket, but that didn't further acceptance in England. More likely, the Australians were a bit more open to this game precisely because they were ready to declare some independence from their English cricket-playing rulers.

For whatever mixture of reasons, the Australians took up baseball fairly readily. At first it was largely a game for schoolboys, but it soon was taken up by colleges and universities, and to this day most Australian players gain their experience in these educational institutions. There are five leagues that make up the Australian Baseball Federation, each league composed of nine or so teams; most of the players are strictly amateurs, often still in college, but many of the players continue after graduation and some are paid, so in effect the teams are somewhat like American semipro teams. The equivalent of winning the American World Series in Australia is the capturing of the Claxton Shield. They form all-star teams that compete in international competition, including the Olympics. There are the equivalent of minor leagues, and young women also play the game.

There are now an increasing number of contacts between Australian and American baseball—American players and coaches go there to play and coach, and some American teams even scout the Australian teams fairly regularly (the New York Mets being among the leaders in this). Several Australians have played in the American minors over recent years, but since Joe Quinn back in the nineteenth century, there has been only one Australian-born and -trained player to make it into the majors—Craig Shipley, who joined the Dodgers as a shortstop in 1986 (although even he honed his skills at the University of Alabama). As might be expected from Australians, who like to take on all physical challenges, Australians play an aggressive type of ball, one that emphasizes fast but intelligent base running.

It is estimated that one hundred thousand Australians now play baseball with some serious skills and commitment, and some Australians are beginning to invest large sums of money in the game with the idea of eventually developing a professional league, complete with a televised schedule and all. As the tempo and level of play increases in Australia, Albert Spalding can chalk up another win.

*The French Curve*  The French—play baseball? Wine tasting, *oui!* Hand kissing, *oui!* But baseball—*jamais!* In fact, baseball is being played these days by perhaps ten thousand French youths and men, and their quality of play is ranked at the second level in Europe (after the first-level play by Italy and Holland). Most of these young men play on amateur club teams; as yet there is no really serious play at the high schools or universities. But France's teams appear in various European and international competitions and there are signs that baseball may finally be catching on as the new generation of French youths abandon their countrymen's traditional coolness to imported culture.

The first baseball game to which the French were exposed was the one played in February 1889 by Spalding's touring teams. It was played, of all places, in a field near another new phenomenon on the Paris scene, the Eiffel Tower, then being erected for the Exposition of 1889. The French evidently weren't too impressed, nor were they moved to take up baseball when John Philip Sousa's band played a game in Paris in 1900. Spalding, not surprisingly, wouldn't take *non* for an answer and he was still trying in the early years of the twentieth century to get the French to take up baseball by offering a bronze trophy to the best schoolboy team. By 1913, this effort was being led on the scene by some Americans resident in Paris, W. H. Burgess and T. Edward Roosevelt, but baseball never really spread outside Paris. (Newspaper accounts of the day observed that French boys simply couldn't catch or pitch like American boys.)

Then along came World War I, when the French had other things to worry about, but the war eventually brought the American forces, and when young American males appear, baseball is never far behind. Sure enough, in 1918, the YMCA in Paris published a French translation of the *"Guide Officiel de Baseball,"* clearly designed to perpetuate the game after the American troops would withdraw. The translators did their best to come up with French equivalents of baseball terms—*une frappe* is a strike, *une triche* a balk, *champ-valide* the playing field—and to explain the rules of this strange American invention:

> *Tout bunt qui roule hors du champ-valide est compté comme une frappe.*
> (Each bunt that rolls out of the playing field is counted as a strike.)

As for the umpire, even the individualistic French had to accept:

> *Ses décisions sont indiscutables sauf par le capitaine d'une des équipes, et seulement dans le cas où il s'agit de savoir si le code a été dûment observe.*
> (His decisions are "undiscussable" except by the captains of the teams, and only then in situations where it is a question of knowing if a rule of play has been properly observed.)

Unfortunately, as soon as American forces departed France after World War I, baseball also left the French scene. Although American troops played some baseball during World War II, again it failed to take root. Now, although baseball may never become a truly popular sport on any scale in France, at least some ballplayers want to show that 40 million Frenchmen were wrong to reject this game.

*Latin American Baseball*   Most North Americans who know anything about baseball beyond yesterday's box scores are aware that baseball is big in many Latin American countries. Just how big, though, and how extensive its presence is, can hardly be imagined by anyone who hasn't either experienced it firsthand or read about it with some focus. Taking all of Latin America—Middle, Central, and South America, the Caribbean islands, and including non-Hispanic lands such as Brazil—it may be admitted that soccer remains the number-one sport in terms of sheer attendance and fan frenzy. But in a few countries, at least, baseball and its players hold a position that surpasses even that held by the game in the United States. It has been pointed out in Chapter 4, for instance, what a role baseball plays in the tiny Dominican Republic; clearly, just to have so many former and present major leaguers driving about in their fancy cars in that small and impoverished country (about the area of

Vermont and New Hampshire, with the population of Massachusetts) has to have a greater impact than major leaguers can make while spread out all over the United States. When was the last time *you* saw a major leaguer speeding down your main street? Meanwhile, on another level of society, both Batista and Castro have shared at least one goal for Cuba: championship baseball teams.

Earlier in this chapter, too, it has been claimed that the spread of baseball on the international scene can be plotted simply by following the expansion of the American empire. It is also true that different countries in Latin America can lay claim to slightly different variations on this basic historical theme. Mexico, Venezuela, and Colombia, three major countries where baseball is highly popular, were never actually taken over by U.S. troops, but economically they became dependent on the United States, and where the "big stick" came, the baseball was not far behind. (The role of American oil companies in spreading baseball throughout the world could be a chapter unto itself.) Panamanians, clearly, wouldn't be playing baseball if it weren't for North Americans because their country wouldn't even exist if the United States hadn't carved it out of Colombia; for most decades of its existence, moreover, U.S. military and other personnel were a dominant presence and not unnaturally the youth of Panama took up baseball. Likewise, Puerto Rico fell under United States governance after the Spanish-American War, and it was not long before U.S. military and civilians assigned there began to introduce the Puerto Ricans to baseball. As early as August 3, 1901, *The New York Times* was carrying a small story on its sports pages, datelined San Juan:

> Baseball is becoming a great fad here. Most of the American colony are great patrons of the game. Several clubs have been organized and nearly every Saturday afternoon a game has been played between two picked nines. The interest has become so great that a league was proposed. The plan took well with the people and six clubs have been formed from the clerical force of the various Government offices. A number of Americans employed by private concerns and several Puerto Ricans are members of the different clubs. All the clubs have sent to the United States for uniforms. . . . A large subscription list was raised to defray expenses.

There, in a horsehide, is the story of how baseball "followed the flag" in parts of Latin America, and with far more success than Spalding's attempts to transplant it whole into various societies elsewhere. Part of the success of baseball in these Latin American countries must also be attributed to the fact that their less-developed societies did not offer as many indigenous and entrenched alternatives as did such countries as Britain or France. A Roberto Clemente in Argentina, let alone Spain, might have become a bullfighter or a soccer player, a horseman or a cattleman, or for that matter something not even requiring physical skills. Baseball, after all, continues to offer young boys in many "disadvantaged" neighborhoods a way out of dead-end lives.

*Latins and the Majors*   All this is quite apart from yet another special contribution of Latin America to the realm of baseball—the winter season of the various professional teams in Mexico, Panama, Puerto Rico, Venezuela, and the Dominican Republic, plus other varied contacts and exchanges between Latin American players and teams and North American teams and players. This is a subject not for a chapter but for a separate book—the emergence of professional teams in the Latin American countries, the first appearances of individual North American players on the rosters of these teams early in this century, the ongoing appearances of many major leaguers in these winter leagues, the exhibition games played by U.S. major league and All-Star teams and Latin American teams over the decades, the abortive attempt by the Pasquel brothers of Mexico to set up an independent Mexican League in 1946, the establishment of minor league farm teams in Mexico and elsewhere, the abandonment of Cuba's minor league and professional teams to isolate Castro, and so on. One entire chapter in this book would be about the special status held by Latin American players who become stars in the majors and return to play in their countries' winter season—Roberto Clemente, Dave Concepcion, and such. Most North American fans have little awareness of how many of their recent favorite stars—Luis Tiant, for instance, or Ozzie Virgil—are not only superstars in their own lands but also the sons of baseball heroes in those lands.

Some active and former major leaguers also manage teams in the Latin American winter season, and this bears on U.S. baseball in yet another way: Before Frank Robinson was allowed to become the first black manager in the major leagues, he had managed a team in the Puerto Rican Winter League for five years, and there is some sentiment that many other minority managers could long ago have been brought up from these winter teams to manage in the majors. The fact is that these Latin American teams have effectively been integrated from the outset; as early as 1900 they were willing to play all-black U.S. teams as well as all-white major league teams. In fact, many a U.S. white player who wouldn't or couldn't play alongside U.S. blacks in the majors went down and played alongside them on the winter league teams.

Meanwhile, early in this century a team known as the Cuban Stars regularly came over to the States to play all-black teams. It was two of their lighter-skinned players, Rafael Almeida and Armando Marsans, who became the first Latin Americans signed on by a major league team (the Cincinnati Reds, in 1911), and it was this that gave some U.S. players and managers the idea that U.S. blacks could "pass" as Cubans in the majors. The Cuban Stars, by the way, are not to be confused with the Cuban Giants, a team of U.S. blacks formed in New York City in 1885; speaking gibberish on the field to pretend they were Cubans, this was the first of several barnstorming black-American teams that adopted the name *Cuban.*

In the 1920s, the newly formed Negro leagues in the States signed up Cuban teams, and Cubans and black Americans moved back and forth freely between these leagues' teams as well as between Puerto Rican, Panamanian, and other Latin American teams. Many of the great names of the Negro leagues went down there as individuals or on all-star teams and outperformed these Latin teams. Others have written about these matters, but the point to be made here is that Latin American baseball deserves recognition for having put pressure on the dam that Jackie Robinson eventually breached. Literally pressured: Jules Tygiel reminds us that in order to avoid problems in then-segregated Florida, Rickey moved the Dodgers spring training camp to Cuba and staged an exhibition tour in Panama during spring 1947 so that Robinson could be eased onto the team. Rickey used Latin Americans, already accepting of blacks, to show North Americans where the wave of the future of baseball was heading.

*Nicaraguan Baseball*　Nicaragua provides yet another variation on the basic historical pattern of baseball "following the flag." Baseball's initial introduction into this tiny land came about 1900 when some upper-class Nicaraguans who had been attending colleges in the United States returned with this new game. But the big boost came when the U.S. Marines occupied Nicaragua much of the time between 1912 and 1933; like American servicemen since the Civil War, they played baseball on their time off, and Nicaraguan youths soon picked up the essentials. By the time Anastasio Somoza took over as dictator in 1937, there were enough teams to make up a national league and baseball was already regarded as the country's national sport. Somoza recognized the importance of baseball by providing government funds and building a thirty-thousand-seat stadium in the capital, Managua, naturally named the Somoza Stadium; he also erected a statue of himself on a horse in front of the stadium. After the great earthquake of 1972 destroyed the stadium, Somoza made sure it was rebuilt (presumably with funds for the earthquake victims).

Somoza's statue was torn down in the revolution that overthrew Somoza in 1979, but the Sandinistas are no less aware of the importance of baseball in their people's lives. More than the national pastime, it is the national passion, played by Nicaraguans from six to sixty. Poets write about it; government leaders think about it; the newspapers are filled with columns about it; the games are carried over the radio and TV. Baseball, in fact, may be one of the few threads of unity left in the increasingly unraveling society of this country. Even the fact that baseball is imported from and still linked to the *yanquis* who are trying to overthrow them does not keep the Sandinistas from supporting the game—and detailed accounts of the U.S. teams and season are carried in the heavily censored press. The most recent defense minister has also served as Nicaragua's baseball czar, and threw his support behind one of the several top-level teams, the Dantos; this has led to rumors that the Dantos get better equipment and other special privileges, and they did not exactly win the hearts of Nicaragua's baseball fans when they took the national championship in 1988. The Sandinista government knows very well, though, that baseball can be used as a weapon in the propaganda war: Robles Stadium in Boaco, for instance, is named after a young ballplayer murdered by forces supporting Somoza, and when it fell into disrepair, the Sandinistas allowed a group from the United States called Baseball for Peace to come down in 1987–88 to help reconstruct it.

Objective observers of baseball in Nicaragua admit that the quality of play has declined in recent years—there is little money for equipment, able-bodied men are needed for more pressing tasks (the teams are amateurs, but good players were traditionally given plenty of time off), and the general poverty and disarray of the country in recent years has inevitably taken its toll on something so close to the texture of life. Still, famed U.S. Marine Colonel Oliver North could not have been more off base when, at a briefing on Nicaragua where he displayed blow-up photographs of what were clearly baseball fields, he said this proved the Nicaraguans must be trying to hide something—because they don't play baseball.

*Cuban Baseball*   Even Colonel North must know that the Cubans play baseball, although he, like most North Americans, might be forgiven for not knowing just how long baseball has been part of Cuban life. It was as far back as 1864 that a Cuban who had studied in North America is said to have returned with the first baseball bat and ball. Then in 1866 an American ship put in at the port of Matanzas and showed the Cuban dockworkers how to play baseball. (Another version claims that it was several North American–educated Cuban students who introduced it in 1866.) Whether there were other "introductions" is not certain, but the game caught on quickly; by 1874 the first game between organized teams from Havana and Matanzas was being played, and by 1878 there were enough teams to hold a Cuban championship. So popular did baseball—called *pelota* by the Cubans—become that the Spanish who ruled the island banned the game; they could see that it was not part of any Spanish tradition and they also suspected that money collected by "passing the hat" at games was being turned over to the opponents of the Spanish regime.

After the Spanish were thrown out in 1898, Cubans were free to pursue baseball with a passion that has never let up. Teams and leagues grew up all over the island, a National League of Amateur Baseball of Cuba was formed in 1914, and today, out of a population of some 10 million there are estimated to be 1.3 million Cubans who play baseball (most, despite the revolution, still males). Baseball is played everywhere in Cuba—on any available crossroads

*Today most people associate Cuban baseball with Fidel Castro, but the dictator he overthrew, Fulgencio Batista—pictured here with some of his top staff at a baseball game in Havana in the 1950s—was equally supportive of baseball.*

in cities, on any field in the countryside, in schools and factories, even in psychiatric hospitals: Baseball is one of several games used as a form of therapy. Since 1889 Cubans themselves have been writing histories of baseball in their land, games are carried on TV, newspapers and sports magazines are full of baseball stories and statistics, and fans can recite the latest accomplishments of their favored teams and players.

During the early decades, Cuba's teams were all amateurs, but after World War II some turned professional; these latter are not to be confused with the minor league farm teams maintained by U.S. major league teams from the 1940s until the United States broke off relations with Cuba in 1961. Under Castro, baseball has returned to amateur teams, but the best of them are given so much government support and the star players so much time off to practice and play that they are practically professional. Certainly the all-star Cuban teams dominate amateur competitions, not only the Central American and Pan American Games but also in the amateur World Championships—no other country has won as many World Championships as has Cuba. This dominance by Cuba began long before Castro came to power, but his government has undeniably placed great emphasis on national achievement in sports in general and baseball in particular: "I do not know a revolutionary youth who is not a sportsman" is one of Castro's pronouncements painted on baseball stadiums, and for years Fidel himself liked to join in baseball games to show his solidarity with the people.

*Besuboru Japanese Style*   When it comes to Japan, there is no need to convince Americans that baseball plays a major role in another country. Even if relatively few have read one of the excellent recent books on the subject— *The Chrysanthemum and the Bat* and its follow-up, *You Gotta Have Wa!*, both by Robert Whiting, and *The Rise of Japanese Baseball Power* by Robert Obojski—numerous magazine articles and frequent newspaper items now inform even the most casual American reader of the depth and extent to which baseball permeates Japanese life. Reports of the long hours that players are required to give to practice sessions and pregame warmups, the intensity of the fans' dedication, the sheer noise level at the games, the total concentration on every technical detail of the game by broadcasters, the omnipresence of amateur and youth contests throughout Japan, the loyalty exhibited by (and expected from) the players to their teams, the widespread Japanese press coverage, the close ties between the corporate world and teams—all this is now a staple of the American media, the small talk of sportscasters.

Meanwhile, the overlap of North American and Japanese baseball realms increases year by year. Since there will soon be no more Impressionist paintings left to buy, some wealthy Japanese will be buying one of the North American franchises. It has long been commonplace to read of major leaguers whose careers seem stalled and who go off to play a season or two in Japan for great salaries; increasingly American fans are waking up to find that players still in good shape are being signed by Japan for fabulous salaries. Many American baseball fans even know the name of at least one Japanese baseball great, Sadaharu Oh, whose 868 career home runs are a world record. Few, however, know the name of another player, Sachio Kinugasa, who in June 1987 broke Lou Gehrig's record of playing in 2,131 consecutive games. And how many can recall the name of the Japanese player who pitched a few games in 1964–65 with the San Francisco Giants? (Masanori Murakami: He got homesick and went home.)

One fact many American baseball fans may prefer to forget: The Japanese team defeated the U.S. team in the revival of baseball as a demonstration sport at the 1984 Olympics in Los Angeles. These same fans will want to remember that the U.S. team got its revenge by defeating Japan in the final at the 1988 Olympics. The 1992 Olympics, when baseball becomes a full medal competition, should prove to be a true showdown. The assumption that these two teams will meet once again in the finals may seem risky—even though Japan and the United States are generally conceded to be the two baseball "powers," in a class by themselves—because the fact that they are the only two countries that maintain openly professional teams can work against them when it comes to assembling Olympic teams against countries like Cuba.

The general outline of the history of baseball in Japan can be sketched from any number of sources. It was introduced there in 1873 by Horace Wilson, an American visiting professor at Kaisei School (which would become the University of Tokyo) who taught Japanese youths how to play the game; soon it was taken up by college and university students. American college teams, starting with the University of Wisconsin's team in 1878, came almost every year over several decades to play Japanese teams.

The next great impetus to the game came after a whole series of visits from American professional teams. The first, in 1908–09, was organized by A. J. Reach & Co., a sporting-goods company, and featured a sort of all-star team that totally dominated its Japanese opponents. But the most famous one was that of 1934 by the American League Stars, led by Babe Ruth, Lou Gehrig, Jimmy Foxx, and Charlie Gehringer (all four were struck out in succession by a nineteen-year-old pitcher, Eji Sawamura). Ruth, a legendary player even before he arrived, hit thirteen homers and batted .408 in the sixteen-game series and left a superhero. And it was this tour that inspired some Japanese to organize their first professional teams.

The Japanese continued to play baseball during World War II (and their soldiers were alleged to shout insulting epithets about Babe Ruth to demoralize American forces). After the war, they eventually built up two leagues of twelve professional teams, now all owned by corporations; colleges and universities function like farm teams to produce generations of talented players who remain totally loyal to their first teams. However, it seems that even any over-the-hill American major leaguer can all but dominate the Japanese teams.

*Besuboru's Other Face*   Those are "the facts" of Japanese baseball history as widely purveyed, and it is not that they are wrong but simply that there are so many more interesting facts to go along with them. For instance, much is made of Murakami's pitching for the San Francisco Giants in 1964–65, but this only complicated his relations with the Japanese when he returned. It is also overlooked that, after a disappointing career in Japan, he returned to the United States and tried out again in 1983, but never made it back into the majors. Or another example: Japanese players are said to be forced to work under far more Spartan conditions. Yet which American team has what the new stadium in Tokyo offers its teams: soundproof bullpen rooms so that relievers can concentrate before entering a game?

Or consider the question of why baseball should have taken hold in Japan so quickly and so profoundly; after all, American missionaries, teachers, servicemen, and other "torchbearers" had introduced baseball into many corners of the world where it didn't "take" to such a degree. Close observers such as Whiting and Obojski offer several explanations: There was some similarity between baseball and Japan's traditional martial arts; baseball rewards discipline and the "group harmony" that the Japanese value so; there is the rational, rules-oriented element to the game that appeals to the Japanese; aspects of the game have even been compared to elements of traditional culture such as the samurai or Kabuki drama; and so on.

But close students of the history of the game also know of other factors. It was a Japanese nobleman, Baron Hiroshi Hiraoka, who, after seeing what the American professor Wilson had introduced, went to the United States in 1877 and returned with a Japanese translation of the rules of baseball. This as much as anything allowed the game to be adopted in those early years, for the Japanese prefer some protocol and structure in all that they do.

Much is made of the early visits by touring American college teams, and their influence was undoubtedly important, but Whiting stresses that the first

*In April 1927, the Philadelphia Royal Giants, an all-black team, made the first of two visits to Japan and played a series of games against Japanese teams. Although they easily defeated their Japanese opponents, they did it with such sensitivity to the Japanese that some credit them for playing a major role in encouraging the Japanese to pursue the sport.*

great burst of national pride in the game was due to a Japanese team from the First Higher School of Tokyo defeating a team of Americans resident in Yokohama in 1896. It was no accident that Japan, on the verge of entering the modern international world, realized it could compete with Westerners—and within a few years it would take on Russia in a war. Still more credit for advancing the game in Japan is given to the tour of major league All-Stars of 1934, and it was important.

Kazuo Sayama, on the other hand, has made a good case for the equally influential role played by virtually ignored tours in 1927 and 1932 by the Royal Giants, an all-black team from Philadelphia. Sayama argues that the exhibition tours by the major league stars were in some ways too spectacular, too overwhelming (and often condescending in their exhibitionism), while the more low-keyed visits by the all-black team left the Japanese feeling that the game was more accessible, more within their grasp:

There is no denying that the major leaguers' visits were the far bigger incitement to the birth of our professional league. We yearned for better skill in the game. But if we had seen only the major leaguers, we might have been discouraged and disillusioned by our poor showing. What saved us was the tours of the Philadelphia Royal Giants, whose visits gave Japanese players confidence and hope.

It is equally simplistic to believe that all Japanese went crazy for this imported sport from the outset. Early in this century, a doctor was claiming that the game put undue "mental pressure" on the brain and that the constant throwing and bending could deform the bodies of youths. A prominent educator in 1911 attacked it as "a pickpocket's sport, in which players try to swindle their opponents . . . to steal a base." Behind this opposition to baseball was the fact that it was imported from abroad, and there remains to this day a xenophobic streak in the Japanese, a desire not to contaminate their race, culture, and society. (Indeed, ever since World War II, when the Japanese wanted to rid their language of Americanisms, *besu boru* has been more generally called *yakyu,* or "field ball.") They limit each major league team to hiring two foreigners—fair enough; but ask American players how the Japanese feel about American blacks or Hispanics coming over. (Japanese like to overlook that the great star, Sadaharu Oh, is in fact half Chinese.) Not much is made of the fact that many of the three-hundred-odd Americans who have played in Japan have not had that happy an experience there, through a combination of their own inability or refusal to adjust to a foreign culture and the Japanese resistance to all outsiders. There are some exceptions, one of the more notable being Randy Bass, who has played in Japan for six years (through 1988); yet, when he came into the final game of the 1985 season needing only one homer to tie Sadaharu Oh's season record of fifty-four, even Bass was thrown bad pitches by the Yomiuri Giants—under the management of none other than Oh.

So although baseball is definitely wildly popular as well as the national sport in Japan, it is a much more complex and interesting phenomenon than is commonly portrayed. In this sense, baseball in Japan gets much the same treatment as Japan's economic, industrial, and educational systems: They all tend to be touted as having attained a state of perfection. In fact, baseball in Japan is not without its problems, financial and otherwise. In recent years, for example, half of its twelve major teams have operated with a deficit. And most North Americans would not be comfortable with the mixture of feudal demands and fanatic hero-worship that Japanese ballplayers are subject to.

Beyond that, there are far more fascinating nooks and crannies to the history of baseball in Japan than are usually illuminated in the mass media. Merritt Clifton, a freelance writer on baseball, in an article in *The National Pastime* (Spring 1985), traces baseball all the way back through Japan's traditional cultural traditions to its roots as "a fertility rite, a ritual symbolizing human reproduction from conception to birth":

> Pitchers stand on the mound, the sacred pedestal, as ovulating females, whose egg becomes vulnerable to the phallus-swinging batsmen. Their objective is to avoid unwilling impregnation; they are protected from rape by their clans, behind them, whose own phallus menace other women in their turn. Yet each pitcher is also carrying the child of her clan, the hope of victory, which must be nourished through nine increasingly difficult innings corresponding to the period of gestation. Today, though not in baseball's first half century, midwife relief pitchers may help her.

One need not go along with all of that to accept that baseball, in Japan as well as in America, has deeper roots than even the history of the reserve clause.

Or consider the article "Pearl Harbor: A Failure of Baseball?" (*Journal of Popular Culture,* Spring 1982) by Richard Crepeau, one of the new generation of baseball-social historians, who reveals how baseball relations between the United States and Japan during the 1920s and 1930s and up through Pearl Harbor directly mirror Japanese-American political relations during that era. At first baseball was promoted as a link between the two countries, one that would promote world peace. Despite the fact that in 1924 the United States passed an immigration law that clearly discriminated against Asians, all the prominent spokesmen for baseball kept promoting the goal of eventual parity between the two countries' ball teams. Immediately after the famous all-star tour of 1934, a member of a reactionary-nationalist group in Japan assassinated the man who had arranged the tour, but some argued that this called for a renewal of efforts to "fight it out on the diamond [rather] than on the battlefield." By 1940, though, Japan began to try to mask the American element in the game by getting rid of all English-based words: Thus, *besuboru* became *yakyu.* And with the attack on Pearl Harbor, American baseball promoters were suddenly left looking as though they had been collaborating with the enemy. Crepeau reproduces some incredible examples of spokesmen for the baseball establishment turning on the Japanese with a vitriolic racism and absolving those Americans who had, in the words of J. G. Taylor Spink, the editor of *The Sporting News,* helped the Japanese to "share the benefits and the God-given qualities of the great game with us." Most definitely, the full story of baseball in Japan goes well beyond Sadaharu Oh and his home runs.

*Olympic Heights*    The acceptance of baseball by the Olympics as a medal competition (the twenty-fifth summer sport) starting in the 1992 games is generally conceded to have put baseball on the world map once and for all. It then follows that the two previous appearances of baseball as a demonstration sport—at Los Angeles in 1984 and at Seoul in 1988—are accorded the honors of assisting in this achievement. This is true, but not the whole truth. Most everyone has forgotten that baseball was a demonstration sport at six previous Olympics. The first time was in 1904 at the third of the modern Olympics, and it came about because the games were held at St. Louis, Missouri. The second time was in 1912, at Stockholm. The third time has been completely overshadowed by the other events of the 1936 games at Berlin. Baseball was also played as a demonstration sport in 1952 at Helsinki, in 1956 at Melbourne, and in 1964 at Tokyo. Only four teams were allowed to compete at the finals of these games, little publicity was given to the contests, and there was not much sense of any truly international support for the game.

What happened next seemed to barricade the road to the Olympics forever: In 1972 the International Olympic Committee (IOC) voted to eliminate all demonstration sports from the Olympics. What pushed aside that barricade was a series of events. The autocratic Avery Brundage, who ran the IOC as a personal fiefdom, retired; the 1984 Olympic Games were awarded to Los Angeles and Peter Ueberroth, definitely a friend of baseball, was appointed to run them; and, little known to the public at large, the International Association of Amateur Baseball was lobbying hard behind the scenes on behalf of baseball. The result was that not only was baseball a demonstration sport in 1984 but it was guaranteed promotion to full medal status in 1992. But it should not be thought that this has come about just because of some individual personalities and in-group lobbying. It is a recognition that baseball has arrived as a world sport.

*World Wrap-Up*    It begins to look as though there is more baseball being played around the world than most Americans realize. And the histories recapped and stories recounted here are only the beginning of a complete survey of baseball on the international stage. Country after country, from Argentina to Zimbabwe, has a baseball story to tell. Much has been made of the role of baseball in the Western Hemisphere outside North America, yet nothing was said of the active baseball programs in Ecuador, Chile, Guatemala, Aruba, or the Virgin Islands (British and American). The story of baseball in Great Britain and France has been set forth, but nothing has been said of countries in Europe where baseball is actually much more advanced in terms of level of play and fan enthusiasm—Italy and the Netherlands are in fact the two amateur powerhouses in Europe (and Italy supports a professional league). Right behind those two are such countries as Spain, Belgium, and Sweden, while in the next rank are Germany, Switzerland, Austria, and Finland. North Americans must be astonished to know that Zurich is becoming a hotbed of baseball—the home town of such teams as the Coconuts and the Lions—even though it wasn't until 1980 that the first serious game was played in Switzerland.

Nor is this activity confined to West Europe. Czechoslovakia has for some years been extremely active in amateur baseball, with fourteen clubs maintaining schedules of forty to fifty games a season, including national championships and international contests. Yugoslavia also supports a strong baseball program and Poland is gaining fast in its level of play, and thanks to support from Polish-Americans it has become the first East European country to have a Little League program. Communist countries traditionally depend on government departments to lead the way, but much of the support for baseball in East Europe is grass roots. In any case, these countries have come a long way since 1922 when the first baseball game was played in Budapest, Hungary, by two amateur teams of Americans, and a dispatch to *The New York Times* reported: "Hungarian sporting writers were of the opinion that the game was too exciting for the Hungarian temperament, and declared that Magyar teams would be sure to leave too many dead on the diamond."

Australians' enthusiastic and expanding support of baseball has been set forth, but nothing has been said of the other nations and territories of Oceania where baseball is also on the rise: the Philippines, Guam, American Samoa, Micronesia, the Marianas, the Marshall Islands, Tonga, and Tuvalu. Baseball was introduced on Guam by U.S. servicemen stationed there in World War I, but it wasn't until 1974 that it really took off; now this tiny island supports one hundred teams. And on the island of Pohnpei in Micronesia, with a population of only twenty-eight thousand, there are between fifty and a hundred teams. India's baseball program is expanding, while offshore, Sri Lanka—where Spalding's touring teams played in 1889—has been supporting a growing baseball program since 1980. At the other corner of Asia, Israel also has an increasingly active baseball program.

The Chinese are yet another story. Many Americans have been aware that baseball must be played on Taiwan ever since it won the Little League

World Series in 1969. That inspired the Taiwanese to take up baseball with a passion, and now the older youths of Taiwan are also a force on the international amateur baseball scene—they took the bronze medal in the '84 Olympics and were one of only eight teams that made it to Seoul in the '88 Olympics (where South Korea, by the way, took the bronze). Not much has been heard from the bleachers of mainland China, but that may soon change. American missionaries introduced baseball into China early in the century, but it never took hold much outside schools. When the Communists took over in 1949, they purged their society of most things American, but in 1952 *The New York Times* reported that baseball was featured in a ten-day athletic meet held by the Red Army—and the trophies were weapons captured from the Americans in Korea. During the most rigid years of Mao's rule, baseball vanished completely from the scene, but in recent years, old baseball equipment began to be literally pulled out of closets and the game is being actively encouraged. The Los Angeles Dodgers, with Peter O'Malley taking the lead, have been especially supportive of baseball in this new China and have been sending coaches to teach the Chinese; Tianjin, China's third-largest city, also now boasts a brand new ballpark, Dodgers Baseball Field, designed and financed in part by the Dodgers organization.

Africa is the next continent that the apostles of international baseball hope to convert. And they are already out there—both the African ballplayers and the apostles. These days the latter are by no means confined to American flagwavers like Albert Goodwill Spalding. There is a whole international cadre of baseball missionaries, now generally operating under the auspices of the International Baseball Association (IBA), the same organization that began life in 1975 as the International Association of Amateur Baseball. The IBA is headquartered in Indianapolis, Indiana, and its president is an American, Dr. Robert Smith (a college administrator when he is not encircling the globe to promote baseball), but its other officers are from various other countries, and the organization counts on the efforts of numerous baseball supporters, some paid, some volunteers, all over the world.

The IBA, at last count, included sixty-five countries as formal members (meaning they had organized baseball programs at some level) but points out that it is already being played in another fifteen countries—a total of 90 million people play the game, says the IBA. The goal is to bring the IBA's formal membership up to one hundred countries in the next decade. The IBA is essentially an umbrella association for the many national federations and organizations around the world, and in addition to supporting these it works to develop more of them in new countries. The IBA publishes a quarterly magazine, *World Baseball* (with all text printed in both English and Spanish—a great way for parents to get their baseball-playing children to work at their Spanish); it sends baseball equipment (usually in conjunction with Rawlings Sporting Goods) to emerging baseball countries; it arranges for all sorts of international manpower assistance projects, like coaching and instruction, or umpire training; and it sanctions and administers most of the major international amateur baseball tournaments. (The International Olympic Committee now recognizes the IBA as the sole governing body for amateur baseball.)

North Americans are vaguely aware of the Little League World Series and the Pan American Games, but few are aware of all the other international amateur baseball competitions—the biennial World Championship, World Youth Championship of the Amateur Athletic Association, European Baseball Federation Championship, Asian Baseball Federation, Intercontinental Cup, South American Youth Championship, and Central American and Caribbean Games, not to mention countless matches now played each year between two or more countries sharing geographic or other elements. (Czechs, for instance, travel to the Soviet Union to play the Russians.) These contests go on, year in and year out, and attract large and enthusiastic fan support: When the World Championships were held in Holland in 1986, 220,000 spectators showed up, and millions of Europeans watched the games on TV. The Netherlands already has its own National Baseball and Softball Museum and Hall of Fame—and the IBA is working toward an international hall of fame for baseball.

So although Spalding may have chosen the wrong itinerary and idiom, he was on to something, after all. Forty million Frenchmen may have been wrong, but not even Spalding could have dreamed of a billion Chinese baseball fans.

JOEL ZOSS AND JOHN BOWMAN

# Epilogue

If our book has an overriding thesis, it is that baseball reflects American history and society. Small wonder, then, that developments and events that have occurred on and off the field since this book was revised nearly a decade ago demand comment.

One might assume that the facts surrounding the beginning of the game would be a settled matter by now, but in fact the history of baseball continues to be a lively and open-ended subject for debate. As in the past, members of the Society for American Baseball Research (SABR) lead the way in the study of baseball archeology, but many other researchers have made significant contributions as well. Among recent developments, SABR member David Block has presented convincing evidence that the game of rounders, though clearly related to the game of baseball that emerged in North America, is not an ancestor of baseball in a direct line of descent. Published records show bat-and-ball games called "base ball" were being played in North America as early as the first half of the 1700s, while rounders is not mentioned in an American context until 1828.

In the spring of 2001, George A. Thompson Jr., while researching old newspapers in New York, discovered a brief article in the April 25, 1823, edition of the *National Advocate* that at present stands as the earliest known newspaper account of an "organized" team of young men (not boys) playing baseball with some regularity. Thompson's finding antedates the organized game of the New York Knickerbocker era by some two decades, but it is important to remember that the definitions of "organized" and "baseball"—or, specifically, the definition of the "New York Game of Base" that became baseball—are still open to dispute.

In 2002 SABR member Brian Turner published his discovery of what appears to be the earliest record of the existence of an integrated baseball team. Drawing on a late-nineteenth-century account, some old newspaper articles, and the recollections of an elderly neighbor, Turner has established that Luther B. Askin, an African American, was a full-fledged member of the Florence (Massachusetts) Eagles, a team of young men (not boys) wearing uniforms and playing scheduled games in 1865 and 1866 against similarly organized teams from elsewhere in Massachusetts. (Florence is now part of Northampton, Massachusetts.)

In the area of collectibles and pop culture, the baseball card bubble has greatly shrunk, if not burst, as we anticipated more than a decade ago. The truly rare originals continue to hold their value, but today's massive print runs of reissues and new cards mean that quite a few collectors are holding cards that cost them more than they are ever likely to get back. Autographed photos and baseballs have also been devalued because players put so many into the marketplace; they may profit from this arrangement, and perhaps rightfully so, but the commercialization of autographing has diminished the value of any single signed artifact. Ron Halper, acknowledged in our opening chapter as far and away the leading collector of memorabilia, has auctioned off most of his collection. Reflecting the ever ubiquitous hand of marketing in American culture, more modern marketing arrangements seem to be the order of the day. In August 2003 Commissioner Bud Selig announced that between 2005 and 2009, the thirty teams of Major League Baseball will receive at least $500 million in licensing fees for on- and off-field equipment and apparel in deals described as "unprecedented in their size and scope" by MLB executive vice president for business Tim Brosnan. (MLB-licensed retail products, which gross about $2.3 billion annually, sell at a rate comparable to products from the National Basketball Association but fall short of the National Football League's, the fourth-largest licensed brand in the world.)

At another point along the American cultural spectrum, baseball novels, poems, and paintings have proliferated beyond tracking. Richard Greenberg's play about the crises confronted by a gay baseball player, *Take Me Out*, won a Tony Award for the best new play of the 2002–2003 Broadway season and represents baseball's metaphysical entry into the wider culture's grappling with gender issues. Baseball players' use of drugs of all kinds—from steroids to narcotics—continues to be as major a source of scandal and controversy in the twenty-first century as it was in the nineteenth and twentieth.

Some new faces and trends have appeared on the playing field itself. Notably, the attempt to start a women's professional baseball league, begun in 1994 through the sponsorship of Coors Beer, fizzled out after a few seasons. Meanwhile, Japanese players, although still few in number, are no longer just novelties in North American Major League baseball and have even become popular stars (in Japan they are lionized as superstars). Three Japanese players—Ichiro Suzuki of the Seattle Mariners, Hideki Matsui of the New York Yankees, and Hideo Nomo of the Los Angeles Dodgers— earned the attention and respect of fans on both sides of the Pacific during the 2003 season.

While our book does not particularly emphasize statistics or records, many major benchmarks have been revised or broken. Perhaps the most remarkable longstanding record to fall was the number of home runs in a season, first broken by Mark McGwire in 1998 with 70, and then again by Barry Bonds in 2001 with 73. Another major landmark was passed when Cal Ripken Jr. retired from baseball in 1998 after playing in 2,632 consecutive games, breaking the apparently immortal record of 2,130 set by Iron Man Lou Gehrig. (Numerous other records have been broken since this book was originally issued, and the reader is advised to check for the latest figures, most of which are now available on the Internet.)

Interestingly enough, despite the heroics of Jackie Robinson and the significantly broader integration of American society since the 1940s, participation in the game by African American players and fans has decreased. At their peak in 1978, U.S.-born black players represented about 25 percent of major league players; in 2003, they represented only about 10 percent of major league rosters (or slightly less than the percentage of African Americans in the U.S. population). This trend reflects an overall cultural trend among the African American demographic—which increasingly prefers basketball over baseball—that has led Major League Baseball to worry publicly over black fans' waning interest and declining attendance at major league games. It seems that even though baseball is officially integrated, the sport has never made blacks feel completely welcome: regardless of their on-field percentages, since the Negro Leagues disappeared, black Americans have not felt comfortable in the ballpark as players or as fans. Although baseball was a true pioneer in racial integration, paradoxically it may have succeeded in remaining true to its white conservative roots. Many of the greats of the Negro Leagues have finally been admitted into the Baseball Hall of Fame, thanks in large part to the efforts of SABR members, but even if this gesture was not too little, it may have been too late to help save the game for African Americans. As one black inner-city basketball coach put it, baseball is a "suburban" sport.

A striking cultural development reached its apotheosis at the 2003 World Series when singing "God Bless America" during the seventh inning stretch replaced singing "Take Me Out to the Ball Game." In the wake of the September 11, 2001, attacks on the New York World Trade Center, "God Bless America" began supplementing or replacing baseball's unofficial anthem in many Major League parks. Some fans bemoaned the passing of their traditional communal sing of the lighthearted tune, as beloved by Americans as "Happy Birthday," but the phenomenon of the adoption of "God Bless America" neatly paralleled the adoption of the pregame performance of "The Star Spangled Banner" during World War II.

Although many Americans have recently expressed concern over an at least perceived decline in the general popularity of baseball—as measured by lower major and minor league game attendance figures, a decline in the popularity of youth leagues, and the rise in popularity of longer and longer seasons of basketball and football—the popularity of the game abroad appears to be growing slowly and steadily. Many European countries now have active baseball leagues, and some of their best players have emigrated to American minor league teams; unfortunately, having been a part of the Olympics since 1992, baseball has been threatened with removal from the Games after 2008. A more vital sign of the internationalization of the game is the budding tradition among some U.S. teams to play their opening games abroad—in Mexico in 1999 and in Japan in 2000. In 1998, in an effort to hold and win over fans, Major League Baseball introduced regularly scheduled interleague games, which are now a popular fixture of each season.

One of the best recent examples of baseball's distinctive role as America's cultural barometer was the Baltimore Orioles' decision to play two exhibition games with the Cuban National Team in 1999—one in Cuba, one in Baltimore. Although the exchange was roundly criticized by some and praised by others—and in the end did not lead to immediate changes in Cuban-American political relations—the Orioles' groundbreaking move showed once again how baseball continues to be a bellwether of American society, influencing and evolving out of the attitudes of the nation that gave it birth and fulfilling, as a uniquely American game, a uniquely American function. Whatever else may be said of our national pastime, baseball promises to remain one of the clearest lenses through which to observe the issues and passions of American life for a long time to come.

# ILLUSTRATION CREDITS

60 Courtesy Albert G. Spalding Collection, Rare Books and Manuscripts Division, The New York Public Library, Astor, Lenox and Tilden Foundations.
61 The New York *Herald.*
69 *Puck.*
71 U.S. Patent and Trademark Office.
74 U.S. Patent and Trademark Office.
79 Courtesy Mark Rucker, *Frank Leslie's Illustrated Newspaper.*
82 National Baseball Library, Cooperstown, New York.
90 National Baseball Library, Cooperstown, New York.
94 Courtesy *The Sporting News* Archives.
96 Courtesy Bison Picture Library.
99 Signal Corps, Bison Picture Library.
103 Courtesy Mike Mumby.
106 Courtesy Mike Mumby.
108 Courtesy Mike Mumby.
110 National Baseball Library, Cooperstown, New York, credited to Ray Ramon
116 National Baseball Library, Cooperstown, New York.
137 Courtesy Oberlin College Archives, Oberlin, Ohio.
141 David Maxwell.
147 Courtesy William Weiss.
153 Courtesy John Holway.
157 Courtesy Bob Peterson, National Baseball Library, Cooperstown, New York.
160 National Baseball Library, Cooperstown, New York.
198 David Maxwell.
201 *Harper's Weekly.*
205 Courtesy Vassar College Library, Poughkeepsie, New York.
207 Courtesy Smith College Archives, The Sophia Smith Collection, Northampton, Massachusetts.
211 Courtesy Kelly Candaele and KCET.
224 Courtesy John Holway.
230 Courtesy The New-York Historical Society.
231 *Frank Leslie's Illustrated Newspaper.*
232 Library of Congress.
234 Library of Congress.
236 Library of Congress.
239 Courtesy General Research Division, The New York Public Library, Astor, Lenox and Tilden Foundations.
240 Courtesy Fogg Art Museum, Harvard University, Cambridge, Massachusetts.
244 Courtesy Wayne N. Farr.
246 Courtesy Mark Rucker.
247 Courtesy New York State Library, Print Collection No. 3752.
250 Courtesy John Morrison.
256 David Maxwell.
262 Stephen Crane Collection, George Arents Research Library for Special Collections at Syracuse University, Syracuse, New York.
264 David Maxwell.
266 Courtesy John Thorn.

291 Courtesy Albert G. Spalding Collection, Rare Books and Manuscripts Division, The New York Public Library, Astor, Lenox and Tilden Foundations.

295 Courtesy Mark Rucker.

297 David Maxwell.

307 Courtesy Albert G. Spalding Collection, Rare Books and Manuscripts Division, The New York Public Library, Astor, Lenox and Tilden Foundations.

312 David Maxwell.

353 Courtesy Albert G. Spalding Collection, Miriam and Ira D. Wallach Division of Arts, Prints and Photographs, The New York Public Library, Astor, Lenox and Tilden Foundations.

362 Courtesy Mike Mumby.

367 Courtesy John Ripley Slide Collection at Kansas State Historical Society, Topeka, Kansas.

370 Courtesy John Ripley Slide Collection at Kansas State Historical Society, Topeka, Kansas

371 Courtesy The Print Department, Boston Public Library.

389 Courtesy Jan Bagin and Lloyd Johnson, S.A.B.R.

390 *Harper's Weekly.*

393 Courtesy Mike Mumby.

395 David Maxwell.

396 David Maxwell.

398 Courtesy Albert G. Spalding Collection, Miriam and Ira D. Wallach Division of Arts, Prints and Photographs, The New York Public Library, Astor, Lenox and Tilden Foundations.

407 National Baseball Library, Cooperstown, New York.

411 Courtesy Kazuo Sayama and John Holway.

# INDEX